"Benidickson's environmental-legal history of the Lake of the Woods area considers the tensions between the geographical integrity of the river basin and various geopolitical entities that have sought to assert their will over parts of it. The book is a rare example of regional history that effectively situates the local within the administrative scales and networks of power bearing on it."

– Shannon Stunden Bower, Department of History and Classics, University of Alberta

"Professor Benidickson travelled to a fascinating corner of the Canada-US border, explored its every nook as a paddler and historian, and gathered a treasure trove of stories along the way. His comprehensive study of the Lake of the Woods region reveals how political boundaries and water bodies shape us and are shaped by us. As we consider erecting walls along our border waters, Professor Benidickson's story of cooperation and conflict offers a much-needed history lesson."

– Noah Hall, founder of the Great Lakes Environmental Law Center

Levelling the Lake

The Nature | History | Society series is devoted to the publication of high-quality scholarship in environmental history and allied fields. Its broad compass is signalled by its title: *nature* because it takes the natural world seriously; *history* because it aims to foster work that has temporal depth; and *society* because its essential concern is with the interface between nature and society, broadly conceived. The series is avowedly interdisciplinary and is open to the work of anthropologists, ecologists, historians, geographers, literary scholars, political scientists, sociologists, and others whose interests resonate with its mandate. It offers a timely outlet for lively, innovative, and well-written work on the interaction of people and nature through time in North America.

General Editor: Graeme Wynn, University of British Columbia

A list of titles in the series appears at the end of the book.

NATURE | HISTORY | SOCIETY
GENERAL EDITOR: GRAEME WYNN

Levelling the Lake

Transboundary Resource Management in the Lake of the Woods Watershed

JAMIE BENIDICKSON

FOREWORD BY GRAEME WYNN

UBC Press • Vancouver • Toronto

28 27 26 25 24 23 22 21 20 19   5 4 3 2 1

Printed in Canada on FSC-certified ancient-forest-free paper
(100% post-consumer recycled) that is processed chlorine- and acid-free.

Library and Archives Canada Cataloguing in Publication

Benidickson, Jamie, author
    Levelling the lake : transboundary resource management in the Lake of the Woods Watershed / Jamie Benidickson ; foreword by Graeme Wynn.

(Nature, history, society)
Includes bibliographical references and index.
Issued in print and electronic formats.
ISBN 978-0-7748-3548-0 (hardcover). – ISBN 978-0-7748-3550-3 (PDF)
ISBN 978-0-7748-3551-0 (EPUB). – ISBN 978-0-7748-3552-7 (Kindle)

    1. Natural resources – Lake of the Woods – Management. 2. Natural resources – Rainy Lake (Minn. and Ont.) – Management. 3. Lake of the Woods – Economic conditions. 4. Rainy Lake (Minn. and Ont.) – Economic conditions. 5. Lake of the Woods – Environmental conditions. 6. Rainy Lake (Minn. and Ont.) – Environmental conditions. I. Title. II. Series: Nature, history, society

FC3095.L34B46 2019   333.709713'11   C2018-905834-X
                                                               C2018-905835-8

Canadä

UBC Press gratefully acknowledges the financial support for our publishing program of the Government of Canada (through the Canada Book Fund), the Canada Council for the Arts, and the British Columbia Arts Council.

This book has been published with the help of a grant from the Canadian Federation for the Humanities and Social Sciences, through the Awards to Scholarly Publications Program, using funds provided by the Social Sciences and Humanities Research Council of Canada.

Printed and bound in Canada by Friesens
Set in Garamond by Artegraphica Design Co. Ltd.
Copy editor: Joyce Hildebrand
Proofreader: Kristy Lynn Hankewitz
Indexer: Noeline Bridge
Cartographer: Eric Leinberger
Cover designer: Gabi Proctor

UBC Press
The University of British Columbia
2029 West Mall
Vancouver, BC V6T 1Z2
www.ubcpress.ca

For Heath and the Palmerston gang.

Contents

Illustrations

Reflections
from the North Country

Graeme Wynn

Jamie Benidickson is a professor in the Faculty of Law in the University of Ottawa where he specializes in Canadian and International Environmental Law, Water Law, Sustainable Development Law, and Canadian Legal History. His authoritative text, *Environmental Law,* entered its fourth edition in 2013, and his social, legal, and cultural history of wastewater and flushing (published in 2007) has been widely praised for its exploration of the murky histories of sewage disposal in Canada, the United States, and the United Kingdom through two hundred years. Long interested in policy issues, he has participated in a number of public inquiries and Royal Commissions and has also served as the executive director of the Academy of Environmental Law for the International Union for the Conservation of Nature.[1]

Over the years, Benidickson's enthusiasm for canoeing, as a hobby and recreational pastime, has also led him along numerous Canadian waterways, and into print; his 1997 book *Idleness, Water, and A Canoe: Reflections on Paddling for Pleasure* is a social history of recreational paddling.[2] Towards the end of that work, Benidickson quotes (approvingly and perhaps even somewhat autobiographically) a passage from a 1915 issue of the Canadian outdoors magazine, *Rod and Gun:* "There is a secret influence at work in the wild places of the North that seems to cast a spell over the men who have once been in them. One can never forget the lakes of such wonderful beauty, the rivers, peaceful or turbulent, and the quiet portage paths, or the mighty forests of real trees."[3]

Mighty forests, beautiful lakes, and rivers both quiet and frenzied are defining characteristics of the Lake of the Woods area of northwestern Ontario and Minnesota on which Benidickson here focuses his attention. But "canoe" appears a mere handful of times in these pages. Fond though Benidickson may be of the scenic and recreational attributes of Ontario's north country, *Levelling the Lake* is about the challenges of watershed management rather than the joys of paddling. It is an analytical rather than a nostalgic book. By tracing the course of resource developments in the Lake of the Woods catchment through the last 150 years or so, it sheds new light on the ways in which piecemeal responses to a succession of environmental challenges have spawned unanticipated consequences and tested attempts to sustain the watershed.

This is no simple story. Watersheds encompass several "interlocking and interacting" considerations; they require engagement with "numerous interests simultaneously, and the promulgation of solutions which concurrently balance benefits and costs for many different parties."[4] They present what Benidickson and others characterize as quintessential polycentric problems, in which the consequences of actions (deliberate and inadvertent) are often poorly understood and "multiple forms of resolution and re-alignment" are possible. These problems are only compounded by history and precedent, and by radically different understandings of rights and entitlements among participating interests. They are further exacerbated when political jurisdictions cross drainage systems, because water knows no borders, while politicians and bureaucrats are notoriously attentive to the reach of their authority and that of their counterparts.

Lake of the Woods is a remnant of the former glacial Lake Agassiz that once covered much of present-day Manitoba, northwestern Ontario, eastern Saskatchewan, North Dakota, and northwestern Minnesota. It straddles both the international border and a geological boundary, between glacial till (to the south) and Precambrian rock (to the north). Broad and shallow, Big Traverse Bay in Minnesota is bordered by wetlands and peat deposits. The remaining two-thirds of the lake, almost all of which is in Ontario, is an intricate mosaic of open water, 14,500 islands, narrow channels, inlets, and bays; thin soils and mixed forests cover many of the islands and much of the land around this part of the lake.

Feeding into the Winnipeg River from an outlet near Kenora, Lake of the Woods is part of an extensive drainage basin carrying water from the southern third of northwestern Ontario and the northern reaches of Minnesota (approximately 150,000 square kilometres) into Lake Winnipeg and hence to the Hudson Bay.[5] Benidickson focuses his attention on the southern, largely Canadian section of this system. For the most part, his gaze extends upstream from Lake of the Woods, along the Rainy River (that forms the international boundary) to Rainy Lake. This is undoubtedly the most storied part of the entire Winnipeg River drainage basin. Occupied by Indigenous peoples for 10,000 years, it became part of Rupert's Land in 1670. Early the following century, fur traders from the St. Lawrence were travelling regularly along the Rainy River – the "voyageurs highway" – to access the interior. La Vérendrye, Benjamin and James Frobisher, Alexander Henry, David Thompson, Daniel Williams Harmon, Peter Pond, Alexander Mackenzie, George Simpson of the Hudson's Bay Company, and others all came this way. So, too, did General Wolseley, his 400 British troops, and 800 Canadian militiamen of the Red River Expedition in 1870. Three years later, most of the Winnipeg River drainage basin was included in Treaty #3 between local First Nations and the Crown. Soon, twenty-eight reserves were established for the Indigenous signatories, and provincial and federal politicians turned to settle the location of the boundary between Ontario and Manitoba.

Levelling the Lake begins with these developments of the late 1860s and early 1870s. Then it turns to trace evolving patterns of resource use – and the controversies and consequences they generated – in the Lake of the Woods–Rainy Lake area through the following decades. Late in the nineteenth century, exploitation quickened considerably. Forests were heavily used for the production of lumber and, later, pulp and paper. Minerals promised a new Eldorado, in the minds of investors and promoters, at least. Hydroelectric power generation spawned dams, changed water levels, and remade river flows and local ecologies. Many of the interests behind the dams, mills, and mines discounted the environmental costs of their activities and adopted a common mantra of the day – "the solution to pollution is dilution" – to answer concerns about the release of noxious substances into the environment.

Yet, lake waters were prized and tapped for urban supply as cities grew in the watershed and beyond. Farmers and fishers, both recreational and commercial, had their own interests in, and ecological effects on, the region, as did those who came, increasingly in the twentieth century, to hunt big game or to build lakeshore cottages and resorts. Competing priorities and conflicts were common. Should lake levels be high or low? Should they be controlled or allowed to fluctuate "naturally"? Answers differed because high water levels flooded low-lying farmsteads, some industries wanted to store water for later use, and some interests preferred stable water levels year-round. Was flow (for electricity generation) more important or more valuable than the aesthetic that pleased recreationalists? How might one weigh the purity of the drinking supply against the wages and profits generated by mines and mills? Such questions were (and are) hardly unique to the Lake of the Woods region, but (in Benidickson's telling) this area was particularly scarred by repeated failures to address such conundrums effectively. Through most of the last century and a half, he tells us, there has been surprisingly little concern for the overall well-being of the watershed.

At one level, this claim seems entirely banal: the world offers us more than a few examples of environments despoiled by some combination of short-sightedness, disregard, ignorance, or wilful pillage. From a different perspective, it seems more than a little bewildering, however. In 1978, US legislation designated more than a million acres (4,400 square kilometres) of this watershed, on the American side of the border, the Boundary Waters Canoe Area Wilderness (BWCAW). Here, in a tract that extends more than three hundred kilometres along the international boundary, from the height of land above Lake Superior to the threshold of Rainy Lake, logging, mineral prospecting, and mining are banned; motorboat and snowmobile use is severely restricted; and visitor access is tightly controlled. Offering visitors opportunities "to canoe, portage and camp in the spirit of the French Voyageurs of 200 years ago" and providing "freedom to those who wish to pursue an experience of expansive solitude, challenge and personal integration with nature,"[6] the BWCAW is the most-visited wilderness area in the United States.

All of this was made possible by a long history of concern. Early in the twentieth century, Christopher Columbus Andrews, soldier, diplomat, and Minnesota forest commissioner, discovered the beauty of the area and sought to protect it from logging. Within a few years, he persuaded President Roosevelt and members of the Ontario legislature of the value of "an international forest reserve and park of very great beauty and interest"; 1909 saw the establishment of Superior National Forest (in the United States) and the Quetico Forest Reserve, which became an Ontario provincial park in 1913.[7] In the mid-1920s, the US Secretary of Agriculture designated 2,600 square kilometres of Superior National Forest as roadless wilderness. A few years later, Congress prohibited logging and the construction of dams to maintain water levels in this area. On the eve of World War II, it was renamed the Superior Roadless Primitive Area. An Executive Order in 1949 excluded low-flying aircraft from the skies above the roadless wilderness, which became known as the Boundary Waters Canoe Area in 1958. Six years later, the Wilderness Act incorporated the

BWCA into the National Wilderness Preservation System. Similarly, regulations prohibited logging (1971) and the use of motor boats (1979) in Quetico. Together, Quetico-Superior and neighbouring La Vérendrye provincial and Voyageurs national parks protect almost 22,000 square kilometres of the southeastern reaches of the Winnipeg River catchment from rash environmental assault.

How to explain this juxtaposition of protection and neglect, preservation and despoliation, along the Rainy River? The geographer David Lowenthal limned an answer of sorts years ago, in a series of reflections on the American landscape. After acknowledging that the sheer size of the continent influenced both its landscape forms and the ways in which people reacted to them, he insisted, nonetheless, that societies shape their surroundings and that landscapes reflect landscape tastes. In this view, the US scene mirrored important oppositions, or cleavages, in the American mind: "Americans build for tomorrow, not today"; they diminish the present and embrace an idealized, immutable past ("history expurgated and sanitized"); they emphasize parts rather than wholes (individual features at the expense of aggregates); they neglect the nearby and typical in favour of the remote and spectacular; and they make both history and nature "objects of isolated pleasure and reverence," fencing them off and enshrining them "in historical museums and wilderness preserves." No one has tried to encapsulate Canadian attitudes towards the environment in similarly bold strokes, but one might suggest that, at this level of resolution, neither the international boundary nor Canadian experience with the land served as an effective prophylaxis to such ways of thinking. On both banks of the Rainy River, experience and places are dichotomized: admired features "are set apart and deluged with attention"; beyond them, a more utilitarian functionalism prevails, and environments are brought to terms – developed, exploited, subdued, and despoiled in pursuit of workaday human ends, until, in effect, they are "consigned to the rubbish heap."[8]

Beguile though they may, such sweeping pronouncements about national attitudes offer only weak and partial explanations of particular outcomes. They provide a context for thinking about specific developments and point to general parameters that make certain actions or results more likely than others, but they cannot account for idiosyncratic behaviour or contingencies. Social structures (rules and resources) and societal attitudes constrain and influence human actions, but individuals have their reasons for choosing to act (or allowing others to do so). Change is never simply the consequence of collective actions that mirror societal attitudes (the cumulative aspirations, beliefs, and inclinations of a group). As sociologist Anthony Giddens once put it: "The only *moving* objects in human social relations are individual agents, who employ resources to make things happen intentionally or otherwise."[9] All of this is to say that a tight focus is required to understand why any actual place – town or countryside, landscape or watershed – developed as it did. Only a fine-grained analysis of the factors at play (of the type exemplified in *Levelling the Lake*) can identify the real drivers of change – the mechanisms and the reasons behind the variety of actions that transform localities.

Recognizing this, and challenging the view that the places we inhabit are but passive reflections of economic, social, and attitudinal forces, cultural geographer Marwyn Samuels argued, in 1979, that places are created (authored) by individuals and small groups of people, and that understanding landscapes requires a biographical approach.[10] Using modern New York City as a case in point, Samuels acknowledged the effects of the city's changing economy, and the influence of industrialization, architectural fashion, and the Progressive movement, on its development, but insisted that we will "not understand either the making or meaning of that landscape without reference to the brothers Roebling, Louis Sullivan, ... the Rockefellers and Harrimans, and especially Robert Moses."[11] Parallel instances abound: Capability Brown was surely the "author" of numerous widely admired parkland landscapes associated with grand English estates; the Olmsteds left their signatures on Central Park in New York City and parks and suburbs across the continent; and *The Plan of Chicago*, authored by Daniel Burnham in 1909, influenced the development of that city for several years thereafter.[12]

But do the elite – the city officials, urban planners, landscape architects, project developers, and others who most obviously exercise power and influence – write the whole script? Looking down on Manhattan from the top of the former World Trade Centre, in 1984, French historian and philosopher Michel de Certeau identified another level of landscape authorship. In his view, the "real authors" of urban space are those who live and work and move through the city every day, the *Wandersmänner* or "walkers whose bodies follow the thicks and thins of an urban 'text' they write without being able to read it."[13] There are complicated issues here, but the essential points of de Certeau's observation are that the story of any landscape (urban or rural) is written – at least in part – from below, and that any attempt to understand it must recognize – as that devoted interpreter of the American scene, Donald Meinig, observed – "that life must be lived amidst that which was made before."[14]

These observations carry us a step closer to understanding the contrasting landscapes of protection and neglect along the Rainy River. Different authors wrote the script for these sections of the watershed, although they did not do so alone, or in circumstances entirely of their own choosing. As the pages that follow make abundantly clear, Minnesota-based timber baron and entrepreneur Edward W. Backus played a large role in shaping the destiny of the Rainy Lake area. Down to his last $5 bill, Backus became a bookkeeper at a small sawmill in Minneapolis in 1882. Within a few years, he owned it. By 1920, he held directorships at the Northern Pacific Railway, the National Bank in Minneapolis, and several other firms while serving as president of the Backus-Brooks lumber company and its many subsidiaries. Regarded to this day as "the key man in the development of Koochiching County" (which encompasses the US bank of the river between Rainy Lake and Lake of the Woods), he established a vast empire of saw and pulp mills, dams, power plants, and woodlands in the Minnesota-Ontario boundary country. After acquiring the Keewatin Lumber Company in 1906, he built dams and a pulp and newsprint mill near Kenora, as well as generating stations on the Seine River that supplied 25,000 horsepower to his pulp and paper mill in Fort Frances. Backus was used to getting his way, on both sides of the border. Powerful enough to "obtain a respectful hearing before distinguished political groups on both sides of the international dividing line," he was also characterized, by a contemporary newspaperman, as "brutal, remorseless, ruthless and not always (to say the least) ethical."[15]

Backus's barnstorming expansion of his industrial interests in the Rainy Lake watershed faltered in the mid-1920s, however. Plans to build a series of dams for power-generation and storage east of Lac La Croix (one of which would raise water levels by 80 feet) drew the ire of an influential group of Americans who envisaged an alternative future for the upper reaches of the river.[16] Led by Rainy Lake resident Ernest Oberholzter, they set about writing their own script for the area. Taking their case first to the International Joint Commission, established in 1909 to address boundary and transboundary water issues, they argued that the dams were a misuse of public resources and lamented the loss of scenic beauty they would entail. With growing public support, the group formed the Quetico-Superior Council. Its lobbying led, in 1930 to the Shipstead-Nolan Act in which the US congress explicitly, and for the first time, protected land as wilderness. The act withdrew all federal land in the Superior Forest from homesteading or sale, prevented the alteration of natural water levels by dams, and prohibited logging within 400 feet of shorelines.[17]

Among those involved in the Quetico-Superior Council, Sigurd Olson, an educator, writer, and avid outdoorsman, played a crucial role in protecting the area through the 1930s and beyond. After wartime service, he returned to Ely, Minnesota, to write about, and advocate for, wilderness preservation. President of the US National Parks Association for six years in the 1950s and then vice president and president of the Wilderness Society between 1963 and 1971, he played a major role in the passage and implementation of the 1964 Wilderness Act and the designation of the Boundary Waters Canoe Area Wilderness. Praised as a "voice of nature" whose responsiveness to "the Song of the North" placed him among the giants of the twentieth-century wilderness movement, Olson published nine books between 1956 and 1982. Blending the pro-wilderness arguments of preservationists, recreationalists, and ecologists and celebrating the spiritual and intangible qualities of the wild, they helped redefine the environmental movement, and won Olson renown as the "Evangelist of the Wilderness."[18] They were also instrumental in defining Quetico-Superior as canoe country and setting it apart from the lower reaches of the Rainy River system. Olson was, clearly, at the forefront of the small group of individuals who scripted and secured Quetico-Superior as wilderness.

For Olson, wilderness was a vital antidote to the troubled clamour and superficiality of contemporary technological society. His convictions rested upon this dualism. As he wrote in his 1976 book, *Reflections From the North Country*: "Wilderness can be appreciated only by contrast, and solitude understood only when we have been without it."[19] He believed that people could rediscover, in wilderness, "the timeless, creative force of the universe," regain a sense of being part of that force, and in so doing glimpse "the land beyond the rim." Wilderness was "a stepping stone to cosmic understanding"; Olson, observed his biographer, professed a "wilderness theology."[20] All of this makes Olson's musings about the Rainy River country categorically different from Benidickson's scholarly engagement with its lower reaches. Both reflect on the north country in search of understanding, but Benidickson's careful detailing of the historic experience of implementing resources and environmental management in the Lake of the Woods basin is a world apart from Olson's cosmic reveries.

By focusing upon institutional responses to resource and environmental challenges, *Levelling the Lake* forces us to think again, and more deeply, about the complexities of the north country and the ways in which landscapes are made. We find ample evidence, in the pages that follow, that both elites (power brokers) and ordinary men and women (*wandersmänner*) had important parts to play in shaping the development of the Lake of the Woods region over the years. Edward Backus orchestrated the cutting and milling of forests and the damming of waters through a series of corporate entities. Limited liability companies assumed similar leadership in the mining sector. Commercial enterprises quickened the depletion of fish stocks. Individuals and the organizations they led enabled the assault on regional resources. But their actions were guided by the unheralded work of timber cruisers and mineral prospectors, their success depended upon the labour of countless employees, and their activities impinged on (and were to some degree moulded by) the presence of Indigenous and other inhabitants of the region. From the first, environmental disruption drew critical, albeit sporadic, attention from public officials, early conservationists, and First Nations leaders. Yet all of this, Benidickson forcefully and insistently reminds his readers, took place within – and was conditioned and constrained by – an evolving web of statute and regulation spun by various institutional actors. Complicated by jurisdictional boundaries (between countries, provinces, and reserve and Crown lands) and tangled by competing and conflicting agendas, development in the Lake of the Woods area was far from straightforward. Here, legal and bureaucratic structures shaped land and life at least as significantly as did the actions of elite and ordinary individuals. In this liminal territory, "legislative authority and proprietary rights over slippery fish," powerful waters, and shiny metals were by no means congruent. The consequences impelled at least one investor to lament that the venture in which he was involved was a "blooming tangle."

Intricate as this century-and-a-half long story of development in the Rainy River–Lake of the Woods watershed is, it warrants attention in the second decade of the twenty-first century. The reasons for this are many and complicated. But anthropologist Tim Ingold perhaps summarized them best when he wrote: "The landscape tells – or rather *is* – a story, a chronicle of life and dwelling ... [that] unfolds the lives and times of ... [those] who, over the generations, have moved around in it and played their part in its formation."[21] Environments are palimpsests. They carry the evidence of generations of human interaction with the earth. They are, as Ingold put it, "pregnant with the past." Writ large and reduced to its essence, the history of the Winnipeg River catchment is a history of transformation, of one sort or another and in varying degree, in the name of progress. Here and there, opposition movements won battles large or small. Across most of the time and space of concern here, however, logging, mineral development, water regulation, pulp and paper mill operations, and recreational activities had a wide range of environmental effects. Some of these consequences were little understood at the time they occurred; some were accepted as the price of progress; yet others were discounted, in prevailing conceptions of the capitalist market system, as externalities (or the inconsequential side-effects of human actions). None of them was truly ephemeral. In the final decades of the twentieth century, as the discourse of "sustainable development" began to supplant the aggressive, oppositional, preservationist stance of the early environmental movement in North America, an increasing number of legislative and regulatory initiatives sought to curb or ameliorate the most egregious environmental consequences of untrammelled growth. Seen in a new light, many of the results of development came to be understood as evidence that "the gods of progress have a darker side."

From this perspective, it has become clear that Indigenous peoples in northwestern Ontario have been disproportionately, tragically, and often unwittingly, enveloped by the darker side of progress. In the nineteenth and early twentieth centuries, their interests were scanted. Later, efforts to consult with and include the concerns of First Nations in resource management often foundered for want of administrative capacity, flawed processes of consultation, and fundamental differences in expectations. Among many such instances noticed in these pages, two – involving the Grassy Narrows (Asubpeeschoseewagong) and Whitedog (Wabaseemoong) First Nations and the residents of the Shoal Lake 40 Reserve – stand out. The plight of the Grassy Narrows Nation (dealt with in Chapter 11 below), has been the focus of much attention – and anguish.[22] Forced to relocate to a new, compact reserve by the Department of Indian Affairs in 1963, and then poisoned by mercury discharged into the English-Wabigoon River from a chemical company/pulp mill in Dryden, these people endured deep demoralization and the radical disintegration of their society's social fabric. Meanwhile, the provincial government sanctioned industrial logging across much of the traditional territory of the Grassy Narrows First Nation. Despite frequent blockades and protests since 2002, the exploitation has continued. About half of the Nation's land has been logged, and the boreal forest is in rough shape.[23] The Asubpeeschoseewagong Nation's efforts "to find a pathway out of a state of desperate dependency" has continued for decades; compensation has been paid out; commitments to clean up the river have been made; but even in 2017, Indigenous leaders were protesting the failure of governments to "get to the bottom of the science, and [take] the next steps necessary to deal with [the mercury] issue once and for all."[24]

As a discrete part of the Lake of the Woods, Shoal Lake appears many times in the pages that follow – as a focus of concern about the continuing viability of the fishery, as a water body in danger of toxic contamination from mining, and as a source of water for the City of Winnipeg. Its urban water-supply function began early, in 1919, with the completion of a costly 135-kilometre aqueduct and has, as Benidickson notes, been a source of significant and persistent controversy and conflict with other water users for nigh on a century. Celebrated at its completion as an engineering achievement, the aqueduct has been more commonly interpreted, in recent years, as an example of Indigenous dispossession and maltreatment in the interests of colonial progress. To build the aqueduct, the federal government allowed approximately 1,200 hectares of the Shoal Lake 40 Reserve to be expropriated. Efficient functioning of the aqueduct also required the diversion of water between a pair of western bays on Shoal Lake. The canal cut for this purpose made an island of the peninsula on which most inhabitants of the reserve lived. Deprived of secure, year-round overland access, the community has suffered many consequences, including an inability to establish a viable water treatment plant.[25] It has existed under a boiled-water advisory for almost two decades, even as the aqueduct has delivered 225 million litres of "clear, tasty, plentiful and cheap" water to the city each year. Invoking a strong sense of irony – as well as injustice – Indigenous leaders noted in 2014 that the taps and reflecting pools of Winnipeg's newly built Canadian Museum of Human Rights would be filled with Shoal Lake water. They characterized the new $350 million edifice as "a towering shrine to hypocrisy" and invited "Canadians and the world" to visit the Shoal Lake 40 Reserve, "a more realistic museum, the Museum of Canadian Human Rights Violations ... the living museum of our community."[26] Continuing a strong publicity-protest campaign aimed at revealing the real price of water and the injustice of their circumstances, the people of Shoal Lake 40 finally won commitments from the governments of Canada, Manitoba, and Winnipeg to construct the "freedom road" they had long sought. Construction began in 2017, and completion is projected for 2019.[27]

Levelling the Lake is, first and foremost, a careful local history, a richly detailed account of the interactions between people and place in a relatively thinly settled and, politically perhaps, somewhat peripheral part of Ontario. But it is a regional history with a broader message. In describing the development of natural resources (a term, it is worth recalling, that elides the way in which human appraisals shape the valuation and use of nature), and the often contentious ways in which these resources were allocated, used, and managed over time, this book invites readers to think hard about the importance of context in political, institutional, and personal decision-making. Much of what happened in the Lake of the Woods area was complicated by jurisdictional questions. Institutions – state, provincial, and national governments, local authorities, and the International Joint Commission established specifically to grapple with transboundary water issues – wrestled with questions of governance. Responding often to particular problems or disputes, they often came up with ad hoc or piecemeal "solutions." Circumstances – and societies' priorities – shifted as they did so. Individuals and groups within and beyond the region had different interests and widely divergent capacities to articulate and implement them. In such conditions, decision makers walk a tightrope.

The history of the Winnipeg River catchment includes environmental and human losses unusual in their scale and severity – "an immensely valuable fishery, ... [and] the essential destruction of aboriginal communities as a result of toxic contamination" among them. But such losses are neither *sui generis* nor beyond explanation and understanding. By telling the particular story of how these events unfolded, *Levelling the Lake* offers perspective on the larger continuing challenge of understanding both ourselves and the trajectory of development that created the present. In the twenty-first century, it is well to remember that the impacts of particular actions on people, landscapes, and ecologies may only become evident years or decades after they are taken. By the same token, it is also important to recognize, as this book demonstrates, that knowledge grows, that commitments change, and that power comes in different forms to be exercised in various ways. Rather than judging earlier institutions and historical actors by the light of the present, Benidickson's reflections from the north country encourage a broad rather than narrow view of the past and offer a timely reminder that the conjoined twins of environmental and social injustice are as often the products of avarice and ignorance as they are of wilfulness and presumption.

Acknowledgments

It is no easy task to read a draft manuscript punctuated with unhelpful references like "insert to follow," so I am enormously grateful to a number of friends and colleagues who not only worked their way through some early versions of these pages but also provided invaluable guidance ranging from "What are you really getting at here?" to "This discussion adds nothing as far as I can see." Thus, immense thanks to Lynda Collins, Murray Clamen, Jane Mather, Dan Macfarlane, Alan B. McCullough, Heather McLeod-Kilmurray, Todd Sellers, and John Wadland. I am also the beneficiary of thoughtful independent assessments provided to me as a result of UBC Press's manuscript review process. These assessments, along with the insightful guidance of Graeme Wynn as general editor, were also the source of extremely worthwhile suggestions, which are much appreciated.

Archives and government records used here have been preserved in numerous libraries and archives across Canada and the United States. They are listed more formally in notes throughout the volume. At this point, I simply acknowledge my appreciation as a researcher for the determined efforts of dedicated custodians to safeguard and maintain access to the unique and invaluable sources that contributed to this book. I also wish to thank museums, historical societies, and other repositories of images found throughout the volume for permission to use items from their collections as noted alongside each of the illustrations. Frank H. Johnston's 1922 painting, *"Serenity, Lake of the Woods,"* as photographed by Ernest

Mayer appears on the cover thanks to the Winnipeg Art Gallery, whose assistance is greatly appreciated.

I also benefited from the work of research assistants who, thanks to their diligence and perseverance, recovered many important elements of the complex history of the Lake of the Woods basin: Melinda Nicole Andrews, Michelle Bloodworth, Lindsay Chan, Kerith Gordon, Tim Groves, Dillon Fowler, Ben Hiemstra, Ellen Kaine, Shahira Khair, Stacey Mirowski, Samantha Santos, Izabella Sowa, and Gil Yaron. Although all the words contained here might have been launched into the digital world on the basis of about six clicks, they have ultimately emerged between the covers of a book thanks to the conscientious and professional guidance of editorial and production personnel at UBC Press – again, greatly appreciated.

Introduction

County Sheriff Art Lux of Baudette, Minnesota, promised to "drain the lake if we have to" in order to find a missing person in Tim O'Brien's popular mystery novel, *In the Lake of the Woods*.[1] It's not that simple.

Managing watersheds in the twenty-first century is a vital, urgent, and potentially overwhelming task. From the Murray-Darling basin in Australia to the Colorado River system, North America's Great Lakes basin, or the vast Nile network extending across Africa, conflicts and intense debates have surfaced against the backdrop of environmental change. Proposals for institutional innovation and, sometimes, elaborate legal reform aimed at reconciling competing expectations with respect to flows, levels, and water quality are continuously emerging.[2] There is a lot at stake.

The American legal scholar Lon Fuller has reflected on the persistent interaction of competing objectives and varied preferences that are inherent in water management and characteristic of certain public decision-making challenges with multiple forms of resolution and realignment. He describes these situations as polycentric, a concept he effectively illustrates using the metaphor of a spider's web:

> A pull on one strand will distribute tensions after a complicated pattern throughout the web as a whole. Doubling the original pull will, in all likelihood, not simply double each of the resulting tensions but will rather create a different complicated pattern of tensions ... This is a "polycentric" situation

because it is "many-centred" – each crossing of strands is a distinct centre
for distributing tensions.[3]

Watersheds represent quintessential polycentricity problems, challenging
citizens and policy makers alike to match their eight-legged counterparts
as the creators of resilient regulatory and institutional webs that – barring
catastrophe – are exceptionally well-suited to the redistribution of strains
and tension. Can we, in other words, design adaptable and resilient institutions capable of achieving divergent social and economic aspirations
while sustaining watersheds as fundamental ecological frameworks?

I explore this question in this book with reference to the region that
encompasses the Lake of the Woods basin or watershed.[4] This is a transboundary basin, shared between Canada and the United States, with the
consequence that some form of collaborative international management
is required to address differences arising between the two countries and
to pursue joint objectives. Writing in 1983, John Edward Carroll included
the Lake of the Woods experience among "success stories in the resolution
of Canadian-US transboundary environmental problems." This transboundary success story is not earth-shaking, he suggests, but the issues
were satisfactorily resolved, and the story is therefore valuable as a potential source of guidance to those concerned with managing other shared
water systems.[5]

My title, *Levelling the Lake*, invokes one early twentieth century episode
centring on hydroelectric power production, which was successfully resolved in its day but, like the resolution of many other water management
controversies, is regularly subject to reconsideration and possible readjust-
ment as circumstances and environmental understanding change. Indeed,
this account of the Lake of the Woods basin describes a sequence of ongoing
responses to water-related issues that arose from decisions whose impacts
on water were rarely anticipated, let alone fully appreciated from a watershed perspective.[6]

Geographically, the Lake of the Woods basin extends approximately
400 km east to west and about 260 km north to south, covering roughly
70,000 square kilometers (25,000 square miles) in Ontario, Manitoba,
and Minnesota. It forms part of the still larger Winnipeg River watershed,
which stretches to the east across the Boundary Waters of the Quetico-
Superior National Forest district to the height of land separating flows
to the Great Lakes system. The numerous internal sub-basins of the
Lake of the Woods watershed include Rainy Lake, from its headwaters
down through the Rainy River to Lake of the Woods; the Big and Little

Fork River basins, among other southern tributaries; and Shoal Lake to the west.[7]

The overall Lake of the Woods watershed has experienced a succession of uses and demands, including the traditional and continuing activities of Indigenous communities. From the late nineteenth century, resource development in the forest and mineral sectors accelerated significantly. The lumber industry used the main lakes, tributary waters, and the Winnipeg River to transport raw materials or to produce industrial water power at sawmill sites. Pulp and paper manufacturers subsequently placed similar demands on the water system. Commercial fishing and agriculture existed alongside these more prominent industries. Advances in the field of hydroelectric production and transmission technology stimulated interest in dams, local power production, and, eventually, major hydroelectric facilities. Recreational activity has expanded continually for the better part of a century and a half, from early beginnings in sport fishing and the pursuit of big game to cottage and resort development, which was initially stimulated by railway access. Urban growth and the advent of municipal water supply systems resulted in new uses for Lake of the Woods waters, including a very substantial pipeline, or aqueduct, to transmit water from Shoal Lake to Winnipeg.

Each of these activities – including recreational enjoyment – has produced environmental impacts associated with extraction and consumption of water, or with alterations to levels and flow, or with the introduction of waste materials. Certain land-based activities have also influenced water characteristics as a result of nutrient and chemical runoff or siltation.

The experience of stakeholders around the watershed has varied in relation to the benefits of development and ensuing impacts or consequences. Although Ontario, Manitoba, and Minnesota were profoundly interested in activities within the watershed, their priorities and management preferences differed significantly. Manitoba's interest in the Winnipeg River became closely associated with the flow of water for downstream power generation, while Winnipeg's use of Shoal Lake waters for municipal supply emphasized quality. Comparatively low-lying agricultural lands in northern Minnesota were vulnerable to flooding from high lake levels, while Ontario gold mining and timber interests, later joined by a growing recreational community, generally welcomed higher and seasonally stable lake levels. Still further upstream in waters associated with Rainy Lake and its headwaters in Ontario's Quetico Park and Minnesota's Superior National Forest areas, pulp and paper operations emphasized industrial requirements for water storage and control. In doing so, they provoked a forceful response from pioneering conservationists. Aboriginal interests, both commercial and cultural, continue to influence and be influenced by decisions that affect the management of water resources. But in all of this, the overall well-being of the watershed has hardly been a primary consideration.

To the extent that environmental protection measures were implemented within the Lake of the Woods district during much of the nineteenth and twentieth centuries, these were adopted as responses to observed deterioration, sometimes in conditions of emergency and generally too late to avert serious damage. While this sequence of events is by no means uncommon, the region may be distinctive for the scale and severity of certain losses – an immensely valuable fishery, for example – and for the devastation of Aboriginal communities as a result of toxic contamination.

Contemporary environmental protection measures are often framed by concepts such as "sustainable development" or "ecosystem management."[8] Rather than elaborating upon the theoretical complexities of these concepts, *Levelling the Lake* takes their core elements as given and emphasizes the historical experience of implementing resources and environmental management in the Lake of the Woods basin. Nor does this volume seek to identify a preferred mix of principles, policies, or institutions to enhance watershed management, an inquiry that is underway around the world.[9] More modestly, I seek to describe institutional responses, including transboundary and interjurisdictional initiatives, to resource and environmental challenges. Legal, institutional, and governance arrangements have been continuously tested in relation to the environmental implications of economic development around the watershed. They have, accordingly, evolved significantly to acknowledge and accommodate varying perspectives as the resource and environmental agenda has developed from a focus on primary extractive industries towards conservation and sustainability, which now include impacts on invasive species such as the spiny waterflea, rusty crayfish, and zebra mussels, as well as the implications of global climate change.

In order to explore the evolution of environmental decision making, *Levelling the Lake* describes the development of natural resource industries around the watershed in conjunction with Aboriginal resource use – both traditional and commercial – but tries to do more by associating these activities with each other and with associated environmental consequences in the polycentric relationships that Lon Fuller likens to a spider's web.

Legal, institutional, and governance initiatives affecting or potentially affecting water flows and quality as well as land use within the Lake of the Woods/Rainy basin are diverse. These include treaties, as these have been interpreted since the late nineteenth century, as well as the common law, particularly in relation to property rights: Who owns what, and what does ownership mean? Statutory measures such as fisheries licensing regimes and efforts to protect navigable waters are also significant, alongside the introduction of public health legislation, much of it concerned with water quality. Some sectors – pulp and paper, for example – have been subject to detailed regulation and monitoring of their specific operations and effects. Water resources commissions and regional, forest, and land-use planning processes have played a role, along with environmental assessment arrangements.

In addition to national, state, and provincial departments responsible for natural resources and environmental matters, and these departments' respective predecessors, institutions concerned with water management in the region eventually included interjurisdictional arrangements. The International Joint Commission (IJC) and boards with supervisory authority over water levels and pollution control are prominent examples. The inventory of institutions involved in decisions related to or arising from regional resource activity also extends to Canada's Freshwater Fish Marketing Corporation, a Shoal Lake watershed board, and, tragically, a mercury disability compensation board.

Efforts to govern the watershed were generally implemented at the federal and provincial or state levels on a piecemeal or ad hoc basis without much reference to questions of complementarity or integration and without much indication that the effects of previous interventions had been analyzed or understood. The basin is now part of a pioneering transboundary watershed governance initiative that has been encouraged through the work of the IJC. Indeed, institutional reconfigurations are ongoing, as shown by the 2013 consolidation of international water level control and pollution boards together with further proposed institutional development.

Chapter 1 describes late nineteenth-century transitional processes whereby the post-Confederation transfer of lands from the Hudson's Bay Company to Canada and the negotiation of Treaty 3 introduced new and uncertain governmental institutions on the Canadian side of the border. While the circumstances of Indigenous communities were acknowledged in some manner on both sides of the international boundary, intense federal-provincial conflict on the Canadian side coloured much subsequent history. Known as the Ontario boundary dispute, the intergovernmental struggle over land and jurisdiction exerted a continuing influence over regional affairs.

In Chapter 2, I examine the unfortunate fate of the valuable Lake of the Woods fishery, a resource contested between Aboriginal and commercial users whose claims were dependent, at least to some degree, on lingering federal-provincial disputes and on the virtually complete separation of Canadian and US fisheries regulation regimes. As Chapter 3 demonstrates, forest resource use and mineral development were similarly affected by assertions derived from Treaty 3 and the ongoing struggle between Ontario and the Canadian federal government respecting ownership and authority over forest and mineral resources. Chapters 4, 5, and 6 describe how waters and water powers, along with an emerging international pulp and paper sector, became directly entangled in complications derived from divergent preferences and perspectives, which were also traceable to competing federal, provincial, and Aboriginal visions of a regional destiny. Municipal and recreational interests around the watershed simultaneously contributed distinctive perspectives to the unfolding debate over water use and protection, emphasizing, in particular, considerations of water quality and public health.

Chapters 7 and 8 review and assess important public deliberations about "levelling the lake" in a manner that might reconcile priorities among a wide range of established and prospective users of the watershed's levels and flows. Beginning in 1912, consultations were conducted by the newly established Canada-United States International Joint Commission. Negotiation and deliberations continued – with national, state/provincial, and local government involvement – for several decades. As described in Chapter 9, alongside resource and industrial activity in the watershed, traditional Aboriginal users continued to seek access, while recreational interests on both sides of the international boundary asserted the importance of a broader set of environmental and conservationist values.

The 1950s and 1960s witnessed a significant attempt to restore water quality and habitat – particularly along the Rainy River and in Rainy Lake – the deterioration of which was attributable to the combined impacts of hydroelectric power production, pulp and paper effluent, municipal wastes, and wartime mining activity (Chapter 10). Even as those systematic remedial measures were being formulated, a tragic and devastating episode involving mercury contamination unfolded in the Wabigoon-English-Winnipeg River system to the north and west, which is detailed in Chapter 11.

Focusing on the forest sector, Chapter 12 examines the emergence of the principle of sustainable development in an era of significant conflict over resource use, environmental values, and Aboriginal rights. Chapter 13 discusses the late twentieth-century fishery as the subject of continuing controversy, with competing claims advanced by Aboriginal communities and commercial interests on both sides of the Canada-US border. Aboriginal treaty rights, the international trade regime, and the status of long-standing fishing licences were all invoked to defend entitlements to a diminishing resource. Contemporary attempts to establish more effective and collaborative institutions within and around the watershed are addressed in the final chapter, which emphasizes once more the potential contribution of the International Joint Commission as a forum for bringing together divergent views and voices in an attempt to identify common interests and concerns across the watershed. The Lake of the Woods experience thus provides a valuable opportunity to observe the progressive implementation of a framework for watershed management in a complex transboundary setting.

Levelling the Lake

I

Building Boundaries

A s the winter of 1868 approached, twelve to fifteen thousand residents of the isolated settlement at Red River, their crops devastated by locusts, faced "imminent danger of starvation." The Canadian government – in the belief that the Hudson's Bay Company (HBC), which then exercised authority across the region, had done nothing to address the "threatened calamity" – allocated $20,000 to relief supplies and road work linking the imperilled community with the Lake of the Woods.[1] For its part, the company deemed the fledgling Canadian government's initiative "most unusual and improper." The HBC strenuously objected to road construction from the settlement to the Lake of the Woods, describing the undertaking as "a trespass upon [its] freehold territory."[2] This early skirmish between remote competing authorities foreshadowed numerous land-use disputes soon to unfold within the territory, entangling incoming settlers and Indigenous inhabitants in contests about the rights of occupants, the quality of land ownership, and the relative authority of rival jurisdictions.

A Contested Territory

Canada's formal response to the HBC's protestations could not have been unexpected: "Canada ... denies ... the pretentions of the Hudson's Bay Company to any right of soil beyond that of squatters, in the territory through which the road complained of is being constructed."[3] Georges Etienne Cartier and William McDougall, then in London to represent

3

Canada in negotiations with the HBC concerning surrender of the fur trading company's North American domain, took advantage of the exceptional circumstances to claim humanitarian high ground. They insisted that the simple objective was "to supply food to a starving community about to be imprisoned for six months in the heart of a great wilderness." Since the settlement lacked roads and other means of communication, the government sought to provide a link "and to supply it in the way most acceptable to a high-spirited people, viz. in exchange for their labour."[4] Canada's ambassadors ventured further to suggest that the HBC might actually appreciate the transportation initiative as offering "valuable protection to those under their government against similar dangers in the future."[5] The Canadian negotiators took full advantage of the HBC's public relations misstep to condemn the company's stewardship. Had the company "performed the first duty of a government towards its people" by establishing an "easy means of communication with the outer world," or had it demonstrated some capacity to address the threatened calamity by forwarding provisions and supplies in a timely fashion, then "the Canadian government would have rested happy in the belief that neither humanity nor public policy required or justified their interference."[6]

In January 1869, Canada was pleased to report that relief supplies had arrived from St. Paul, the capital of neighbouring Minnesota, and that a second shipment was on hand in the Dakota Territory for spring delivery.[7] Yet collaborative good works in difficult circumstances hardly ensured harmonious international relations in the continental interior, for Canadian aspirations to secure HBC territory formed part of a more ambitious strategy to extend and solidify the authority of a youthful national government.

Much was at stake in connecting Canada's newly federated eastern provinces with the North-West Territories and British Columbia. The formation of a chain of settlements and communication linkages was of great public interest given "the danger of the Red River Settlement, from its close connection with Minnesota, consequent on its isolated position with regard to Canada, becoming imbued with American principles and views." The risk of losing Red River to "our rivals" threatened to deprive the country of trade with British Columbia, and ultimately with China.[8]

British and US negotiations over territorial boundaries had previously been contested within the frameworks of the 1783 Treaty of Paris and the 1814 Treaty of Ghent. The former, acknowledging American independence, apportioned this section of North America according to a line originating at Sault Ste. Marie and "thence through Lake Superior Northward of Isles Royal & Phelipeaux to the Long Lake; Thence through the middle of said

Long Lake, and the Water Communication between it & the Lake of the Woods ... Thence through the said Lake to the most Northwestern Point thereof."[9] The latter treaty, concluding the War of 1812, made provision for survey commissions and other required procedures to determine the boundary line on land and water and to identify the northwesternmost corner of the Lake of the Woods. At stake was the possibility that east-west traffic – including HBC trade – between Rainy River and the Red River settlement might be forced to enter American waters in order to pass around the vast Aulneau Peninsula, which would mean the potential further complication of tariff duties and American regulation.[10]

Transfer of the HBC's lands to Canada in 1869 may have forestalled American aspirations and, eventually, facilitated exchange with China, but it also introduced more immediate challenges. These included questions associated with the rudimentary track – or "simple road" – linking Fort Garry and the Lake of the Woods: What lands had actually been acquired, and by whom might the newly added territory be governed? Quite apart from American territorial aspirations, real or imagined, the Canadian contenders included the Dominion government as purchaser or in some other capacity, the ambitious Province of Ontario, neighbouring Manitoba (after 1870), and adherents to Louis Riel's alternative vision for the territory. Long-established Aboriginal communities also exercised governmental authority until such territorial claims as they might assert could be satisfactorily resolved. Thus, the relief road linking the Lake of the Woods to the West was a pathway to uncertainty. Decades later, even the HBC remained ensnared in residual controversy over the extent of its ongoing rights to land and water in the "disputed territory."

Cultivating Amicable Relations

In the late 1850s, Simon James Dawson became engaged in detailed reconnaissance of the territory between Lake Superior and the settlement at Red River.[11] He identified a route across the region designed to take advantage of navigable waterways while anticipating railway construction and simultaneously serving to forestall the northward expansion of American ventures.[12] Dawson, later an elected representative from the region that became Northwestern Ontario, was well acquainted with the resident Saulteaux or Ojibwa.[13] He met personally with community leaders around the fur trade post at Fort Frances on the Rainy River in 1868 with a view to facilitating construction of his proposed transportation corridor.[14]

The Ojibwa, Dawson affirmed, "are very intelligent and are extremely jealous as to their right of soil and authority over the country." He believed that "extreme prudence will always have to be observed by the officers in charge of men to keep them from coming in contact with the Indians." Through extensive interaction during fishing season along the Rainy River with their counterparts from Red Lake in the neighbouring state of Minnesota, the Indigenous Canadian population had learned from "expert diplomatists" and was well aware of ongoing treaty-making arrangements on the US side. Accordingly, Dawson cautioned that "anyone who, in negotiating with these Indians, should suppose he had mere children to deal with, would find himself mistaken."[15]

Accepting the Saulteaux as trustworthy, Dawson thought that they would adhere to treaty provisions, so long as these were equally respected by the incoming population. He anticipated that the Aboriginal inhabitants of the Rainy Lake and Lake of the Woods region would be prepared to accept a right-of-way across their lands, but he recognized their apprehension about the impact of settlement, particularly any interference with the fisheries, "their chief means of subsistence." Dawson, accordingly, considered that it would be "imprudent to introduce settlement in the particular section which they occupy."[16]

In an 1869 report, Dawson observed that the international boundary line ran through the territory, such that some of the Indigenous people lived on the US side and some to the north of the border.[17] "Permanent residents," however, were more numerous on the British side, while those from the United States appeared in greater numbers during the summer fishing season. He advised: "They are sufficiently organized, numerous and warlike, to be dangerous if disposed to hostility; and standing as they do in the gateway to the territories to the North West, it is of the highest importance to cultivate amicable relations with them." Dawson urged the government to address the question of a right-of-way as a matter of great significance, for the Indigenous residents "would be keenly alive to any imagined slight in opening a highway ... through a territory of which they believe themselves to be sole lords and masters, and to which, if a lengthened period of occupation can give a claim, they have unquestionably some title."[18] A hundred and fifty years later, the extent of "some title" remained under discussion.

In anticipation of treaty negotiations, Ojibwa leaders outlined an initial proposal.[19] They sought annual payments, forever, of $50 for each chief; $20 for council members; and $10 for every man, woman, and child. Chiefs also expected to receive livestock, tools such as saws and grindstones, provisions, and household equipment, as well as guns and munitions. In due course, requests were made for free passage on the expected railway – "things that run swiftly, that go by fire – carriages."[20]

Notwithstanding one unflattering prediction that the region could anticipate "a destiny of perpetual sterility," pressure for settlement and resource development intensified.[21] Mineral prospectors were active and passenger traffic was set to increase with the construction of numerous steam-powered vessels. W.F. Butler, a British military adventurer, describing the Lake of the Woods in the summer of 1870, forecast that "its shores and islands will be found to abound in minerals whenever civilization reaches them."[22] By early 1870, a thousand men or more were engaged in clearing and construction to facilitate Colonel Garnet Wolseley's expedition to quell Red River resistance to Canadian authority. Reporting his encounter with Wolseley's troops along the Rainy River in mid-summer, Butler counted seventeen large and well-provisioned vessels.[23]

The *Globe*, a Toronto newspaper, promoted Dawson's route, leading to significant government expenditures on roadways, portages, dams, and canal work to enhance navigability. Koochiching Falls, on the Rainy River, became a hub of construction as engineers excavated solid rock to produce a lock-and-canal complex to facilitate movement between Rainy Lake and the Lake of the Woods. Alongside these early stream flow alterations, an early lumber operation at Fowler's Mills introduced sawdust and slabs to the waterway.[24] Far more transformative impacts on regional waterways lay ahead.

By the end of May 1873, more than two hundred people had travelled the Dawson route by stage and steamer to reach Manitoba.[25] Vessels, including locally constructed steamboats, transported two thousand passengers during one season in the mid-1870s.[26] Yet travellers unaccustomed to the northern interior faced notoriously difficult conditions, including the rumoured threat that "every mosquito who has been turned out of doors by his parents or who has failed to earn a livelihood in other parts of the world, has emigrated to the Dawson Route."[27]

Despite heavy investment, the Dawson route remained vulnerable to competition, whether from alternative passageways through the United States or from the ambitious prospect of an all-Canadian railway. Ottawa's 1874 decision to pursue such a railway along a more northerly corridor connecting Fort William on Lake Superior with Manitoba via Rat Portage, a fur trade post located where the Lake of the Woods empties into the Winnipeg River, "brought the beginning of the end for Simon Dawson's magnificent dream."[28]

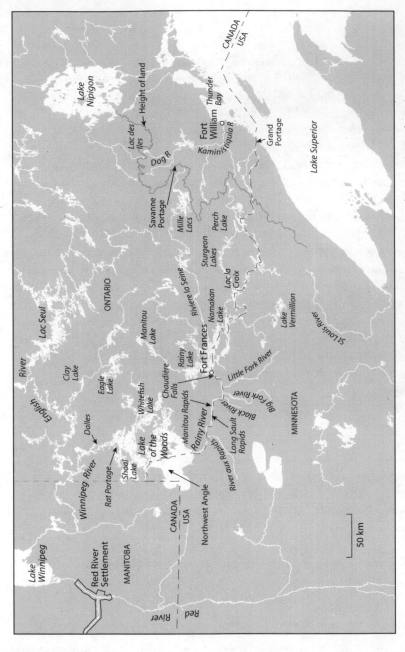

MAP 1.1 Regional Overview. *From Grace Lee Nute, Rainy River Country (Minnesota Historical Society: St. Paul, 1950). Map adapted by Eric Leinberger.*

As the 1870s began, Ojibwa fishing, hunting, and trapping continued. Garden plots and extensive wild rice harvesting activities further contributed to sustenance.[29] As Dawson had noted, the Ojibwa were determined to maintain their interests in these resources in the face of mounting external pressures. They clashed with settlers, prospectors, railway surveyors, and other work crews entering the district.[30] Chief Blackstone, in particular, resolutely resisted the activity of miners who had neither secured consent nor offered compensation to Indigenous residents. He disrupted developments around Shebandowan and carefully monitored the movement of both military and civilian expeditions. When steamboat construction and associated requirements for building supplies and fuel-wood foreshadowed greater flows of settlers and transients, Blackstone became a leading figure in the ranks of protesters.[31]

Benefits from development, though often welcome, did not alter the Ojibwa understanding of resource allocation. Thus, early business operators – steamboat builders, for example – readily purchased forest resources from the Indigenous inhabitants, who were also occasionally employed to provide timber and fuel-wood or to participate directly in building and transportation.[32] Individuals appreciated these sources of income, particularly when fish were in short supply.[33] However, the Ojibwa associated such payments with their collective interest in the region's forest resources, and so, during one round of treaty negotiations, Ojibwa representatives responded firmly to a suggestion on the part of a Canadian commissioner that timber resources were available for all to use: "What was said about the trees and rivers was quite true, but it was the Indian's country, not the white man's."[34]

Robert J.N. Pither had served nearly a quarter of a century with the HBC, including most of the decade from 1853 to 1863 at Fort Frances, when, in March 1871, he accepted an appointment from Joseph Howe, superintendent of Indian Affairs, to represent Canadian interests at Fort Frances. On advice from Simon Dawson, and after recent "unfortunate occurrences" at Fort Garry, Howe assigned Pither a "delicate and confidential mission" for maintaining good relations with the Indigenous people pending eventual negotiation of a treaty. The specific assignment was "to keep up a friendly intercourse with them and disabuse their minds of any idle reports they might hear as to the views and intentions of the Government of Canada in reference to them."[35]

In the fall of 1873, following earlier and unsuccessful rounds of negotiations and with government steamers already operating on the water system, Canadian representatives pursued the broadened goal of securing

FIGURE 1.1 Hudson Bay Company Post, Rat Portage, 1857. *Courtesy of Toronto Public Library.*

the full extent of Ojibwa territory.[36] Alexander Morris, Albert Norbert Provencher, and Simon Dawson met at Northwest Angle on the Lake of the Woods with Ojibwa leaders from Northwest Angle, Rat Portage, Lac Seul, Whitefish Bay, Grassy Narrows, Rainy River, Rainy Lake, Kettle Falls, Eagle Lake, Nepigon, and Shoal Lake.[37] Three regional chiefs – Blackstone of Rainy Lake, Mawintopinesse of Rainy River, and Powassan of the Lake of the Woods – figured prominently in negotiations.[38]

Governor Morris explained land transfer arrangements and his authority to establish Indian reserves. He offered land for farming as well as reserves approximating a square mile for every family. "It may be a long time before the other lands are wanted," he added, explaining that "in the meantime you will be permitted to fish and hunt over them."[39] In one of his most elaborate statements on cultivation and food, Governor Morris advised the chiefs of his objective to "do everything to help you by giving you the means to grow some food, so that if it is a bad year for fishing and hunting you may have something for your children at home." More specifically, he offered "two hoes, one spade, one scythe, and one axe for every family actually settled," along with communal agricultural equipment, oxen, cattle, and seed. In addition, Morris undertook to provide "ammunition, and twine for making nets, to the extent of $1,500 per year, for the whole nation, so that you can have the means of procuring food."[40] Difficult negotiations culminated in Treaty No. 3 (hereafter referred to as Treaty 3).[41]

The interpretations of the agreement of 3 October 1873 – what was in the minds of the commissioners and what Indigenous negotiators understood about the expectations captured in the treaty text – became questions of profound importance for the general configuration of Canadian society's later relationship with Aboriginal communities. Historian Donald Smith frames the inquiry with these questions: "What was the legal scope of the Indians' title? In what ways might native title properly be extinguished? And what was the effect of treaties that ceded lands to the Crown?"[42] Nearly a century and a half after the treaty, ethnohistorians, anthropologists, and political theorists debated the intentions of Governor Morris and his associates, the origins of Canada, the rationale underlying federal constitutional responsibility for "Indians and Lands Reserved for the Indians," and how Ojibwa representatives might have envisaged the treaty-based relationship they agreed to enter.[43]

One Ontario judge concluded in 2011 that the Indigenous communities would not have anticipated "increasing and cumulative negative impacts on their way of life."[44] According to her assessment of documentary evidence and oral testimony, the Ojibwa expected traditional harvesting practices to continue. She further suggested that the treaty commissioners also understood the importance of traditional Ojibwa harvesting and, for that reason, recognized "the importance of promising continuing Harvesting Rights to induce the Ojibway to enter the Treaty."[45] Moreover, in the judge's view, the route through the Treaty 3 territory was the primary interest of Canada and its commissioners, who were "less concerned with the prospects of the territory itself." With a view to securing the Dawson route and completing the Canadian Pacific Railway within the Treaty 3 area by 31 December 1876, "they needed to get the Treaty done."[46]

In the aftermath of negotiations, the creation of reserves was of pressing concern. Even before the formal approval of Treaty 3, Dawson launched the reserve-selection process through consultations. Yet it proved impossible to designate reserves in conjunction with the treaty itself. Hoping to forestall conflict, Morris specifically recommended against issuing patents or licences for mineral or timber lands until the reserves were allocated.[47] Shortly thereafter, explicit instructions were issued to avoid including mineral lands in designating reserves.[48] Unfortunately, however, conflicts arising from mineral prospects associated with reserve lands proved unavoidable.[49]

Dawson and Pither negotiated the selection of Treaty 3 reserves in the summer of 1874. By this time, Ojibwa chiefs had highlighted the urgency of the matter, emphasizing the importance of garden sites and fishing grounds. Dawson quickly identified the valley of the Rainy River as a location where agricultural reserves "could interfere with the progress of settlement." To mitigate potential conflicts, he sought to confine Rainy River reserves to about six square miles, land that encompassed sites previously occupied as camping grounds, fishing stations, and gardens.[50] Reverend George M. Grant, who accompanied the railway engineer Sandford Fleming through the district, also highlighted agricultural prospects along the Rainy River, where "every mile seemed well-adapted for cultivation and the dwellings of man."[51] The most fanciful nineteenth-century estimates even imagined "two million agriculturalists" in the "extremely luxuriant" district.[52]

INTERGOVERNMENTAL FRICTION

While it appeared that Canada and the HBC had successfully completed land transfer arrangements respecting the North-West Territories, and with Treaty 3 concluded, other matters represented potential sources of contention among neighbouring jurisdictions. Settlement and resource development were advancing northwards in Minnesota – soon to be accelerated by iron ore discoveries in the state's northeastern corner – while an epic federal-provincial struggle for control of land and resources emerged within the Canadian portion of the region.

Even before the treaty had been agreed, Ontario and the federal government were contesting provincial boundaries and natural resources.[53] In an 1871 memorandum prepared for Conservative prime minister John A. Macdonald, Dominion Surveyor General J.S. Dennis reviewed the origins of the provincial boundary dispute. The controversy centred upon the interpretation of language in the 1774 Quebec Act, in which the westerly boundary of Quebec, after reaching the northwest angle of what was then the Province of Pennsylvania, was set out. From that point, Quebec's boundary continued "along the western boundary of the said Province (Pennsylvania) until it strikes the River Ohio, and along the bank of the said river westward to the banks of the Mississippi, and northward to the southern boundary of the territory granted to the Merchant Adventurers of England trading to Hudson's Bay."[54]

Dennis explained two views as to the meaning of this description. Those committed to locating the Ontario boundary as far west as possible argued that "the term 'to the banks of the Mississippi, and northward to the southern boundary of the territory, etc., etc.,' means that in going northward, the banks of the Mississippi are to be followed to its source, and that they were in fact so intended in the Act." In contrast, an interpretation more favourable to the Dominion government suggested that the phrase "to the banks of the Mississippi" should be understood as meaning "to the banks of the said river at the point where it is joined by the Ohio, and the words which follow, 'and northward to the southern boundary etc,' was intended to be construed as upon a due north line."[55] A greater or lesser Ontario lay in the balance, as did a greater or lesser Canadian federal domain. And much else besides.

Oliver Mowat, premier of Ontario as of 1872, set out to establish his province's boundary as running north from the source of the Mississippi, a point slightly west of the Lake of the Woods.[56] With a more receptive Liberal government then in office federally, efforts to resolve an inherently contentious matter proceeded in as orderly a manner as could be expected. David Mills, a Liberal MP and a constitutionalist, was appointed special commissioner for Ontario in relation to the boundary issue in March 1872, reporting back in 1873 and again in 1877. Mills' reports facilitated an interim boundary determination in 1874 and an award by an arbitration panel four years later.[57]

In 1874, David Laird, federal minister of the Interior, and Timothy Blair Pardee, representing Ontario's Crown Lands department, agreed that following the final settlement, each of their respective governments would confirm and ratify land patents "issued by the other for lands then ascertained not to be within the territory of the government which granted them" and would account financially for proceeds or revenues derived from lands determined after resolution of the boundary dispute to belong to the other.[58] This worthy effort to provide clarity and stability was most welcome, yet it was inconclusive on at least two grounds. First, the mutual recognition of land patents failed to address vast acreages over which claims would arise under leases, licences, and other forms of entitlement. Further uncertainty derived from the fact that parts of the relevant terrain were simply unknown.

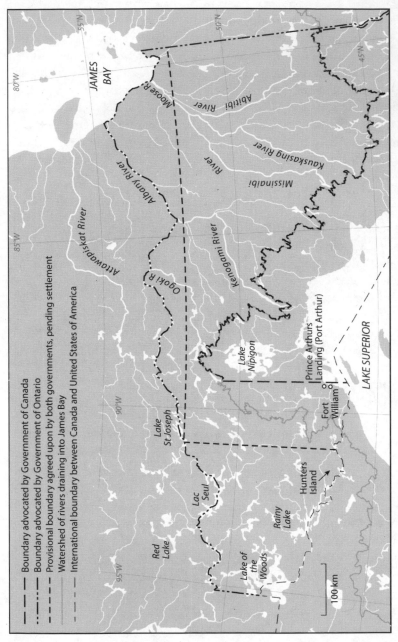

MAP 1.2 Boundary Dispute. *From Norman L. Nicholson, The Boundaries of the Canadian Confederation, (Macmillan of Canada for the Institute of Canadian Studies, Carleton University 1979). Map adapted by Eric Leinberger.*

As geologist Robert Bell explained, the height of land – that magisterial divide separating waters presumed to flow northwards from those draining to the Great Lakes-St. Lawrence, should that be identified as a boundary – was more readily conceived on a map than located on the ground. The level landscape and the interlocking headwaters of numerous small streams presented great challenges: "The water soaks through the moss and swamps and one cannot tell on which side of the watershed he may be."[59] The precise location of watershed boundaries remained elusive well over a century later, when a new generation of surveyors and officials set out to delineate ecological rather than political space. But Bell's quest for political lines that corresponded with the flow of waters underscored an enduring theme in the region's development.

Provisional boundaries were agreed by orders-in-council in 1874, with Ontario accepting the award in advance.[60] But when Ottawa rejected the arrangements, the Ontario legislation was never proclaimed.[61] The dispute soon found its way to arbitration.

The 1878 board of arbitrators consisted of a provincial nominee, Ontario chief justice R.A. Harrison; Sir Francis Hincks, who was named by the Dominion; and Sir Edward Thornton, Britain's representative in Washington, who acted as the neutral third member. Prime Minister Alexander Mackenzie accepted the arbitrators' findings, which largely favoured Ontario's position, but following a Conservative election victory, John A. Macdonald returned to the office of prime minister and refused to ratify the award. The federal-provincial boundary conflict escalated thereafter, with the interests of neighbouring Manitoba becoming more prominently engaged.

With a growing need for lumber supplies and a covetous eye on port facilities at Lake Superior, the Manitoba legislature approved an eastward extension of its boundaries in December 1880.[62] The next spring, the federal government extended Manitoba's boundaries to the north and east so as to meet the "westerly boundary of Ontario."[63]

The Toronto press relentlessly emphasized the commercial basis for Ontario's acrimonious opposition to Dominion interference in the northwest, metaphorically invoking a creative understanding of upstream-downstream relations: "Where is the future growth of Toronto to come from if one half of the country tributary to the city is to be chopped away?" With support from Ottawa, Manitoba's ambitions threatened Toronto's ambition to become the political capital of the disputed territory and to dominate the trade of the country.[64]

Officials representing their respective provincial interests pursued conflicting agendas, soon triggering intense skirmishing. In response to a petition from merchants at the new lakeshore community of Rat Portage and
elsewhere along the railway line when construction of the transcontinental
CPR got underway, Ontario established Division Courts for the District
of Thunder Bay in May 1880. In the absence of civil courts, local business
operators found it impossible "to enforce payment of our outstanding
debts" against subcontractors, traders, and labourers who simply moved
on following completion of the works along portions of the railway.[65] The
matter of squatters also called for attention: that category included a wide
range of occupants of unsurveyed lands along the Rainy River, around
the townsite of the new community of Keewatin, and on Shoal Lake, an
important body of water linked through a short channel to the Lake of the
Woods and shared – sometimes controversially – between Manitoba and
Ontario.

George Burden, an Ontario-appointed commissioner, reported as squatters a number of butchers, carpenters, general labourers, and lumbermen,
as well as a railway conductor and an engineer, while assuring Premier
Oliver Mowat that no irregular inducements had ever been offered to
secure their political allegiance to the government candidate in local elections.[66] Conflict and political uncertainty intensified following simultan-
eous elections for the overlapping constituencies of Varennes in Manitoba
and Algoma in Ontario. As the Manitoba merchant and journalist
Alexander Begg wryly observed, "the people of the district had the unique
privilege of voting in both Provinces, for members to represent them in
two Provincial Legislatures."[67] Begg was simultaneously entertained and
appalled by the interjurisdictional shenanigans: "One day a Manitoba constable would be arrested for drunkenness by an Ontario constable, the
next, Manitoba would reciprocate by arresting an Ontario official." Amidst
these distractions, Begg imagined that "gamblers and whiskey pedlars
enjoyed almost complete immunity," for not even the most industrious
constable could monitor the miscreants "while he was himself a fugitive
from justice, engaged in dodging a warrant for his own arrest."[68]

Judicial Resolution

Following one inflammatory episode involving the arrest by eager Ontario
officials of Manitoba's police chief, Attorney General Mowat and his Manitoba counterpart, James Millar, arranged to coordinate policing and various

FIGURE 1.2   Manitoba Jail, 1883. *Courtesy of the Lake of the Woods Museum.*

civil matters and to submit a joint case on the boundary dispute to the august Judicial Committee of the Privy Council (JCPC).[69] This would be the first of a remarkable number of opportunities offered to the JCPC to familiarize itself with the contested geography of this granitic corner of empire.

Toronto's *Globe* reported the JCPC's boundary decision as a provincial triumph: "From Glengarry to the Lake of the Woods and from Hudson Bay to the Pelee Islands – these are the magnificent distances between the utmost bounds of the province we may now call our own! It is a splendid victory!" Even if the geographical reference points do not fit harmoniously to the tune of *This Land Is Your Land*, the message was unmistakeable: "Ontario wins! The once Disputed Territory is ours!" In addition to most welcome spoils, Ontario enjoyed – and embellished – the experience of the successful struggle that had pitted "all the force against all the right!" The reputation of Prime Minister Macdonald, "a lifelong enemy" of the province, had been "shattered by this crushing verdict, this unanswerable exposure to the baselessness of the pretensions upon which he has founded his six years of rancorous hostility to Ontario."[70]

Yet even before the "crushing verdict" against a boundary demand grounded on an interpretation of historical maps and documentation, Prime Minister Macdonald had reformulated the foundation of federal claims: "By seven treaties the Indians of the Northwest conveyed the lands to Canada; and every acre belongs now to the people of Canada, and not to the people of Ontario," the argument began. As a consequence, "there is not one stick of timber, one acre of land, or one lump of lead, iron or gold that does not belong to the Dominion, or to the people who purchased from the Dominion government."[71]

The intergovernmental contest unfolded on several planes, combining bold and intricate legal manoeuvres with determined political engagement. Political struggles at the local electoral level were deeply coloured by the boundary controversy as rival parties allied with local newspapers to rally supporters in vigorous electoral combat.[72]

But land management proved to be the most contentious issue, one Canadian centennial history reporting that "chaos reigned in the woods over federal and provincial licensing."[73] Charges that Macdonald "gave away literally dozens of timber limits to his political friends provoked acrimonious parliamentary exchanges: for example, one MP, in a House of Commons debate in 1886, declared: "All the grants of the public domain which have been made by this Administration have been made to supporters of themselves, either in or out of Parliament."[74] Beyond partisan considerations, however, was the underlying determination of Ontario to secure control of valuable natural resources in the face of persistent federal unwillingness to implement the boundary award.

In November 1883, St. Catharines Milling and Lumbering Company, whose backers and advocates included identifiable Conservative supporters, obtained a federal timber licence for land south of Wabigoon Lake, about twenty miles southeast of what is now Dryden, along the Canadian Pacific Railway (CPR) line.[75] To supply rail-line construction ties, St. Catharines Milling and Lumber Company cut timber pursuant to a federal government licence on land that Ontario believed to be its own. The St. Catharines Milling licence formed the basis of a "test case," an initiative that would firmly demonstrate Ontario's commitment to provincial timber resources and the revenue stream they represented. Ontario seized timber cut by St. Catharines, sold it, and successfully obtained an injunction against the federally licensed company in early 1885.[76]

The federal view, following Macdonald's revised line of argument, was that the Dominion owned the disputed lands and resources through acquisition under Treaty 3. Ontario, having rested its own claims for years on the documentary record that had stood it in good stead through the arbitration process and the 1884 JCPC decision, was initially ill-prepared to confront the new formulation of federal claims.[77] As historian Barry Cottam explains, the legal challenge facing Ontario was to advance an alternative analysis of the significance of the treaty: "Indian title had to be established as something less than full ownership for Ontario's counter-claim to stand."[78]

In the House of Commons, Liberal MP David Mills contributed force-fully to Ontario's cause. His partisanship towards the province was clear: "Anything like hesitation in the total exclusion of Manitoba from any exercise of authority is injurious," he declared.[79] Mills drew upon his deep knowledge of Indian affairs from his previous experience as minister of the Interior in Alexander Mackenzie's cabinet to actively challenge Macdonald in Parliament over Dominion resource licences. In March 1885, Mills set out a long statement on the nature of Indian title that contributed to Ontario's evolving legal position.[80] Cottam sums up the Ontario gov-ernment's assertions "that the Indians had no concept of property recog-nizable in law, and that, whether they did or not, the title to the lands of North America lay in the Crown of England by virtue of the processes of discovery, conquest and settlement." Accordingly, "if the Indians had any rights at all, they came through the generosity of the Crown."[81] Thus for-mulated, the debate over the validity of the St. Catharines company's Dominion licence to cut timber set the stage for a legal contest of funda-mental importance.[82]

As judicial proceedings opened in Toronto on 18 May 1885, the Riel Rebellion was underway.[83] Only one witness, Alexander Morris, the com-missioner who had negotiated Treaty 3, appeared in Chancellor John Alexander Boyd's court. The proceedings were otherwise confined to legal presentations. D'Alton McCarthy, representing St. Catharines and thus arguing for the validity of the Dominion timber licence, insisted that the St. Catharines licence had been issued on the basis of ownership transferred from the Ojibwa to the federal Crown pursuant to the treaty. Oliver Mowat, in his capacity of attorney general, and William Cassels represented Ontario.

Oliver Mowat directly attacked the foundations of Macdonald's revised assertion of Dominion authority: "We say that there is no Indian title at law or in equity. The claim of the Indians is simply moral and no more."[84] Ontario's position was more fully set out as the case advanced. In the Court of Appeal, Ontario asserted that the Ojibwa right to land was "at most only a right of personal occupation during the pleasure of the Crown, by the band of Indians occupying the same as hunting grounds or otherwise, and was not transferable." Based on the view that the Ojibwa enjoyed only a "right of personal occupation," Ontario insisted that "the so-called sur-render of Treaty 3 (regarding it as having extinguished the so-called Indian claim), did not and could not transfer the lands or any interest therein to the Dominion."[85]

Following Chancellor Boyd's judgment in June 1885 and the Court of Appeal decision almost a year later, the St. Catharines case proceeded to the Supreme Court of Canada, where Justice Samuel Henry Strong – in a dissenting opinion – introduced the notion of usufructuary rights. Although lacking precise legal definition, this concept, as Strong expressed it, "nevertheless sufficed to protect the Indians in the absolute use and enjoyment of their lands, whilst at the same time they were incapacitated from making any valid alienation otherwise than to the crown itself, in whom the ultimate title was, in accordance with the English law of real property, considered as vested."[86]

While "absolute use and enjoyment" represented a high level of respect and protection for Indigenous interests in land use, the entitlement to use traditional lands would not be sufficient to uphold the Dominion's claim to own the disputed territory. Nor, in the longer term, would it satisfy Aboriginal claims to ownership that had been expressed in the context of treaty negotiations: "We have a rich country, it is the Great Spirit who gave us this; where we stand upon is the Indians' property, and belongs to them."[87]

In proceedings before the JCPC, advocates for Ontario, now including Lord Haldane, and for the Dominion, which participated directly in support of its timber licence holder, restated their respective positions.[88] The 1888 JCPC ruling rejected the Dominion government view, while endorsing the concept of usufructory rights. Although distancing itself from the extreme position of Chancellor Boyd, the JCPC grounded Indian possession of traditional lands on the *Royal Proclamation of 1763*. At this point, however, the concept of usufruct underpinned the analysis: "Indian possession was not a fee-simple title but merely a right to occupy the land."[89] With this burden on the Crown's underlying title being extinguished or removed by treaty, the lands passed, by virtue of section 109 of the British North America Act (1867), to the province.

Against this new backdrop, implementation of the earlier boundary award resumed. Provincial boundaries were confirmed in 1889 on the basis of a JCPC recommendation for imperial legislation, which was requested from Canada by means of a joint address to the imperial Parliament.[90]

The legislative confirmation of new boundaries in 1889 failed utterly to forestall continuing and future controversies over land and resources arising from the intergovernmental conflict.[91] Ontario, following the protracted dispute with federal officials, had little inclination to compromise a hard-fought legal victory. Among those affected by the province's firm defence of its interests were the Ojibwa, whose reserve boundaries remained in abeyance.

TREATY IMPLEMENTATION

In 1875, to confirm the selection of reserves (which had still to be settled), Surveyor General J.S. Dennis conferred with Indigenous communities.[92] At about the same time, Robert Pither was appointed as Dominion Lands agent to give him the authority to deal with trespassers cutting timber on reserves.[93] There were, however, extraordinary delays in confirmation of the reserves, attributable largely to the federal-provincial boundary conflict. Regrettably, uncertainty, confusion, and controversy over the location and status of reserve lands persisted until 1915, forty-two years after the conclusion of the Treaty 3 negotiations.[94]

Formerly occupants of their own lands, the Ojibwa, following resolution of the provincial boundary dispute, found themselves to be residents of Ontario. They were living on unconfirmed reserves designated through consultations with federal officials on lands that were understood to be part of the province, lands that had perhaps even belonged to Ontario from the date of Confederation, six years before the treaty. The conundrum arising from the *St. Catharines* decision and the boundary legislation was difficult indeed: as Barry Cottam puts it: "How could amends be made to Ontario for past actions of the Dominion upon lands it was now seen as having no right to act upon without disturbing the expectations of the Indians upon those lands who were signatories to the treaty as well?"[95]

Taking the position that the province now enjoyed "absolute ownership of all the Treaty 3 lands" while insisting that it had not consented to the use of those lands for the creation of reserves, Ontario questioned the validity of federally allocated reserves.[96] Prolonged efforts to resolve this and other federal-provincial differences lingering in the aftermath of the boundary settlement included negotiation, legislation, and further court proceedings that extended over several decades. But these efforts involved comparatively limited direct participation on the part of the Aboriginal communities affected, some of whom – especially along the Rainy River – eventually obtained reserves falling short of original expectations.

Governments made some headway in the immediate aftermath of the JCPC decision as Oliver Mowat pressed to secure his understanding of the *St. Catharines Milling* result. Mowat sought to clarify the foundations of resource development and settlement, including the residual status of hunting and fishing rights. As his point of departure, the Ontario premier declared that "the meaning [of the Treaty] of course was that such matters should be determined by the authority, whatever it was, from which grants for settlement, etc, should come." Given Ontario's success in the courts, he suggested that "the Province becomes the rightful authority to make grants, etc., free from the Indian right of hunting and fishing." In an attempt to avoid further uncertainty or even friction and litigation, Mowat requested a federal order-in-council, to be confirmed by legislation. He took the liberty to "enclose draft of such an Order etc as I think would do."[97]

Concurrent federal and provincial legislation emerged in 1891, followed by a ratification agreement three years later.[98] The combined effect of these measures has been described as an amendment to the treaty, but the 1894 agreement was at least expected to facilitate Ontario's acceptance of the location and extent of the Treaty 3 reserves as previously selected.[99] The agreement also provided for a process to resolve any questions if the province was not satisfied with the proposed reserves.[100] The basis of such dissatisfaction was already beginning to emerge.

Provincial inspection of reserves allocated by federal officials revealed that their extent significantly exceeded the formula of one square mile per family, as set out in 1873.[101] Although E.B. Borron, who reported on the location of the proposed reserves, was anxious to avoid any appearance of bad faith, he was equally of the view that Ontario should be compensated by the federal government, which had generously allocated valuable provincial lands to reserves.[102] This factor, among others, further delayed the confirmation of reserve lands.[103]

Beyond challenges arising from the boundary award, regional affairs were further complicated by the changing status of adjacent lands. Lying to the north of the disputed territory, the vast District of Keewatin remained under federal authority as part of the old North-West Territories until a portion was annexed to Ontario by statute in 1912. A century later, in a twenty-first-century controversy involving Aboriginal rights and environmental issues, an Ontario court signalled the continuing significance of boundary matters and the status of the 1891 legislation in the Keewatin Territory. Justice Marie Sanderson noted that "the lands in issue in this litigation are *not* in the Disputed Territory but in Keewatin, which at the time was unaffected by the 1891 Legislation. If the 1912 annexation did not affect it, the 1873 Treaty Harvesting Rights continue in respect of Keewatin to this day."[104] But the resolution of this riddle lies ahead, one of many examples of the complex intermingling of past and present in this region's history.[105]

Persistent controversy continued, not only about boundaries but about resources affected by those boundaries – whether trees on the ground, precious minerals beneath it, valuable fisheries within regional waters, or regulation of the waters themselves. Fisheries issues were particularly challenging because of the wide range of interests, jurisdictions, and values involved in the exploitation and management of the resource.

2

Cultural, Commercial, and Constitutional Fishing

Two years after being described by US fisheries officials as "the greatest sturgeon pond in the world," the Lake of the Woods fishery had declined "almost to the vanishing point."[1] Fisheries threatened with exhaustion were not uncommon, although distinctive circumstances rendered the Lake of the Woods resource particularly vulnerable. One contributor to damage from exploitation was competition in various forms – between Aboriginal and commercial resource users, within commercial ranks, between licensed operators and poachers, between Canadian and American fishing interests and their governments, and between federal and provincial regulators on the Canadian side. Shoreline developments and new structures that were introduced to control water-level fluctuations or to generate electricity threatened habitat, including spawning grounds, thereby undermining regenerative capacity and presenting further sources of conflict between competing authorities over long-term arrangements for water management.[2]

CULTURAL FISH

Fur trade records indicate that under Ojibwa management, "a sustained sturgeon fishery of considerable size" existed from at least the 1820s to the advent of the non-Native commercial fishery in the 1880s.[3] European explorers from La Verendrye, in the 1730s, through the artist Paul Kane and the mid-nineteenth-century military observer W.F. Butler, remarked on the abundance of the fishery, notably sturgeon. After purchasing a few sturgeon at the Manitou Rapids along the Rainy River in 1859, John Jessop confirmed their special significance: "The Indians of that region subsist chiefly on that species of fish; in fact it is as much the staff of life among them as bread is with us."[4]

Researchers estimate that Aboriginal fishers employing a variety of techniques involving hooks, lines, nets, and spears harvested slightly above 140,000 kilograms per year of sturgeon between 1823 and 1885.[5] The cultural significance of the annual sturgeon harvest was striking. Simon Dawson reported that with the opening of spring navigation, the Ojibwa left their hunting grounds to "congregate in considerable numbers" in search of fish.[6] Councils were held and feasts celebrated along the Rainy River, where sturgeon were plentiful, if not always as forthcoming as W.F. Butler once recounted: "During the long night a large sturgeon, struck suddenly by a paddle, alarmed us by bounding out of the water and landing full upon the gunwale of the canoe."[7] As many as fifteen hundred people attended gatherings around Fort Frances, where an abundant fishing harvest supported social activities. Alongside marriages and dances, elders met in council to deliberate on community affairs, "while matrons with some regard to the future, dry the flesh of the sturgeon in the sun and store it past a day of want."[8]

In early July, as river flows declined, the population relocated to sandy plains and rocky islets in search of blueberries, another valuable staple, which were sun-dried and compressed into cakes for storage.[9] The coming of the railways facilitated a transition to blueberries as a valuable cash crop.[10] In the late 1890s, berrypickers collected 150 tons of blueberries or more in the Lake of the Woods area, an important harvest worth around $9,000 in 1901, and one that continued to grow.[11] The wild rice harvest, next in the annual cycle, was of even greater significance.

Concern for the fishery was evident as early as 1873. In the words of an Ojibwa chief: "One thing I find, that deranges a little my kettle. In this river, where food used to be plentiful for our subsistence, I perceive it is getting scarce." Making a direct link to the integrity of the water system, he emphasized that "the river should be left as it was formed from the beginning – that nothing be broken." Preservation of the fishery was not an issue that Canadian negotiators had been prepared to address, and their responses fell well short of the desired assurances. For his part, Governor Morris declared: "This is a subject I cannot go into," while Simon Dawson cautioned that future circumstances could not be guaranteed: "Anything that we are likely to do at present will not interfere with the fishing, but

FIGURE 2.1   Blueberry Pickers, 1912. *Courtesy of the Carl Linde and Minnesota Historical Society.*

no one can tell what the future may require, and we cannot enter into any engagement."[12] In connection with the selection of reserves, further efforts, which were not entirely effective, were made to preserve community access to traditional fisheries.

Surveyor-General J.S. Dennis learned first-hand of the Rainy River fishing grounds in the early fall of 1875. In considering reserve boundaries, he noted specifically that fisheries opposite reserve lands would be "open to Indians generally." Moreover, given the possibility that canal construction might harm or destroy fishing grounds, it was understood that "the Indians [are] to be fairly dealt with in consequence."[13] Additional protections were suggested fifteen years later, in the aftermath of the boundary settlement when Ontario and the federal government sought to resolve some of the practical issues created during the extended period of jurisdictional uncertainty.

When, for example, the suggestion arose in the context of concurrent 1891 federal and Ontario legislation that reserve boundaries might be drawn across the water to extend from headland to headland (i.e., from one shoreline point to the next), the objective was presumably to secure food sources – fish and wild rice – for Indigenous communities.[14] Such an arrangement to substantially increase the size of reserves while simultaneously excluding non-Aboriginal people from fishing inside the new boundaries met with firm opposition from Ontario. By this time, competition for the fishery had expanded dramatically and fears of overfishing were already being expressed.[15]

Although the federal and provincial governments affirmed that the Ojibwa would retain the "right to pursue their avocations of hunting and fishing throughout the tract surrendered ... subject to such regulations as might from time to time be made by the Government of the Dominion of Canada," Indigenous representatives expressed a different understanding of the agreement.[16] In the words of Conducumewininie, a Northwest Angle chief who had signed the treaty: "When we gave up our lands to the Queen we did not surrender our fish to her, as the Great Spirit made them for our special use."[17]

To encourage commercial fishing, Ontario refused to recognize Aboriginal fisheries while licensing twenty-five gill net operations on the Lake of the Woods and Rainy Lake in 1894.[18] Native resource users found it increasingly difficult to sustain their communities and grew deeply disheartened by official interference with their efforts to support themselves through hunting and fishing.[19] Representatives of the Rainy River, Rainy Lake, and upstream Seine River bands expressed their dissatisfaction through the years, stating emphatically in a petition to the federal government in 1909:

> We are not seeking anything new but only want our dues between us our fathers and this Government at North West Angle in the year 1873 ... We also wish to Fish for ourselves all the year and no reserve seasons for us. It's our daily food. We don't want to be stopped and Game Inspectors cutting our lines and taking our nets.

"Reserve seasons" were among the prominent conservation measures designed to preserve stocks, but they interfered with traditional harvest practices. Similar restrictions on hunting also frustrated the Indigenous harvest and aroused grievances. "We want to know the reason why?" the petitioners wrote. "The White Man's laws are all right for them – we live and let live in our hunting they do not, just shoot and destroy." Expectations associated with the treaty arrangements had not been met: "Are your words or the word of the Great White Queen our Mother to be as smoke? We trust you will remember the Queen's man's word is his bond."[20]

At about the same time, the chief of the Couchiching community along Rainy River protested that expectations of continued access to the fishery were being largely undermined by overfishing on the US side. He complained that two or three car loads of fish taken from Rainy Lake were shipped by rail daily from Ranier to Chicago or New York: "Americans are fishing all the time in Canadian waters. Is there no remedy to this fraud? If not, where will we get our fish in a very near future?"[21] Such apprehension was by no means unwarranted as the commercial harvest expanded.

COMMERCIAL FISH

A modest commercial but unlicensed fishery was underway by 1884 to take advantage of new railway connections. Two seasons later, Alex McQueen, the Winnipeg-based federal inspector of fisheries, reported that thirty-five thousand pounds of fish were "shipped by a few small traders" out of Rat Portage.[22]

A flurry of commercial fishing licence applications during the 1880s prompted Canada's federal government to contemplate a suitable regulatory approach that would control access to the resource while generating some income from fees. In July 1888, D.F. Reid and Company, an American venture associated with Baltimore Packing, secured the first federal gill net licence on an experimental basis.[23] Following this initiative, further licences were issued: three in 1892, twenty-four in 1893, forty-seven in 1894, and a hundred the next year. Government revenues from the permit program increased from $70 in 1892 to just over $1,000 in 1894, reaching $4,140 in 1895.[24] Meanwhile, US authorities at the mouth of the Rainy River collected $300 to $400 per month in revenues and duties on fish imported from Canada.[25]

Lacking rail facilities at the southern end of the lake, US fishermen generally barged their catch of sturgeon and sturgeon roe to the D.F. Reid operation at Rat Portage for packing, freezing, and shipment via the Canadian Pacific Railway.[26] Ventures of this kind proliferated into the mid-1890s as experienced fishers relocated to the Lake of the Woods from Wisconsin, Lake Michigan, or Lake Erie, among other locations. The Sandusky firm, for example, abandoned Lake Erie, shipping nine car loads of nets and equipment as well as a fishing tug to the Lake of the Woods in 1894.[27] In 1896, the Minnesota Fish and Game Commission licensed 211 nets, including allocations to the Baltimore Packing Co. (50), Sandusky (50), Coffee Bros. (25), Minnesota Fish Co. (50), Lake of the Woods Fish Co. (14), and H.P. Asmus and Sons (18).[28] Both the number of tugs and boats operating on the Canadian side and employment in the fishery peaked in that same year.[29]

Effective techniques for catching fish – gill nets and pound nets – accompanied the advent of commercial operations. Gill nets, generally machine made, were run in straight lines between marker buoys in fairly shallow water. Small fish could pass through while larger fish were trapped by the gills. Gill nets could be brought into Canada free of duty if used by the importer.[30]

The more controversial pound nets were substantially larger and placed in deeper waters for more extended periods of time. Wooden piles from fifty to a hundred feet in length were driven into the lake bed at intervals of about seventy-five feet to form a square roughly five hundred feet on each side. A vast net, equal in depth to the water, was then hung inside the poles and fastened, forming a pen. A long leader net running out from one side of the pound was largely impassable; most fish would simply have to travel alongside it until they came to a passageway, about two or three feet wide, allowing them into the pound. Sturgeon, pickerel, and whitefish were the primary species captured in this fashion. Crown timber agent William Margach informed Aemilius Irving, who was carefully investigating intergovernmental administrative and financial matters on behalf of the Ontario government, of about ten pound nets under Canadian licence along the Rainy River, where he believed they were not authorized by US officials.[31] In the overall water system, however, pound nets on the US side vastly outnumbered Canadian usage.[32] Indeed, US observers reported fourteen pound nets in Canadian waters and more than ten times that number on the American side in the spring of 1894.[33]

The sturgeon catch expanded dramatically. Noting that sturgeon "swarmed ... in almost incredible numbers," Warren Evermann and Homer Latimer, in a study for the US Bureau of Fisheries shortly before World War I, declared the Lake of the Woods to be "the greatest sturgeon pond in the world."[34] With more promotional ends in mind, George Barnes, mayor of Rat Portage in the mid-1890s, asserted that "the Lake of the Woods produces seventy-five per cent of the caviar supply of the world."[35] His assessment of the fishery suggested that it brought $200,000 to the local economy, affording employment to five hundred men.[36] Sturgeon shipped out by rail in the winter months were "stacked like cordwood."[37] The sturgeon harvest was not to be confused with a sport fishery; as Canadian federal officials explained in 1891: "Its sluggish nature renders its capture comparatively easy, as they can be herded into nets with little difficulty."[38]

The principal products of the fishery, ranked by value, were caviar; isinglass, a product of the swim bladder; the flesh – salted, smoked, or otherwise prepared; sturgeon oil, highly regarded in the leather industry; and fertilizer, produced from entrails and scrap. Further minor uses included glue-making, while somewhat esoteric delicacies were offered to markets in Russia, China, and Astrakhan.[39]

On average, each female sturgeon yielded ten gallons of roe, estimated to contain 1 to 3 million eggs.[40] The bulk of production was destined for Hamburg merchants supplied out of New York. Canada's Dominion commissioner of fisheries, the highly qualified Edward Ernest Prince, who arrived in Canada with a solid track record of research in Scotland, remarked: "The final destination of much sturgeon roe secured in Canada was either Germany, Russia or London, and much of it no doubt returned to this side of the Atlantic put up in characteristic European packages and marketed at exorbitant European market prices."[41] Experimental shipments estimated at eight to ten thousand pounds travelled from Rat Portage to London in the late 1890s under the direction of an English buyer. The Canadian Department of the Imperial Institute was credited with another trial shipment, heralded as "a new Canadian product of an unusual sort." This fifteen hundred pounds of caviar travelled from Rat Portage in cold storage so as to reach London in a condition that satisfied the consignee in both its quality and condition. "It is said that the appearance of the Canadian product closely resembles the best Russian," noted Prince.[42]

The International Joint Commission (IJC), formed under the Canada-US Boundary Waters Treaty of 1909, gathered data on the fishery in order to assess the impact of water-level regulation. Between 1888 and 1909, almost 23 million pounds of whitefish, yellow pike, jackfish, and sturgeon were taken from pound nets in the Lake of the Woods, with 18 million pounds credited to the US side and 5 million allocated to Canada. Officially, peak production occurred in 1894, when the reported catch reached 3,125,835 pounds, valued at $88,225.[43]

Unsurprisingly, observers reported that "the sturgeon are not half as abundant as they used to be" and began to call for conservation measures.[44] Apprehension about the long-term prospects for sturgeon was not universal, however; one US commentator, supervising Sandusky operations on Oak Island, denied that the population faced depletion: "We are only fishing just in one corner for them and they are all around these islands."[45]

The IJC statistics may actually have captured only that portion of the Canadian catch shipped through Warroad, neglecting Canadian-sourced shipments sent out through what was now Kenora (renamed from Rat

FIGURE 2.2   Curry Sturgeon Fishery on the Lake of the Woods, c. 1900.
Courtesy of the Lake of the Woods County Museum.

FIGURE 2.3   Warroad Fishermen. *International Joint Commission,* Lake of the
Woods Reference, *1917.*

Portage in 1905).[46] Nor does it appear that the IJC incorporated information concerning an important Canadian fishery at Shoal Lake, whose waters are directly connected with the Lake of the Woods. The Norman Fish Company alone took nearly a million pounds of fish from Shoal Lake in 1895 for delivery to Selkirk, Manitoba.[47]

The harvest from Rainy Lake and upstream waters was also significant. In 1908, some 160,000 pounds, valued at $4,050, came out of the nets. In 1916, a more comprehensive review indicated that sixty-two Canadian fishermen operated with Ontario licences and contributed to a total catch valued at $46,413.19. Canada's Rainy Lake fishery involved thirty-six boats, including eighteen gasoline vessels reportedly worth $8,290. Pound nets were valued at $5,500 and gill nets at $4,610. Ice houses, freezers, wharves, and piers represented a further investment of around $3,000.

In the same year, forty-three licence-holders authorized by the Minnesota Game and Fish Commission to fish on Rainy Lake and upstream on Kabetogame, Namakan, Sand Point, and La Croix Lakes landed a substantial $58,104.62 worth of fish. The Indigenous subsistence fishery in both Canadian and US waters, while difficult to assess in the absence of reporting, was thought to be worth more than $5,000 for 1916.[48]

The rapid expansion of commercial sturgeon harvesting in the early 1890s was succeeded by a precipitous decline. Thus, while 1.3 million pounds of fish, valued at $26,000, were taken from American waters in 1893, by 1903, the sturgeon catch had been reduced to forty-five thousand pounds, worth roughly $2,700.[49] Despite modest fluctuations, the American catch remained low from 1903 onwards.

Ontario experienced a similar rise and decline in harvest levels. From a reported catch of forty thousand pounds in 1888, production rose to 1.65 million pounds in 1893, remaining at approximately that level until 1896. By 1909, the catch had fallen to below fifty-four thousand pounds.[50] The devastating peak harvests of sturgeon in the mid-1890s were thus several multiples of the average Aboriginal catch of 140,000 kilograms (roughly 300,000 pounds) during the earlier decades of the nineteenth century.[51] In fact, federal officials in Canada were on record at the start of the 1890s in noting that excessive fishing threatened to deplete the Lake of the Woods entirely. For conservation purposes and in order to maintain the fishery "as a means of livelihood to the Indians," officials called for a prohibition on pound nets.[52]

Visiting officials such as Archibald Blue of the Ontario Bureau of Mines fully appreciated the risk of overfishing. Following his 1895 tour of northwestern Ontario, Blue reported that "at the rate at which operations have been carried on during the last two years it is feared that the waters will soon be fished out."[53] Margach, the Crown timber agent, expressed similar alarm following the introduction of pound nets along the Rainy River: "This I think is an offul [sic] mistake. If they are going to clean out the Inland Lakes and Rivers God help Lake of the Woods."[54]

Well before this point, very significant increases in the volume of fish taken from the Lake of the Woods in the late 1880s accentuated Ojibwa concerns, prompting Canadian federal officials who assumed they enjoyed relevant constitutional authority to consider further safeguards. Timber operators, for example, were regularly instructed to provide fishways or ladders to allow passage around dams.[55] Federal officials continued to discourage pound nets, while Simon Dawson, in his capacity as MP for Algoma, regularly denounced the threat posed by commercial fishing to Ojibwa fishing interests in Treaty 3.[56] Believing that the treaty recognized the right of Indigenous communities to fish throughout their former territories, Dawson expressed concern if the commercial fisherman "is allowed to go wherever he likes, and to make a speculation in sweeping the fish out of the lakes and sending them to the markets of the world."[57] The use of "destructive appliances" by fish traders to secure "car loads of fish for export" from the Lake of the Woods was sufficiently disturbing that Dawson, who was overlooking the international character of regional waters, felt that Ontario "should ... reserve the whole lake for the use of the Indians."[58] He maintained that if the extensive commercial assault on the fisheries had been contemplated during treaty negotiations, even stronger protection for Aboriginal interests would have been written into the agreement.[59]

To safeguard the interests of Indigenous fishers in the district, specifically in relation to food supply, Indian officers at Rat Portage were authorized in 1889 to enforce the Fisheries Act.[60] The need for action was underscored by the powerful complaints of Chief Conducumewininie, communicated to Ottawa through the Indian Agent at Rat Portage: "We see someone fishing out in the lake. Who is he and where does the evil spirit come from? Is he a big-knife (an American) from the United States?" The chief then turned to food security: "We wish our children and children's children to live, but he is destroying their food, and they will die of hunger."[61]

In the midst of an elaborate constitutional struggle, the Dominion agreed to transfer fisheries regulation to Ontario, excluding waters in Indian reserves.[62] Deputy Superintendent General Lawrence Vankoughnet approved the transfer of authority but specifically recognized the vital fishing interests of the Treaty 3 communities: "As regards the Fisheries of the Lake of the Woods, they should be reserved for the common use of the Indians of Treaty 3." This recommendation flowed from his understanding that the lake had always been the source of the Indigenous population's "principal sustenance" and his fear that if they were excluded from the fishery or if other fishers became established, "it would in either case prove most disastrous."[63] Dawson's interventions were thus echoed in departmental policy to safeguard the subsistence fishery.

Several months earlier, the situation had deteriorated to the extent that a combined force of Treaty 3 Ojibwa and Chippewa from Minnesota seized a fishing station operated by D.F. Reid and Company at Garden Island in US waters. The raiding party destroyed the company's nets and fishing gear as a means of preserving their own access to the threatened resources.[64] The Canadian government immediately attempted to close the commercial fishery of the Lake of the Woods.[65] But Canada's interventions were unable to forestall the collapse of the fishery, which experienced increasingly intense pressure.

In recognition of the significant impact of American fishing on the shared resource, Vankoughnet initiated discussions with his counterparts in Canada's Fisheries department to formulate an international agreement "under which the fishing in the Lake of the Woods might be reserved and protected in the interests of the Indians on both sides of the line and licenses to all other parties refused."[66] Senior Canadian officials, including the minister of the Interior and the minister of Fisheries, subsequently urged the United States to control American fishing on the Lake of the Woods "in order to conserve the fisheries as a means of livelihood to the Indians."[67] Common concerns respecting the fate of fisheries shared between Canada and the United States in the Great Lakes contributed, in 1892, to the formation of a joint commission of inquiry to consider preservation of the fisheries in contiguous waters between the two countries. Though this was a milestone in efforts to regulate transboundary resources, little came of proposals respecting a uniform approach to fisheries regulation.[68] Native access to traditional fisheries remained troubling, not only around the Lake of the Woods but across Canada.[69]

E.E. Prince, as commissioner of Fisheries, undertook a detailed examination of the sturgeon and caviar industries in 1905, a decade or so after the substantial value had been recognized.[70] Sturgeon were still found widely in Canada, but the Lake of the Woods was "remarkable even amongst Canadian lakes for the incredible quantities of sturgeon, of the very finest quality, which it has supplied to the markets." Prince noted the extraordinary pace of commercial expansion and decline, which he attributed to the failure to enforce Canadian regulations, exacerbated by the fact that "a very small corner of the lake falls within the United States border, and there the most unsparing destruction of sturgeon was carried on."[71] Prince concluded that "the propagation of sturgeon by protecting the parent fish in their natural habitat is the only really trustworthy method at present." He anticipated, accordingly, that if the spawning grounds could be identified and marked and if a reasonable number of adult sturgeon were permitted to reach these areas, extermination of the species could be avoided.[72]

But even as this hopeful official forecast was issued, intense efforts were underway to dam the Rainy River, now understood to be, or to have been, a valuable spawning area. The situation soon deteriorated to the point that following its inspection of the Lake of the Woods and Rainy River areas in 1908–09, yet another international fisheries commission called for a four-year closure of the sturgeon fishery.[73] Widespread warnings went unheeded, in considerable measure as a result of divided and uncertain authority. This included regulatory authority over the fishery itself and over hydro-power developments, which, given accelerating technological advances, had begun to attract investors.

CONSTITUTIONAL FISH

In 1882, shortly before the Lake of the Woods fishery came to commercial attention and as the federal-provincial boundary conflict intensified, the *Globe* reflected upon the "vexed question of riparian rights" and navigable waters.[74] In a recent decision, *R. v Robertson*, the Supreme Court of Canada had confined the federal government's authority over seacoast and inland fisheries to fisheries in navigable waterways. Henceforth, provincial governments – not including Manitoba and the North-West Territories, where Crown lands remained under Dominion government control – enjoyed the right to issue licences for fishing in nonnavigable streams that passed through Crown lands and to confirm the right of private landowners to fish in such waters without a licence. In future land grants, the newspaper noted, provinces might take action in the public interest to reserve the right to grant fishing licences for any nonnavigable streams included in land grants. As further developments around the Lake of the Woods would soon reveal, the anthropocentric distinction between navigable and nonnavigable waters would have implications extending well beyond governmental authority over fishing permits.

The *Globe* challenged provincial authorities to safeguard their fisheries against at least some of the perceived risks associated with uncontrolled access and unauthorized fishing techniques. With their powers over fishing in nonnavigable waters so clearly affirmed, the paper urged provincial governments to "take such further measures as may be necessary for the protection of fish and the prevention of their destruction out of season."[75]

Indeed, the *R. v Robertson* decision functioned like a vacuum to draw in provincial legislative action, since the fledging federal regime had been weakened by judicial interpretation. Thus, in 1885, Ontario took steps to fill any newly created constitutional space with the province's first fisheries legislation of the post-Confederation era. Provincial leases and licences were now applicable "to all fisheries and rights of fishing in respect of which the Legislature of Ontario has authority to legislate."[76] The phrasing demonstrated Ontario's determination to assert jurisdiction that it was simultaneously groping to define. The Ontario fisheries legislation authorized regulations ("so far as the Legislature of Ontario has authority so to enact"), including regulations "to prevent the destruction of fish."[77]

During the 1890s, both levels of government in Canada issued commercial fishing licences in Ontario but seemed less inclined to implement and finance a suitable program of supervision and enforcement.[78] Thus, while overfishing in the Lake of the Woods was destroying the lake's rich sturgeon population, the federal overseer, Charles Walter Chadwick, was left to perform his water-based duties without a patrol vessel. Nor was Chadwick's provincially appointed counterpart properly equipped to get around the lake. Thus, to inspect fishing grounds, these two officials travelled as paying customers on commercial freight and passenger steamers, whose regular routes and recognizable profiles on the horizon would have been well known to any fisherman with an eye to avoid inspection. Chadwick somehow managed to bring a good number of charges against unlicensed fishermen, customarily resulting in a conviction leading to a fine of $4 plus costs.[79] Despite limited resources, the federal overseer contemplated the use of smaller lakes to promote sturgeon spawning as well as the creation of fenced sturgeon sanctuaries among the islands of the Lake of the Woods in the interests of what later generations might describe as sustainability: "We do not want to fish this lake out in a few years, but want to make it a permanent business."[80]

Equally damaging to the fishery was the tendency for governments to look to each other when complaints were raised in the Rainy River area about sturgeon being poached for their caviar during spawning season.

While provincial officials insisted that they were powerless to act in the absence of federal legislation creating a "close season" on sturgeon, the federal deputy minister treated the matter as a provincial licensing and enforcement issue.[81]

As Ontario officials grew increasingly concerned about fisheries conservation and public revenue, they took measures to address the situation. Various recommendations from a provincial inquiry into fish and game in early 1892 were immediately reflected in legislative changes. The fishery, in particular, came under scrutiny – at the federal as well as the provincial level – in the face of allegations that some Indigenous fishermen had "abused" the "privilege" of fishing for their own use during close seasons by selling fish to commercial dealers.[82]

Aemilius Irving, whose diligent investigation of fisheries administration has been noted, was called to the bar in 1849. He thus had four solid decades of professional experience, much of it in the service of his province, when his attention was directed to federally granted fishing leases and licences within the Treaty 3 region. Matters coming to Irving's attention usually stayed there until they were satisfactorily resolved, a significant problem for federal officials with whom he courteously exchanged correspondence. W.D. Hogg, solicitor to the Dominion government, received several polite inquiries concerning leases and fishing licences issued by federal authorities. Irving's curiosity persisted alongside ongoing intergovernmental conflict over lands, revenues, and authority in the old disputed territory. He requested, for example, copies of leases and licences that the federal Department of Fisheries might have recently granted "to Fish in the waters within Ontario, the beds of which are the property of Ontario, and the waters speaking generally, unnavigable."[83] In their turn, these casual references to the ownership of the lake or riverbed of waters that might or might not be considered navigable generated intense conflict.

As his understanding and analysis were refined, Irving revealed his strategic motivations to provincial representatives. One objective revolved around the federal licensing power itself and the corresponding scope of provincial authority. His inquiries therefore were underpinned by the desire "to show that the Dominion had not the right to grant these Fishing licenses," as this would be inconsistent with his intent to establish "that Ontario has control over its own lands."[84] In due course, and with equal professional tenacity, Irving also explored compensation for lands "being taken out of Ontario" to constitute Indian reserves.

The rivalry and confusion that plagued Canadian fisheries administration was in some respects consistent with other sources of intergovernmental friction – liquor licensing, for example. A possible pathway towards orderly resolution emerged around 1890 amidst signs of antagonism between Ontario and the federal government over the Indigenous fisheries of Treaty 3. When John Thompson, representing federal authorities, met with Premier Mowat to address a lengthy series of irritants on 28 November 1890 – just two weeks after Ontario launched the MacCallum inquiry into fish and game – Treaty 3 fishing regulation was on the agenda. One of the agreed measures called for Canada to confirm that "the Regulations as to fishing in the territory covered by the Morris Treaty as thereby approved, other than on the Reserves for Indians, shall be made by the Government of Ontario as respects the lands of the Province, without prejudice to the jurisdiction of the Dominion Parliament with respect to Fisheries under the B.N.A. Act." Another term concerning "The Fisheries Question" provided – presuming the concurrence of Quebec – for the matter to be referred to the courts for advice. Mowat would arrange for a draft to be prepared.[85]

Using a distinctive advisory procedure known as a "reference," governments turned to the Supreme Court of Canada in 1894 for an opinion to clarify and resolve the overall fisheries dispute, which proved to be a very elusive objective.[86] "The case is so complicated," editorialized the *Globe* following the Supreme Court of Canada's decision, "that it is difficult to say off-hand what the precise effect of the judgment is, except that it is generally in favor of the Provinces ... The Ontario fishery act is good, and the Dominion fishery act almost wholly bad."[87] With respect to non-navigable waters, the reference decision confirmed provincial authority as previously described in the *R. v Robertson* case. Now the same rule was extended to navigable waterways, "the beds of which are wholly within the Provinces, the right of fishing therein being a public common right subject to Provincial legislation."

It was henceforth understood, as reported by the *Globe*, that "the lakes great and small, the rivers navigable and unnavigable, with the fish and all other things therein contained, are the property of the Provinces owning the adjacent land and not of the Dominion as a whole." Harbours, having been conveyed to the federal government in the Confederation arrangements, constituted the only exception. The federal government was in a singularly unenviable position: "It has the right to protect, preserve and propagate fish if it wishes to do so, while the Provinces have the sole right to catch the fish so preserved and protected." According to the *Globe*, it seemed unlikely that federal authorities would long be willing to finance hatchery programs to "put fish into the great lakes that become the property of the Province of Ontario whenever they enter the water."[88]

The Supreme Court's conclusions on the fisheries question reached the Judicial Committee of the Privy Council (JCPC) in 1898, to be followed by similar controversies in 1912 and 1920. Aemilius Irving, as a young member of Parliament in the 1870s when the Supreme Court of Canada was created, had opposed the JCPC's appeal jurisdiction over the judgments of Canadian courts. But losing one large constitutional principle did not preclude him from eventually arguing the 1898 *Provincial Fisheries Reference* in London on behalf of his province.

Following the 1898 JCPC decision, the federal government retained the right to regulate inland fisheries by creating open and close seasons, for example, or by controls on fishing practices and nets. The provinces, for their part, enjoyed administrative authority on the basis of their proprietary interests in the fish themselves, taking advantage of the restrictive view of federal powers to insert their own preferences into a regime that they had tended to criticize as largely unresponsive to local conditions and needs.[89] The provincial proprietary interest, it might be added, appeared to bolster resistance to fisheries-related claims pursued by the federal government on behalf of Indigenous fishermen.

Stakeholders, as we might now describe all those with interests in the nineteenth-century Lake of the Woods/Rainy Lake fisheries, were many and diverse. Traditional Indigenous fishers encountered powerful competition for a limited resource from commercial operations on both sides of the Canada-US border. The fishery was limited, perhaps, in all respects other than governance, for national and provincial or state regulatory, licensing, and customs officials all exercised some form of authority around the watershed, generally without institutional capacity to enforce the fragmented but modestly restrictive measures that might have prolonged, even if they could not have sustained, a rich and productive fishery.

The state of Canadian fisheries regulation following the JCPC decision has been described as "confusion worse confounded," with one consequence being the collapse of the Lake of the Woods sturgeon fishery, followed a few years later by the formal closing of sturgeon fishing elsewhere.[90] But "confusion worse confounded" in the fishery paled in comparison with the clouds of uncertainty surrounding ownership and control of mineral, forest, and water resources in the disputed territory. These matters were even more deeply affected by the legacy of contested boundaries and competing jurisdictional claims across the region.

3

This Land Is My Land –
It Can't Be Your Land

The legacy of the disputed boundary extended well beyond the courts, intergovernmental friction, or deliberations concerning Indian reserve boundaries. This experience, sometimes celebrated as an epic federal-provincial struggle, simply established the framework within which the practical ordering of civic and commercial life would be put in place. Like the fishery, the forest industry and mining endured endless complications. It was necessary, for example, to address disputes over land ownership and the status of rights to resources that had originated while the boundary conflict raged. Investors and developers sometimes asserted competing interests on the basis of conflicting federal and provincial grants to the same property.

Situations of this nature required detailed consideration by the courts or designated arbitrators. Nor, of course, had the post-treaty concerns of the region's Aboriginal communities – notably, respecting fish and game and reserve lands – conclusively been addressed. In other words, following high-level missteps around northwestern Ontario's place in the evolving Confederation arrangements and the resolution of Indian treaty issues, regional residents were wrong-footed on numerous other issues.

FOREST RESOURCES AND THE LUMBER INDUSTRY

Commercial grade timber abounded around the Lake of the Woods, on its numerous islands, and along tributary waters. And it was actively exploited.

Between 1879 and 1886, the resource base attracted lumber operations of various sizes to lakeshore settlements where essential water power and transportation services were available.

Early lumber mills at Rat Portage and the nearby communities of Norman and Keewatin produced railway ties, timbers for bridges and trestles, telegraph poles, and navigational markers, as well as building products for mines, houses, and, eventually, cottages. After completion of the rail link between Rat Portage and Winnipeg in 1882, lumber was also shipped westward, some of the timber originating from US sources upstream and sometimes in competition with US suppliers. But alongside the universal challenges presented by markets and competition, distinctive difficulties concerning access to forest resources continued to arise. Several of the operations requiring introduction, for their trials and tribulations, sometimes over decades, had important ongoing implications for regional development, including management of regional waters.

Finding the forest resources near Swan Creek, Manitoba, inadequate in the early 1870s, Richard Fuller and several associates from Hamilton, Ontario, applied for new timber limits on the islands of the Lake of the Woods. Following the Treaty 3 agreement, they obtained a federal lease.[1] Then, after corporate reorganization in 1878–79, the Lake of the Woods rights of the original firm were taken over by the Keewatin Lumbering and Manufacturing Company (KLM), with Fuller as president.[2] Another investor, John Mather, an immigrant from Scotland and veteran of the Ottawa Valley timber trade, initially served as manager before recruiting his sons to run operations. Thus began Mather's wide-ranging involvement in the economic affairs of the region.[3]

From Canadian federal officials in Ottawa, KLM obtained a charter to operate in the Lake of the Woods district in July 1879. Supplies and equipment were barged in from Minnesota's Northwest Angle following delivery via St. Paul, the Red River, and wagon teams along the Dawson Trail, and mill construction got underway in the late summer amidst ongoing discussion of timber limits.[4] The proposed mill site, at a location later known as Tunnel Island to acknowledge a railway construction landmark, covered rugged territory between the two outlets of Lake of the Woods waters, where the lake enters the Winnipeg River. This strategic water power location would become the subject of prolonged corporate and intergovernmental struggle, although KLM's initial development plan for the property foundered because of delays in the construction of railway connections. The company began operations closer to the Keewatin townsite, where a planing mill was added to the plant facilities in 1880–81.

Over twenty-five years, the company cut 166,327,526 feet of timber, an average annual cut of about 7 million feet.[5] However, even prosperous lumber operations experienced side effects from the federal-provincial boundary dispute. KLM's difficulties arose over claims to the islands in the northern portion of the Lake of the Woods, where cutting rights had been acquired from Richard Fuller and his associates. When William McCarthy occupied Coney Island – a short distance from Rat Portage and Keewatin – and began to cut timber and to build, KLM found its avenues of legal recourse severely constrained: the company's original timber lease, issued by the federal government when the boundary dispute was under-way, was of little value without ratification or endorsement from Ontario after the province successfully asserted its territorial claim in the courts.[6] Moreover, Dominion officials threatened to seize KLM logs on the grounds that they had been taken from Indian reserve lands, a situation that en-tangled Mather with Ottawa officials. As Aubrey White, of Ontario's Crown Lands Department, remarked with evident approval: "I presume they will endeavour to bulldoze him down there."[7]

After a decade of operations, KLM relinquished the federal privileges it had once enjoyed in exchange for provincial permission to continue cutting on the islands of the Lake of the Woods for a further period of ten years from 1891.[8] Even this agreement did not end contests over the scope of the company's access to forest resources.[9] Lands across the watershed were still required to supply some of the larger wood needed for railway ties.

The distinctive conditions facing Canadian lumber operations around the Lake of the Woods, sometimes advantageous but occasionally quite onerous, included the availability of American timber supplies and the presence of rival US-based operations. Immense quantities of wood crossed the Lake of the Woods from the Rainy River district on both the Can-adian and the US sides.[10] Starting in the 1880s, timber production also originated in Minnesota's Northwest Angle, geographically isolated from the rest of the state through the idiosyncrasies of early international treaty negotiations.[11] In 1885, about half of the 4 million feet milled at Keewatin and Rat Portage originated in Minnesota. American timber, both more plentiful and of better quality, could be purchased from private landowners along the Big Fork and Little Fork Rivers. Supplies flowed down the Rainy River and were then towed northward to the mills. But when St. Paul lumbermen extended their influence northward across the height of land, access to American timber was largely curtailed, a difficulty accentuated by railway development. The Canadian Northern line, constructed south

The Lumber Mills, Kenora, Ont.

600.769.

FIGURE 3.1   Lumber Mills, Kenora, n.d. *Courtesy of the Lake of the Woods Museum.*

of the lake in 1900, "cut off all the American territory and all the south end of the Lake of the Woods, for the mills there at points such as Fort Frances, could get the logs with less expense."[12]

Minnesota lumberman W.J. Macaulay acquired extensive Canadian timber limits in the Lake of the Woods district from Canada's federal government in the early 1870s, when Ottawa still claimed ownership of the lands in question. Macaulay undertook to construct a sawmill even before the arrival of the CPR.[13] His proposed mill site on the Winnipeg River between Portage Bay and Winnipeg Bay required excavation to create a mill race for water power production. This action led eventually to distinctive legal proceedings pitting the claims of those who had re-directed the lake's outflow using an artificial channel against the interests of others who relied on natural environmental conditions for access to the same water.

Dick and Banning, founders of a Winnipeg lumber firm dating from 1872, acquired Macaulay's Lake of the Woods properties at the start of the next decade. With the boundary dispute between the Canadian and Ontario governments still underway, they withheld part of the purchase price pending documentation confirming Macaulay's title from federal officials. To obtain the balance of the sale proceeds, which he desperately needed for a new venture in northern Minnesota, Macaulay petitioned

Prime Minister John A. Macdonald for a formal water power lease and title to twenty-seven acres for lumber yards. "I never would have gone and built the power which cost me ten thousand dollars besides putting up a Mill at the cost of $25,000.00," Macaulay pleaded, "only I had your verbal promise I could have the power provided it did not interfere with the Rail Road." Macaulay bristled about the possibility that Mather and KLM, who had entered the district later, might enjoy better treatment. He implored the prime minister to take up his case and "not make fish of me and flesh of Mather."[14]

Two years intervened before Macaulay finally received a patent to his property and a licence to occupy log-booming grounds on Portage Bay. The new owners, Dick and Banning, then applied, in 1885, to Ontario officials for a two-and-a-half-acre extension on the west side of the property to expand the mill yard.[15] In its own turn, this application was caught up in an elaborate controversy surrounding claims to the beds of navigable waterways, a surrogate for control of water-power sites, whose industrial value and strategic importance was on the rise.

In the nearby lakeshore community of Norman, the Cameron and Kennedy firm built their first steam-operated mill in 1884 and supplied it with sawlogs from Whitefish Bay on the Lake of the Woods. In the same community, the Minnesota and Ontario Lumber Company established a steam saw and planing mill in 1886. Employing 150 men at the peak of summer operations, this firm could produce 120,000 feet per day.[16] The third mill at Norman, the Safety Bay planing mill, belonged to the Bulmer family of Montreal. The Bulmers' mill began as one of many small lumber operations that relied on annual cutting licences from the federal government. The Bulmers eventually confirmed their timber rights with provincial authorities, only to become deeply mired in a further round of controversy over mineral rights.[17]

With timber licence uncertainty largely resolved, cutting at the Norman, Keewatin, and Rat Portage mills reached unprecedented levels. In 1890, the operating companies prepared to utilize 40 million logs cut in Canada in addition to 25 million cut in the United States.[18] By this point, Rat Portage lumber shipped to Winnipeg had displaced US lumber, which had previously reached the city via the Red River.[19] In other respects, difficulties arose and would continue to mount. Sales from Lake of the Woods mills to Manitoba declined intermittently, while competition undermined commercial prospects for all local producers.

Although business amalgamation alleviated some local competitive pressures, external challenges persisted. In the 1890s, new spruce supplies from northern Manitoba and Saskatchewan came to market. West coast lumber provided further competition in the early twentieth century, driving out supplies from other sources, including the Lake of the Woods.[20] But more importantly, as they had done in the past, Minnesota lumbermen again exported successfully to Manitoba. D.C. Cameron, president of the Rat Portage Lumber Company (a product of local consolidation) reported that Minnesota imports to Manitoba had grown from 4 million feet in 1894 to 38 million feet in 1898.[21] Against this backdrop, lumbermen in northwestern Ontario petitioned for various forms of relief, including a duty against US lumber imports.[22]

Lake of the Woods lumber mills experienced further challenges from the neighbouring Rainy River area, which had once served primarily as a source of supply for raw materials. Stephen H. Fowler, who obtained a federal grant from the Mackenzie administration immediately following the 1873 treaty agreement, was the key exception.[23] Proponents of the early Rainy River ventures had selected the best blocks of pine on the different lakes and rivers leading to their mills, "leaving the scattered timber almost worthless to anyone but themselves and closing the door to all rivals."[24]

Rainy River activity expanded again following new exploration work in the 1890s, and activity in the district rivalled or surpassed that at Lake of the Woods mills.[25] Small mills, active in the 1890s, were replaced by larger, generally American operations. D.J. Arpin of the Pigeon River Lumber Company, the Backus-Brooks interests, and the Shevlin, Clarke, Carpenter group all entered the Canadian side of the district in the late 1890s or early 1900s.[26] Yet, though some wood was being cut, lumber sold, and licence fees paid, the overall economic performance of the district was far from what Mather and other investors had anticipated. Competition was but one element of the problem.

On the US side of the watershed, Backus-Brooks acquired all of KLM's Minnesota timber lands in 1906 as a result of state legislation restricting ownership of forest lands to American citizens. Backus took over the entire Keewatin Lumbering and Manufacturing Company, including its Canadian timber limits, in June of the same year, and changed the name to the Keewatin Lumber Company. By 1917, investment in the firm had reached $1.5 million, and Keewatin Lumber employed 350 people.[27] The lumber operation, however, was only one element in Backus's evolving plan to integrate water power and forest resources along the Ontario-Minnesota border. In addition to building a railway line linking Brainerd to International Falls, his ambitions to produce hydroelectricity for an emerging pulp and paper sector generated resource- and water-management conflicts along and across the boundary, from the upper Rainy Lake watershed to the Winnipeg River.[28]

Gold Mining on Unstable Foundations

As Magistrate Lyons forthrightly recounted for the benefit of Premier Mowat, the unsettled federal-provincial boundary also had implications for the mining sector. Lyons cited an 1881 announcement concerning prolongation of joint jurisdiction in criminal matters. This was interpreted as signalling that the boundary question remained unresolved and threw prospectors and miners into "a state of despondency." They had already endured difficulty and disappointment in anticipation of eventually re-couping vast commitments of time and significant personal investment. As Lyons explained: "They have expended all their money exploring and in surveys expecting an early return for their investment and toil which they felt sure they would if the boundary question was settled, so that a deed could be procured for their locations." Such deeds represented secur-ity and were crucial for mining investors, who would not otherwise be prepared to invest in risky ventures.[29]

Lyons expected many miners to be ruined, encumbering local merchants and others with severe financial losses. While many area residents suffered from the absence of officials with authority to register their deeds, those in the mineral sector would be most severely disadvantaged: "All is uncer-tainty and confusion," Lyons lamented. "The mineral lands will be so mixed up before long that the men who own them will not be able to recognize his own property." Conflicting and inconsistent surveys inspired his dire prediction that "we will have fighting and perhaps murder over these claims."[30]

Interest in Lake of the Woods gold prospects began in the late 1870s, following a discovery on Hay Island. A minor flurry of activity, with the Argyle Mine on Clearwater Bay producing the region's first gold bar in 1883, was short-lived.[31] Some early ventures conveyed to potential investors the unfortunate impression that owners of mining locations were merely promoters rather than committed developers. As a consequence, in 1890, northwestern Ontario "remained a land of uncertain or even suspect mineral promise."[32]

Despite apprehension over titles and ownership, mining activity flour-ished intermittently. On Big Stone Bay, on the north shore of the Lake of the Woods, the Winnipeg Consolidated mine operated briefly in 1883 before deteriorating into "a melancholy ruin."[33] Another promising venture, the Pine Portage mine, was equally short-lived when no suitably qualified mining engineer could be recruited. The shortage of suitably trained personnel was thus another obstacle to development in both the United States and Canada.[34]

Gold prospects in northwestern Ontario continued to suffer from the initial round of disappointment, even though the Ontario Bureau of Mines, in its 1893 report, promoted the regional industry as stable and reliable: "Other occupations may afford larger profits, but there are none in which there is less uncertainty in making sales, and none in which the fluctuations of prices are maintained within narrower margins."[35] Despite this favourable assessment (overly optimistic, as the future would reveal), investment again failed to materialize. Mining officials attributed the situation to depressed business conditions throughout the United States, while occasionally lamenting the need for foreign capital: "It does seem to be a deplorable situation that where nature has been so bountiful the citizen folds his arms and the enterprising foreigner is invited to step in to win and carry away the treasure."[36] Often enough, the "enterprising foreigner" was a British investor, who introduced another distinctive perspective to regional development.

Elsewhere in the district, new gold prospects were coming to light around Shoal Lake. This body of water sometimes drained through Ash Rapids into the Lake of the Woods and at other times benefited from inward flows. Shared between Ontario and Manitoba, Shoal Lake has presented management challenges for over a century. In the mid-1890s, with a touch of wistfulness, commentators heralded a transformation as new mining locations such as Shoal Lake were identified: "It is likely that this hitherto lonely lake, visited only by Indians or Scandinavians interested in the pickerel and whitefish drawn from its clear waters, will shortly lose some of its beauty."[37]

One strong Shoal Lake prospect, the Mikado, delivered the best results of any Lake of the Woods area mine in the mid-1890s and attracted investment. The owners – a Rat Portage HBC official and Dr. S. Stuart Scovill, a physician with the CPR – who had previously purchased the location from its Ojibwa discoverer sold the property to an English investor, Col. Engledue, who had become disillusioned with deteriorating conditions in the gold districts of South Africa.[38] Engledue expanded operations and continued to acquire prospects in the region, including further Shoal Lake sites.[39] The Mikado's success encouraged additional exploration and development.[40]

In 1900, with twelve properties under development in the Mikado area, it was noted that "more activity has been displayed in the Shoal Lake or Bag Bay region than during any previous year."[41] The Tycoon Mining and Development Company of Ontario, for example, headquartered at Rat Portage with a prominent local figure, James Conmee, as president, operated a site three quarters of a mile directly north of the Mikado on three small islands and the surrounding waters. The specific history of several Shoal Lake ventures tracked global gold prices for a century thereafter, with late twentieth century efforts to revive some Shoal Lake properties – especially island mines – giving rise to an environmental cause célèbre.[42]

Small or isolated northwestern Ontario mining ventures depended heavily upon local transportation services and sometimes even upon centralized processing arrangements in the form of reduction works accessible by water at Rat Portage. As the *New York Engineering and Mining Journal* wrote: "The whole region is a network of lakes, rivers, and streams, which afford not only excellent means of communication ... in summer, but also in the winter."[43] By the end of the century, sixty steamers of various sizes were in active use across the Lake of the Woods, transporting numerous barges owned by the mines or provided by companies dedicated to ore milling.[44] The traffic, in turn, stimulated interest in navigational improvements – the removal of reefs and obstacles, for example, or damming and managing channels such as Ash Rapids between Shoal Lake and the Lake of the Woods, as John Mather proposed to the Ontario government. Such developments were only the forerunners of far more substantial engineering interventions, including hydroelectric facilities that would alter water flows and quality over many years.

The Rat Portage Gold and Silver Reduction Works began operation in 1892 and was soon processing about nine tons of ore per day, although this performance could not be sustained. The facility passed to American and then British owners before all work on the site was discontinued in 1897.[45] Plans for another ore-reduction facility at Norman never materialized.[46]

With the backing of Ottawa investors, John Mather organized another milling operation, the Ottawa Gold and Milling Company, to take advantage of hydro-power production from the Keewatin Power Company, with which he was closely associated. Ottawa Gold contemplated a fifty-stamp mill to assist smaller mines by saving them the need to put up mills and allowing them "to reap a return from their ore from the very outset." Savings in several forms were anticipated from these arrangements. For example, water power would eliminate the costs of coal imports or wood fuel, and one large and well-equipped mill would replace the need for several smaller and less efficient operations. The costs of skilled management would be more evenly distributed across a range of enterprises that would enjoy access, if required, to more varied processing techniques.[47] Keewatin Power's contributions to regional infrastructure were celebrated internationally; the venture was described as "what will be, when completed, one of the greatest power plants in the world."[48] Commentators endorsed a complementary intervention in water management: "By the erection of an immense dam at this point they have converted the Lake of the Woods into a reservoir 3,000 square miles in extent."[49] The large-scale environmental transformation of the watershed from a natural transportation network and sturgeon pond to a managed system of power-storage reservoirs was underway.

Despite significant initiatives, the ebb and flow of promising ventures and harsh setbacks compelled investors and officials alike to revise the story of the region's prospective fortunes on a regular basis. By 1895, a respectable stream of gold discoveries supported renewed optimism.[50] Yet a modest boom in 1897, suggesting the possibility of a permanent mining industry, was followed by a slight relapse.[51] As the 1890s drew to a close, even supportive commentators were forced to acknowledge that gold production had not met expectations and that predictions had been "unduly inflated."[52]

By the turn of the century, mining activity was slowing down throughout northwestern Ontario, although a few steady producers remained in operation.[53] Such properties included the Mikado and the renowned Sultana, a mine whose story exemplifies the uncertain legacy of the boundary controversy for those engaged in mining and forestry and for Aboriginal communities.[54]

SULTANA

Some of the complications that arose with respect to mining lands such as Sultana had been anticipated during the 1873 treaty gathering. When one Ojibwa chief called attention to "gold beneath our feet," Governor Morris discussed their interests in precious metals.[55] "If any important minerals are discovered on any of their Reserves," Morris wrote, "the minerals will be sold for their benefit with their consent."[56] He clarified that this would not apply in relation to other lands where band members might make discoveries. In these circumstances, he explained, "the Indian

is like any other man. He can sell his information if he can find a purchaser."[57] On the basis of such an understanding, for example, local investors later acquired the site that became the Mikado.

In conformity with treaty provisions, pursuant to the process for select-
ing reserve lands and consistent with the Dominion government's assertion
of ownership, Sultana Island was included within Indian Reserve 38B in
1879, although the designation was not formally confirmed at that time.[58]
The island, about eight miles by lake travel from Rat Portage, was initially
distinguished from the mainland by swamp or marsh, and then more
distinctly separated when water levels rose behind early dam construction
at the Winnipeg River outlet.[59]

Persistent investors, assisted by well-connected legal advisers who solicited the intervention of the HBC's experienced chief trader Alexander
Matheson, diligently pursued access to Sultana mineral locations.[60] On 8
October 1886, the Rat Portage Indian Band surrendered some 600 acres,
including Sultana Island's roughly 520 acres, to the Dominion government
in trust to be sold for their benefit.[61] Keewatin Lumbering and Manufacturing remained keen to assert its rights to cut pine timber on Sultana
Island, arousing first the ire of Indian Affairs, which viewed the timber as
belonging to the reserve, and then mining interests, who proposed to
utilize on-site timber resources for their own operations.[62] Fire eventually
left "scarcely a living tree" in sight: "The brown and naked rocks of the
west shore now stand out prominently, and the contrast with the green
islands in front is striking."[63]

Interest in the mineral content of Sultana's brown and naked rocks officially originated with Jacob Henesy, a Michigan copper miner, who staked
location X42 on the island's western shore in 1881.[64] Henesy thus formally
initiated a prolonged and convoluted contest over Sultana's mineral potential. In the face of the boundary dispute, the uncertain status and extent
of the Indian reserve, and entanglements with competing claims, including
the interest asserted on behalf of KLM, Sultana disappointed early enthusiasts.[65] On 27 November 1888, despite warnings from Ontario about
unresolved matters between the two governments, the federal Indian
Department issued a patent for X42 to Henesy and Charles A. Moore,
who had (independently) asserted his own entitlement to the site. Two
other investors – Henry Bulmer Jr., of the Montreal-based lumber firm,
and the enterprising Dr. Scovill – contributed financially. The prolonged
effort to secure their claim, followed by a discouraging mineral assessment
of the property, prompted this group to sell to John F. Caldwell of

Winnipeg.[66] Caldwell also acquired the neighbouring X43 location, the site of another stalled development, the Ophir mine.[67]

In 1889 and 1890, Dominion government officials issued letters patent to other portions of Sultana Island. Albert C. McMicken, Hamilton G. McMicken, and George Heenan obtained separate parcels totalling about 110 acres. Each of the properties was subject to royalty payments of 4 percent on minerals produced. Heenan and the McMickens later sold their lands to the Ontario Mining Company, which was incorporated for this purpose in August 1889.[68] Ontario Mining thereby (or so it assumed) secured all of Sultana's mineral lands other than the locations held by Caldwell.[69]

With Sultana developing slowly, a local newspaper expressed editorial regret that government had not addressed the contending "real or imaginary claims" so that the "practically inexhaustible mineral wealth" could be exploited.[70] By 1891, Caldwell appeared ready to proceed actively, despite residual concerns about ownership or title. One keenly interested observer remarked that "the matter about the title of Sultana is not settled and he [Caldwell] would perhaps prefer to put his mill on ground where he could not be injuncted."[71] After actual mining got underway in 1892, weekly production levels at Sultana were variously reported at $2,000 or even as high as $3,000.[72]

When English investors took over at the end of the decade, Rat Portage residents generally welcomed this change, which they expected would result in good publicity for the Lake of the Woods in English mining circles.[73] Further reorganizations followed as engineering challenges mounted and production prospects declined. In relation to a prospectus prepared for potential further investors, critics denounced "glaring untruths and absurd misstatements" alongside "untrue and perverted statements" about the value of the property.[74] As difficult as controversies in the realm of finance and promotion may have appeared to developers, investors, and regulators, they were overshadowed by mounting legal turmoil.

Caldwell, who continued as manager following the arrival of English backers, always recognized that solid legal foundations were essential. He had accordingly reinforced his initial claim, founded on the Dominion grant he acquired from Bulmer and his associates in April 1890, with a subsequent patent from Ontario for X42 and X43.[75] It would be hard to imagine a better defence against uncertainties arising from the intergovernmental boundary controversy than to consolidate an endorsement from Canada with the provincial equivalent. But this was not enough.

FIGURE 3.2   Sultana Mine, 1900. *Courtesy of the Lake of the Woods Museum.*

J. Burley Smith dearly coveted the opportunity to participate somehow in the Sultana venture but found himself excluded from the prospect
of riches. Yet Smith, a mining engineer, was evidently rich in ideas, for he
imagined the continuation of the Sultana ore body out under the waters
of Bald Indian Bay into the Lake of the Woods. In association with A.F.
Fraser, an Ottawa lawyer, Smith founded the Burley Gold Mining Company and secured a claim to an offshore prospect. Then, using drilling rigs
operated from above the winter ice of 1896–97, with supplementary exploration by a diver, he determined a location for his mine.[76] To pursue
active exploitation, Smith envisaged a massive crib sixty feet square that
would be towed into position, sunk, and secured above the proposed access
point to the ore body. The structure, delivered in 1897, was suitably filled
and extended six feet above the surface to prevent flooding.[77]

Caldwell responded firmly to the offshore competition.[78] On the basis
of his own prior grant from Canada and subsequent Ontario patents for
X42 and X43, he asked the Ontario courts to set aside the Ontario patent
that supported Smith and Fraser's quest to exploit lands covered by water
adjacent to Sultana Island.[79] Despite the belt-and-suspenders approach
to safeguarding his investment in the form of both Dominion and provincial authorizations, Caldwell came up short.

In a carefully reasoned decision, Justice Rose determined that no one was
entitled to deal conclusively or independently with the lands in question.[80]

Rose's analysis drew heavily upon the *St. Catharines Milling* decision about timber licences in the disputed territory. This case, he believed, confirmed that "as there was no power in the Indians to sell or transfer their interest in the land, but only to surrender their right to the Crown by formal contract, no act of theirs could confer on either the Dominion or the Province the power of sale."[81] As a consequence, the right or power of sale must exist elsewhere, independent of any treaty or legislative authorization. Rose was entirely satisfied

> that the Crown might dispose of the lands without reference to the title of the Indians or their claims but the policy has not been so to do, and by the *British North America Act*, there was not, I think, vested in the Province the right to sell these lands or interfere with the Indians until after a formal surrender of the lands to the Crown.[82]

Rose reminded readers of his keenly anticipated decision that the Dominion power of legislation and administration in regard to Indians did not extend to the power to sell their lands: "The Parliament of Canada could not have given the Indians power to sell the lands to a stranger," he stated, "nor could it by legislation have validly asserted the right to sell the lands." Furthermore, he reasoned: "It would seem anomalous that if the lands and the proceeds of the sale of the lands should belong to the Province, the Dominion could interfere with these lands, fix the price, and sell them without regard to the interests of the Province." Even federal constitutional authority respecting "Indians and lands reserved for Indians" would not support such actions. After eliminating the alternatives, the judge found only one option remaining. He concluded, accordingly, "that any surrender or session by the Indians of their lands or their rights left the power of sale exactly where it was prior to such surrender or cession." In consequence, "that power was in the Province, subject to the surrender or other extinguishment of the Indian title."[83]

Concerning reserve lands, Rose determined – with reference to the 1894 agreement in which Canada had accepted Ontario's authority to approve reserve selection – that the entire Treaty 3 area had been surrendered in 1873, such that Indian reserves would subsequently be selected from Ontario lands. Yet he took the trouble to speculate about an alternative theory whereby the Ojibwa might have withheld unspecified reserves from the surrender with the consequence that reserve lands would never have come under provincial authority.[84] Despite Justice Rose's deft resolution of the clash between Caldwell and the Smith-Fraser venture over

control of the shoreline mine site, the complexities of Sultana Island en-
gulfed many other hopeful investors.[85]

As early as 1894, the Ontario Mining Company applied for Ontario
confirmation of the Dominion titles it had acquired from George Heenan
and the McMickens, and in 1897, the company petitioned Ontario's commissioner of Crown lands to the same effect. This company joined the
chorus of those adversely affected by the uncertain foundations of their
mineral claims. Ontario Mining wanted "the questions of doubt and difficulty" resolved before it would go forward with proposed investments.[86]

In November 1898, the commissioner of Crown lands ruled that Ontario Mining was entitled to a one-third interest in the lands, with the remainder lawfully in the hands of yet another group of contenders, Edward
Seybold, Edmund B. Osler, John W. Moyes, Elizabeth Johnston, John W.
Brown, Edward H. Ambrose, and John S. Ewart.[87] The decision was
specifically subject to the condition that Ontario Mining should abandon
all other claims that it was pursuing under Dominion patents and accept
the one-third interest as its entire entitlement. When Ontario Mining chose
instead to launch legal proceedings, the Crown lands commissioner cancelled his provisional ruling.[88]

Like other disputes over the resources and potential riches of northwestern Ontario, the struggle over Sultana was no mere tussle between
private claimants, with the stakes confined to their own personal prospects
and fortunes. Aboriginal communities anticipated payments, which federal
authorities endeavoured to provide. Ontario, also expecting revenue flows,
was not unconcerned.

Always attentive to provincial interests, Aemilius Irving kept a watchful
eye on contentious litigation. On 19 February 1899, he recorded that the
Dominion government was expected to assert a claim to precious metals
in Treaty 3 lands on behalf of the Ojibwa communities, who may have
believed that they were entitled to the "gold which was heard to be rustling
under their feet." Christopher Robinson, another prominent Toronto
lawyer, advocated the federal view, under which Indigenous communities
might expect not only the payment of annuities and reserve lands but also
the gold located within reserves. Irving confidently judged Robinson's
opinion to be "very incorrect." He reached that conclusion on the basis of
his own firm understanding that "Governor Morris was not authorized
to deal with the Prerogative Precious Metal Rights: which rights were the
property of Ontario."[89] Had Irving found a trump card?

Ontario Mining's challenge to the claims of Edward Seybold and his
investor group was argued before Chancellor Boyd, who had presided over

the *St. Catharines Milling* controversy and was thus no stranger to north-western Ontario's convoluted legal circumstances. Boyd identified two crucial questions: Was the Dominion government in a position to convey a valid title to the Sultana Island lands? And did that government have the right to deal with Sultana's mineral resources, specifically gold? He attributed the Dominion's action in granting Sultana mineral rights to its belief that Ottawa's legislative authority in relation to Indian reserves "conferred such plenary form of control as to amount virtually to exclusive ownership."[90] But as the experience of the *Fisheries Reference* had awkwardly demonstrated, legislative authority and proprietary rights over slippery fish are by no means congruent in Canada. Perhaps the same was true of shiny metals.

With reference to the *St. Catharines Milling* decision, Boyd systematically explained why nothing in the history of the Indian treaty and subsequent surrender could have grounded a Dominion claim to ownership. First, he explained that Canada was indeed entitled to exercise legislative and administrative jurisdiction over Reserve 38B "while the territorial and proprietary ownership of the soil was vested in the Crown for the benefit of and subject to the legislative control of the Province of Ontario." Turning to the reserve overall, he indicated that it had been "set apart out of the surrendered territory by the Dominion: that is to say, the Indian title being extinguished for the benefit of the Province, the Dominion assumed to take of the Provincial land to establish a treaty reserve for the Indians." In connection with the subsequent surrender of part of the reserve in 1886, he concluded that "the effect was again to free the part in litigation from the special treaty privileges of the land," leaving ownership exclusively to Ontario.[91]

This sequence of events and procedures supported Boyd's opinion that "no estate in fee simple could pass to the lands except from the Crown as represented by the Ontario Government." For clarity, he added that the effect of the surrender had been to confer the proprietary interest upon the province "freed from Indian claim." Ottawa, accordingly, had no authority whatsoever to transfer any interest in the land.[92] As a procedural response to the hopes, interests, and expectations that his decision so clearly frustrated, Boyd urged a tripartite mechanism whereby the interests of the Ojibwa and of the Crown in its dual federal and provincial character might all be appropriately respected.[93]

As for gold, Boyd unequivocally determined (as Irving had anticipated) that "the Indians had no concern" and that Ontario was entirely responsible for the disposition of precious minerals.[94] Boyd's conclusions were repeat-

edly upheld through successive levels of appeal. Rather bluntly, the
Divisional Court stated that when the Government of Canada sold the
lands in question, it was "not selling 'lands reserved for the Indians,' but
was selling lands belonging to the Province of Ontario."[95] Canada's
Supreme Court, in a short statement by Chief Justice Strong, endorsed
Boyd's analysis without elaboration, as did the Judicial Committee.[96]

Only one judge viewed with approval the claim of the Ontario Mining
Company derived from the Dominion grant. John Wellington Gwynne,
later described as "the most committed centralist on the Supreme Court,"
had nearly seven decades of legal experience at the time of the appeal.[97]
That experience had included – a half century earlier – legal work on behalf
of the superintendent of Indian Affairs.

The "honour of the Sovereign" underpinned Gwynne's entire perception
of the Sultana Island transactions, the broad historical context in which
they had occurred, and the interpretation of all relevant documentation.
The "inviolable" character of treaties and the manner in which they had
been observed were crucial considerations. Against this background,
Gwynne emphasized a distinction between "Indian lands" and "the public
lands of the province" that was "conspicuously apparent" and had been
maintained "in a most unequivocal manner" up to Confederation.[98] To
Gwynne, this distinction was understood and preserved by the makers of
the constitution.

In Gwynne's mind, the meaning of the Dominion's exclusive jurisdiction regarding "Indians and lands reserved for the Indians" was determined
accordingly. "Exclusive" should be given its precise ordinary meaning, with
the result that no provincial authority should be entitled to interfere with
Indigenous communities or their resources.[99] As Gwynne assessed the record, pledges, promises, and conditions associated with the surrender of
Indian lands to the Crown had been consistently maintained and should
indeed be so maintained. This principle naturally applied in connection
with the Northwest Angle Treaty of 1873 and the ensuing land transactions
affecting Sultana Island, which fell within Dominion authority as having
been reserved for the Ojibwa. This elaborate analysis was intended to
distinguish these lands from lands subject to the earlier *St. Catharines
Milling* decision, a distinction that Gwynne asserted forcefully: "Lands
reserved by treaty with the Indians and retained by the Crown as the lands
in question here were upon a trust accepted by the Crown for the exclusive
benefit of the Indians." In contrast, no trust in favour of Indigenous residents applied to the public lands considered in the *St. Catharines Milling*

case, which formed part of the 34 million acres surrendered by the treaty.[100] The JCPC responded harshly to Gwynne, albeit in a decision that appeared sometime after the latter's death.[101]

Further efforts to clear up matters between the federal and provincial governments had no immediate effect, although as the final appeal was under consideration by the JCPC, Edward Blake, representing Ontario, and E.L. Newcombe, Canada's deputy minister of Justice, explored opportunities to implement the 1894 Canada-Ontario Agreement and to address unresolved mineral issues. Among other things, the two representatives agreed, in 1902, that Ontario would confirm titles to the reserves previously negotiated by Canadian officials. In addition, Ontario agreed that the precious metals on the reserves would be recognized as belonging to the reserves and could be disposed of for the benefit of the Indigenous residents. In 1924, these arrangements were endorsed in federal and provincial legislation.[102]

The View from Sabaskong

Apart from intergovernmental relations and judicial proceedings at the highest levels, land and mineral rights commanded the attention of individual investors and developers. Henry Bulmer Jr., after the loss of his family's Lake of the Woods lumber mill to fire in 1893, shared gold mining interests with a hopeful contingent of investors. He remained stalwart in his loyalty to one particular venture, although he had occasion to view its evolution as a "blooming tangle," a "further muddle," and a "blunder."[103]

As Bulmer closely monitored his Lake of the Woods investments from Montreal, he attributed much of his disappointment to his associate Charles Walter Chadwick, sometime fisheries inspector, Rat Portage mining broker and insurance agent, and, later, president of the local board of trade. In 1888, Chadwick had undertaken to make applications on behalf of a group of gold mining enthusiasts with interests in twenty-one specific locations. He duly filed all twenty-one claims in Toronto, while presenting only fourteen of these to officials in Ottawa. Bulmer found Chadwick's unexplained failure to deliver the other seven applications incomprehensible, for members of the group who had organized themselves under what they called the Sabaskong Agreement assumed that federal authorities had primary responsibility and only by way of precaution were applications filed with the province.[104]

Alexander Matheson, the HBC agent who had helped facilitate the Sultana surrender in 1886, was a regular recipient of Bulmer's lamentations.[105] He was also aware that many of the mining locations in question were – like the Sultana mine – adjacent to or perhaps even within Indian Reserve 38B.

In his capacity as trustee for the Sabaskong Group, Matheson was approached in 1897 by James Conmee, a railway contractor, mining investor, and member of the provincial legislature who was then taking his turn in search of a resolution to the blunder, muddle, or tangle that so frustrated Bulmer and associates. Conmee offered no immediate solution to the clouded status of the mining locations. His initial focus was rather a reorganization of the existing interests to accommodate a new group of Toronto-based investors. In the first iteration of his proposal, Conmee undertook to pay for the land and all further cost of acquiring title, together with $20,000 working capital. He was also to contribute "certain water areas" for which he had applied personaliy.[106]

As the machinations unfolded, Matheson, as trustee, was actively petitioned from all directions. Conmee advised that Ontario was ready to issue title to a portion of the lands when several original investors protested his initiative to preserve a greater proportionate share.[107] Shortly thereafter, Conmee pressed Matheson to endorse his proposed arrangement, now warning that if his proposal were not pursued, the province might take no action at all and "all parties will lose the benefit of the property." He thought this all the more probable following a rumoured sale of Sultana "for a very large price," which might lead to the withdrawal of any remaining lands from sale.[108]

One month later, the Sabaskong applications faced rejection in Ottawa for technical deficiencies: field notes had not been filed, nor had payment been made of half the purchase price in a timely manner.[109] So Hartley Dewart, an interested observer with legal and Liberal credentials, urged collaboration with the rival syndicate, who agreed to contribute "all water lots adjoining 38B or the Sultana Island, for which they have applications pending, when granted."[110] Dewart wrote to Matheson, offering a further rationale for a consolidated approach: "I would prefer to have a smaller interest in the large area with its greater possibilities, than the larger interest in a fraction of the whole area applied for."[111] Bulmer condemned Dewart's plan and was particularly dismissive of the offer to contribute water lots.[112]

But somewhat unexpectedly, Ontario, as we have seen, granted at least a few water lots – properties that Caldwell had failed to obtain – to Fraser and Smith.[113] As Caldwell's legal challenge to the new rivals unfolded,

Bulmer remarked, ominously but insightfully, that "the question as to whether the Ontario gov't has any rights to administer the Indian lands will probably come up. And if it is held by the Court that the Ontario Gov't have not that right an entirely new phase may be put on this Sabaskong question."[114]

As multiple contending factions pressed their competing claims and proposals for restructuring investment arrangements, the moose in the canoe could no longer be ignored. Amidst mounting doubts over Ontario's authority, rumour circulated that Crown Lands Commissioner Gibson might delay his decision on the Sabaskong Group's mining applications until Caldwell's case against Fraser and Smith was resolved.[115]

Whether Ontario or the Dominion would administer Reserve 38B's mining lands remained undecided in February 1898, but when Bulmer ascertained that the seven outstanding locations from the Sabaskong Group's original proposal had still not been applied for in Ottawa, he determined to do so himself.[116]

Conmee, offering continued assurances that title would be granted if the investors' squabbles among themselves could be resolved, eventually secured sufficient support to proceed with a revised reorganization of the various claimants. Many of the smaller investors were "tired of wrangling," and who could blaim them?[117] When George Drewry, acting as secretary of the newly reconstructed Sabaskong Company, set out to put corporate records in order in the summer of 1898, he noted that "many of the old Rat Portage shareholders have sold their interests. Some of the Montrealers too have unloaded."[118] For good measure, steps were also taken to put in claims regarding Conmee's promised water lots, for – following disputed authority over fisheries, timber licences, and mineral claims, as described here – water rights and interests were surfacing on the regional agenda.

4
Water Rights and Water Powers

Pioneering lumber producers and their gold mining counterparts whose efforts had been complicated by disputes over resource ownership never imagined that water rights along the Rainy River system, the Lake of the Woods, and connected waterways would produce equally protracted wrangling. Yet alongside revolutionary power developments at Niagara and extraordinary expansion of the western Canadian economy, difficult water issues emerged within the uncertain legal legacy of the Ontario boundary settlement. With international complications not far behind, the diversity of affected interests made water governance exceptionally contentious.

Until the end of the nineteenth century, Ontario lacked comprehensive water power legislation, while federal officials – to the extent they had authority in the matter – showed irregular interest amidst expressions of concern about monopoly privileges.[1] International considerations were also at play, particularly along the Rainy River system, an important corridor for both Canadian and American business interests. Whether using mechanical power or hydroelectricity, timber operations – and later mining, flour milling, and especially pulp and paper enterprises – faced delays and unexpected costs as they sought to secure water flows. Many became caught up in legal disputes ranging from ownership of a desirable site to international control of waters whose quality and fluctuating levels affected, and might even transform, the environment and the economy of the entire watershed.

THE BUSINESS OF BOOMING

Upstream from the operations of Keewatin Lumbering and Manufacturing (KLM), John Mather pursued ancillary ventures to buttress and secure his business interests. In about 1886, he sought Canadian authorization to establish the Rainy River Boom Company. Considerations related to international boundary waters stalled the application. To meet its immediate needs in the area, KLM then associated itself with the Minnesota and Ontario Lumber Company, which had mills at the town of Rainy River and obtained a boom charter for the American side of the river between its mouth and the Sault rapids. This operation was known as the Rainy Lake River Boom Company.[2]

In 1888, the Ross, Hall, and Brown Lumber Company proposed to incorporate the Rainy River Boom Slide and Navigation Company and to obtain Ontario government approval to operate timber slides. Such works facilitated the passage of logs around various obstructions. The promoters aspired to engage in several aspects of the transportation sector on the grounds that this was necessary in remote northern regions: "A pioneer in any kind of business who goes in to develop the resources of the country must take with him and be prepared to deal in almost everything wanted for himself, his work people and his business."[3]

Premier Oliver Mowat showed less concern about the operational range of the venture than about its geographical breadth and the imprecision of proposed territorial limits. These were described simply in terms of "adjoining water." Mowat redefined the limits to confine the company's activities to the Rainy River "and to rivers and streams in this province emptying into Rainy River." Crown Lands officials consulted timber limit holders about the charter proposal and the suggested toll because, as assistant commissioner Aubrey White recognized, the river was "an international stream and one of the largest rivers in the province, and will be the highway of millions and millions of logs to reach the mills at Rat Portage."[4]

The possibility that forest operations with connections to Ross, Hall, and Brown might gain special advantages aroused consternation among rival enterprises. The owners of an existing Rainy River mill objected that the application, if granted, would make their own business almost impossible. Dick and Banning – always alert to a competitive threat – questioned the extent of territory applied for the proposed tolls.

By the time the Ontario government's review of the Rainy River Boom Slide and Navigation Company proposal was underway, Mather's group

had reapplied for federal incorporation of the Rainy River Boom Company.
Mather planned river "improvements" in order to transport saw logs and
square timber downstream to the Lake of the Woods and reported having
spent $16,000 for a boom "capable of handling the entire cut of the District"
by the time he was invited to comment on the Ross, Hall, and Brown
application. Mather contemplated amalgamation with the American Rainy
Lake River Boom Company as a means to deal with the international
status of the waterway. Ross, Hall, and Brown had intended to incorporate
separately in Minnesota for the same reason: operating on border waterways
clearly entailed complications beyond anything that strictly domestic
businesses would need to address.[5]

Boom operators were entitled to "reasonable tolls" when their facilities
were used to store, handle, or deliver someone else's logs. In the absence
of formal agreements, however, it was not clear that lumber companies
with logs in the river either required or intended to avail themselves of these
services. Disputes arose – and arose regularly – when boom companies
held back logs owned by unrelated lumber firms in order to increase their
chances of receiving payments. Ontario and Minnesota courts were repeatedly asked to determine who was entitled to what. Along an international
waterway, the further complication arose that the very validity of the
legislation establishing boom companies might be questioned when they
extended operations across the boundary or held back timber that originated in the neighbouring jurisdiction.[6] To float logs presumes water of a
certain depth, as, of course, does towing them by steamer. This too might
require environmental intervention.

ONE DAM AFTER ANOTHER

To enhance commercial navigation in the interests of fishing, mining, the
timber trade, and settlement, Rat Portage residents petitioned as early as
1884 for approval of a dam on the Lake of the Woods. Business and prosperity were undermined, they believed, by low and decreasing water levels.
Some mills were compelled to operate well below capacity, and steamers
were unable to maintain regular connections between lakeshore settlements and the CPR.[7] With cabinet approval and funding in the spring of
1887, although apparently without authorization under Canada's *Navigable
Waters Protection Act,* John Mather oversaw construction of the Rollerway
Dam during the following winter.[8] Lake levels were then held between
one and a half and three feet higher. By 1891, the Rollerway structure had

deteriorated to such an extent that arrangements were made to replace it with a more substantial installation, the Norman Dam.[9]

The clash of commercial rivals pursuing economic advantage against an evolving and uncertain legal backdrop soon triggered controversy over the fate of water power sites at the Winnipeg River outlets from the Lake of the Woods. One might imagine an elaborate game of musical chairs played by resolute and ambitious investors, in which a valuable water power location represented an extremely desirable place to sit down. Disputes arose about what one was entitled to do while seated, and artificially cut channels later introduced the possibility of special treatment for those who brought their own chair. It was equally unsettling that both federal and provincial governments might stop or start the music – and change the tune. Neither authority assumed this role in the spirit of harmony. And yes, American officials had their own interests in the seating arrangements. The key participants in the quest for power sites included grain milling, hydro-electricity, and lumber operations, along with municipal officials, railways, and the long-established Hudson's Bay Company.[10]

The Lake of the Woods Milling Company was incorporated in 1887 to operate grain elevators across western Canada and a flour mill at Keewatin. Almost immediately, the company inquired about twelve acres of land alongside Portage Bay to the west of Dick and Banning's lumber yard. Leaders of the grain venture, again including John Mather, were anxious to confirm their rights before embarking on a $200,000 construction program. Some of the land was unoccupied and available, yet Ontario's Crown Lands Department declined to grant the request. There were prior applications and other claims, including Dick and Banning's interest in a westward extension of their lumber mill property.[11]

The task of reconciling competing commercial interests provided provincial officials with opportunities to influence both the process of land allocation and industrial development. Rights respecting the western mill race location were particularly controversial, as Dick and Banning were already in possession of its upper end through the Dominion deed that W.J. Macaulay, the persistent Minnesotan, had extracted from Sir John A. Macdonald. Dick and Banning's application to the province covered the lower portion of what all parties recognized as one potential site for an artificial water power channel.

A real estate guide to a small property destined for flooding is not ordinarily of much value or significance. In this case, the bigger picture ultimately came to involve the competing interests of Ontario, Manitoba, and Minnesota and a unique international water management framework that began to take shape early in the twentieth century. Even taking hyperbole into account, a fair estimate of the perceived stakes is evident in published assessments: "There is no other point on the continent of America possessing water power of such magnitude or situated so advantageously as those of the picturesque falls on the Winnipeg River at 'Portage du Rat.'"[12]

Lake of the Woods Milling wanted two pieces of land in the vicinity – the ungranted property at the lower end of the mill race location and the upper property already belonging to Dick and Banning. Negotiations foundered: "Dick impracticable," wrote Mather in his diary.[13] Mather appealed for provincial support for his company's efforts to introduce new industry in Ontario's northwest. He argued emphatically that the Dominion government clearly intended to grant one water power for the operation of Macaulay's sawmill, certainly not two.[14]

Provincial officials, while refusing to be drawn into the wider conflict, acknowledged Mather's arguments respecting the lower portion of the mill race. The province was more inclined to scorn the federal government, which "actually pretended to issue a patent," as Mather wrote, than to assume responsibility itself, at least while the *St. Catharines Milling* case concerning the authority of Ottawa and Ontario in the region was still in the courts.[15]

In spite of their unwillingness to intervene, provincial officials sympathized with Lake of the Woods Milling and dispatched a commissioner to investigate. The Lake of the Woods Milling Company claim was but one of 159 specific land title disputes on the 1889 agenda.[16] After examining applications for Portage Bay lands and consulting interested parties, Ontario's commissioner recommended that the grain milling company should get as much of Dick and Banning's land as was required for the mill race. The price would be settled by arbitration if no other means could be found. Mather had been persuasive.

Anticipating success and finally assuming that a satisfactory price could be determined, the flour milling company proceeded unilaterally to occupy a small portion of Dick and Banning's lumber yard: Mather, convinced that Dick and Banning's federal title was of little use without provincial confirmation, resolved that "there is no course left but to go on and occupy and let Dick stop us if he can."[17] Dick and Banning protested acrimoniously, but when it was firmly intimated that necessary provincial confirmation of their Dominion deed would be more readily forthcoming if the grain miller's progress was not obstructed and that the CPR might retaliate against interference with a major shipper's interests, the smaller enterprise acquiesced.[18]

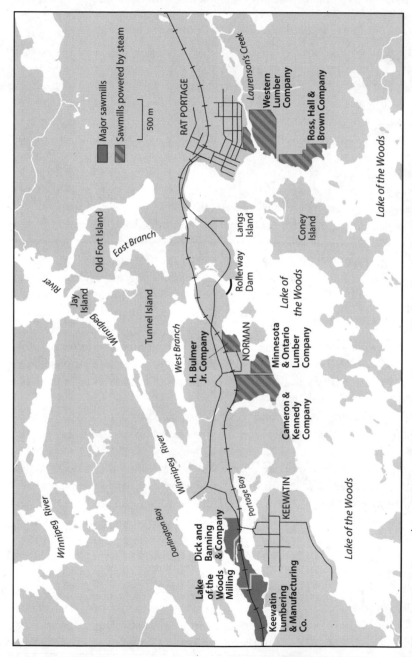

MAP 4.1   Water Power Sites at Winnipeg River Outlets. *Courtesy of Ogilvie Flour Mills. Map adapted by Eric Leinberger.*

To complete its land holdings, Lake of the Woods Milling awaited the even more drawn-out process of Ontario's transfer to the federal government of lands long occupied by the CPR before it could acquire the desired Keewatin site.[19] The CPR's Keewatin property also interested Mather for its proximity to a tavern that was having undesirable effects on operations at the new grain milling facility.[20]

Elsewhere along the shoreline, the Keewatin Lumbering and Manufacturing Company campaigned for a patent to Tunnel Island between the two branches of the Winnipeg River, which it claimed by virtue of rights acquired in 1879 from Richard Fuller's pioneering venture. In 1888, Mather renewed the effort to obtain Tunnel Island and informed Crown Lands Commissioner Pardee – somewhat prematurely, as it turned out – that the Keewatin Lumbering and Manufacturing Company was anxious to begin the development of water power at Tunnel Island.[21]

After a provincial investigation of the Tunnel Island matter, Keewatin Lumbering concluded an agreement with the Ontario government in 1891.[22] The province granted the Keewatin Lumbering and Manufacturing Company most of Tunnel Island and twenty-three additional acres near the lower falls along the south shore of the west branch of the Winnipeg River, the location that became the Norman Dam. In exchange, the company agreed to invest $250,000 for power development, with 60 percent of this investment to be made within three years. The company further agreed to lease power and lands for buildings and factories at rates to be fixed by a provincially appointed engineer.[23]

The next move to advance the development of the west branch power site was the transfer by the Keewatin Lumbering and Manufacturing Company of its Tunnel Island rights to the newly formed Keewatin Power Company. This step depended upon the transferability of property rights in one of the important water power chairs that Mather and his associates had begun to occupy when the federal and provincial musicians finally stopped playing – temporarily at least. The transfer was accomplished in 1893, and again, Mather was to play a central role in a process that would soon engage public interests alongside the private corporate agenda, before further impacting international relations across the entire watershed.[24]

Keewatin Power constructed the Norman Dam with a view to eventual power production, but in 1898, in cooperation with Ontario's Department of Public Works, the company briefly assumed responsibility for regulating water levels of the Lake of the Woods for navigational purposes. Keewatin Power then transferred actual control to the Department of Crown Lands, confirming that the commissioner would "have the right to regulate the

THE DAM, KENORA, ONT.

FIGURE 4.1 Norman Dam, built 1893–95. *Courtesy of the Lake of the Woods Museum.*

height of the water and to control the dam as necessary."[25] This simple language encompassed the power to determine how high the water might rise, how low it might fall – and how fast. Such decisions had the potential to affect almost everyone in the watershed.[26]

Despite vigorous efforts to attract or to create consumers, Keewatin Power experienced great difficulty in selling the available electricity. Initially – in the 1890s – it was hoped that substantial quantities of electricity could be marketed in Winnipeg: cost estimates were prepared, and right-of-way problems and engineering issues were examined. The failure of the proposal was attributed to "the indifference of the Winnipeg public" based on the expectation that power would soon become available from other sources along the Assiniboine or Red Rivers.[27] Continuing discouragement next prompted consideration of a scheme to obtain wood for pulp and paper mills to be established on Keewatin Power's property.

In an interesting example of a potential power producer seeking to create a large-scale consumer to stimulate demand, Mather negotiated for pulp limits between 1898 and 1900.[28] Despite some encouraging signs and the prospect of a thousand local jobs, the Ontario government's unwillingness to approve the necessary arrangements undermined this proposal as well, before agreement on a pulpwood concession was finally reached in 1901.[29] Other possible electricity markets seemed equally elusive.

After a ten-year effort, the Keewatin Power directors contemplated an outright sale of the company's rights and assets. The City of Winnipeg, where municipal ownership of power was under active consideration, could have obtained the entire property at Keewatin in 1905 but either never received or did not accept the proposal offered.[30] A further decade passed before arrangements were concluded to transfer complete control to the Minnesota-based empire of E.W. Backus, who would, with characteristic determination, set out to raise the water levels and the stakes.

A Fur Trader Turns Power Broker

The last of the major private interests in the water power struggles was, in fact, the oldest commercial proprietor in the district. The directors of the Hudson's Bay Company, shrewd and strategic observers of Canada's evolving economic and political landscape, were keenly attentive to the potential of the company's landholdings.[31] Having relocated its Rat Portage trading post from Old Fort Island in the Winnipeg River to a clearing on the mainland in 1861, the HBC found itself in possession of Main Street property as a community formed around it. The company was thus well positioned to benefit from future commercial development.[32]

CPR construction stimulated a frenzy of land sales in the early 1880s.[33] The CPR itself was soon intimately concerned with the status of HBC lands as the railway contemplated its own real estate requirements. The fortunes of the community directly impacted operations at the HBC sales shop, as well as property values. Thus, with the town at one point in a "stagnant condition," the HBC faced commercial challenges, and the depressed state of mining operations after 1900 resulted in a "visibly decreased" population.[34] Survey and construction crews working nearby on building the Grand Trunk Pacific and double-tracking the CPR modestly boosted regional economic activity, although the latter project ultimately reduced the need for resident railway employees.[35] In 1918, following a number of unsatisfactory years, the HBC closed its doors in Kenora, as Rat Portage had been renamed.[36]

Clarence Campbell Chipman, an experienced senior public servant, had joined the ranks of the HBC in 1891 and soon exercised responsibility for the company's lands and properties. From a real estate perspective, successful land sales in the prosperous mid-1890s encouraged him to make additional lots available in a manner "most likely in the future to lead to the development of the Town in the Company's interests."[37] A decade later, though, Chipman had become much less exuberant as he foresaw little prospect "of any material development or increase of population," and by 1912, the speculative era had run its course.[38] Clearing the land inventory at fair values was the order of the day. When the town offered to buy two lots for "full present value," the company, foreseeing no prospects of significant price enhancement, considered the terms appropriate.[39]

By the terms of its Deed of Surrender, the HBC had retained all the fur trade posts actually occupied anywhere in British North America, together with certain lands in the vicinity.[40] Under this agreement, in addition to its townsite holdings, the HBC selected a block of land at Kenora and later extended its holdings prior to the JCPC decision on the Ontario boundary. Thus, the company acquired land – including shoreline property on the mainland side of the Winnipeg River's east branch – to which it would not have been entitled but for the date at which the land was selected and the Ontario government's later willingness to recognize the HBC's rights to the property. The company had no active plans to utilize the east branch water power but was fully aware of the site's potential. Two enterprising local developers – John A. McCrossan and Harding Ridout – established the Citizens' Electric Light and Telephone Company and constructed a small power plant at this site in 1892, under carefully supervised lease from the HBC.[41]

This array of private interests jostling for riparian advantage along the crowded shoreline was enough to cloud the fate of important Lake of the Woods water powers, as rival claimants had similarly affected gold mine development. But the introduction of governmental interests – municipal, provincial, and federal, not to mention the concerns of Minnesotans – added greatly to the entanglement: as representatives of many other parties and interests were forced to experience, there would be transaction costs, more conventionally recognized as complications.

POWER REGULATION AND THE PUBLIC INTEREST

The vital importance of provincial water powers in a period of rapid technological innovation in hydroelectricity generation and transmission was officially emphasized in 1891. In his *Report on the Lakes and Rivers: Waters and Water-Powers of the Province of Ontario*, E.B. Borron explored the advantages and economic significance of electricity, highlighting public interests in continuing to control the resource. He insisted that public rights "are to be most jealously and carefully guarded" and recommended specific means to achieve this result. First, he proposed that water, apart from domestic or sanitary requirements, "should be reserved to the Crown as trustee for the benefit of the people of the province generally" in the context of all future land sales. In addition, he proposed that water powers should be leased rather than sold, with rent varying according to such circumstances as the location of the falls or rapids, difficulties involved in power production, and the nature of anticipated usage.[42]

Prompt development of available water power sites was increasingly considered desirable as a means of stimulating industrial development, particularly in the northern mineral sector. Many who saw cheap power as essential for sawmills, planing factories, pulp mills, and other woodworking industries, together with mining operations and textile and chemical works, also regarded water power as the foundation of a provincial industrial strategy. As much as one might admire Borron's foresight (even extending to the idea of a public trust in water), perhaps he defined the franchise in too limited a fashion.

Borron's recommendation that legislative measures be taken to consolidate control in government hands was ignored until 1898, when the province gave notice of its intention to regulate the terms and conditions of private water power development. The *Water Powers Act* authorized the Crown Lands commissioner to reserve water powers and adjacent property from sale and to prepare regulations to establish terms for disposal and development.[43]

At least theoretically, the *Water Powers Act* and accompanying regulations established procedures and standards to control the allocation of leases and several operational aspects of hydroelectric power production.[44] Conflicts and problems arose, however, with respect to the administration of the regulatory framework and its application to certain water powers in Ontario, especially those secured by private interests prior to the legislation. The latter category included the HBC's Winnipeg River lands.

In October 1897, the London Committee of the HBC rejected a lease arrangement with the Citizens' Telephone and Electric Company of Rat Portage because of the lengthy twenty-year term. Senior company officials were "looking to the rapid rise in values which rapidly occurs in new countries" and were concerned that "future development might be hampered."[45] In the ensuing talks, HBC negotiators insisted upon a fixed limit to the horsepower the Citizens' venture might produce at the site, and, indeed, the HBC intermittently contemplated undertaking power development itself.[46] The lessees acceded to the HBC's demands, including the possibility of further power development by the HBC, but a new obstacle arose when Citizens' realized that it was unprotected against such costs as the interruption of power service if the HBC decided to develop the property further.[47] There were many steps to climb on the learning curve.

Civic officials were beginning to imagine a public enterprise of their own to oversee power production and town lighting. The ambitious municipal leaders were anxious to ensure that the electrical potential of Steep Rock Falls on the east branch of the Winnipeg River be used in a manner most advantageous to their community. H.N. Ruttan, Winnipeg's city engineer who had been interested in the power site for many years, advised the HBC about a municipal power scheme, particularly as a means of circumventing the "comparative standstill" in development activity and, accordingly, the prospects for the company's property.[48] He cautioned prophetically that "as power at the Lake of the Woods becomes valuable, the question of the quantity of water used by the several powers may have to be one of arrangement or litigation."[49] Mayor D.C. Cameron was unimpressed by the terms of the lease that was on offer in the fall of 1902. And so, after the HBC notified McCrossan and Ridout that their lease for Citizens' would terminate, but prior to the actual date of termination at the end of March 1903, the town acquired the power house and associated works from the Citizens' Telephone and Electric Company. The defiant community then refused to vacate, nor would it pay rent to the HBC.

The company took to the courts to regain possession of its property. Sabre rattling in the form of threatened expropriation soon followed.[50] Chipman, astute and experienced, correctly anticipated that the town would secure expropriation authority and prepared in that event "to secure the highest possible price for the property."[51]

In the summer of 1904, municipal representatives initiated expropriation proceedings and declared a specific interest in eleven and a quarter acres of HBC lands, together with one shoreline acre from the Keewatin Power Company site, for payment of $1,167.50 and $100, respectively. These modest valuations rested on the proposition that the potential water rights were not directly associated with the shoreline property.[52] Indeed, having begun to operate the McCrossan and Ridout facilities, the community applied to Ontario for a patent covering the stream bed. Thus, a potential concern about the ownership of riverbeds, which Amelius Irving had flagged in passing many years earlier, began to work its way into the headlines of the day. Newton W. Rowell, acting as solicitor for the town, used his solid Liberal connections to circumvent Crown lands officials by dealing directly with Premier George W. Ross.

With his party's fortunes in evident decline and an important provincial election pending, Ross signalled his willingness to grant the town's application to the bed of the stream. That prospect induced representatives of the parties to convene in Toronto for crucial talks in late January 1905. Allen Aylesworth, who had just declined appointment to the Supreme Court of Canada and was about to become federal minister of Justice in the Laurier cabinet, represented the HBC, with Christopher Robinson on hand for Keewatin Power. These two spoke forcefully against a government grant of the stream bed on the grounds that as property owners of lands adjacent to the Winnipeg River, their clients already owned the adjacent bed to the halfway point in the stream. Chipman, despite his confidence in the HBC's legal position, acknowledged the consensus conclusion that Premier Ross would grant the patent to the town: "With a Government at its wits end to keep in power, there is, unfortunately, the political outlook to be kept in view."[53] Eventually, it was agreed that arbitration over the question of property valuation would be postponed until after the elections.

The landmark 1905 Conservative election victory brought into office the administration of James Pliny Whitney, which soon resulted in the celebrated introduction of provincial public power under the auspices of the Hydro-Electric Power Commission (HEPC) and its energetic champion, Adam Beck. Very early in its mandate, the HEPC ventured west to investigate the contentious application for a water power lease. At the time of Beck's mid-August visit in 1905, Kenora was producing about four hundred horsepower to power electric lighting from "a very dilapidated and antiquated plant." While careful to avoid any pronouncement on the underlying legal entitlements, the HEPC recommended issuance of a lease subject to the possibility of additional terms following a broader review of existing regulations.[54]

The HEPC took inventory of local power production and potential: Keewatin Lumber Company (250 hp), Lake of the Woods Milling (2,000 hp), Keewatin Milling (1,500 hp proposed from an artificial channel), and Keewatin Power at the western outlet (estimated potential 17,000 hp). Respecting the eastern outlet, partially used by the town, one engineering report suggested potential as high as 6,370 horsepower, although the town hoped to produce 4,500 horsepower "as necessity demands."[55] Any increase in power production, though, would have to come from technological innovation and efficiencies, for the 1903 expropriation legislation specifically denied any authority "to withdraw from the Lake of the Woods a larger volume of water than the present natural flow of water in the east branch of the Winnipeg River at the outlet of the said lake into the said east branch of the said Winnipeg River."[56]

Yet in the absence of lawful authority to pursue the water power opportunity, mere engineering *potential* was unlikely to induce investment. With much of the legal framework unsettled in the region, that lawful authority was difficult to secure. In the case of power development, in particular, the ownership of riverbeds where construction would occur remained unresolved. The dispute over ownership of the bed of the Winnipeg River propelled the controversy into the realm of general law. The outcome of this specific case eventually put the matter back onto the public legislative agenda. In the years ahead, both the extent of acceptable intervention and technological innovation, as well as the scope of natural flow, would also be vigorously contested.

Who Owns the Riverbed?

The application of the Water Powers Act to certain Ontario rivers depended upon the ownership of the beds of navigable waterways where shoreline property had been granted by the Crown. Control of a number of major hydroelectric power sites thus depended on whether the Crown was presumed to have granted or retained ownership of the riverbeds associated with shoreline properties. In *Keewatin Power Company and Hudson's Bay Company v Town of Kenora* (1906), the issue was tested in a dispute involving the Winnipeg River. The key question in the property valuation became the nature of private rights in the riverbed of a navigable waterway.

From the outset, possible intervention by the provincial attorney general attracted attention. Chipman, as the Hudson's Bay Company's land commissioner, wired Premier Whitney to oppose rumoured provincial involvement in the case. He was sharply rebuked: "Your telegram received," stated the premier, "and I reply simply to draw your attention to the objectionable tone and language of it." The response could hardly have been unexpected. Nonetheless, one of the HBC's Toronto solicitors continued to urge that "the clearer Mr. Whitney and his government are shown that your company intends taking a strong position, I think the less trouble we will have with them."[57] On their side, Kenora officials favoured Crown participation and, with qualified success, pressed the province to join the litigation.

W.H. Hearst, who later became premier, represented the provincial interest. He travelled with N.W. Rowell, who was still counsel for the town and subsequently became leader of the provincial Liberals, to Kenora, where the *Keewatin Power* case opened before Mr. Justice Anglin in July 1906. Hearst formally secured the attorney general's right to intervene but decided there was nothing to be gained at trial that might not also be accomplished on appeal. The matter of Ontario's formal participation was therefore left open.[58]

After preliminary matters in court, judge and counsel adjourned to visit the disputed power site with several engineers. The legal contingent "no doubt got a very clear conception of the situation."[59] Then, following only one day of testimony, the HBC and Keewatin Power dramatically abandoned the injunction they had previously secured against development by the town and acknowledged Kenora's right to possession. An agreement between the parties settled most matters, apart from valuation associated with ownership of the riverbed. As the week ended, forty labourers returned to work on a coffer dam, with the workforce climbing back to a hundred by Monday as courtroom activity resumed: "Now that the injunction is removed," reported the local newspaper, "it is not so important to have a quick judgment as was considered a few days ago."[60]

Justice Anglin's decision was largely favourable to Kenora's arguments about the nature of a navigable waterway and to the proposition that a Crown grant of lands bordering navigable rivers conferred ownership only to the water's edge.[61] This conclusion was founded upon the judge's willingness to modify or adapt English common law doctrine on waterways in applying it to the rivers and lakes of Ontario.

In anticipation of an appeal, provincial officials reassessed the public interest raised by the Kenora case. Hearst warned that if the companies succeeded, "the grantees of the land on navigable waters have obtained greater rights than it was intended." Similar consequences would follow if the court accepted that the same rights as enjoyed by riparians on nonnavigable streams also applied to the nonnavigable portions of otherwise navigable waterways. To avoid the possibility that future Crown leases might perpetuate a serious – and costly – problem, Hearst urged that the agreements be reworded, "making it clear that where lands are granted bordering on navigable waters, that the grant does not extend beyond high water mark." To protect water power rights on nonnavigable streams, he also proposed to clarify the *Water Powers Act*.[62] But these preventive initiatives failed to resolve the practical question of the Crown's best course of action in the current litigation.

Rowell pressed the attorney general to become a party to the judicial proceedings, with the alarming prediction that a successful appeal "would disturb titles from one end of this province to the other, and would largely destroy the government's plans for control of water power." Rowell, of course, was aware that the Crown could advance new arguments and additional evidence related to long-settled granting practices for water lots far more effectively than the town would be able to do on its own behalf. He even invoked the benefit of "the moral effect" that would flow from the Crown's participation to support his view that direct government involvement would mark the difference between failure and success.[63]

Yet the attorney general remained unwilling to participate. Perhaps the provincial government did not expect the company's legal argument to succeed, and the residual response of legislation was always available to overturn an inconvenient judicial decision. Perhaps, too, the provincial government would have preferred a favourable judicial solution to legislative action.[64] Ironically, the Court of Appeal varied the trial decision and affirmed the private parties' claims to the bed of the Winnipeg River. In the view taken by two members of that court, precedent and statutory interpretation necessitated a conclusion that it was not open to the judiciary to alter or circumvent. Richard Martin Meredith doubted that "judicial legislation is the proper or is at all a permissible remedy."[65] Chief Justice Charles Moss was equally forceful in his opinion that the legislature alone was the proper forum for any necessary changes to the law.

There were no further appeals, but three years later, in 1911, with important power developments along the St. Lawrence River then in contemplation, the legislature reversed the result of the Kenora case.[66] Henceforth, in the absence of an express grant, it should be presumed that ownership of the bed of a navigable water was not intended to pass to the grantee of the shoreline lands.

Paralleling the chain of provincial actions respecting the broader public interest in the underwater foundations of hydroelectric power production across Ontario was the fate of the now less prominent stretch of Winnipeg River shoreline whose proposed municipal expropriation had triggered the epic battle. The HBC celebrated the 1908 Court of Appeal judgment as a "sweeping victory." When the town's opportunity to appeal lapsed, negotiations returned to the matter of price.[67]

By way of overture, the town ritually inquired: "How much are you asking?" only to receive a response of "What are you willing to offer?" The landowners calculated the value of their fiercely contested water power somewhere between $1.2 million and $2.45 million.[68] As arbitrators were being selected to determine a final purchase price, Keewatin Power – to the dismay of the HBC – declared itself entitled to 50 percent of the proceeds. In September 1911, Kenora eventually paid about $100,000 plus legal costs to the two companies.[69] With the lengthy controversy nearing conclusion, Mayor Currie remarked to Leighton McCarthy, solicitor to the HBC: "I might add, with the best of feeling to yourself, that I think you did us to a brown turn on this arbitration business."[70]

The 5.5 percent debentures issued by the town to finance municipal hydro-power ownership were considered a secure investment. As one adviser reported to a prospective investor, "the whole town of Kenora is liable for payment of principal and interest, in addition to which the bonds represent a first charge upon the plant and revenues of a modern Hydro-Electric power development having an assured market for its output."[71] The potential of falling water to elevate neighbouring levels of industrial activity stimulated other lakeshore investments.

FLOUR AT KEEWATIN

Langholm, the setting of Frederick Philip Grove's novel *The Master of the Mill*, "overlooked the rock-strewn plain to the west where, fifty miles beyond, it merged into the prairie."[72] Langholm, in fact, is the fictional representation of Keewatin, the Lake of the Woods community whose "merger" with the prairie was now as much commercial as geological.

In 1890, Canada's largest grain mill had thirty-nine employees, with six more making barrels in the cooper shop and four loaders.[73] An entire train load of ten cars, each laden with hard wheat from Manitoba, arrived daily at the Lake of the Woods Milling Company facility, a six-storey building with a milling capacity of fifteen hundred barrels per day. Looked at another way, on a daily basis, the plant handled the production of ten farms, each yielding twenty bushels of grain per acre from twenty-five acres.[74] These volumes, modest by later standards, were at least sufficient to inspire literature and ambition.

The fortunes of Minneapolis, home to numerous flour mills, were often invoked as a point of reference.[75] A *Globe* correspondent proclaimed the superiority of Lake of the Woods water power over that of the US comparator: the power was situated on the line of the Canadian Pacific Railway, in effect "the highway from the wheat fields of the prairie region leading to an eastern market," and thus offering the possibility of a milling industry that would be "equal to any on the continent of America."[76] The water powers of the Lake of the Woods were central to the integration between prairie agriculture and European markets at a time when new milling technology offered significant efficiencies.[77] Characteristically, and on the basis of a lifetime of experience in Scotland and the Ottawa Valley, John Mather was deeply involved in the details of mill construction.[78]

It proved more challenging to realize the industrial vision than to imagine it. Capital, land assembly, and railway rates were only some of the contentious matters to be addressed. With railway linkages now established between Winnipeg and Lake Superior, CPR investors anxiously awaited enhanced freight and passenger traffic. By 1887, when Lake of the Woods Milling was incorporated, better than half of the initial investment was subscribed to key individuals associated with the CPR.[79] The participants included Sir Donald Smith and Sir George Stephen, of the CPR syndicate, as well as J.J.C. Abbott, the railway's Montreal solicitor and a future prime minister of Canada.[80]

In March 1888, Lake of the Woods Milling initiated wheat shipments to Keewatin from Deloraine and Glenboro in southern Manitoba.[81] To strengthen its supply chain, the milling company subsequently purchased country elevators in western Canada.[82] Additional facilities were constructed, thereby offering the Keewatin lumber mill important sales opportunities to supply building materials. Having held their investment for nearly fifteen years, the original investors in Lake of the Woods Milling resolved, in 1902, to sell shares on the public stock exchange. A few months later, Ogilvie Flour Mills secured a controlling interest in the company.[83]

Lake of the Woods Milling was the first but not the last flour milling venture to take advantage of the water powers and railway access available in northwestern Ontario. John Mather was again instrumental in the formation of the Keewatin Flour Mills Company, an initiative at least partially financed by proceeds from the sale of his Lake of the Woods Milling Company stock. The other crucial ingredient in the Keewatin Flour venture was the Dick and Banning property, finally secured in 1897. The clear failure of the Ottawa Gold Milling and Mining Company on this site made it available for transfer to the next enterprise, a process concluded in 1904–05.[84] As the Keewatin Flour project was envisaged, developers anticipated an initial milling capacity of four thousand barrels per day. But prior to completion, arrangements were concluded to permit Lake of the Woods Milling (now under Ogilvie control) to assume control of the Keewatin Flour venture for a purchase price of $950,000. Federal legislation confirmed the commercial agreement, with Lake of the Woods Milling enjoying the particular satisfaction of securing control of the

"Keewatin" name.[85] Having marketed "Keewatin" flour for many years, the older milling company had deeply resented the prospect of competition from a rival company called Keewatin Flour.

The benefit or burden of names and reputations was also central to the emergence of yet another flour milling business attracted by water power and transportation advantages. D.C. Cameron had accepted the town's name in his Rat Portage Lumber Company but found a potential association with rodents less suited to his grain processing ambitions. As the new enterprise, the Maple Leaf Milling Company, launched operations in 1905 at two thousand barrels per day, Rat Portage assumed the new identity of Kenora.[86]

Public and private interests in water rights and the control of power sites had been vigorously contested by early industrialists, as well as by provincial and municipal officials who recognized their exceptional economic value. With the rapid emergence of pulp and paper development in the early twentieth century, the stakes would rise still further as new contestants vied to gain advantage from the use and control of regional waters. These developments, accompanied by legislative intervention and the construction of substantial regulatory works, soon had important and ongoing environmental impacts on water flow and quality throughout the watershed.

5

Pulp and Paper:
From Emergence to Emergency

Minnesota-based entrepreneur E.W. Backus sought to promote pulp and paper development in the mid-continental region. He campaigned relentlessly to secure suitable wood supplies and to establish favourable water management arrangements, coming close to agreement with the Ontario provincial government, under Premier George Ross, before the Liberal Party's dramatic electoral defeat in 1905.[1]

While lobbying public officials on both sides of the Canada-US border, Backus defended his interests vigorously against rivals, challengers, compensation seekers, and government regulators.[2] Overall, his ambitious industrial vision for Rainy-Lake of the Woods waters engaged the attention of state, provincial, and national governments before an array of regional concerns expanded the scale of potential conflict across the watershed and eventually landed on the international agenda. Largely unanticipated environmental consequences emerged as stream flow and water levels became subject to artificial control, disturbing aquatic habitats and shoreline conditions.

RAINY RIVER POWER

With years of Minnesota lumber industry experience behind him, Backus, in partnership with William F. Brooks, a railroad and water power engineer (and later a state senator), established the Backus-Brooks Company, with an eye to Canadian prospects.[3] In the late 1890s and early 1900s, Backus

79

pursued business expansion around Rainy Lake and the Lake of the Woods, where substantial water powers and timber resources were available.[4] He systematically acquired dam sites along the Ontario-Minnesota border through the Quetico-Superior Forest area and initiated industrial development at International Falls on the US side of the Rainy River and at Fort Frances on the Canadian side.

With a provincial charter for his Ontario and Minnesota Power Company, he concluded a controversial agreement with the Liberal government, then led by George Ross, to dam the Rainy River between International Falls and Fort Frances. The latter community subsequently protested that amendments to a proposed fifty-fifty power split in the agreement unfairly left Canadian interests with a much lower fixed allocation.[5]

Backus also pursued a Canadian federal charter for the same enterprise, hoping to have the works declared to be "for the general advantage of Canada," a designation that he expected would provide some constitutional insurance against future provincial interference. Forced to settle for less supportive legislation in 1905, Backus established power facilities and mills between 1904 and 1914, by which time the Canadian plant supplied ground wood pulp for a sulphite mill on the US side.[6]

The strategic significance of upstream water power was readily appreciated, just as the valuable sites at the Lake of the Woods' Winnipeg River outlets were being contested at the local level. Intense controversy over power production extended to debate over the authorization of power exports, for, as Fort Frances's mayor greatly feared, "whoever controls the water power will have a practical monopoly of the pulpwood on this vast area and can buy it at his own price."[7]

Backus's proposals presented sensitive and complex problems regarding the protection of public interests in water in the face of aggressive private claims. In an effort to eliminate ambiguity concerning the respective rights of Rainy River water power developers and Canadian electricity consumers in Fort Frances, provincial legislation enacted in 1906 authorized power exports from the Ontario and Minnesota Power Company facilities, provided that at least half of the energy was available for use in Canada, "as and when demanded." Subject to this condition, cabinet was given responsibility to establish terms for export.[8]

Applications by the Ontario and Minnesota Power Company to export Canadian power generated heated debate in Fort Frances – and more widely across the province. The municipality insisted that Backus had acted in bad faith, even alleging that the Ontario and Minnesota Power Company had and would continue to "in every way discourage, hamper and render impossible the development of industries on the Canadian side of the river."[9] According to the Fort Frances District Board of Trade, Backus "never did intend and does not now intend that one horsepower shall be sold for use in Canada if he can prevent it."[10] The town insisted that no export from Canada should be permitted until all the water power resources on the US side were fully used. Civic spokesmen rejected the suggestion that any Canadian power could be regarded as not being in demand for use on the Canadian side of the river. It should be seen as needed, they argued, until such time as a fair and reasonable chance had been given to the people of Ontario to promote their own industries and utilize their own power. Mayor Williams of Fort Frances posed the spectre of a "dead village on the Canadian side of Rainy River, a prosperous city on the Minnesota side, all because our provincial and federal government have not the backbone to say 'We will retain our resources for our own people.'" The Kenora Board of Trade joined the chorus of criticism.[11]

In June 1910, the provincial legislature concluded that the export conditions had been met and granted a temporary export authorization that could be revoked at any time. In combination, the Fort Frances and International Falls facilities were soon producing 350 tons of paper per day for sixty-five newspapers across North America. Between twelve and fifteen hundred men were engaged in woods and river operations in the district tributary to Rainy River.[12]

To enhance water flows for his power production facilities, Backus contemplated further storage upstream. His attention focused on Lake Namakan and its Kettle Falls outlet in the heart of an area of increasing interest to conservationists and recreational users from the United States and Canada. He pursued legislative authorization on both sides of the border before the international character of the development triggered the interest of the International Joint Commission (IJC), an institution newly established under the 1909 Boundary Waters Treaty.

The first item of transboundary water business considered by the IJC was the Backus proposal for an international dam at the Kettle Falls outlet from Lake Namakan. The application on the US side, in the name of the Rainy River Improvement Company, corresponded with efforts by the Ontario and Minnesota Power Company to secure Canadian approval. As each of the national governments had authorized development as proposed by the two business ventures that shared common controlling ownership, the IJC concluded that it had no jurisdiction in the matter.[13] Thus, an early water development with widespread implications moved forward without comprehensive scrutiny.

In connection with power exports, Backus had also overcome local opposition and was positioned to transfer unsold portions of the power generated on the Canadian side to his Minnesota operations. Nevertheless, the intricacies of local property and tax assessments kept company lawyers busy for many years as Fort Frances officials doggedly maintained their understanding that access to the falling water remained a valuable source of community revenue.[14]

Backus's rights to deal with water were also contested on the environmental front by riparian owners whose lands were adversely affected by the new dam across the Rainy River.[15] One trial judge concluded that "greed was the ruling motive in the defendants' method of operating their works. They disregarded the rights and interests of adjoining proprietors and took a chance to make all the money they could."[16] But Backus was not alone in facing closer scrutiny for the impacts of developmental activity on regional water resources and on the interests of other users.

THE ENVIRONMENT, RESOURCES, AND THE CANADIAN CONSTITUTION

Within about a week of commencing operations in the spring of 1913, the Dryden Timber and Power Company came under official examination for environmental impacts.[17] Dr. Robert E. Wodehouse conducted a sanitary survey, having been alerted by Ontario's chief medical officer to concerns about the mill expressed by residents.[18]

Wodehouse noted that after bark removal, pulpwood was "macerated to a fine chip condition." The chips were then conveyed to cooking digesters, where steam was directed into vats containing sodium hydrate and lime. A chemical process followed the digestion so that as much as possible of the lime and soda could be recovered for reuse. The plant engineer advised that 90 percent of the soda could be captured in this way. Of the remainder, 4 percent stayed in the wood pulp, while 6 percent entered the waterway. This was described as a vegetable carbonate, rendered essentially neutral in the digestion process, and harmless, according to the plant engineer.[19]

Putting the damage issue aside, the visual impact of the effluent discharge in the form of froth foam or suds was widespread. The plant engineer's calculation suggested that six thousand pounds of organic soda compound and eighteen thousand pounds of lime carbonate entered the river every

FIGURE 5.1 Dryden Mill. *Courtesy of the Lake of the Woods Museum.*

twenty-four hours. Given resinous matter in pulp wood, this resulted in the formation of froth foam and the proliferation of complaints.[20]

One remedial response then in contemplation (at least to ameliorate the visual impact of foam) was to locate the effluent pipe underwater to reduce frothing. There was no suitable soil in the area to use as irrigation beds for the effluent, but Wodehouse noted a nearby ravine that might be filled in for the purpose if this form of treatment was judged to be feasible or desirable. Wodehouse found "nothing unsanitary" about the resulting condition of the river, nor did he consider that the effluent constituted a nuisance. But to permit further assessment of impacts, he ordered samples for analysis.[21]

Around nearby waterways, flooding attributable to power development severely disrupted traditional Aboriginal wild rice harvesting arrangements and forced Indigenous communities to transplant some of the beds.[22] The impact of hydro development on the elaborate wild rice cultivation practices of Indigenous residents was but one illustration of the interconnected nature of water uses. The importance of this feature of water power development was not unknown to early twentieth-century observers, although it was commonly dismissed or inadequately considered. "Too often it has been the tendency in reports on water-power resources to consider power development exclusively without giving adequate place in them to such related subjects as navigation, agriculture, and domestic water supply," began an important Canadian conservation report in 1911. The authors went on to insist: "It is incumbent upon us to determine whether there will be any prejudicial effect upon these other related interests, which depend upon the same source of supply and which have a claim upon our fresh waters, both surface and underground."[23]

Linking the supply of water to forest cover, the same report elaborated upon the environmental consequences of the deforestation sometimes associated with large-scale pulp mill operations: industries proposing to use water power could menace their surroundings. For that reason, pulpwood mills, "which might completely denude the timber lands of trees, at, or near, the head waters of important waterways had better not be established at all; or if established, then only under the strictest regulation and supervision designed to conserve the forest growth," since deforested areas were incapable of effectively retaining groundwater. Summing up the conservationist message, the authors explained that "water is necessary to the soil, and the soil, with its plant growth, is necessary to an economical disposition of the water."[24]

Similar concerns about safeguarding the natural and ecological foundations of the country gave rise to various proposals to maintain what would later be known as ecological services. For example, the future of the forest industries and public objectives for water management were linked in an unsuccessful Canadian government proposal to extend a system of forest reserves across northern Ontario to the Lake of the Woods.[25] Prior to 1930, federal officials had responsibility for the natural resources of the Canadian Prairie provinces of Manitoba, Saskatchewan, and Alberta.[26] Rapid growth and the expansion of western settlement in the years before World War I stimulated consideration of regional water power potential and particularly the needs of burgeoning urban centres such as Winnipeg. This community depended for its hydro-power supply on production from the Winnipeg River.[27]

Advocates of forest reserves – that is, areas permanently set aside for the conservation of forest resources to be used on a sustainable basis over the long term – generally emphasized opportunities for public revenue from forests as their key rationale. John Bow Challies, superintendent of Water Powers for the national Commission of Conservation, was thus somewhat unusual in calling for the area in Canada draining into the Lake of the Woods to be segregated as a forest reserve "so as to render the run-off as uniform as possible."[28] Building his argument around anticipated population expansion in Manitoba and that province's need for dependable water power, Challies stressed that "stream flow is so dependent on forest cover." Indeed, he asserted that adverse impacts on stream flow resulting from the loss of forest cover were among the most important considerations facing anyone interested in water power, irrigation, water supply, navigation, or any other water-dependent activity.[29]

In Challies's view, the Lake of the Woods forests already faced severe threats. Challies believed that without supervision and restrictions on lumbering, combined with reforestation, water storage and runoff conservation would be impaired. A forest reserve in the Lake of the Woods basin, however, "would probably be one of the most important in Canada, in so far as the water-power interests are concerned." The Winnipeg River and those relying upon its ability to generate hydroelectric power would benefit, Challies insisted, from "practically uniform" year-long flowage.[30] The proposal was all the more crucial, it appeared, because the international character of the Rainy-Lake of the Woods drainage system made it impossible to construct dams that would "unduly" raise lake levels. But thoughtful reflection on questions of water retention, flow, and lake levels rarely extended to the implications of industrial development on, for example, water quality or the fishery.

Sentiment favouring the long-term conservation of natural resources was not confined to far-sighted public servants. In 1910, the Kenora Board of Trade sought to preserve what is now called natural capital by invoking, among other principles, the notion of a public duty or trust associated with equity between generations. "The first and most vital duty [of governments]," wrote the board to Premier Whitney, "is the faithful conserving for Canadians, not only those of today but more essentially for those of the generations to follow, the natural wealth and the wealth-producing opportunities of the Country."[31] The Board of Trade then proposed to allocate responsibility for that "vital duty" to the national level in order to prevent pioneering developers from overexploiting resources in the short term at the expense of longer-term public benefits. Others specifically advocated a greater federal role in the region, among them MP Frank Keefer, whose background in mineralogy and a lengthy legal career in northwestern Ontario grounded his deep-seated interest in natural resources.

In connection with the proposed transfer of natural resources to the Prairie provinces at the end of the Great War, Keefer considered an appropriate allocation of ownership and control between the federal and provincial governments on the basis of certain core principles: "Canada is a trustee for these Provinces of these natural resources. She is also a trustee, it might be argued, for the whole Dominion of Canada, including, of course, the

Prairie Provinces themselves, for some of these natural resources." Accordingly, Keefer endeavoured to distinguish resources of a "purely domestic" nature from those of interprovincial or international significance. Assuming the possibility of such classification, Keefer advised assigning domestic resources to the provinces, with more careful consideration to those of broader interest and concern.[32]

Keefer analyzed natural resources – including lands, timber, minerals, and water – and often suggested a functional rationale for federal authority. In the case of forests, he concluded that the control of runoff through forest practices was of more than local or provincial importance because of obvious interprovincial effects. For example, "the head waters may be situated in one Province and the water power or the detrimental flood effect is in another." In order to promote common benefits, authority over "forestration" should be allocated to the federal government.[33] Keefer's confident assertions were not universally accepted.

Keefer's survey of resources eventually brought him to water powers and their defining characteristic of being "a natural resource which originated from a very wide area although it may be available at a particular point." Interrelationships among storage, the location of power production sites, and ultimate points of use or consumption underscored the overall relevance of watersheds, which were as essential to power production as the head or drop of water at the point where power would be generated. The uniform continuous flow of certain water powers depended entirely on regulation of the watershed of an adjoining province. Keefer illustrated that proposition using the Winnipeg River in Manitoba, whose water power potential was influenced by, and might possibly be impaired by, "improper control" of the dam at Kenora, where Lake of the Woods levels were controlled.

As Keefer was well aware, the Norman Dam had already produced international irritation as a result of flooding claims from Minnesota residents. Together with the Milk River controversy over western irrigation flows between Alberta and Montana, Keefer regarded the example of regulating water levels on the Lake of the Woods as sufficient demonstration that "it is most advisable that any of the streams that cross the boundaries of the Provinces internationally or as boundary waters, should be federally controlled." He applied the same principle to interprovincial flows. Keefer's extension of his analysis to the interprovincial context rested on his further suggestion – widely asserted and widely contested – that "the Dominion can be trusted by each Province to do what is best for both with no particular selfish interest to serve."[34] For decades to come, it would be easier to acknowledge the importance of a watershed perspective than it would be to devise institutions to incorporate that perspective within the framework of political boundaries, let alone to accommodate the so-cial, economic, environmental, and cultural interests existing within and across those boundaries.

In correspondence with Prime Minister Arthur Meighen, Keefer reiter-ated his analysis, referring directly to the situation respecting Manitoba water powers as demonstrating the desirability of national control: "The power is on the Winnipeg River and on the Nelson River," he wrote, "but the watershed and storage is in Ontario, e.g., the Lake of the Woods and Rainy Lake and tributary waters. It is international and has caused inter-national difficulties. Why repeat such possible difficulties?" Keefer urged Meighen to retain federal control over water power, along with several other broad resource domains, while allocating to the provinces respon-sibilities for such areas as public lands and homesteads, timber, and nonfuel minerals.[35]

The federal government's position regarding Manitoba's interests in certain water powers that depended upon vast flows originating in Ontario (as well as in Minnesota) eventually demanded a great deal of political attention, prime ministerial and otherwise. But apart from such issues on the watershed scale, there were still more localized water-related disputes to be resolved. As in the case of timber licences and mineral rights, water conflicts derived from persistent uncertainties associated with Treaty 3 and the federal-provincial boundary dispute.

INDIAN RESERVES AND WATER LEVELS

In anticipation of legislative resolution of the lingering Indian reserve situation, Ontario's Aubrey White recalled the prolonged narrative in 1915. In 1894, the Dominion government had authorized reserve selection by Ontario, and "the Indians confidently expected they would get these re-serves." When the boundary award confirmed provincial title, Ontario, not having been consulted, refused to recognize the allocation, and the matter became largely dormant. Despite the 1894 agreement, nothing de-finitive was done until December 1914, when Indian Affairs agreed that surrenders should be taken from the Indigenous communities respecting all but one of the eight reserves on the Rainy River. Manitou Rapids was the exception. The agreement extended to the so-called Wild Lands Reserves. In addition, White reported agreement with Ottawa that Reserve 24C, located upstream in the Quetico district, would also be abandoned as a reserve.[36] Provincial legislation to confirm Canada's title to the reserve lands in Treaty 3 was finally enacted in 1915.[37] In a reference to survey plans that would become more controversial than perhaps initially appeared, the statute stated: "The said Reserves as shewn on said plans, with the exception of Indian Reserve 24C in the Quetico Forest Reserve, are hereby transferred to the Government of Canada, whose title thereto is hereby confirmed."[38]

The extended intergovernmental process failed to reflect the agricultural influx that took place on both sides of the Rainy River during the 1890s and early 1900s. Indeed, Aubrey White had once indicated Ontario's willingness to accept the reserves as originally delineated but had sought compensation for interference with settlement.[39] Even as sixteen hundred men were at work on the Ontario and Rainy River Railway in 1901, the steamer *Keenora* delivered settlers and their livestock to shoreline destinations along the Rainy.[40] One journalistic account of a trip up to the Sault and Manitou rapids described a farmer's disembarkation. As plow, churn, furniture, and household gear were unloaded, "we saw his horse and his cows taken off and watched them begin at once to munch the green grass."[41] What appeared idyllic to travellers on the boat may have seemed more unsettling to Indigenous observers.

Thus, in refusing, until 1915, to confirm seven out of eight reserves along the Rainy River in order to retain access to prime agricultural land, the province – according to a subsequent judicial assessment – had "disregarded specific promises Canada had made to the Ojibwa during the negotiations that their gardens would be specifically reserved to them for their exclusive use."[42] Conditions facing the Ojibwa then deteriorated further: not only had they lost prime agricultural lands, but the province severely limited their ability to hunt for subsistence outside their designated reserves.

Remarkably, the ownership and delineation of reserves that was apparently concluded by legislation was not yet resolved despite four decades having passed since the signing of Treaty 3. The forces of nature and industry combined to take the question of reserve boundaries to the courts after an exceptional flood in 1916 affected shoreline lands, including reserve lands, along the Rainy River system upstream from Backus's industrial works. The flooding damaged crops and other property, eroded soil, and destroyed trees. If these injuries had not occurred – or had been much less severe – in the absence of the dam, it was worth asking whether Ontario and Minnesota Power, as owner of the structure, might be liable to pay compensation or, alternatively, whether the company enjoyed some form of immunity in the face of extraordinary occurrences like the high water of 1916.

On behalf of reserve residents who had suffered losses, and on its own behalf as a landowner, the federal government launched a claim against Backus's power company in 1918. The original judgment disappointed plaintiffs. Judge Audette expressed the opinion that the Dominion government had no interest in the damaged reserve lands prior to the 1915 legislation. Thus, the lands were subject to the prior rights of the power company as conferred by the authorization it received in 1905, a grant that permitted flooding of Crown lands in Ontario. Moreover, Audette concluded that the reserves' boundaries did not coincide with the water's edge. Rather, the actual boundaries were two chain lengths, or about 132 feet, inland, since the border – as recorded clearly on the original map or plan held by the Department of Indian Affairs – showed a shoreline allocation for public purposes such as roads or timber booms. For damages experienced inland beyond the two-chain allowance for public purposes, Audette awarded $500.

The federal government's appeal produced a much more favourable and sympathetic decision from the Supreme Court of Canada.[43] Justice Idington, in an effort to protect Indigenous residents from intergovernmental crossfire, used the opportunity to endorse an opinion expressed at the trial level in earlier Sultana Island gold mining litigation, stating that this expressed "more exactly than any other ... what I feel."[44] Unquestionably, Idington began, the surrender of traditional lands was subject to the treaty obligation to set aside reserves "for the special use and benefit of the Indians." For this reason, the Province of Ontario "could not without plain disregard of justice take advantage of the surrender and refuse to perform the condition attached to it." Equally plain, however, was the fact that Ontario's "ownership of the tract of land covered by the Treaty was so complete as to exclude the Government of the Dominion from exercising any power or authority over it."[45]

After reviewing the treaty and subsequent relations between Ontario and the Dominion with respect to the reserves, Idington concluded with assurance that, apart from explicit exceptions, the 1915 legislation represented "a clear ratification of all that may have been done by the Indians concerned in assertion of their rights in the premises." In considering the effect of the grants to Backus for power development following his initial discussions with federal authorities and subsequently with the province, as well as the 1915 legislation, Justice Idington found no support for "any alleged right to raise the water beyond its natural level."[46] And with reference to the details of the agreement, he suggested "that it was never the intention of the Government of the province to go so far as to flood lands never before flooded."[47] The pulp mill dam had raised the water far beyond levels ever contemplated, at least by Ontario. Despite contrary assertions from the power company, Idington preferred evidence offered by the environment on its own behalf: "The dead trees are better witnesses of what the actual facts were before and after the construction of this dam."[48]

On different grounds, other members of the court called for compensation payments exceeding $20,000. Justice Brodeur, for example, took the view that when the federal government permitted Ontario and Minnesota Power to obstruct navigation and the free flow of the river, it did so "on the assumption that the company would pay all the damages that a rise of the water level would occasion."[49] Still more dramatically, Justices Mignault and Anglin concluded that the federal government's original delineation of the reserves, dating from the 1870s, took precedence over all subsequent dealing with these lands. They insisted, accordingly, that "the title of the Dominion relates back to the time when the reserve was laid out and is unaffected by any rights which the Ontario government may have conferred upon Backus and his associates by the agreement of January 1905, insofar as the Indian Reserve is concerned."[50]

Once more, in the context of the power company's appeal, a panel of Law Lords in London contemplated the intricacies of northern Ontario law and geography. The Judicial Committee of the Privy Council (JCPC) determined that the federal title to Indian reserves confirmed by Ontario legislation in 1915 was subject to the 1905 grant to Backus. This conclusion, in the view of the JCPC, rested on the federal government's own acknowledgment of the grant to Backus when it approved the dam. Their lordships confirmed that damages were owed for flooding of reserve lands, even though the boundary of those reserves was found to be two chains inland from the water line.[51]

Compensation payments for lands flooded along the Rainy River in 1916 were of fractional significance in comparison with other charges and constraints that Backus faced at the time. In particular, legal challenges against wartime governmental measures and regulatory decisions would again (and not for the last time) place the fortunes of Rainy River industry on the docket of the highest court in the British Empire.

The Wartime Price of Paper

The outbreak of war in August 1914 coincided with and contributed greatly to the expansion of North American newspaper sales and readership. That growth depended heavily upon the availability of newsprint, which came increasingly from Canadian producers, who supplied both domestic and US markets. In responding to intense pressure affecting newspapers and newsprint producers, the Government of Canada established agencies to oversee pricing and supply allocation. These exceptional wartime bodies, beginning in 1917, included a Paper Commissioner and Controller and a Paper Control Tribunal, and were all established pursuant to legislation introduced at the outset of hostilities. That legislation, the *War Measures Act*, authorized, among a broad range of unprecedented initiatives, actions taken with regard to "trading, exportation, importation, production and manufacture."[52]

Backus's Fort Frances Pulp and Paper Company supplied a number of western Canadian publishers with newsprint during the war and in a period of postwar adjustment.[53] When a dispute arose with the *Manitoba Free Press* over newsprint pricing and refunds following an order from the Paper Control Tribunal, Backus attacked the regulator's constitutional foundations. The argument that Backus's distinguished counsel, Blake and Redden, eventually presented to the Law Lords was that the work of the Paper Control Tribunal largely concerned matters of property and civil rights, which were designated under section 92 of Canada's constitution as matters of provincial rather than federal responsibility.[54] True enough, the JCPC confirmed, before introducing to Canadian jurisprudence a limited but important constitutional exception applicable in case of emergency.

In the litigation between the Fort Frances Pulp and Power Company and the *Manitoba Free Press*, Lord Haldane, whose personal knowledge of northwestern Ontario extended back to *St. Catharines Milling*, observed that in wartime "the national life may require for its preservation the employment of very exceptional means."[55] To maintain peace, order, and good government for the country overall, it may be necessary for "the interests of individuals ... to be subordinated to that of the community."[56] While careful to emphasize that the general constitutional division of authority remained in place, Haldane's interpretation established that "there is implied the power to deal adequately with that emergency for the safety of the Dominion as a whole."[57]

It was, of course, a matter of great contention whether a state of emergency actually existed in the postwar period when the Paper Control Tribunal set the disputed prices and the contested contracts were formed. Again, however, their lordships deferred to the federal government's determination that while hostilities had ceased, "the effects of war conditions might still be operative."[58] Few residents of communities still recovering from the aftermath of wartime hostilities in 1919 or 1920 would have found this conclusion difficult to accept.

In little more than a decade and a half, the emerging pulp and paper industry and its interests in the Rainy-Lake of the Woods waters had, in addition to important economic impacts, triggered the introduction of complex arrangements affecting international power exports from Canada. The industry had been implicated in the delineation of Indian reserve boundaries, and its operations had provided the setting for an important interpretation of Canada's constitution in circumstances of emergency. These and other long-term impacts, including impacts on water flows and environmental quality, continued to be felt along the water system and to demonstrate the challenging significance of place, context, and environmental integrity for law, politics, and public policy.

6

Bacterial Waterways

As the nineteenth century drew to a close, the sportsman's magazine *Rod and Gun in Canada* reflected growing appreciation of recreational lanscapes in showering praise on the Lake of the Woods district: "Mix Temagaming, Parry Sound and the Thousand Islands together, flavour with a dash of Constantinople and the Isle of Wight, and the result is Rat Portage."[1] An early mayor of Rat Portage, George Barnes, also regarded municipal promotion as inherent in his civic mandate. He believed that his community could be aptly described as the "Saratoga of the West" and that it was by no means unexpected that, thanks to new railway connections, opportunities to experience picturesque shorelines were more conveniently available to the urban workforce. Those fortunate enough to have secured one of the lake's "miniature islands" could live like Robinson Crusoe.[2] Mayor Barnes assured sojourners that they would not encounter "the crushing magnificence or stern ruggedness which, in connection with so much of the primeval in nature, appals and saddens the imagination." Lake of the Woods scenery instead tended "to soothe and charm, to cheer the mind and imbue it with a healthy admiration for the works of the Creator." An indescribable labyrinth of intricate channels entranced sightseers and vacationers.[3] The perceived value of regional waters thus extended well beyond the industrialist's focus on water power storage and production.

Alas, not long after summer visitors began to enjoy the health-giving, spirit-lifting, and restorative features of outdoor experiences in the "Saratoga of the West," the need to conserve, sustain, and safeguard the natural environment from harmful exploitation and menacing pollution had to be acknowledged. This was a direct consequence – unanticipated by some, unsurprising to others – of resource development, population influx, and even growing recreational activity itself.

Summering

Glowing tributes to the landscape had proliferated since W.F. Butler's travels in the 1870s, when this military adventurer marvelled at a maze of narrow channels, luxuriant vegetation, and infinitely varied island scenery.[4] Such praise was winning out over less appreciative views, including the sentiments of Lady Dufferin, who remarked disdainfully in 1877 that "this part of the country is wooded, and there is no scenery at all."[5]

The CPR line between Winnipeg and Rat Portage, completed in 1882, inaugurated a chain of key linkages to markets and population centres that soon included St. Paul, Minneapolis, Duluth, Fort William, and Port Arthur. By 1885, trains were running three times weekly between the Manitoba capital and Rat Portage, with daily service established by 1894.[6] The Winnipeg Sanitary Association came into existence in 1881 with the object of establishing resort facilities at the Lake of the Woods, which became a "summer suburb" much like Muskoka, populated by Toronto in the holiday season.[7]

In contrast with the exorbitant costs of other resort districts, the Lake of the Woods was considered affordable. If an island retreat could be purchased for $200 or $300, "it is certainly not an expensive luxury, and about the cheapest form of absolute monarchy available."[8] Or so it was argued.

Many cottages were valued in the late nineteenth and early twentieth centuries at $100 to $600, although some of the more elaborate camps were estimated as high as $3,000, with one or two thought to be worth $5,000.[9] Coney Island, subdivided in the late 1800s and serviced with both electric power and access to the Rat Portage municipal water supply – referred to as "town water" – as of 1904, was the location of many early summer homes.[10]

As early as April 1885, the Keewatin Lumbering and Manufacturing Company advertised its willingness to build summer houses, but with nothing underway by July, the initiative was abandoned.[11] Ten years later, amidst prospects for a major subdivision of over forty lots on Coney Island's western shore, KLM's interest in cottage construction was renewed.[12]

In addition to cottagers, other vacationers arrived for shorter campground stays or by way of an excursion. The one-day return fare from Winnipeg at the turn of the century was around two dollars, with still lower group rates available.[13] Hotel development accelerated to meet visitor demand, prompting one local commentator to proclaim: "Real estate is going wild."[14] In a less inspiring observation, he noted that "a 4 story building and two large hotels are going up all on the muskeg."[15] Thirteen hotels were in operation by 1900, with Hilliard House, the Russell, and the Queen's among the most comfortable and well-appointed.[16] Estimated summer tourist numbers ranged between a thousand and twenty-five hundred people during the final years of the nineteenth century, providing the foundation for further growth and economic diversification.[17] Although the economy was not yet directly linked to the scenic and recreational value of regional waterways, it did not go unremarked that "many thousands of dollars are annually spent among the merchants" by summer visitors.[18]

Local residents also enjoyed the Lake of the Woods, some taking advantage of Wednesday afternoon store closings to get out on the water, others commuting from cottages on the north or beach side of Coney Island or along Big Stone Bay when road access became available. Camping, fishing, and fall hunting for ducks and game were also popular activities and began to constitute elements of the lifestyle choices of northerners.[19] Outside the summer season, northwestern Ontario had a particular appeal for prewar moose hunters, for whom frontier conditions in more remote quarters offered a sense of adventure.[20]

Vacationers would be likely to travel in or perhaps own a launch, runabout, or skiff – some purely functional, others handsome – including a number manufactured locally by the J.W. Stone Boat Manufacturing Company. The quality and scale of this firm's production in the early decades of the twentieth century placed it in the front ranks of the industry. Beginning with an hour on the waters of the town bay, boaters progressed to circumnavigate Coney Island, with the truly adventurous passing through the swift current at Devil's Gap for a more remote outing, often oddly described as "going down the lake."[21] Those without a vessel of their own might book a cruise on one of the elegant lake steamers.

Local resident Jacob (Jake) Gaudaur (1858–1937) generated a distinctive further interest in watercraft – sculls, to be precise: as a world champion professional oarsman, his international fame reflected favourably on the community. An uptick in visitorship and hotel occupancy coincided with

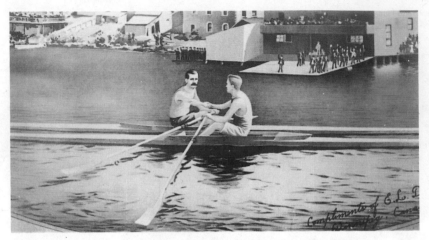

FIGURE 6.1 Gaudaur vs. Towns, 1901. *Courtesy of the Lake of the Woods Museum.*

a much-heralded race between the local favourite and his Australian chal-
lenger.[22] Alongside a well-established rowing tradition in the area, international sailing competitions were initiated shortly before World War I.

By 1913, it was estimated that two thousand to twenty-five hundred
people could be found summering in the Kenora area. The CPR itself
contemplated entering the tourist accommodation business in the Lake
of the Woods region and, in the early 1920s, began construction of the
Devil's Gap Bungalow Camp. When the new facilities, consisting of bungalow cabins and a central club house, opened in July 1923, the local
newspaper enthusiastically announced that guests would "have a delightful
time, build up their constitution, refresh their spirits and secure a better
and happier outlook of life, and this all for the nominal charge of $5 per
day or $30 per week."[23] The CPR was thus able to compete more effectively
with the commercial recreational attractions of Minaki on the Canadian
National Railway line some twenty miles downstream from Kenora on
the Winnipeg River. These water-based railway resorts, soon featured
among the "Playgrounds of Canada," were already drawing visitors from
Chicago, St. Paul, and Minneapolis.[24]

A day's sport fishing, generally guided, complemented many vacations
and increased visitor appreciation of the district. W.F Butler, in 1870, spent
time fishing downstream from Rat Portage on the Winnipeg River, where
the potential for competition between recreational anglers and commercial
and Aboriginal subsistence fishers was foreshadowed. Butler was delighted
with the results obtained from "a bright spinning piece of metal," which

FIGURE 6.2   Holst Point Lodge, 1925. *Courtesy of the Lake of the Woods Museum.*

he had acquired in Minnesota. He estimated his catch at three to one in comparison with an Ojibwa man fishing nearby from a canoe and "casting every now and then a large hook baited with a bit of fish."[25] Emerging concern for resource conservation and recognition of the valuable economic potential of recreational and sport fishing contributed to restrictions on the subsistence fishery and represented a continuing challenge for reconciliation among users of the watershed. Recreational opportunities were also influential in encouraging the introduction of smallmouth bass as a sport fish as early as 1903 and the establishment of a fish hatchery in 1914, initially to support pickerel and whitefish before being converted to promote the development of lake and speckled trout.[26]

The level of services and amenities available for summer visitors increased dramatically from the early 1880s, when Sandford Fleming, who described himself as "not difficult to please," reported a meal in Rat Portage that fell below his estimation of the acceptable "lower depth."[27] Hot summer days stimulated consumption of other local offerings, notably the beverages available from the Western Liquor Company or the Lake of the Woods Brewing Company. The latter, in its heyday, saluted the fortunes of the gold mining industry while seeking to cultivate brand loyalty among visitors and the labour force with Sultana Lager, Mikado Pale Ale, and Regina Porter, named after some of the best-known gold-producing properties.[28]

WINNIPEG WATER

Even as sizable numbers of its residents began to enjoy the water-oriented attractions of northwestern Ontario, Winnipeg's civic leaders struggled with municipal water supply challenges. Before a franchised water works operator came on the scene, river water was delivered to Winnipeg residents by wagon and then replaced with an artesian source, which soon proved inadequate. A severe typhoid outbreak in 1905, alongside mounting pressure to ensure water for firefighting, set the stage for a municipal Water Supply Commission inquiry in 1907. Although consultants identified Shoal Lake water as the best source of supply, water from the Winnipeg River was still a far more economical alternative.[29]

With five years of procrastination under its belt, city council assigned Judge Hugh Amos Robson to re-examine the water supply options in 1912. Unequivocally, he recommended the Shoal Lake supply "solely for the reason that it is the best." Shoal Lake was not the cheapest option, but Robson considered it unnecessary "to weigh too nicely the cost of such a project."[30] Robson's conclusion was supported by Dr. Charles S. Slichter, an experienced water specialist from the University of Wisconsin. Based on his examination of Shoal Lake in August 1912, Slichter concluded that "the water of Shoal Lake would require no treatment" and that "the Lake of the Woods constitutes an enormous reservoir of clear, pure and soft water."[31]

Situated three hundred feet (ninety-one metres) above the city of Winnipeg and within one hundred miles (160 kilometres) of the city, the source was accessible. Slichter was confident that minor aesthetic concerns associated with algae could be satisfactorily resolved. He did not address the "Cyanide Plant for Cameron Island," announced in a gold mining feature on the front page of Kenora's *Miner and News* on the date of his Shoal Lake inspection.[32] It would take most of a century for such toxic water-quality threats to come to public attention.

Adopting Slichter's advice in 1912, Winnipeg moved vigorously to implement suitable arrangements, collaborating with neighbouring communities through a dedicated institution, the Greater Winnipeg Water District. The Kenora Board of Trade urged caution with regard to the proposed diversion and called for a full investigation by Ontario's provincial hydro officials prior to any decision. The board's letterhead depicted the dam and sluiceways across the Winnipeg River, described as "the great water power of the great west," and these images were accompanied by one of a rugged workman surrounded by light standards under the heading "Cheap

Power" and the promise of "special inducements for manufacturers": the potential for conflict over water management priorities was thus not difficult to imagine.[33]

As three decades of industrial activity and a recent high-profile legal contest between the Hudson's Bay Company and the town had shown, the water powers at the Winnipeg River outlets of the Lake of the Woods were a vital regional asset, and Shoal Lake was a relevant element of storage infrastructure. Thus, the Board of Trade made its point: "The future development of this District depends in large measure upon the development of manufacturing and industrial enterprise induced and stimulated by assurance of the efficiency and permanence of such water powers."[34]

Robson, now utilities commissioner for the Province of Manitoba, prepared draft legislation for the federal government to authorize Winnipeg to take water from an interprovincial source. An *Act to Enable the City of Winnipeg to Get Water Outside the Province of Manitoba* was passed in Ottawa in the spring of 1913.[35] Parliamentary debate was limited, although in response to an inquiry about Ontario's views in the matter, Winnipeg MP Robert Rogers provided assurances that there had been no objections from the neighbouring province, adding: "This lake is in an outlying district, and the Bill cannot affect or disturb anybody."[36] This was not an entirely accurate assessment of the perception in Ontario, where the drawn-out process of finalizing Indian reserve boundaries was still underway. Nor would it have reflected the perception of the actual residents of those long-anticipated reserves whose occupation and mobility within their traditional homelands were severely disrupted by construction and who continue to assert their interests to the present day.[37]

In connection with Winnipeg's interest in Shoal Lake's water, Ontario officials expressed reservations about the possible extension of Treaty 3 reserves to cover headland-to-headland waters in the interests of Aboriginal fishing, as the federal and provincial governments had briefly contemplated in 1894. Such an adjustment to the reserves as originally surveyed "left the door open for all kinds of disputes and misunderstandings." Aubrey White speculated that this "far-reaching" provision might even have implications for Winnipeg's application to draw water from Shoal Lake. He expressed particular concern that "there are rivers of considerable size running through them and it surely never was intended that lands under a river should belong to the Indians."[38] White indicated his expectation that Ontario would confirm Treaty 3 reserves "as actually surveyed, leaving nothing open to argument hereafter."[39]

The Ontario legislature subsequently enacted legislation to authorize water transfer from Shoal Lake in Ontario to Winnipeg.[40] The 1916 legislation confirmed previous executive consent to the removal of Shoal Lake water up to 100 million gallons per day, subject to terms and conditions, including protection for Kenora's power development interests and compensation for private parties whose lands or property suffered interference.[41]

The Greater Winnipeg Water District had also applied to the International Joint Commission (IJC) on 8 September 1913 for approval to use Shoal Lake waters for domestic and sanitary purposes.[42] To confirm the jurisdiction of the IJC in relation to a body of water that lies entirely within Canada, all parties to the proceedings accepted that Shoal Lake was a tributary of the Lake of the Woods, a boundary water. This agreement finessed a source of uncertainty presented by engineering evidence suggesting that while Shoal lake, in a state of nature, "was a tributary water," it was, at the time of the hearings, "an arm or an inlet" of the Lake of the Woods.[43] Immediately following hearings in Washington from 13 to 15 January 1914, the commission granted the request on conditions associated with its own mandate regarding international waters: "That the water so to be diverted from Shoal Lake and from the Lake of the Woods be not used for other than domestic and sanitary purposes; and that the quantity of water so taken and diverted shall never at any time exceed 100,000,000 gallons per day."[44] The IJC added unequivocally that the authorization given to Winnipeg to utilize Shoal Lake waters would be subject to any recommendations that might emerge from a ground-breaking international inquiry then beginning to examine possible arrangements for regulating the levels of the Lake of the Woods.[45]

As construction began, the sill of the Shoal Lake aqueduct was located at 1,050.82 sea-level datum in order to provide for a daily flow of 85 million imperial gallons (158 cfs) with the lake at a minimum stage of 1,058.19.[46] As calculated by the commission, the ordinary and low precipitation experience of the Shoal Lake watershed would be insufficient to furnish this level of use on a year-round basis. The deficiency could be made up by drawing on the Lake of the Woods with "relatively little effect upon the levels of the Lake of the Woods," although the commission concluded that "the proposed diversion will ultimately reduce the flow of the Winnipeg River by about 150 cfs."[47]

The IJC estimated that on a daily basis, the completed aqueduct would deliver about 25 million gallons to supply between eighty-five and a hundred gallons per capita for a population of 230,000 to 270,000 people. It would be some time, therefore, before the full authorized capacity of the

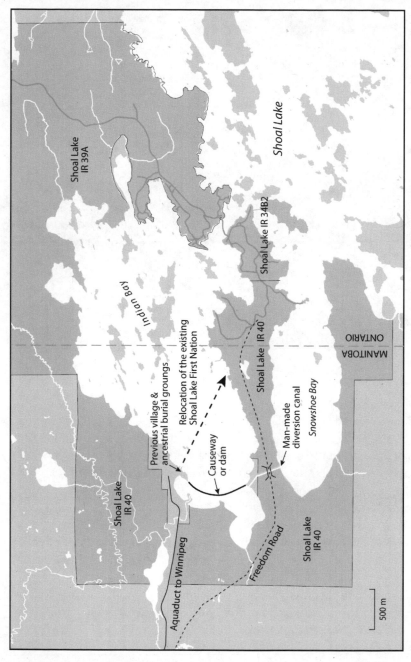

MAP 6.1 Winnipeg Aqueduct. *Courtesy of the City of Winnipeg and NetNewsLedger. Map adapted by Eric Leinberger.*

FIGURE 6.3   Greater Winnipeg Water District. *Courtesy of the City of Winnipeg.*

aqueduct would be used. The IJC anticipated that any temporary shortfall in a period of low water could be managed through "the installation of a small booster pump at the intake [that] could easily lift the balance not supplied at a given level." The consulting engineers had determined that an aqueduct with capacity of 85 million gallons provided for "as much future growth as the present city could afford to finance."[48]

To improve navigation through Ash Rapids, which connected Shoal Lake and the Lake of the Woods, Canada's Department of Public Works removed the crest of a rock ridge in 1912.[49] The alteration facilitated flow between the lakes, which, according to early navigators, had always varied in direction depending on local conditions – depending, that is, "upon the relative run-off into and outflow from each body of water at the given time."[50] A decade or so before the Public Works project, when a local crew cleared out a dam and obstruction at Ash Rapids, Shoal Lake was about three feet above the Lake of the Woods.[51]

In relation to water quality, the consultants assured the Greater Winnipeg Water District that Shoal Lake "is practically free from contamination, that it is clear and practically without color and that it is free from odor and has an agreeable taste." Minute animal and vegetable organisms represented no cause for concern, and no significant taste or odour issues were anticipated.

Two bays, Snowshoe and Indian, were somewhat closer to Winnipeg than the main body of Shoal Lake and thus offered potential cost savings. However, the muddy bottom of the shallow Snowshoe Bay was too easily disturbed by wind and waves, while Indian Bay suffered discoloration from "dark-colored muskeg water" entering from the Falcon River. To secure Indian Bay as an acceptable location for the intake of Shoal Lake waters, the most promising solution was a short diversion of the Falcon River outlet into Snowshoe Bay.[52] This involved not only a land transfer but also the construction of a dyke and channel, which divided the Shoal Lake No. 40 Reserve, leaving part of the Indigenous community isolated from the mainland on an artificial island.[53]

Following six years of construction at a cost of about $13.5 million, the Shoal Lake aqueduct began to supply water to Winnipeg in 1919.[54] These arrangements continue to provide Winnipeg with access to a distinctive interjurisdictional source of supply, but conflicts with other water users and affected parties have generated significant and persistent controversy: the Indigenous community that became physically isolated from the mainland as a result of dyke and canal construction has endured the unfortunate consequences for a century.[55]

MUNICIPAL AND INDUSTRIAL OUTFLOWS

Even as Winnipeg sought to secure a reliable source of municipal water supply by focusing on what is now called "source protection," a powerful impulse to utilize water for waste disposal was gaining momentum in cities across Europe and North America. Even smaller communities, including several in the Lake of the Woods watershed, introduced sewage systems in order to discharge an array of municipal wastes into available waterways.

Between four and five hundred students at Rat Portage's newly constructed public school placed significant demands on the basement trough latrines − nine closets for girls and seven for boys, with the latter also enjoying privileged access to a large urinal. Municipal officials envisaged sewers to drain the school and to remove surface water from the site of a proposed park . The intended destination of this outflow was Laurenson's Creek, which was within the confines of the growing community. In anticipation, the main sewer line was set for completion pending consideration by the Provincial Board of Health.

Sewerage arrangements were first introduced in Rat Portage in 1899.[56] The town sought approval of its plans to discharge school and other domestic wastes into Laurenson's Creek to address a nuisance and to safeguard the health of the school children. Provincial officials firmly rejected the Rat Portage proposal on the basis of an on-site investigation by Dr. Charles A. Hodgetts, one of Ontario's senior public health officials.[57]

Hodgetts and his colleagues were thoroughly familiar with the sanitary challenges facing remote and isolated communities. On numerous occasions, these officials had carefully examined similar situations. Following studies of the northern districts in the early 1900s, for example, public health representatives declared in unmistakable terms: "The emptying of excreta directly into the lakes needs no words of condemnation from us for such a procedure is in our opinion criminal and should be stopped forthwith."[58] As far as possible, officials were committed to applying the very recent insights of bacteriological research in the public health arena. This required diversion of waste flows away from sources of water supply; treatment of sewage, as techniques for doing so evolved; and the introduction of drinking water purification arrangements such as filtration and chlorination.

The surveillance capability of determined provincial administrators was such that in the 1905 annual report of the Board of Health, Rat Portage's municipal representatives were confronted with a frank review of their town's performance. "It will be remembered that Rat Portage ... applied for permission to drain into Laurenson's Creek and was refused," the report began, before indicating that "it would appear that the municipality has ignored the Board and run the sewage into the creek at a point lower down the stream than proposed instead of running it into the general system."[59] But northwestern Ontario communities were hardly unique in their unwillingness to finance timely investments in the costly wastewater infrastructure that provincial inspectors urged upon them; foot dragging has always been a characteristic step in the intergovernmental dance, one that all the partners have mastered.

The provincial inspectorate also scrutinized drinking water arrangements. Dr. Robert E. Wodehouse, whose investigation of pulp mill effluent at Dryden has already been mentioned, was responsible for a district stretching from Manitoulin Island in Lake Huron to Kenora. Wodehouse covered

35,552 miles in 1913 to report on twenty-eight organized municipalities, to visit forty-nine other population centres, and to assess epidemics as they arose. Among that year's more encouraging accomplishments, he was pleased to note chlorination of the water supply at Kenora, Fort Frances, and Rainy River.[60]

The Fort Frances initiative was especially gratifying, for Wodehouse had specifically pressed the mayor on chlorination during a previous visit. He had observed lamentable conditions at the Fort Frances pump house – located downstream from numerous residential and industrial facilities – where water was drawn from the Rainy River without filtration or other treatment. Among the threats on the Canadian side was an Indian industrial school accommodating about fifty residents. This facility drew its own water supply from the lake and discharged sewage back into lake again a mere fifty feet away and less than a mile above the town's intake. Industrial sources worsened deplorable water supply arrangements, for two miles upstream were two large mills "with some privies on rock at edge of water, others higher up on rock but which surely would overflow during spring freshettes into lake." A large CNR construction camp was a bit beyond this, again draining refuse and excreta into the lake about three miles above the town's water supply. Animal remains, the "bi-catch" of lumber operations, added to contamination as game animals such as moose and deer often died while trying to cross log booms. Decomposing carcasses then drifted down to the water intake.[61]

The American shoreline was of equal concern, with privies along the rocky banks. Moreover, a large fish plant above the intake steadily dumped refuse into the stream. Wodehouse lamented that citizens seemed unaware of the endangered water supply but were quick to protest offensive sights and smells along the waterway. These priorities were not uncommon in a period when public understanding of waterborne diseases and the invisible perils of bacteria was still limited. People objected to "rotten animals because of unpleasantness for picnic parties going up past boom in launches," while remaining largely oblivious to the risk of typhoid.[62]

The proliferation of tourist facilities and summer residences across the Canadian Shield, including very significant expansion throughout the Rainy-Lake of the Woods watershed, was a further source of public health concern. One senior public health official singled out resort operators for attention in the hope that tourist facilities could be made attractive and safe in the interests of summer visitors. To encourage suitable improvements in accommodation and in relation to water supplies and sewage disposal arrangements, the same official proposed inspection visits, after which he would "use discretion in publishing for the benefit of the public, a list of places approved of or otherwise."[63]

By 1911, provincial regulations had spelled out sanitary precautions. Summer resorts were specifically prohibited from depositing garbage, excreta, manure, animal and vegetable matter, or filth in Ontario's lakes, rivers, and streams. Vessel operators faced similar controls against creating a nuisance or polluting inland waters of the province.[64] Despite such regulations, problems persisted. Holst Point Inn, on the Winnipeg River, had installed a basic sedimentation tank, but, as observed with some regret by the district officer of health, the sewer outlet pipe was located only a short distance upstream from the water intake. Conditions at the CNR's fashionable Minaki Resort were more elaborate but still in need of upgrading.[65]

Practices common within the camping and cottaging community also produced disturbing conditions, as many summer residents took their water supply from the same bay or shoreline into which their privies and kitchen slops drained. Arrangements for sewage treatment, or even earth closets, were rare, with the consequence that "the greatest source of danger ... is from the residences themselves."[66]

Summer resorts and cottages constituted a potential danger to anyone in the vicinity and not only to the seasonal inhabitants. Wodehouse was particularly apprehensive on behalf of Keewatin residents who drew water from the Keewatin Channel or had it delivered by barrel from the same source.[67] A few years later, another inspector repeated words of caution: "The summer population in this area is large; and is a source of danger to the water supplies of Kenora (including the supplementary supply at Norman) and Keewatin."[68]

About a decade after the rejection of the proposed discharge of sewage into Laurenson's Creek, local officials were advised that "the sewerage system of your town requires the first and earnest attention of council."[69] A subsequent sanitary survey of the Kenora District highlighted deficiencies.[70] Not all wastes from the shoreline hospital were being disinfected prior to discharge into the bay, and some town sewage also found its way directly to the lake. Kenora had four separate sewer systems at this point, with aspirations to treat its effluent for deposit into beds rather than for discharge into the lake. Yet there were no concrete plans to accomplish the transformation. The summer cottage population, estimated at three thousand just before the war, represented a continuing source of concern. "Possibility of infection," advised Ontario's medical health officer for the Kenora District, "in my opinion, is very great."[71]

Early in the century, Kenora implemented chlorination treatment, at least during the summer season, before delivering the supply to the mains for distribution. The new arrangements, however, serviced only a limited proportion of the community. Despite a ban by the local Board of Health, private wells were still widely used. These, alas, were poorly constructed, shallow, and often located in muskeg, contributing "an amber shade to water and a slight odour and flavor of swamp."[72]

After the war, another provincial inspector, G.L. Sparks, urged local officials to consult with Ontario's sanitary engineering staff as to the most suitable purification arrangements. His inspection around the waterworks intake and of the pumping station and treatment plant was far from re-assuring. "The present chlorinating apparatus at the Kenora waterworks pumping-station is not effectually purifying the Town water," he reported.[73] Sparks concluded that the chlorination process was a matter of guesswork, and he described several of the eight sewers draining untreated wastewater to the waterfront, one of which was but a quarter mile from the municipal water intake. Typhoid cases in the Coney Island population directly op-posite that intake were alarming; "it is presumed they were infected from lake water while bathing in the bay," wrote Sparks.[74] Equally disheartening findings were replicated in other district communities, leading to remedial recommendations.[75]

To the extent that water quality was a regional concern, general en-vironmental conditions were less worrisome than matters of public health. Thus, in 1894, the Joint International Commission on Fisheries ultimately commented positively on the presence of algae, sometimes blue-green or of "a dense bright green color," that penetrated as deep as the eye could see and formed extensive patches of green scum. While the Big Traverse on the Lake of the Woods was sometimes described as stagnant, it was also understood to serve as a "nursery" for species that favoured a rich growth of algae and water of this character.[76] However, more troubling and no-torious conditions existed along the Rainy River, where municipal and in-dustrial sources of pollution were found in combination with local, state, provincial, and international interests and institutions.

THE RAINY RIVER AND INTERNATIONAL POLLUTION

Only a few years after the 1909 Boundary Waters Treaty ushered the International Joint Commission into existence, Canada and the United States called upon this remarkable binational organization for guidance

concerning international pollution. In August 1912, the two national
governments asked about the extent and causes of pollution in boundary
waters, which rendered them "injurious to the public health and unfit
for domestic or other uses."[77] This original pollution reference was
amended to incorporate transboundary effects in addition to impacts on
boundary waters. Given contemporary concerns around the transmission
of diseases such as typhoid and dysentery, the focus of the inquiry became
bacteriological.

As early as 1914, in initial findings from locations along the international
boundary, investigators referred to gross pollution from Fort Frances and
International Falls travelling downstream and even affecting the Lake of
the Woods.[78] This observation, one result of bacteriological tests described
as "the most extensive that have ever been made in the world," came only
a few years after an engineering report unequivocally assured Fort Frances
that no problems would arise from the town's proposed sewage works:
"The large volume of water constantly flowing over the falls, or through
the tail race, will so dilute the sewage that no nuisance of any kind whatever
can possibly take place."[79] Key findings from the comprehensive international inquiry completely discredited such blinkered optimism. As a
consequence of sewage discharges, Rainy River waters – along with those
of other boundary rivers, including the St. Mary's, St. Clair, Detroit, and
Niagara Rivers – were declared by the IJC in 1918 as "no longer fit for domestic use unless subjected to extensive treatment in water-purification
plants."[80]

The specific investigation into the conditions of Rainy Lake, Rainy
River, and the Lake of the Woods involved the assessment of 995 samples.
Rainy Lake suffered from agricultural drainage and from the impact of
extensive railway construction.[81] The drinking water supplies of Fort
Frances and International Falls were "seriously contaminated," a condition
attributed to "the discharge of polluting matter in the vicinity of the respective waterworks intakes."[82] Indeed, statistics gathered for the IJC's
report showed that typhoid death rates at Fort Frances dramatically exceeded those of other communities.[83] Downstream, along the Rainy River
below the falls, "a very considerable pollution" persisted.[84]

Responsibility for this state of affairs rested with Fort Frances and
International Falls, the two main towns whose sewage entered the waterway
without treatment. Farms, small villages, and additional sewage discharged
from the towns of Rainy River and Baudette further contributed to pollution. Overall, then, the Rainy River was deemed "unfit for domestic
uses." Extensive water purification would be required to permit the river

to serve as a source of drinking water supply. As for the Lake of the Woods, analysis at the mouth of the Rainy River was less alarming. "It appears," the commissioners observed, "that the self-purification and dilution had here operated to lessen pollution of the river."[85]

The Rainy River, among other interjurisdictional watercourses, was also the subject of pollution complaints associated with sawdust and other lumber mill wastes. These produced nuisances "by making the shores and bed of the stream unsightly, unclean and malodorous," with chemical waste from pulp operations as the primary contributor. Investigators confidently concluded that pollution of this type "is also injurious to fish life and the fishing industry." Signalling the international implications, the pollution report confirmed that sawmill and pulp mill wastes regularly resulted in "transboundary effects detrimental to property and health."[86]

Investigators did not otherwise address pollution from chemical and industrial wastes, noting that "contamination from these sources is at present so limited and local in its extent" that further scientific assessment was unwarranted. Nevertheless, acknowledging that "a very injurious effect" would "unquestionably" arise in future if preventive measures were not taken, the commission took this prospect into account in preparing its overall findings and recommendations.[87]

The Rainy River, along with the St. Mary's, St. John, Niagara, and Detroit Rivers, illustrated international boundary considerations for Canada and the United States in the form of "a well-marked crossing of pollution from one side to the other."[88] Building on these findings, the IJC proceeded to discuss "injury" in relation to pollution, an analysis that was required in order to connect the scientifically observed results with the threshold of legal concern:

> In the case of the Detroit and Niagara Rivers pollution exists on one side of the boundary line which unquestionably is an "injury" within the meaning of the treaty to health and property on the other. In the case of the Rainy River and the St. John River, pollution also exists on one side of the boundary line which is an "injury" within the meaning of the treaty to health and property on the other.

The findings and analysis thus supported the inquiry's conclusion that "the pollution is trans-boundary both in its effect and extension."[89] But this recognition of pollution impacts along and across international waterways was not accompanied by a joint or collaborative institutional and remedial response.

While the international inquiry was underway, and following the release of the final report of the IJC in 1918, Ontario health officials endeavoured to promote local improvements. When the town of Rainy River,
for example, proposed a pumping station rather near the site of the sewage
outlet, provincial officials pointedly indicated that "the sewage of the town
should not be discharged in a raw condition into the Rainy River."[90] The
pumping station and intake pipe were duly located well upstream of the
town – above a substantial lumber mill – where they operated satisfactorily
for a decade or more until the town acquired the powerhouse. By this
point, the lumber mill had burned to the ground and the town wanted
to relocate the water supply intake to the powerhouse site. Provincial inspectors concurred with the suggestions, subject to the removal of boathouses and other measures to guard against shoreline disturbance.[91]
However, municipal officials at Rainy River resisted encouragement to
implement liquid chlorination in the early 1920s to the point that Dr.
Sparks believed that only compulsion from the Provincial Board of Health
would stir them to action.[92]

Members of the local Board of Health at Rainy River eventually inquired why they had been compelled to install a septic tank to treat sewage
while Fort Frances, sixty miles upstream, continued to discharge municipal
wastes without any treatment whatsoever. By 1921, a new waterworks
plant was finally being contemplated at Fort Frances, with an estimated
cost of about $6,000. Its primary goal of increasing water pressure was
really intended to satisfy fire insurance companies sufficiently that they
would agree to lower premiums in the community.[93] As to drinking water
quality in Fort Frances, Sparks was dismayed by the lack of attention town
officials gave to chlorination, describing the local system as a "ridiculous
farce." This assessment followed a round of aqua-roulette, a once fashionable though highly questionable procedure for evaluating water quality by
taste. None of the life-threatening experiments reported by Sparks detected
the taste of chlorine.[94]

If general disregard for the merits of chlorination at Fort Frances required
any reinforcement, further incentive to abandon all pretense of safeguarding public health through drinking water treatment reached civic officials
in December 1921. When Ontario's deputy minister of Game and Fisheries announced plans for the Fort Frances fish hatchery, the department
required "a supply of pure water free from chlorination during the pickerel
season." Sparks, stunned by news of the trade-off between pickerel and
public health as proposed by another provincial agency, sought guidance
from his superiors and requested an order prohibiting Fort Frances from

discontinuing chlorination arrangements for any purpose whatsoever without prior approval.[95]

Alongside the growing popularity of northern Ontario waterways as a mecca for recreational visitors, contaminated water supplies and deteriorating water quality conditions were widespread in the early twentieth century. Indeed, these situations were sufficiently common that the Provincial Board of Health sketched out typical – and highly predictable – pathways to pollution. First, it was noted that "the degree of dilution which occurred at the time of the installation of a particular system does not remain constant," as a result of an increasing number of house connections and the growth of factory and trade wastes such that "the solid portions carried down the sewers accumulate and spread beyond an area at first contemplated." Thus, without actual awareness on the part of those in control of the water supply, "the limit of safe dilution of water when it passes from a potable to a non-potable article is passed." It was only following a severe outbreak – of dysentery or enteric infection, for example – that officials took note of deteriorating conditions. Sparks reported to the Provincial Board of Health: "It is at this point they awake from their lethargy and institute systematic inquiries to find a condition of affairs which is the result of municipal carelessness or indifference."[96]

Fort Frances's dalliance with fish hatcheries and the village of Rainy River's reluctance to install chlorination equipment may have strengthened Dr. Sparks's resolve to post notices along the north shore of the river: "Persons using raw Rainy River water are advised that it contains the untreated sewage of a large population and may communicate typhoid fever. Boiling raw river water will destroy the disease-producing germs."[97] Even after Rainy River introduced chlorination, laboratory reports showed disappointing results, supporting a call for more elaborate measures. Yet the prospects were not encouraging from a public health official's perspective: "Rainy River is a boundary water between Canada and the United States; and it is apparently useless to expect any improvement in the conditions resulting from the discharge of sewage" from communities on either side of the waterway.[98] The shared status of the divided watershed was once again noted as both pathway and obstacle to satisfactory protection arrangements over the long term.

As for the Laurenson's Creek situation, for which Kenora officials had been publicly reprimanded early in the century, the town received engineering assurances in September 1924 that "the Creek apparently is not suffering from the discharge of sewage thereto, as to cause any local nuisance. The nuisance that exists there now is one due to the presence of the unsightly shore." One month later, however, a provincial health inspector took issue with that conclusion. Pointing to insufficient water in the creek and the slowness of the current, which made it impossible for solid fecal matter to be carried into the waters of the town bay and ultimately to the Winnipeg River, he felt the statutory conditions for nuisance were established. A trunk sewer along the banks of the creek seemed the preferred solution.[99]

Water quality along the Rainy River and around the Lake of the Woods was certainly on the public policy agenda, even arousing scrutiny and concern at the international level. But the practical utility of these waters for navigation, power production, and irrigation generally remained of greater concern to policy makers than public health, environmental, and recreational considerations. This array of interrelated water uses became the subject of a remarkable international inquiry in the World War I era, an exercise that presented a unique opportunity to contemplate the future of the watershed on a comprehensive basis.

7

Levelling the Lake

When Canada and the United States first invoked the distinctive reference mechanism established in conjunction with the International Joint Commission, they requested guidance on Lake of the Woods water levels. Three commissioners appointed by Canada prepared to deliberate alongside three counterparts from the United States in conformity with agreed arrangements. Not only would the proceedings directly affect developments across a major international watershed; this pioneering initiative afforded a fledgling institution an opportunity to establish its credentials with governments, professional constituencies, and the general population. Oriented around water levels, the Lake of the Woods inquiry necessarily addressed the varied interests and expectations of regional water users, with every potential for disappointment.

1,056 Low – 1,061 High

Commissioners recognized responsibilities associated with implementing an innovative process on behalf of a novel institution and articulated a wide-ranging interpretation of their mandate consistent with ambitious aspirations for the first reference ever assigned to their ground-breaking organization. The binational reference, declared the commissioners, "calls for a report upon all matters pertaining to the regulation of the levels of the Lake of the Woods and the advantageous use of its waters, shores, and harbors, and the use of the water flowing into and from the lake, and the

113

effect of such regulation on all public and private interests involved."[1]
Beyond this, they gave "advantageous use" a broad meaning as including
"not only all practicable uses to which these waters can be put on their
own watershed, but also all beneficial uses which the energy developed
thereon may serve in the adjacent territory."[2] Water use was elemental to
the inquiry, and this priority was reflected in economic, legal, and engineering terminology – "advantageous," "beneficial," "practicable."

To convey the territorial scope of the mandate, the commissioners
summoned up familiar comparisons. For the benefit of the US audience,
they pointed out that the surface area of the Lake of the Woods and Shoal
Lake substantially exceeded that of Rhode Island. The wider drainage basin
exceeded the combined area of New Hampshire, Massachusetts, Rhode
Island, Connecticut, and Delaware – or, to orient Canadian readers, an
area five thousand square miles larger than the province of Nova Scotia.[3]

To situate their work in relation to cross-border concerns about water
levels that led to the reference, the commissioners reported their understanding that "the outlets of the Lake of the Woods remained in their
natural condition until 1879."[4] Construction and operation of dams on
the Canadian side, initially the short-lived Rollerway Dam and then the
Norman Dam, altered water levels on the US side, which increased "over
the levels which would have prevailed with the outlets in the state of
nature." Those increases varied from 0.9 feet in 1899 to as much as 6.3
feet in 1913.[5] The significance of new or expanded outlets attracted less
commentary.

Most of the south shore residents had settled their grievances after the
Norman Dam raised water levels, but in periods of high water, protests
concerning submerged lands persisted. From an official perspective, acre-
age had certainly been lost, for during the survey between 1893 and 1896,
the US Land Office ran subdivisional lines out over the flooded lands, in
some cases more than a mile. Meander posts marked the border of the lake
along a shoreline then dividing open water from willow brush or marsh
grass. US homesteaders had received patents according to Land Office
maps, "even though a portion of the platted area was and ever since has
been under water."[6] During low water, however, navigational improvements in Warroad harbour could not be used effectively, at least not without
dredging. The fact that Minnesota residents had divergent interests in
higher or lower water levels somewhat moderated the risk of acrimonious
conflict between the neighbouring countries.

An unfruitful exchange between the two national governments over
some of the irritants, together with mounting protests about other matters,

FIGURE 7.1 South Shore Flooding, 1916. *International Joint Commission,*
Lake of the Woods Reference, *1917.*

encouraged US interest in the reference procedure established by the
Boundary Waters Treaty in 1909. Canada's inclination to pursue an inquiry
into friction along the border was then stimulated by a proposed diversion
of the waters of Birch Lake in northern Minnesota out of the Lake of the
Woods watershed towards Lake Superior.[7] Between 1904 and 1913, the
Minnesota Canal and Power Company repeatedly sought permission to
close off the flow of Birch Lake waters into the Rainy River in order to
provide power at Duluth. Despite Canadian opposition, protests from the
town of Fort Frances, whose concerns made their way across the border
via Ottawa and the British embassy in Washington, and reservations expressed by the International Waterways Commission, the company secured
a permit from the US Secretary of War in 1910.[8] The decision was supported by the legal opinion of Chandler Anderson, a New York lawyer
who expressed the then-fashionable Harmon doctrine in his advice on
the Birch Lake matter to the US secretary of State: "The jurisdiction of the
nation within its own territory is necessarily exclusive and absolute ... no
restriction upon the use of these tributary waters within the borders of the
United States can be admitted."[9]

Further Canadian protests from the City of Winnipeg and the Lake of
the Woods Milling Company, and the residual force of the 1842 Webster-
Ashburton Treaty safeguarding "the free and open use of the boundary

waters from Lake Superior to the Lake of the Woods by the citizens and subjects of both countries," delayed but never fully deterred the power company from its ambitions.[10] But Birch Lake was a tributary water rather than a boundary water and was thus subject less directly to the new treaty arrangements.[11] Issues also arose respecting the proposed Long Sault Dam on the Rainy River as contemplated around 1900 and later taken up by the Western Canal Company.[12]

Once charged with the Lake of the Woods assignment, IJC officials embraced admirable technical and participatory procedures. The commission highlighted a feature of considerable significance: "Perhaps for the first time in history two nations are being furnished by a commission, created to protect and conserve their mutual interests, with a very complete and accurate international map representing, without regard to political boundaries, the limits and details of a great and important watershed."[13] Whether or not this was indeed a global precedent, the welcome collaboration evidently helped to elevate the commissioners' aspirations for their own performance.

Over a period of years, expert engineering research, alongside public consultations, confirmed "the diverse requirements of the various interests."[14] This finding, or acknowledgment, made the conventional impulse to impose a human preference for order and certainty in the form of a fixed level for the lake – or a regimen of seasonal levels – "an impossibility." As an alternative to this "impossibility," the commission ultimately called for collaborative supervision. The IJC proposed an international board and recommended that it be given authority "to exercise supervision and control over the operation of all dams and regulating works extending across the international boundary," as well as regulating works across the Canadian channel upstream at Kettle Falls and works at the downstream outlets of the Lake of the Woods, but only "when its level rises above 1061 or falls below 1056 sea level datum." So long as water levels remained within this five-foot range, supervision and control would fall to a designated Canadian agency, thereby reducing significantly the prospect of short-term squabbling. Nevertheless, the design and implementation of that institution presented its own federal-provincial challenges.[15]

Absolute security against future flooding was never on offer. Measures to increase the outflow capacity to the Winnipeg River provided some assurance against floodwaters at the exceptional levels reached in 1916, while the commission was still conducting its work; nevertheless, still greater flood inflows could not be ruled out. And there were other risks, such as high northeasterly winds, which could cause levels in southerly portions of the lake to rise as much as a foot. Accordingly, the commission believed that "all land lying below the 1064 contour will be either submerged or injuriously affected under the proposed regulation and maintenance of the recommended level."[16] What regulation did offer, though, was maintenance of "a distinctly more uniform level than actually prevailed in the past" or than would have prevailed under natural conditions.[17]

In its recommendations, the commission identified a number of primary considerations: navigation, agriculture, logging and lumbering, fishing, summer recreation, water supply and sewage disposal, water power development, and manufacturing.[18] Given this array of interests, neither an engineering nor a political solution to the challenge posed by the reference was readily available. As the commission explained, "both uniform level and uniform outflow could be obtained only if the inflow into the Lake of the Woods could be completely equalized." Since much of the inflow was beyond control, there was no possibility of securing both uniform level and uniform outflow.[19] Anyone likely to confuse management of a large watershed with filling a bathtub was thus on notice to expect disappointment.

Moreover, "any method of regulation which aims to secure either uniform level or uniform outflow, or any combination of the two, will affect the various interests involved in different ways." As a result, "no single method or combination of methods of regulation will be most advantageous to all of the several interests."[20] Challenging situations of this nature have aptly been described as polycentric – like a spider's web, where pulling and tugging anywhere sends stresses and strains across the net.[21] In the circumstances, the commissioners concluded that "the most advantageous use" of Lake of the Woods waters would have to reflect "the maximum aggregate advantage to all interests involved."[22] The commissioners may well have imagined that "all interests involved" had in fact been accommodated in their assessment, but this was not an era in which environmental considerations received much official attention, let alone appropriate valuation. Furthermore, Aboriginal concerns on the Canadian side were largely represented through the reports and interventions of Indian Affairs officials, who were not generally equipped to provide direct or personal accounts of anticipated impacts on the fishery, wild rice harvests, or reserve lands that might result from regulation of water levels.[23]

Water power operators had enjoyed attractive hydrological conditions in the years preceding the completion of the commission's work in 1917, including the exceptionally high levels of 1916. Yet such favourable circumstances could not be relied on, supporting the conclusion that "the

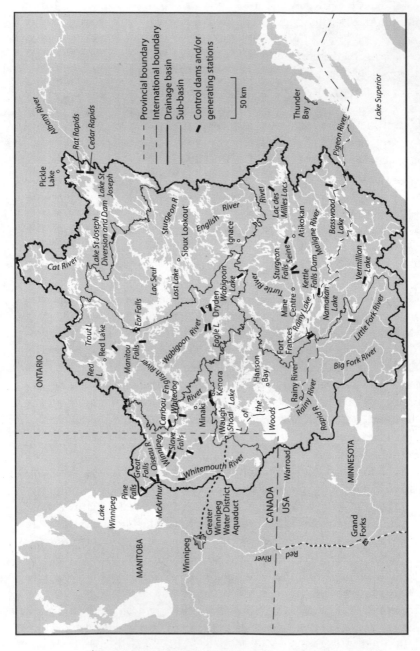

MAP 7.1 Lake of the Woods/Winnipeg River Drainage Basin. *From Lake of the Woods Control Board, "Winnipeg River Drainage Basin," at: https://www.lwcb.ca/permpdf/detail_map.pdf. Map adapted by Eric Leinberger.*

water power interests at the outlets will be better served by the proposed regulation than in any other way, provided no portion of the cost of providing this regulation is assessed against them."[24] But the apparent windfall for power producers and an unprecedented disaster that the high water of 1916 represented for agricultural interests at the south end of the lake had to be seen through a wider lens: the solution preferred by owners of flooded Minnesota farm lands in 1916 might not be entirely congruent with a recommended response when considered alongside the long-term expectations of hydro producers and other lake users.

The commission identified enhanced outflow capacity into the Winnipeg River as crucial to maintaining the recommended water level range. The existing outlets, which provided for a discharge of about thirty-two thousand cubic feet per second (cfs), could not prevent lake levels from rising during seasons of extraordinary precipitation. Accordingly, expanding outflow capacity to about forty-seven thousand cfs was judged very desirable, although it was recognized that even with this increase, "it will be impossible to discharge the water as rapidly as it will blend into the lake in time of exceptional floods."[25]

The technical recommendation to expand outflow capacity afforded the commissioners one of many opportunities to explore and explain their overall objectives. "If the questions of the reference were limited to the maintenance of a reasonably uniform level on the Lake of the Woods," they wrote, "that end could be attained by acquisition of the necessary flowage rights and the provision of the necessary controlling works just indicated." Yet a uniform lake level was not really a goal that anyone had in mind. Rather, "the most advantageous use" of the lake's waters was the holy grail.[26] Achieving that objective called for equalizing the outflow as far as was practicable, because, given factors affecting power development along the Winnipeg River, "there is little likelihood that these water power interests will ever, in the future, develop more than the dependable outflow from the lake." The quest then became, rather than a uniform lake level or a fanciful expectation of sustaining peak flows like 1916, "the greatest dependable outflow that can be economically secured."

With the objective of dependable flow in mind, the engineering agenda expanded beyond increased control of the downstream outflow as a measure of flood prevention to more challenging issues of retaining upstream waters: "The dependable outflow increases with the available reservoir storage, although at a decreasing rate. The most advantageous use of the waters flowing from the lake, then, can be secured by providing as much storage capacity as the resulting increase in dependable outflow

will warrant."[27] Although "dependable outflow" might readily be defended
as a reasonable, common sense, almost innocuous objective, the concept
generated intense controversy, for it is equally reasonable to be concerned
about reconfiguring a natural system of lakes and rivers into a managed
reservoir. Indeed, the maintenance of natural flow had been fundamental
for centuries and would figure in subsequent legal challenges.

The commission turned its attention upstream to the storage capacity
of Rainy Lake and the interconnection between discharges of water stored
in Rainy Lake and the dependable downstream outflow from the Lake of
the Woods into the Winnipeg River. It concluded that the regulation of
Rainy Lake and upstream waters in the interests of the Lake of the Woods
regime might add as much as twenty-five thousand horsepower to the
Winnipeg River's potential, but this increase would be at the expense of
a loss of about a thousand horsepower at International Falls and Fort
Frances.[28] Here, the commission acknowledged what astute observers
already knew: compromise is essential; prepare for trade-offs. Gains
might be accompanied by losses that would not necessarily be distributed
evenly across the watershed.[29] The subsequent unwillingness of some
interested parties – notably E.W. Backus – to accept the allocative implications contributed to significant delay in reaching agreement and implementing regulatory arrangements.

In addition to increasing dependable outflow from the Lake of the
Woods and Rainy Lake, the IJC's *Final Report* emphasized that "international supervision and control shall be administered in such a manner
as this commission may from time to time deem necessary to protect and
promote the development of all interests involved in both countries."[30]
Again, what was intended by "all interests" seemed more straightforward
or less controversial to the commissioners than some later observers
would be inclined to assume.

Even within the recommended range, water level fluctuations had implications for shoreline properties and activities around the lake. This was
still the case even after expenditures were directed towards protecting public
and private lands from the impact of regulation. Properties in Baudette,
Minnesota, and Rainy River, Ontario, were particularly vulnerable.
Alternatively, funding might be required to compensate for unavoidable
impacts. In this regard, the commission offered the opinion that "unoccupied lands in territory far removed from settled ... have at the present time
no particular value beyond that of the timber that may be found thereon."[31]
In due course, owners would beg to differ, some taking their own view of
the value of flooded lands to the steps of the US Supreme Court.

As for the emerging recreational industry, the commission saw no reason for concern that the owners of docks, boathouses, and summer homes around the lake would be disadvantaged by the proposed regulatory arrangements.[32] Agricultural, fishing, and navigational interests were also considered from the perspective of the impacts of high or low levels and of fluctuation. The lumber industry, which needed access to bays and inlets and to certain narrow channels for towing logs, was discussed in conjunction with navigational concerns. Rainy River navigation posed challenges of its own, with the Long Sault rapids and the Manitou rapids presenting particular difficulties. Some consideration was also being given to the creation of locks at Kettle Falls, Fort Frances, and the Long Sault rapids in order to provide a navigable waterway of about 250 miles linking the Lake of the Woods and the Namakan River.[33]

The commission endeavoured to present a moderate compromise between divergent preferences with regard to levels, fluctuation, and rates of outflow: "On the one hand are the navigation, fishing, and summer-resort interests, which desire regulation to secure a uniform level, and on the other are the water power interests on the Winnipeg River, which desire regulation to secure a uniform outflow, necessitating the largest practicable fluctuation in the level." The proposed regulation, the commission asserted, "will subserve all interests reasonably well and ... so far as appears practicable, will admit of the most advantageous use of these waters."[34]

Bearing in mind the inevitable trade-offs around water levels, the commission even suggested a calculated basis or cost-benefit formula for adjustments within the fluctuation range it had identified.[35] Notwithstanding such assurance as the formula appeared to provide, winners and losers had to be acknowledged. Any increase in the ordinary maximum level would most directly affect riparian owners, including the town of Warroad and owners of recreational shoreline, as well as fishing interests, particularly in the United States. A reduction of minimum levels would principally affect water power plants and lumbering interests at the outlets and navigational interests throughout the water system. Fishing interests, and certainly fish habitat, were most likely to suffer from fluctuations. Identifying the impacts was easier than evaluating them, as the commission frankly recognized. Accordingly, the commission's recommendations for ordinary maximum level and regulation arrangements were offered in the stated belief that they "come as near as is practicable to securing the most advantageous use of these waters by all interests concerned."

To later observers, references to "all interests" or to "the most advantageous use" and associated standards such as "beneficial" or "practicable" uses seem to subordinate or even overlook important considerations associated, for example, with environmental values, ecosystem services, and sustainability. Such questions would become central considerations for later generations examining water management alternatives.[36] Nevertheless, the IJC devoted close attention to the concepts of "normal" and "natural."

Notably, the words *normal* and *natural* had generally been used as though they might share the same meaning or constitute equivalents. For example, the commissioners observed that the expression "normal or natural level" had been employed in correspondence preceding the reference and that certain officials clearly treated the two words as synonymous. Upon further analysis, however, *natural* was understood to have only one meaning "that is, signifying a state of nature." *Normal*, with reference to the present condition of the lake, "is always used alone and did not come into such use until after the stage to which it referred had become the ordinary, normal condition." In general, this came to mean, on the United States side, the "mean level of the lake during the open season." To Canadians, normal was "the ordinary summer level," or about 1,060.5 feet.[37]

While suggesting that there was "good ground for concluding ... that the normal level as existing today was believed to be the natural level so far as the ordinary high stages were concerned," the commission took great metaphysical pains to reconcile "natural" and "normal":

> Since the word "natural" was never used in any other sense than as signifying the condition of nature, and since the word "normal" was used to signify both natural and existing conditions, the expression "normal or natural level" cannot fairly be interpreted as meaning any other level than that which prevailed in a state of nature, the commission has so construed it.[38]

Despite such attempts to identify a level that might be termed natural, decision makers displayed limited insight into the function or significance of "natural," apart from that level's convenience or lack thereof from the perspective of human uses. For example, the value of what we have come to know as ecological services provided by the aquatic environment was barely recognized or factored into the decision-making process.

As interventions such as the Norman Dam were completed, the resulting water level conditions came to be accepted as normal, with "normal" similarly equated to a natural level that seemed to be of limited significance, except perhaps as a reference point for determining compensation to property holders. Uncertainty about the actual relationship between normal and natural contributed to a decision-making problem. "Since the United States did not know what the natural level of the lake was," wrote the commissioners, "it was unable to determine the merits of the protests of the riparian owners or the justice of their claims for injury on account of prevailing levels."[39] Historical fluctuations within the natural range, whose ecological importance is now better understood, received limited recognition.[40]

But if there were regulatory losers, there were also distinct beneficiaries. In particular, the Norman Dam was expected to increase in value as a power site for manufacturing, if not necessarily for hydroelectricity production. There was, however, a catch:

> If all the power plants at the outlets are willing to forgo the small increase in head resulting from maintaining the level of the lake as close to the ordinary maximum stage as possible well into the spring, and will agree to the drawing down of the reservoir in anticipation of spring floods, no extreme high rates of discharge will ever become necessary, and the value of the Norman Dam as a power site will be correspondingly increased.[41]

The admonition to play nicely together in the pool rested on the premise that compromise has certain advantages. Yet accommodating new water levels proved to be another area in which experience would suggest that the practicalities of achieving harmonious accord among neighbouring interests might far outweigh any philosophical attractions. Whether we call the obstacles to agreement "transaction costs" or "human nature," controversies were substantial and persistent.

Within the agreed range of fluctuation, authority to implement the proposed water level regime would rest with designated Canadian officials, while the involvement of an international board would be triggered if lake levels rose or fell outside those limits. James A. Tawney, one of the US commissioners, felt compelled to express a personal view in relation to the scope of the proposed supervision and control regime. Although he accepted that supervision at the international level would be limited, Tawney argued that those limited controls should apply to "*all structures* materially affecting the level or the flow of boundary waters, and all structures in waters flowing into boundary waters, as well as waters flowing from boundary waters" whenever their operation might affect the level or flow of boundary waters to a material degree.[42] Tawney illustrated and explained his observation before reiterating that international supervision should apply to "*all the waters* of this watershed so as to permit their most advantageous use, *considered as a whole.*"[43] This perspective was largely congruent with the view repeatedly expressed by E.W. Backus.[44]

In Tawney's view, the national governments had effectively waived article 2 of the Boundary Waters Treaty in relation to exclusive jurisdiction over tributary waters on their own side of the border, at least for the purpose of the reference.[45] With a casual dismissal of the treaty makers' labours and expectations, Tawney expressed the opinion that deviation from the negotiated provisions would appear reasonable in circumstances where so doing might greatly increase beneficial use of the water system as a whole. Why would one country not simply accept compensation for relinquishing a treaty right when the circumstances "would permit its neighbour to enjoy benefits otherwise lost to both nations aggregating many times the value of that which has been relinquished"?[46]

Tawney's position failed to gain general support within the IJC, and the process of national review and implementation of the commission's 1917 recommendations got underway. Yet delays were encountered, due at least in part to a continuing desire on the part of US officials to adopt a wider view of the watershed, including upstream and tributary waters, consistent with Tawney's vision of the watershed as a whole.

CANADIAN CONTROL LEGISLATION

At the IJC hearings on the Lake of the Woods reference, Frank Keefer, while still a Port Arthur lawyer, represented both Canada and Ontario. Despite federal-provincial differences in domestic implementation arrangements, the two governments generally shared international objectives. In his capacity as legal counsel for Canada, Keefer reported directly to Sir Robert Borden, wartime prime minister and secretary of state for External Affairs.

Keefer had failed in his first bid for election to Parliament in 1908 but enjoyed more favourable results in 1917. In November of the following year, in recognition of his service and talent as illustrated in the Lake of the Woods matter, he was designated parliamentary under-secretary of state for External Affairs, serving in that position until mid-July 1920. Keefer's penchant for offering advice may have been appreciated by Robert Borden but was hardly embraced by his successor.

Prime Minister Arthur Meighen rebuffed Keefer's offer to prepare a memorandum on the evolving water management framework, particularly as it affected power production on the Winnipeg River.[47] In light of an anticipated conference with the Manitoba and Ontario premiers, Meighen dismissed the proposal: "I know of no special work which I feel justified under the present circumstances in asking you to do."[48] Undeterred, Keefer voluntarily submitted his memorandum to the prime minister, who ultimately acknowledged its usefulness and forwarded it to Senator James Lougheed, minister of the Interior, with the suggestion that Keefer might be consulted.

Yet relations between the prime minister and northwestern Ontario's parliamentary representative remained awkward when national and regional perspectives diverged. As federal MP for the District of Port Arthur and Kenora, Keefer was deeply concerned about matters arising from the IJC recommendations and for the economic circumstances of his constituents. For Meighen, however, international obligations calling for the attention of the national government took priority when steps towards acceptance and implementation of the IJC report got underway.

Canada accepted the recommendations of the IJC's Lake of the Woods report and, by means of a cabinet decision, made arrangements in 1918 to establish an interim control board pending legislation to remove any doubt about the legal foundations of federal water management authority.[49] There were some delays, however, in connection with a Canadian response to a US dispatch concerning ratification in November 1920. In Keefer's personal view, delay in responding to Washington's message played into the hands of those who opposed legislation to establish the water level control board.[50] Yet after a delegation of Kenora mayors – past and current – visited Ottawa in March 1921, Keefer conveyed their request for delay pending further consultations with Ontario authorities. They saw no urgency in the matter, particularly in light of anticipated provincial legislation and the existing Lake of the Woods Control Board.

Deservedly, Keefer took pride in his contribution to Canada's participation in the Lake of the Woods reference. He had acted as counsel on the water level file for both Canada and Ontario, "with the concurrence of each." He was especially pleased with his success in persuading Ontario authorities to relinquish "their claim to sovereign exclusive jurisdiction" and to agree to reconstitute the existing Lake of the Woods Control Board by appointing two provincial engineers to serve alongside two engineers from Canada.[51]

Unfortunately, the existing Control Board had not secured sufficient authority to function effectively and was simply unable to deal with the expanded scope of Backus's power interests. As Interior Minister Sir James

Lougheed explained, the Minnesota industrialist's plans for a downstream power site at White Dog Rapids could seriously interfere with power development along the Winnipeg River.[52]

Early in 1921, Canada, Manitoba, and Ontario agreed upon the desirability of a joint control board established under statute in order to make control effective in the interests of all parties involved. Accordingly, Canada and Ontario introduced legislation concurrently. The federal legislation proposed to reconstitute the Lake of the Woods Control Board with responsibility "to secure at all times the most dependable flow and the most advantageous and beneficial use of, (a) the waters of the Winnipeg River; and (b) the waters of the English River." To accomplish these objectives, the Control Board would be empowered to regulate the Lake of the Woods, Lac Seul, and the Winnipeg River and "to regulate and control the level and flow of such other waters of the watershed of the Winnipeg River" as the governor general and the lieutenant governor determined.[53]

Lougheed, who introduced the bill in the Senate, informed the prime minister that following concurrent passage of the federal and provincial legislation, water regulation could proceed in the interests of all concerned parties.[54] But before passing the bill without amendment, senators voiced reservations. There were calls for further consultation with Winnipeg power interests, for example, and a warning that great care should be taken in working with Backus, who, on the basis of past experience, "cares nothing for the order or instruction or edict of the Canadian government."[55] Lougheed assured his colleagues, however, that the bill reflected agreement among Ontario, Manitoba, and the federal government "for the purpose of protecting the public interest from private enterprises which, up to the present time, have been a menace to these western water powers."[56]

On 20 April 1921, with the House of Commons in committee to discuss the Senate bill, Keefer reported dissension and lack of understanding in parts of his northern constituency.[57] The fault, he suggested, lay with government officials whose consultations had been deficient rather than with the government itself.[58] Somewhat less obliquely, Keefer had previously conveyed to Meighen the message that his constituents were "dissatisfied, angry, suspicious," and unable to understand "why bureaucracy is to over-ride democracy."[59]

Meighen chose to regard Keefer's intervention as substantive opposition to his plans for a federal water control regime, forcing the latter to rearticulate his position: "As stated, I initiated the Lake of the Woods Control Board and of course believe in control and in having Ontario a party to the control." Keefer insisted that he had fulfilled his duty to constituents by presenting *their* representations. "I was appealing to you," he assured the prime minister, "not at all dissatisfied with you."[60] The proposed Canadian legislation, as he understood it, called for three measures: control of the Norman Dam, control of the Winnipeg River within Ontario, and control of the English River, a tributary of the Winnipeg River below the Norman Dam that does not flow into the Lake of the Woods.[61] Ontario's cooperation was needed in relation to the English River and was desirable in relation to downstream power development.[62]

Keefer recounted the history of various water control installations. The Rollerway Dam was constructed in 1887, following several years of low-water conditions. It was privately built on the instigation of Ontario authorities but with Canadian government support in the form of a $7,000 contribution. When the Rollerway Dam proved ineffective, Keewatin Power built the Norman Dam between 1893 and 1895, with stop-logs added in 1898. As Keefer saw the situation, although it was sometimes called "an outlaw dam," this was a work of a public nature that not only benefited navigation but facilitated power production. "The dam was not put there as a menace or to take advantage of anyone," he wrote, "but to do good, in the public interest."[63]

Keefer acknowledged that the Norman Dam had never formally received Dominion government consent and that it was not a satisfactory power site, but he nevertheless believed that if it was to be controlled and regulated "against the will of the owners," there should be compensation.[64]

Keefer had appealed fruitlessly to the prime minister for sufficient delay to allow Ontario to proceed with corresponding legislation: "If we wait until the Ontario Legislature progresses with this Bill and puts it through (which if they are going to do so will be within a short time now) then the Federal Parliament putting it through cannot cause any dissatisfaction in my Riding." This was the case, he explained, because residents of the western portion of his constituency would have had the opportunity to express their concerns to the provincial legislature. Keefer emphasized that the Kenora people favoured the control plan, "but we can get more by quietly leading them along rather than giving them the idea of compulsion."[65] He elaborated the political situation as he perceived it: "By exercising patience and waiting somewhat upon the dissidents we can still get it through." The legislation would be of no value if enacted only by the federal government and not by Ontario; in that case, the bill "would then merely develop a contest over Provincial rights and develop a strong opposition to the Government in Kenora."[66]

Keefer made every effort to inform the prime minister of local sensitivities relating to water power regulation, concerns heightened by difficult economic circumstances as lumber milling declined and other industries closed. Yet on the basis of available timber and water power, the community had, in the end, agreed with Backus in order to promote local development. Keefer described the desperation of his Kenora constituents, comparing them to "drowning people catching at a straw," and adding, "they were ready almost to give their whole town away to any industry that would locate and put them on their feet."[67] In addition, concerns were emanating from Sioux Lookout to the north about including the English River in the control bill because of potential adverse impacts on power production at Pelican Falls.[68]

Firmly seeking to move the federal bill forward, Meighen insisted that a "most thorough review" had taken place involving Ontario representatives, including the premier; Manitoba representatives, among them the attorney general; and the Dominion government, whose representation, he emphasized, included himself and the minister of the Interior.[69] In the prime minister's view, Canada's interests and responsibilities were at least equal to those of Ontario. He pointed to three dimensions of the federal role, beginning with the importance of governmental authority in relation to an international body of water:

> Shall it be argued for a minute that it should be left to private interests, – the owners of the Norman Dam for instance at the outlet of the Lake of the Woods, – to have control of the levels that they virtually have today and that, they exercising the control, we should be liable for the failure to exercise control in the public interest?[70]

To drive the point home, he raised the spectre of Lake of the Woods control being exercised in a manner that produced flooding in Minnesota: "It is this Parliament and this country that is going to be responsible then."[71]

Second, Meighen highlighted the explicit and paramount constitutional authority of the federal government over navigation. Even if what he disdainfully described as "some joint arrangement" involving Ontario and the Keewatin Power Company had developed in the past, he saw no reason for it to continue: "It surely is not becoming that this Parliament, having imposed upon it by the constitution a distinct jurisdiction and duty should leave to the province of Ontario and Mr. Backus, or the Keewatin Power Company, the carrying out of that duty."[72]

Finally, the prime minister pointed to the federal government's administrative and proprietary interests in downstream power production, a
continuing legacy of Canada's post-Confederation acquisition of the
North-West Territories. Just as Ontario's interest arose from the province's
ownership of power production sites, "we are the owners and administrators of the power properties farther down in Manitoba."[73]

Apart from his strategic differences with Keefer, Meighen appreciated
the core implications of the IJC report for international and domestic
regulation. If the United States was primarily concerned about navigation,
and navigation would be adequately taken care of by levels maintained
between 1,056 and 1,061, explained Meighen in the House of Commons,
"it follows that while they are so maintained the United States does not
need to come in at all." The commission's advice to create a board "to
control the whole matter so long as they keep the high level at 1061 and
the low level at 1056" put control within that range in Canadian hands.
Meighen noted that the maintenance of Canadian national authority thus
depended upon the effective domestic administration of the approved
range of regulated levels: "It is between those two that it must be kept,
and while so kept it is under Canadian control, but if it goes above 1061
on the one hand or below 1056 on the other the jurisdiction of a joint
international board arises."[74]

In correspondence with Keefer, Meighen further sought to explain the
proposed 1921 federal legislation to confirm the creation of the domestic
Canadian control board: "All that this Bill says is that this board shall
have control while the levels are maintained between the limits fixed by
the International Joint Commission or between such other limits as the
two countries may agree to – because we have not yet agreed on the report of the commission." Should water levels fall outside those fixed limits,
no arrangement was then in place, "but if the commission's report is
agreed to by the United States there will be an international board to take
care of it."[75]

Keefer connected Canadian acceptance of the IJC report with the pace
of federal legislation, again counselling delay. Then, taking the unfortunate
tone of "I told you so," Keefer pontificated to Meighen: "I foretold to you
before the result of your policy – viz to force the rejection in the Ontario
House. I foretell to you, now, the result of this policy if pursued, will be
that you will throw away the effect of the report of the International Joint
Commission." The report, he underlined, was of no use whatsoever in the
absence of adoption by the United States, adoption that he believed was

put in jeopardy by the legislative timetable Meighen was determined to pursue.[76] To Robert Borden, Keefer more candidly confided his fears about pushing the bill forward: it afforded Backus a sufficient grievance to petition "his own Legislature," the US Senate, citing the Canadian statute as an example of ill treatment in that he had been denied an opportunity to voice his concerns. He might thus exert his influence to delay or even to prevent adoption of the IJC report. Canada, Keefer observed, would only benefit if the report were to be accepted on both sides of the border, so "why do anything that will throw difficulties in the way of getting that report adopted unless same were necessary? Therefore it is very bad judgment to press the situation now."[77] Bad judgment or not, Meighen pressed forward, insisting during Keefer's absence from a government caucus meeting that the federal government could not avoid its international responsibilities.[78]

As for compensation for Backus, Keefer considered it to be appropriate, even though he firmly asserted that he had no brief from any of the parties, certainly not from the owner of the dam.[79] Meighen, acknowledging the possibility of compensation should a claim be fairly made, went out of his way to discredit claims relating to the Norman Dam by referring to it as "a structure erected or existing in defiance of the *Navigable Waters Protection Act*."[80]

By late May of 1921, when the Lake of the Woods Control Board question returned to the parliamentary agenda, the tenor of debate had deteriorated. Protestations from the Kenora Board of Trade characterized the legislation as "designed to transfer the rights of the province of Ontario over her waterpowers to the province of Manitoba."[81] Keefer, publicly describing his position as "unenviable and unhappy," nevertheless felt compelled to side with his constituents against the prime minister, who remained utterly unsympathetic to any conflict Keefer might have been experiencing.[82]

In the interests of his constituency, Keefer emphasized factors other than federal responsibilities in his account of the IJC's recommendations.[83] Specifically, the control regime would serve "to protect the interests of riparian owners in both countries during seasons of excessive flood inflow into the reservoirs and to protect the interest of navigation against loss and damage due to excessive draft upon the stored water toward the end of a series of dry years." Simultaneously, the supervisory arrangements would permit "advantageous use of the waters flowing from the reservoirs for power purposes."[84] Once again, downplaying the disruptive potential

of the IJC's conclusions, Keefer presented the proposals as largely consistent with existing expectations. Thus, subject to limitations associated with
the proposed international control, he assured the owners of dams and
other works that they would retain their rights as intended by their respective local governments.

The concept of "dependable flow," which IJC officials had taken such
care to ensure, was, in Keefer's estimation, "the whole trouble."[85] He explained that dependable flow would be secured by "placing artificial obstructions in the river, raising the minimum flow up and thus at certain
periods securing more water, and taking away the increased flow naturally
resulting from spring freshets and holding it for use during the summer
when it may be most needed." While acknowledging that this produced
"an artificial state of affairs," he asserted that it was "a very proper thing
to do."[86] There was not much here to echo the "normal" and "natural"
debate that had absorbed a great part of the IJC's intellectual energy.

Keefer succinctly described the key difference between Ontario and
Manitoba electricity interests: the latter "want to get the dependable flow
out of the Lake of the Woods, but they do not want to pay for the dependable flow out of Rainy Lake."[87] In the bluntest possible terms, Keefer
described the conflict as "a water-power dispute between the powers in
Manitoba versus the powers in Ontario."[88]

The prime minister accepted dependable flow as a matter of common
sense and on the basis of the IJC's advice. He rebuked Keefer for his apparent support of natural flow over the dependable flow objective, asking:
"How can you have natural flow when, at the same time, you must, not
naturally at all, but for the general benefit of all, keep the flow of the
lake out of the natural level?" In periods of high water, it must be retained,
the prime minister observed, and in other circumstances you would "do
the very opposite." So, he concluded, "you have the principle of natural
flow interfered with to the general advantage of navigation and in the
interests of all concerned."[89]

Meighen was more than a little impatient with the idea of revisiting
dependable flow. The IJC had consulted power interests, fishing interests,
the navigational sector, and many of those whose lands were flooded before
recommending dependable flow, "and acting upon that report, having accepted it, it is our business to see that we are in a position to carry out that
recommendation."[90] Full stop. Meighen also had very limited sympathy
for Kenora spokesmen. He regarded their opposition as motivated by the
town's immediate economic agenda: "The Backus interests at Kenora ...

do not want dependable flow at the Lake of the Woods, but such flow as suits Mr. Backus. The more it suits him the better pleased they are."[91]

Alongside the contentious issue of dependable flow and the sensitive matter of federal-provincial relations with respect to water powers were some pressing practical considerations. When embarking upon construction at the power site on the eastern branch of the Winnipeg River, Backus had unfortunately neglected to secure the approval of the federal Department of Public Works, the agency then responsible for the relevant exercise of the Canadian federal government's constitutional responsibility for matters affecting navigation. Mayor George A. Toole appealed for permission – that is, for "verbal orders" – from the minister pending formal approval by the governor in council of the plans and applications that were submitted. With high levels of unemployment, especially among railway workers, Toole was anxious on behalf of about 150 men then working on the Backus project and of a further 250 or 300 who might be added to the workforce if the project were allowed to proceed. Those employed and threatened by the work stoppage were "all Kenora men" with families to support. The possibility of delay, perhaps for as long as a year, was, on this basis, quite alarming.[92]

Rumoured developments in connection with the terms of the navigable waters permit appeared – to Kenora observers, at least – designed to provoke a rejection by Backus, leaving the town exposed to further costly delays and prolonged unemployment.[93] The federal government's insistence on safeguarding its navigational interests, even to the point of expropriating the Norman Dam, was doubly infuriating in the context of local experience: for years, municipal officials had petitioned for a dock at Rideout Bay, only to experience repeated denial on the grounds that there was insufficient traffic.[94]

Keefer's interventions with the prime minister on the navigable waters front were ultimately successful; however, in a manner reminiscent of the early battle between the town and the Hudson's Bay Company, much of the 1921 construction season was lost during the interlude before the Kenora water power project gained the prime minister's more or less daily attention in mid-September. When modifications consistent with Kenora's wishes were finally accepted in the early fall, Keefer expressed his appreciation to the man whose peremptory disregard of his earlier advice had complicated negotiations.[95]

Still, for some time, there was not much to show by way of implementation. Despite best efforts by Keefer and others to present the IJC's conclusions as an appropriate compromise in the general interest – effectively a win-win-win story – there were still several all-or-nothing players at the table. It would be more than two decades before the overall institutional framework for managing water levels could be completed, following an extended period of contentious deliberations involving Backus, as well as provincial governments determined to safeguard interests of their own.

8
Power Struggles

As the Great War was drawing to a close, and following the International Joint Commission's (IJC's) final report on the Lake of the Woods, Edward Wellington Backus, the Minnesota industrialist, contended with business rivals and with governments to control power production throughout a complex network of northern waters while those governments contended with each other. Backus's interests included the Keewatin Power Company, which he had acquired in 1913, along with its power sites at Tunnel Island, where the Lake of the Woods empties into the Winnipeg River. Keewatin Power still owned the Norman Dam, which, since 1898, had been subject by agreement to the authority of the Ontario commissioner of Public Works to control the dam in the interest of navigation. The agreement, however, could be terminated by written notice of the company's intention to use the dam for power purposes, after which time Keewatin Power would be responsible for keeping the water "at ordinary Summer level."[1] Backus was also interested in the nearby Kenora municipal power plant, formerly owned by the Hudson's Bay Company and the subject of a prolonged and costly legal dispute. Resolution of these interconnected conflicts would deeply affect water flows and quality throughout the entire watershed. But the focus on power sites, individual facilities, and infrastructure in a watershed context risks overlooking or downplaying broader impacts and consequences, whether these were cumulative and gradual or sudden and catastrophic.

The existence of private regulatory authority over the Lake of the Woods outflow was of immense political concern, not only in Kenora but also in

Ottawa, Winnipeg, Toronto, Washington, DC, and St. Paul, Minnesota. Upstream, but still in Canada, were works on the Rainy River at Fort Frances and International Falls. Beyond that point lay storage opportunities situated in border country extending beyond Rainy Lake to the Namakan system and through the Superior Forest and Quetico parklands and reserves. The desire to regulate these upper waters for his own industrial purposes underpinned Backus's enduring quest for a comprehensive water management treaty rather than an agreement limited to Lake of the Woods levels. This expansive goal, however, accentuated existing conflict with Manitoba power interests and with new rivals. Among the latter, of particular note was an influential group of conservationists on both sides of the international border.[2] These new players initiated an important and continuing re-evaluation of the watershed and environmental resources more generally.

PULP AND PAPER AND POWER

Backus was in default respecting development of the Lake of the Woods pulp limit (1,860 square miles), which he had acquired through the Keewatin Lumber Company in 1914. Critics and wartime financial constraints further delayed progress. Under pressure from the Ontario government of Howard Ferguson in 1919 and, later, from the United Farmers administration, Backus responded with plans for expanded operations. By the summer of 1920, he was prepared to begin production, agreeing to establish a pulp and paper mill in Kenora with 200 tons daily capacity, 150 of which would supply paper. Backus further agreed to assume Kenora's existing municipal power obligations and to supply power to the Maple Leaf Flour mill. The municipality, in exchange, undertook to transfer its hydroelectric plant to Backus's company, to fix property assessment for municipal tax purposes, and to "actively assist and support" applications by Backus to obtain additional pulp limits on the English River as well as an important power concession downstream on the Winnipeg River.[3] Thus, Backus's campaign for water power rights and pulpwood limits around Kenora was more systematically aligned with municipal interests than were his initial Canadian ventures around Fort Frances, where, after fifteen years of lobbying and negotiations, he had still not secured satisfactory timber limits.[4] By 1921, Arthur Meighen's insistence that the voice of Kenora on lake regulation was, in effect, the voice of Backus was close to the mark.

In an agreement that aroused widespread – if not entirely merited – criticism, Backus obtained a commitment from Premier E.C. Drury of the United Farmers of Ontario government to lease a power site at White Dog Rapids.[5] The White Dog deal was stated to be "for the purpose of enabling the company to carry out the terms of their said agreement with the town of Kenora."[6] Failure to construct and operate new facilities, however, might lead to cancellation. Further terms required Backus to respect other established interests, including those affected by regulation of the Norman Dam. It soon became a matter of great controversy whether the Norman Dam clause in the White Dog agreement provided sufficient protection for public control to satisfy the concerns of other Lake of the Woods users, notably Manitoba power producers and municipal consumers.[7]

The next phase of Backus's expansion in northwestern Ontario – and a step closely associated with the White Dog power agreement – involved a pulp limit along the English River, which the provincial government put up for competition after cancelling the unproductive Lake of the Woods concession. The territory in question covered some three thousand square miles, extending eastward from the Manitoba border between the National Transcontinental rail line in the South and the English River in the North. Timber and pulpwood from the area was to be processed in Kenora. This requirement applied equally to newsprint production from pulpwood suitable for that purpose.[8]

Backus enjoyed vocal support from the town of Kenora, whose officials celebrated the new arrangements and expressed great confidence that Backus and his associates were "men who do things. We have seen and investigated their works. They are not promoters or exploiters. They are builders of huge industries."[9] Backus's appeal to local officials and commercial interests rested on his commitment to the region as reflected in extensive and long-standing investments and evident determination to bring resources into production.

When the English River pulp limit was advertised, Backus positioned himself to enjoy exclusive participation rights in a somewhat truncated bidding process. He need not have gone to the trouble of orchestrating dummy bids from two business associates, for his success was assured by his stranglehold on regional water powers. Backus had locked up the key strategic assets, including the Norman Dam site, and had also secured agreement from Kenora for the municipal site and provincial agreement in connection with White Dog Rapids. Without access to a power supply, no potential competitor could satisfy the obligation to develop a mill at Kenora.

FIGURE 8.1   Lake of the Woods Milling, 1936. *Courtesy of the Library and Archives Canada.*

Local sentiment, as expressed by Mayor George Toole and commercial representatives, firmly supported development of the English River pulp stands. Loss of the project would have been a severe economic blow at a critical time.[10] Leaders within the agricultural community spoke out to dispel rumours that farmers opposed the new venture: "If the big interests do not build the railroads and establish the mills, the timber on the English River limit will rot, as it will never be brought out by the small man without assistance of big concerns."[11] Mayor Toole effusively endorsed the deal, expressing hope that Kenora's pulp and paper mill would become a continental leader and gratitude for Backus's contribution, which "without men of your great courage and faith in the future would remain in its dormant state."[12]

Lake of the Woods Milling, then operating the second-largest flour milling facility in Canada, sounded a discordant note.[13] The company sought assurances of continued access to poplar and whitewood supplies to meet its requirements for 175,000 barrels per year. Departmental officials insisted that annual allocations could satisfy any needs of this kind.[14] Lake of the Woods Milling had actually never secured a long-term arrangement but had operated through seasonal cutting permits. Since 1914, it had enjoyed some protection under the Lake of the Woods concession, which reserved poplar and whitewood for the use of local industries.[15]

FIGURE 8.2 Minnesota and Ontario Operations, Fort Frances and International
Falls. *Courtesy of the US National Park Service.*

The "Backus Deal" soon took its place among leading scandals of a
highly contentious era. Cartoonists and pamphleteers honed their skills
on the savoury and unsavoury details as these emerged. Aided by the Drury
government, the Minnesota millionaire, it was widely alleged, had secured
for himself, and at his own price, a timber empire. Not only did Backus
control virtually the entire pulpwood and timber situation, but he was also
portrayed as the industrial dictator of the vast territory between Lake Superior and the Manitoba boundary.[16] The description of the deal alone was
enough to arouse public alarm: "The most cunningly devised and diabolical
scheme to rob Ontario ever perpetrated in the history of the Province."[17]

But if Backus's performance drew criticism, it was the political collab-
orators in the pulpwood arrangements, notably Premier E.C. Drury and
Attorney General W.E. Raney, who faced condemnation. These pillars of
the United Farmers administration had denounced Howard Ferguson, the
Conservative leader, for disregarding legislated and democratic procedures
respecting the disposal of public lands, but they were, according to some
later commentators, equally responsible for circumventing established
arrangements.[18]

Ferguson correctly sensed Drury's vulnerability on what would later be
considered the "optics" of the English River deal. "What a farce to call
such a transaction a public sale," Ferguson cried. "What hypocrisy to say
there was any competition."[19] Although the pulpwood controversy was

essentially a matter of internal provincial concern, its interrelationship with hydro-power production and water management inevitably produced entanglements involving several other governments.

THE INTERGOVERNMENTAL DIMENSION

In the late fall of 1920, the federal government's primary concerns regarding the Lake of the Woods centred on waterways rather than the pulp limit controversy, as shown by the jostling between Frank Keefer, the region's MP, and his prime minister. Canada's interests were nevertheless multidimensional: navigational authority; the expectations of Manitoba power users, to whom the federal government had direct obligations; and the desire of the United States to resolve the water management situation along the Ontario-Minnesota border.[20]

The prime minister initially failed in an effort to convene with the Manitoba and Ontario premiers on the Lake of the Woods question, but Premier Drury did meet Premier Norris and the Manitoba cabinet in Winnipeg in December 1920. In response to Manitoba's concerns regarding the Norman Dam and downstream impacts on Winnipeg River power interests, Drury promised safeguards. Backus, he repeatedly indicated, had agreed to relinquish control of the Norman Dam. Planned legislation would give control to the province, and Ontario offered measures to protect Winnipeg's power interests in connection with White Dog Rapids. As one of Meighen's Manitoba informants explained, however, "the power interests of the Winnipeg River still look to the Dominion Government to protect their interests."[21]

Immediately following the meeting between Drury and Norris, J.B. Challies, the experienced engineer who had earlier defended the watershed through work for the Commission of Conservation and who served with the Dominion Water Powers Branch before taking an appointment with the Lake of the Woods Control Board, recommended that Ontario and Canada pass concurrent legislation. His intent was to confer upon the board clear authority over the regulation and flow of the Winnipeg River between the Lake of the Woods and the Manitoba boundary, as well as that of the English River between Lac Seul and the Manitoba boundary. A conference was scheduled for early February.[22]

At this point in early 1921, the federal government's multiple responsibilities for navigation, for international affairs, and for natural resources in Manitoba produced converging pressures.[23] Both Canadian and Ontario officials were soon engaged in reconsidering the status and powers of the Lake of the Woods Control Board, with the province seriously questioning the legitimacy of federal government participation.[24] But as we have seen, Meighen and his advisers were committed to securing and refining the control procedures established under orders-in-council in 1919. In the first place, federal officials claimed that an agreed legislative basis would reduce the risk of conflict between Canada's constitutional responsibility for navigation and Ontario's authority over water powers. US pressure for an international body to regulate the broader watershed, including Canadian waters, caused further apprehension. But Backus's influence at White Dog Rapids and the persisting uncertainty regarding the strength of provincial authority over the Norman Dam were more pressing.

Backus defended his interests vigorously. Judge Rockwood of Minneapolis, who represented Backus, explained his client's concerns to "The Ministers of the Crown." Rockwood, in effect, attacked the "most dependable flow" principle of water regulation as recommended by the IJC and as adopted in the Control Bill for the guidance of the commissioners. Rockwood charged that the proposed enactment went well beyond simple regulation of water flow. Rather, he insisted, "its fundamental purpose is to abrogate the common law of property in flowing water and to create a new and artificial rule." The redistributive intent, he further alleged, "is to subtract from the value of certain water powers and add to the value of others by the direct and simple process of statutory enactment." In this case, the judge continued, "it happens that the whole injury would be to water powers in Ontario and Minnesota and to riparian rights therein, and the whole benefit to water powers in Manitoba." Rockwood criticized "most dependable flow" on the grounds that it "results in a substantially smaller use of water in the course of a year because of the constant necessity of holding a reserve to insure that the stream shall not fall below the fixed minimum." He argued that the Fort Frances Pulp and Paper Company, the Minnesota and Ontario Paper Company, and the power facilities at Kenora and White Dog Rapids would all experience significant reductions in power production potential.[25] Kenora officials, in their continuing alliance with Backus or his associates, also questioned "most dependable flow."

Challies promptly replied to the arguments raised by Rockwood on Backus's behalf. The "dependable flow" method had been fully considered by the IJC and was "undoubtedly in the best interest of all concerned": to reconsider intermittent flow as Backus desired would require a complete reopening of the international proceedings. Challies insisted that the legislation did not conflict with US preferences and actually went as far as Canada could go to protect US interests in accordance with the IJC report. Canadian officials were adamant that no confiscation of Backus's rights was involved; Challies further defended the proposed measures as a valid exercise of Canada's constitutional authority over navigation.[26]

Ontario perceived Ottawa's authority in the realm of navigation as a threat to provincial authority over hydroelectric power. This subject became increasingly sensitive as provincial officials contemplated development along major waterways, including the Ottawa and St. Lawrence Rivers. Hartley Dewart, of the provincial Liberals, leveraged his criticism of the Lake of the Woods situation against this broader threat to provincial prosperity: "Is the Dominion government under the guise of its superior power with reference to navigation to take control of the rights of the Province of Ontario with reference to its own waterways and to deal with them as it pleases?"[27]

Peter Heenan, a railway engineer and union leader, was elected to the provincial legislature in 1919, along with a cluster of fellow Labour Party members whose legislative support he helped to deliver to the Drury administration. As a Backus loyalist whose personal political fortunes were tied to the Kenora mill, he also weighed in against dependable flow, projecting a potential reduction of 700,000 horsepower in Ontario. Facing vigorous criticism and the possible loss of Heenan's crucial support, Premier Drury withdrew the Ontario bill to establish the Lake of the Woods Control Board in late April, 1921.[28]

Since the federal Lake of the Woods Control Act was explicitly inoperative in the absence of the concurrent Ontario legislation, Canada was left in the position of having made no advances of any kind from the previous situation. Meighen promised Drury that he would "take up the matter of continuing the present Control Board with the Minister of the Interior and can assure you that we will endeavour to do so if the same can be effectively done."[29] This undertaking left a reasonable scope for misunderstanding and for manoeuvre.

The federal government was still engaged in ongoing talks with the United States to implement the IJC's proposals for the Lake of the Woods by treaty, and pressure for action from other quarters was mounting. The City of Winnipeg and the municipalities of Fort Garry and St. Boniface boldly called for expropriation of the Norman Dam and for a declaration that the works regulating the Lake of the Woods waters were – in the language of a powerful constitutional provision – for the "general advantage" of Canada. Amidst high levels of postwar unemployment, Kenora

officials sought federal cooperation to encourage Backus to proceed with
the promised development of the new mill facilities.[30] Meanwhile, newspaper opinion confirmed a hardening of attitudes. The *Ottawa Journal*,
for example, lamented the apparent failure of the concurrent legislation
plan and rhetorically inquired: "Shall Edward Wellington Backus be absolute dictator in the Lake of the Woods district, or shall the King's
governments prevail?" As far as the paper was concerned, "there ought not
to be any doubt about the answer."[31]

When Senator Lougheed introduced the federal Lake of the Woods bill,
he explained that use of concurrent legislation had been intended to avoid
possible conflict over jurisdiction concerning navigation and hydro power.
But with Ontario's recent change of heart, this approach was no longer viable. The *Lake of the Woods Regulation Act,* as the new statute was known,
declared the works on the lake and on the Winnipeg and English river
systems to be for the "general advantage" of Canada and conferred responsibility for the management of these structures on a control board that
would be appointed federally.[32]

Premier Drury, infuriated by the provocative invocation of "general
advantage," immediately protested federal invasion of provincial authority:
"Any effort to take control of the waters and water powers of this Province
further than is necessary for the purposes of navigation will be strongly
resisted."[33] Yet Canada's evident determination to proceed spurred Drury
to action. Six months after assuring his Manitoba counterpart that there
were no difficulties with the Norman Dam controls, Drury finally obtained
written agreement from Backus confirming the latter's willingness to waive
the right to cancel Ontario's control of the Norman Dam while the White
Dog development was being carried out. Drury explained this to Meighen,
challenging the prime minister's contention that existing arrangements
were ineffective. He also questioned the need for legislation to fulfill
Canada's international obligations because "no such engagements have yet
been ratified and because there are means of controlling the private interests
involved."[34]

To Meighen, however, the previous federal-provincial agreement on
concurrent legislation amply demonstrated the inadequacy of the 1919
order-in-council arrangements, and he explained that Canada's obligations for navigation and water levels were already well established in the
1909 *Boundary Waters Treaty.* The proposed legislation, Meighen claimed,
"is to make quite certain that the Dominion Government shall not be
powerless to exercise that responsibility."[35] On the basis of the province's
own legal advice from Newton Wesley Rowell, Ontario threatened to

challenge federal authority in relation to Lake of the Woods control.[36] Backus also remained opposed to the new federal developments. These clearly curtailed his ambitions and left him to face continuing legal liabilities and uncertain future costs, even if they did not actually interfere with rights that he could successfully defend in the political process. From Fort Frances, local officials urged that their concerns should be heard and respected before a decision was taken. In particular, directing its gaze upstream, the town asserted its entitlement to power from "waters flowing into Rainy Lake from Canadian sources exclusively."[37]

Drifting Upstream

In the fall of 1922 – after Drury and Mackenzie King, the next Canadian prime minister to inherit the Lake of the Woods file, had renewed efforts to establish joint control – Backus restated his desire to see the upstream Rainy Lake questions resolved in conjunction with control of the Lake of the Woods. His interests in these waters dated back nearly two decades to early exploration and application for control of Kettle Falls and other sites affecting Namakan, Sand Point, Crane, Little Vermillion, La Croix, Crooked, Basswood, Knife, and Saganaga Lakes along the boundary.[38]

On 20 September 1922, Backus was present in the office of Prime Minister Mackenzie King, along with Premier Drury and Manitoba's new leader John Bracken, their advisers, and Governor Jacob A.O. Preus of Minnesota. Governor Preus, while satisfied with the proposed resolution of the Lake of the Woods issues as they were agreed upon by Canada and the United States, strongly urged that the upper lakes such as Namakan should be dealt with at the same time. He argued that sufficient information was already available to resolve these questions. The governor's reluctance to accept a treaty that failed to address Rainy Lake matters was much influenced by Backus.[39]

At the September 1922 meeting, Backus pressed for commitments on additional upstream storage. He also proposed that the IJC should determine the cost of the new storage infrastructure to be provided for his facilities at International Falls and at the outlet of Lake Namakan, with power interests further downstream contributing to the investment.[40]

A few months later, on the afternoon of 15 November, the group reconvened in the prime minister's office. Backus restated his position and indicated a willingness to leave to the IJC the entire matter of Lake of the Woods control, including the method to be adopted, construction requirements, and the assessment of benefits. On this occasion, however, representatives of other lumber companies (including Shevlin-Clarke and Weyerhauser) and local communities were on hand to oppose any immediate resolution of the upper lakes questions. They argued for a full IJC investigation and report.[41] This, as noted, was the eventual basis for settlement of the international questions in 1925.

THE BATTLE FOR THE NORMAN DAM

With regard to domestic issues on the Canadian agenda, including the status of the Norman Dam, 15 November 1922 was also a day of great significance. At 9:00 a.m., about six hours before Backus and other industrial and community representatives convened in the prime minister's office to express their views about shared upstream waters, a purely Canadian intergovernmental conference got underway.

In the offices of Charles Stewart, the federal minister of the Interior, Mackenzie King, along with Premiers Drury and Bracken, worked out a formula for repeal of the "general advantage" legislation and confirmed an approach to the Canada-US issues. The Ontario-Manitoba-Canada understanding called for expropriation of the Norman Dam, regulation of water levels under concurrent federal-provincial legislation, and procedures for Manitoba power interests to obtain storage of Lac Seul waters on the English River system.[42]

The November 1922 intergovernmental agreement constrained Backus's ability to influence the political outcome. It provided Manitoba with a degree of formal reassurance that was greatly welcomed by Winnipeg municipal and power interests. It shifted Ontario more firmly towards public regulation of water levels. And the replacement of Premier Drury by Howard Ferguson soon further reduced Backus's influence on Ontario's assessment of the overall situation.

The 1922 agreement did not eliminate friction on the Canadian side, but as Winnipeg's city solicitor concisely noted, the core underlying interests might be distinguished sufficiently to permit reconciliation: "Backus needs a power dam at Norman and the Government needs a regulatory dam, and the Manitoba interests must have Government control and operation of the regulatory dam so as to control the level in and the flow out of the waters of the Lake."[43] Even within that clarified framework, the timing of the repeal of the *Lake of the Woods Regulation Act* remained contentious. Manitoba interests urged that it should remain in place until the expropriation questions were fully resolved. If anything, Winnipeg's desire for secure power from the Winnipeg River was strengthened by recent expenditures on an innovative central steam heating system that would rely heavily on off-peak electrical energy.[44]

At the local level, editorial relations between Winnipeg and Kenora deteriorated markedly. When the *Manitoba Free Press* referred to warlike circumstances, the *Kenora Examiner* took up the challenge: "It really is a 'War,' an aggressive war on our rights to the use of our own natural resources ... It is no longer a fight to have Mr. Backus allowed to harness his water power. It is now another fight, or 'war' to defend our rights as a town. This town is in Ontario. Winnipeg is in Manitoba."[45] The decline of water levels to twenty-five-year lows in 1924 accentuated the urgency of work to restore or replace the coffer dam and added to intermunicipal tensions as Kenora residents feared adverse impacts, including reduced output at the pulp and paper plant and at Lake of the Woods Milling. The "war" with Winnipeg intensified as a *Free Press* advertisement under the slogan "United We Stand" summoned local electricity users to a civic meeting on the Norman Dam issue: "The flow of water over these power sites affects your daily life," it declared.[46] Four thousand power consumers rallied on 21 October 1924 at a downtown theatre to demand permanent control.

With the *Lake of the Woods Regulation Act* in place, an effective operating relationship provided Manitoba power interests with satisfactory storage and supply arrangements from the waterways, which were also greatly valued by Backus's forest industries.[47] For his part, the Minnesota industrialist had fully satisfied Kenora officials with his performance of the 1920 agreement. Even as the 1922 negotiations progressed, Mayor Toole reported his satisfaction with the steady pace of construction and development: twelve thousand cords of pulpwood were on hand and ready for grinding, and a new power house on the east branch of the Winnipeg River was nearing completion. Mayor Toole indicated that the new facilities would soon require even more pulpwood and timber than the limit could provide. Perhaps an additional reserve north of the English River should be considered.[48]

On 24 February 1925, Canada's minister of Justice, Ernest Lapointe, and the American secretary of State, Charles Evans Hughes, signed an international agreement to confirm arrangements for regulating the water level of the Lake of the Woods. The objective, once again, was "the most advantageous use" of Lake of the Woods waters on each side of the boundary for domestic and sanitary purposes, navigation, and fishing, as well as for power, irrigation, and reclamation.[49] The agreement, as long anticipated, called for the creation of a Canadian and an International Lake of the Woods Control Board with shared responsibilities for maintaining the ordinary level of the lake between the elevations of 1,056 and 1,061.25 sea level datum and for regulating levels within that range with a view to ensuring "the highest continuous uniform discharge of water from the lake."[50] As long as water levels remained within the agreed range, the authority of the Canadian regulator would prevail. The involvement of the international board, consisting of one Canadian and one American engineer, would be triggered by water levels outside the range, with the IJC itself responsible for a final decision in the case of disagreement within the international board.[51]

Further provisions called for enlargement of the outflow capacity where the Lake of the Woods tumbles into the Winnipeg River "to permit the discharge of not less than forty-seven thousand cubic feet of water per second (47,000 c.f.s.) when the level of the lake is at elevation 1061 sea-level datum."[52] In addition, without governmental approval and authorization from the IJC, diversions out of the Lake of the Woods watershed were prohibited.[53] The watershed – a frame of reference not evidently even contemplated within the Boundary Waters Treaty – was expansively defined as "the entire region in which the waters discharged at the outlets of Lake of the Woods have their natural source."[54] Although a considerable period of time would pass before such a wide-ranging configuration began to receive sustained attention across the many boundaries and jurisdictions that it encompassed, the watershed now enjoyed official acknowledgment.[55]

THE DAMS IN THE COURTS: COMPENSATION AND CONTROL

The new Norman Dam was built during 1924–25 and eventually began operations in 1926. During construction, a temporary coffer dam blocked the outflow from the lake except for water passing through the other smaller outlets – including the artificial channels – to the river below. By the time the dam was opened in 1926, water levels in the Lake of the Woods had risen from the lows of 1924 to above the treaty-level peak and had to be reduced. The discharge of the accumulated water supply took place over three seasons, from 1926 to 1928, an outflow that greatly exceeded the capacity of the downstream power plants. Not only did this discharge cause severe shoreline damage, but the water was considered by Winnipeg River power developers as having been "wasted." Accordingly, they insisted that they had received no benefits from the regulation of lake levels until

1929.[56] Others affected by the protracted series of events – from the IJC reference, to the treaty, to legislative implementation – also waited a long time for the final resolution of their concerns.

Historical riparian grievances had been at the heart of the origins of the 1925 international treaty. The signing of the treaty, Kenora's leading newspaper remarked, "is the culmination of efforts commenced as far back as 1907 when protests were made to the U.S. Govt. by Warroad residents regarding high water levels caused as they thought by the Norman dam."[57] Within the treaty context, Canada and the United States addressed compensation claims associated with earlier fluctuations in water level and assigned responsibility for future damage or injury. Each country assumed responsibility for damage or injury suffered by its residents as a result of the new regulatory regime.[58] With respect to current or existing claims for flooding on the US side, Canada agreed to pay $275,000 in exchange for the United States assuming liability for flooding damage to its shoreline on the Lake of the Woods.[59]

Compensation proceedings affecting American landowners continued into the early 1930s as American courts, the US Department of Justice, and the US State Department struggled over the valuation of losses.[60] Finally, the US Supreme Court was asked to decide how to calculate the fair market value of shoreline land on the Lake of the Woods that was expropriated and flooded in accordance with the international agreement on water level regulation.[61]

Property owners on the American side of the Lake of the Woods had begun to protest intermittent flooding of their lands after the original Norman Dam became fully operational on the Winnipeg River in 1898.[62] When the US Congress moved to make the flooding permanent in keeping with the 1925 Convention, the secretary of War expropriated "flowage easements up to the specified elevation upon all lands in Minnesota bordering upon the Lake of the Woods, the Warroad river, and the Rainy river, and that compensation should be made."[63] Sensing a gold mine, or at least a beneficial outflow from public coffers, landowners who had previously complained of flooding now argued that compensation payments should not be limited to the loss of agricultural lands but should also reflect the value of power production enabled by enhanced storage capacity on the flooded property. In other words, the landowners wanted to supplement a claim for their own personal losses with some of the public gains.

The US Supreme Court eventually ruled that "the fact that the most profitable use of a parcel can be made only in combination with other lands does not necessarily exclude that use from consideration if the possibility of combination is reasonably sufficient to affect market value."[64] However, the value for compensation purposes would not include future enhancements in use or value resulting from or subsequent to the expropriation.[65] In this case, the court concluded – given "the number of parcels, private owners, Indian tribes, and sovereign proprietors to be dealt with" – that there was "no foundation for opinion evidence ... that it was practicable for private parties to acquire the flowage easements in question."[66] Thus, the landowners' just compensation for the condemnation of their property should not include the value later associated with the property as a storage reservoir. Bluntly put: "Nice try."

Flooded riparian owners were not alone in seeking to obtain the fullest advantage from the regulatory transformation of the Lake of the Woods water system. Despite Backus's persistence in various governmental and administrative forums where water management problems were debated, by the early 1920s, he had had limited success in gaining public acceptance for his vision of the watershed. Questions regarding Rainy Lake and upper waters remained unresolved, and legal claims against his companies for previous flood damage were still outstanding in Minnesota.[67] "Dependable flow" was firmly in place as a principle of regulation, and expropriation of the Norman Dam was under active contemplation as a consequence of the November 1922 intergovernmental agreement. By this time, Backus was also fully committed to an extensive construction program at Kenora for mills. So, alongside ongoing federal-provincial, international, and partisan political conflict over water regulation, Backus embarked upon litigation against the occupants of the artificial water outlets on the lakeshore in a practical attempt to strengthen his access to Lake of the Woods power potential. To put the matter another way, he set out to reduce downstream outflows as one means of compensation for his failure to secure regulatory approval to control the upstream inflow arrangements.

In 1916, the Keewatin Power Company, which Backus had acquired three years earlier, launched proceedings to prevent the Lake of the Woods Milling Company and the Keewatin Flour Mills Company from diverting any further lake water through artificial channels. But the injunction claims against the two milling companies did not proceed to trial until 1927, by which time a power plant had been completed at the Backus site.[68]

Through Keewatin Power, Backus claimed rights to all of the hydroelectricity that could be developed from the full volume of water that would ordinarily flow through the natural outlet.[69] The Backus interests further contended that the artificial or "cut" channels used for flour milling had never obtained water rights, so diversion through these mill races infringed Keewatin Power's entitlement to natural flow. In response, the milling companies asserted limitations on the power company's privileges, claiming that their own grants incorporated full recognition of the water flows they had used for many years. Once again, the contending arguments led the courts back to a detailed review of land titles in the old "disputed territory" of northwestern Ontario and of the specific terms of negotiation related to the use of Keewatin shoreline properties. Justice David Inglis Grant interpreted the facts in a way that precluded Backus from restricting the water rights of the flour mill owners. The milling companies' rights under the original federal grants, concluded the judge, had been recognized by Ontario according to the spirit of the provisional agreement between the federal and provincial governments in 1874 – that is, before any grant of a water power was made to John Mather's Keewatin Lumbering and Manufacturing Company, from whom Keewatin Power later obtained it. Provincial authorities were always fully aware of the facts and demonstrated approval of the construction and use of the "mill-races" by the plans prepared by the departmental surveyors and by the references made to such mill races in the descriptions of lands conveyed by Crown grants.[70]

In the Court of Appeal, Keewatin Power reasserted its claim to exclusive use of Lake of the Woods water flowing through the natural outlets. Chief Justice Francis P. Latchford highlighted the stakes by remarking that if the appeal succeeded, "the vast area of the Lake of the Woods – some 1,500 square miles in extent ... would be the personal mill pond of Backus."[71] Latchford confirmed the result of the trial decision, albeit following a somewhat altered process of factual interpretation.[72]

The underlying arguments on both sides were essentially unmodified by their transatlantic passage to the Judicial Committee of the Privy Council in London.[73] Here, counsel for Keewatin Power put forth the view that no Dominion or provincial legislation enabled the Crown to make a grant that could impair the natural rights of lands that had not yet been granted. Otherwise stated, previous grants could not diminish the water power to which riparian owners might subsequently become entitled as a matter of common law. Thus, it was argued, the grantees of the patents upon which the flour millers relied were bound to keep the property in the state in which it was when they applied for the grants, so that the Keewatin Power Company, as subsequent riparian purchasers of the outlet, could use all of the water that naturally flowed through this channel.

In giving judgment, Viscount Dunedin declared Keewatin Power's principal argument to be "untenable" and "so extravagant as to be scarcely worth repeating." This was not even a "nice try." In the end, the positions of the Lake of the Woods Milling Company and the Keewatin Flour Mills Company were protected. The several owners of the neighbouring power sites were each entitled to use the waters of the Lake of the Woods, whether their locations benefited from natural or artificial outlets.

Dunedin perceptively summarized the nature of the private legal battle, which was finally resolved after fifteen years. No damage whatsoever had ever been done to Keewatin Power's water rights, but the plaintiffs nonetheless "conceived the idea of securing a monopoly to themselves of the whole of the water power of this enormous lake – an idea never entertained by the Crown ... when the whole arrangements were still to make."[74]

Despite this forceful judicial rebuke, acquisition and protection of water powers and the flow of water on which their continued operation depended was an enduring preoccupation for E.W. Backus and his enterprises, the principal pulp and paper producers in northwestern Ontario throughout the first third of the twentieth century. In his ambitions for the Lake of the Woods basin and the surrounding region, from its origins in northern Minnesota waters to White Dog Rapids near the Ontario-Manitoba border, Backus was the person most directly concerned with the watershed as a whole, albeit from the narrowly focused conception of economic utility.

While John Mather, and perhaps other early observers, regarded the water powers as a means to promote development of various resources and opportunities on a comprehensive basis and were therefore apprehensive about a potential monopoly, Backus viewed the water system primarily in terms of its adaptability to his own operations. This determination resulted in a complex and prolonged series of investigations and negotiations, which contributed to the new water management program. In one form or another, the quest for a regulated system of water storage and power production continued, eventually clashing with other interests along the Ontario-Minnesota boundary, where environmental interconnections were often at odds with political and jurisdictional divisions.

9

Economy and Ecology

The expanding popularity of angling and hunting, among other outdoor activities and pastimes, added new dimensions to natural resource management and foreshadowed the emerging importance of environmental values.[1] The Ontario-Minnesota border lakes area was no exception. Conflicts soon emerged between recreational users, hydroelectric power producers, and resource developers. For their part, Indigenous residents expressed increasing concern about access to fish and game as well as about impacts on other traditional land use and harvesting practices.

THE SUBSISTENCE ECONOMY

Aboriginal subsistence fishing had initially been exempted from the regulatory framework that emerged from an 1892 inquiry into Ontario fish and game.[2] In the face of mounting criticism from sportsmen and conservation interests, however, official attitudes changed. More restrictive enforcement efforts were soon directed at both the settler community and Indigenous harvesters. When competition arose among local and commercial fishing interests and the angling community, the Toronto Anglers Club petitioned Premier Howard Ferguson to address certain grievances. Taking aim at small-town and rural Ontario residents who enjoyed year-round access to fish and game resources, the Toronto contingent called for "a considerably larger showing of arrests for infringement of the laws amongst the local

FIGURE 9.1 Land Family, 1911. *Courtesy of the Lake of the Woods Museum.*

population," with the thought that "a livelier activity on the part of pro-
tective officers should effect very real benefits to the game fish waters."[3]

Ontario pursued prosecutions, notwithstanding legislation that appeared
to respect Aboriginal wildlife interests. Indigenous fishers were expected to
comply with licensing and conservation measures and also faced prosecution for fish and wildlife harvesting off-reserve.[4] As more provincial charges
were laid, federal Indian Affairs representatives provided limited though
diminishing support and occasionally sought special consideration for those
convicted.[5]

Grievances over restrictions on their access to traditional sources of
sustenance and the neglect of treaty provisions persisted following World
War I. Chief David Land of the Islington or White Dog community, for
example, lamented the lack of agricultural equipment and severe restrictions on hunting: "We are asking the government to be the same agreement
now as when the first treaty was made. That is all."[6] Similar expressions
of frustration and disillusionment became increasingly common. "The
white man Sweep off Every thing on which I should owned and I am kind
of afraid if I don't see what I can make my livings," one Treaty 3 resident
wrote to Indian Affairs.[7]

By the 1920s, federal officials attributed "deplorable" conditions around the Lake of the Woods to provincial interventions: "I have seen many Indians practically starving on the shore," J.H. Bury of Indian Affairs told his deputy minister, "whilst they watched white men fishing commercially in the bays, adjacent to their reserves, the Indians themselves being refused fishing licenses by Ontario, although quite willing to pay the license fee and purchase their nets and equipment."[8] Bury cited disheartening instances of interference by provincial game wardens who, in his opinion, acted without authority. In his estimation, the Indigenous population was "possibly facing today the worst conditions of living that they have ever experienced." In addition to hardships resulting from restrictions on hunting and fishing, the valuable blueberry crop had failed. Bury proposed financial and legal support from the federal government in the form of a test case in which the Dominion, as custodian of Indian rights, would seek to prevent the province from acting in contravention of the treaty. This would, in his opinion, allow Treaty 3 residents to "turn to the future with renewed hope and a conviction that treaties are inviolable documents, not susceptible to alteration or abrogation by parties who were not contributory signatories."[9] For its part, the Hudson's Bay Company explored potential legal defences on behalf of its fur suppliers. The HBC advanced arguments related to the constitutional status of its Indigenous trading partners and to the terms of its own Deed of Surrender but eventually accepted a political resolution that left underlying issues unresolved.[10]

From Fort Frances, Indian Agent Spencer reported the difficult circumstances of the 1930s. The Indigenous residents had no opportunity to support themselves "unless they are permitted to sell a few fish, as fishing and trapping is the only way they have of making a living." Yet provincial licences were difficult to obtain because "nearly all the lake is taken up with white fishermen and the Indians have no place to go." The implications were dire: some members of the community told Spencer that "if they could not sell a few fish to provide for their families, that they would have to go to Jail, because they could not see their families starve." He added a personal endorsement: "I think they are telling the truth in that respect."[11]

Ontario's determination to confine Indigenous harvesting activity to reserve lands persisted, with little apparent regard for troubling consequences. Another Indian Agent, Captain Frank Edwards, was disheartened that "Ottawa apparently has no idea how serious the matter is." Some had faced prosecution for simply travelling off-reserve with a piece of meat killed for food on reserve lands. Subsistence fishing, even "with twine given them by us under Treaty stipulations," had also resulted in fines and the seizure of boats and nets.[12]

In 1946, immediately following World War II, Treaty 3 representatives forwarded their views on fishing, hunting, and trapping rights to a Special Joint Committee of the Senate and the House of Commons, one of a continuing series of federal efforts to address Aboriginal concerns: "Our understanding ... was that we could hunt and fish without hindrance in the territory ceded by us. The Indians who signed the Treaty could not possibly anticipate any future Government regulations which would change this, as Game and Fish laws were unknown to our forefathers." The petitioners insisted that "the white man who arranged the treaty must have known something about Game and Fishery regulations even in those days of long ago," arguing that if the situation had been fully explained, either their ancestors would not have signed the treaty or it would have contained a "positive statement giving the Indians full right to hunt and fish without restrictions."[13] In an enduring expression of discontent, they insisted that "since we made the Treaty with the Government of Canada we believe we should not be forced to have any dealings with the Province of Ontario."[14]

Coincident with this petition to federal authorities, administrative reorganization in Ontario brought the provincial fish and wildlife service under the authority of the Department of Lands and Forests in 1946.[15] Fishing licences and trapline registration arrangements, including quotas, were soon introduced for Indigenous resources users. But if some measure of more regularized access was welcome, the transition from communal management to a more individualized form of operation also produced dislocation and disruption.[16]

Some communities also claimed exclusive access to wild rice, or *manomin*, not only a dietary staple but a sacred plant whose cultivation had been refined over generations.[17] Wild rice was vulnerable to untimely water level fluctuations associated with hydro-power operations. Both the Rollerway and Norman Dams had produced complaints to this effect dating back to the 1890s.[18]

Upstream on the English River, the Lac Seul community was also adversely affected in this respect and indeed suffered much wider flood damage to hay fields, gardens, residential sites, and trapping grounds. As early as 1915, Lac Seul representatives sought information regarding rumoured dam construction. Federal interventions did not prevent power development, but legislation, the 1928 *Lac Seul Conservation Act*, provided for compensation.[19] As reservoir levels rose behind the dam in the late 1930s, however, there were further delays in evaluating losses and delivering compensation.

FIGURE 9.2 Wild Rice, n.d. *Courtesy of the Mabel Silverman Collection, Lake of the Woods Museum.*

Canada, Ontario, and Manitoba eventually assessed damages globally at $100,000 for losses attributable to flooded lands and foregone timber revenues, as well as construction expenses to provide new homes for a number of families while individual claims were deferred.[20]

Across the broader region, flooding was considered in some circumstances to be an inevitable consequence of the statutory operations of the control board and thus not subject to compensation. But it was also acknowledged that to deny compensation in the case of flooding of Aboriginal lands would require "clear and plain indication" of intention.[21] Meanwhile, other interests were marshalling in response to the impacts of water power and resource development on the natural environment.

CONSERVATION AND PROTECTED AREAS

As governments and industry contemplated boundary water flows – whether "advantageous," "beneficial," "practicable," or "dependable," and increasingly with an eye on upstream storage – a more natural vision for those flows emerged in conservationist circles. Inspired by Minnesota forestry commissioner Christopher Andrews and with encouragement on the Ontario side from William Preston, who represented Rainy River in the provincial legislature, extensive tracts on both sides of the international boundary were set aside in 1909. When US president Theodore Roosevelt created the Superior National Forest, Ontario correspondingly established the Quetico Forest Reserve. The limited effectiveness of Ontario's forest reserve framework in safeguarding fish and particularly large game animals from overexploitation prompted the province to proclaim the area a provincial park four years later.[22] The wilderness status of the adjoining protected areas influenced subsequent development of the boundary waters and associated basin.

On the US side, proposals for road access into the Superior National Forest generated controversy during the early 1920s, prompting measures to safeguard a valuable recreational asset. As early as 1922, Arthur Carhart, a landscape architect and recreational planner working for the US Forest Service, envisaged conservation along the boundary region.[23] As Carhart succinctly explained, "there is a limit to the number of lakes in existence."[24] Thus, when Canada and the United States agreed, in 1925, to examine water level regulation for the Rainy Lake watershed, Backus's proposals to raise water levels in border lakes aroused opposition within the ranks of a growing constituency determined to protect scenic and natural values.[25]

Among the forceful wilderness advocates of the time was Aldo Leopold, to whom Carhart's message on the finite number of lakes had been addressed. Leopold – who later wrote *A Sand County Almanac*, a profoundly influential guide to environmentalism – was himself a gifted communicator in the interests of forest conservation and ecology. As he wrote in 1925: "An incredible number of complications and obstacles ... arise from the fact that the wilderness idea was born after, rather than before, the normal course of commercial development had begun." Leopold acknowledged that "the existence of these complications is nobody's fault," but he firmly declared that "it will be everybody's fault if they do not serve as a warning against delaying the immediate inauguration of a comprehensive system of wilderness areas."[26]

At the IJC hearings on Rainy Lake and upstream waters, it fell largely to a small group of conservationists to articulate an alternative to the transformation of the Rainy-Lake of the Woods waters into Backus's "personal mill pond," as his ambitions for water management had once been described. Ernest Carl Oberholtzer was prominent within that group and forceful in expressing the conservationist vision. He was a self-taught naturalist who had briefly studied landscape architecture at Harvard, before extensive wilderness travel in the border lakes in the early 1900s inspired him to take up residence on Rainy Lake and learn the Ojibwa language.[27]

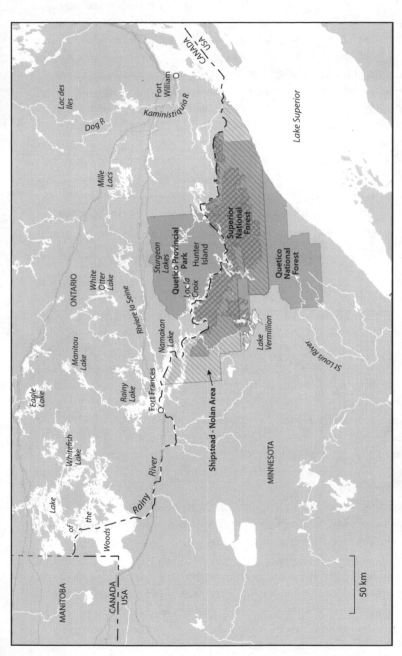

MAP 9.1 Quetico/Superior District. From Gerald Killan and George Warecki, "The Battle for Wilderness in Ontario: Saving Quetico-Superior, 1927–1960" in Patterns of the Past: Interpreting Ontario's History, ed. Roger Hall, William Westfall, and Laurel Sefton MacDowell (Toronto: Dundurn Press, 1988), 328–55. Map adapted by Eric Leinberger.

Oberholtzer envisaged a comprehensive watershed regime encompassing significant portions of Ontario, Minnesota, and Manitoba. Specifically, he forecast "that the lakeland corridor joining the north end of Rainy
Lake to the northern part of the Lake of the Woods at Kenora will be
included within the Quetico-Superior area or will at least have applied to
it the same principles." Oberholtzer was strengthened in his conviction
by proposals for a park in southeastern Manitoba that could help to extend
conservation-oriented management along a four-hundred-mile stretch of
forested lakeland.[28]

J.B. Challies, while serving with Canada's Commission of Conservation, and MP Frank Keefer had previously imagined elements of such
an arrangement, but the specific principles to which Oberholtzer referred
only crystallized later, during an international forestry conference held in
Duluth. Here, a body known as the Quetico-Superior Council promul-
gated general guidance for a treaty-based management framework along
the Ontario-Minnesota border. The framework was based on four key
principles, beginning with the proposal that "park-like conditions, free
from logging, flooding, draining, and all other forms of exploitation, be
established and maintained on all visible shores of lakes, rivers, and islands
under public control." Second, modern forest practices were to be applied
in adjacent areas not visible from the waterways, to ensure a maximum
timber supply. In addition, game, fish, and fur-bearing animals were to
be managed for "maximum natural protection." Finally, these objectives
were to be pursued under the supervision of an international board com-
prising forest, park, and wildlife officials from the two neighbouring
countries.[29] This innovative proposal was particularly significant for its
ambition to address the international character of the watershed through
the participation of land and water management officials from both sides
of the border.

Actual implementation was expected to "transcend both park and forest"
through a progressive zoning system ranging from an outer circumference
where private development would continue, through a narrow inner zone
managed by leaseholds, around "the innermost zone, [which] would be
kept undeveloped and free of all evidences of man."[30] In condensed form,
the proposal called for maximum sustained-yield forestry pursued alongside
wildlife conservation. These goals would be undertaken in association with
a program of shoreline reserves within a buffered wilderness zone, all to
be governed by a binational panel of professional administrators.[31]

Oberholtzer credited Arthur Hawkes, "a brilliant fellow," more explicitly
for practical direction and leadership in pursuing the vision along the

Ontario-Minnesota border.[32] Hawkes was a publicity agent for the Canadian National Railway when he travelled to St. Paul in 1908 to promote a conservation preserve that became the Superior National Forest and Quetico Provincial Park reserves. Two decades later, Hawkes was again instrumental in proposing a treaty between Canada and the United States to perpetuate the resources of the Rainy Lake watershed – economic, recreational, scientific, and historical.[33]

Oberholtzer himself then further promoted the transboundary watershed-based model: "Nature, the original conservationist," he began, "knew no political divisions or sign-posts when she created the Rainy Lake watershed and enveloped its thousands of lakes and streams in a forest of pine." Although the watershed lay in two countries, he noted, "its unity from every other point of view is striking." Common hydrology, geology, biology, and history were readily apparent. The lakes were "intimately connected" with those along the international boundary, dependent upon tributaries from both sides before finally converging in Rainy Lake. The landscape, wildlife, and vegetation were also similar in character throughout the basin. The region, he added with rhetorical exaggeration, "even celebrates the same history." The policy prescription flowed from this essential unity: "Whether looked at economically or from the higher social point of view the problem transcends political boundaries and calls for a comprehensive program applied to the whole watershed."[34]

Years ahead of the more generalized notion of peace parks involving transboundary protected areas as symbols of common interests and collaboration, the proposed initiative was referred to as "a work of peace."[35] At their 1929 annual conventions, both the Canadian and American Legions endorsed the suggestion that much of the Rainy Lake area be dedicated as a peace memorial to veterans from Canada and the United States who had fought together in World War I.[36]

In his insistence on a comprehensive progam, Oberholtzer anticipated substantive management policy integrated with organizational and institutional arrangements. Yet acknowledging common interests did not ensure agreement on the means of pursuing them. It proved easier over time to encourage adoption of complementary policies across the international border than to create overarching institutions, whether by treaty or otherwise.[37] Ontario, in particular, viewed a treaty-based solution as a threat to its authority over natural resources. Still, the province gradually took steps to align its conservation and land-use measures with US initiatives.[38]

As early as the initial years of the IJC's Rainy Lake study, which began in 1925, Ontario Lands and Forests Minister William Finlayson expressed sympathy for joint action and cooperation as far as possible. Examples of practical collaboration included, for example, the introduction in Ontario of shoreline reserves along several prominent border canoe routes to mirror the effect of US legislation that protected shorelines alongside federal lands in the boundary waters area.[39] Yet even while calling for "joint action," Finlayson rejected the Quetico-Superior Council's preference for an international treaty since it might entail the loss of administrative control over provincial natural resources.[40]

Arthur Hawkes's involvement was very much in keeping with the early twentieth century enthusiasm of Canadian railways for recreational passenger traffic, especially to their own highly fashionable wilderness resorts. Minaki Lodge and the CPR bungalow facilities at Devil's Gap contributed significantly to regional tourism. Fort Frances, accessible by rail from Duluth as of 1909, drew significant numbers of American vacationers to lodges and resorts on Rainy Lake and the southern stretches of the Lake of the Woods. Nestor Falls flourished in this era as well, with one particular establishment able to accommodate two hundred guests per week, many from Duluth, Minneapolis–St. Paul, or Chicago.[41] Quetico emerged more prominently as an alternative recreational destination, again most accessible from the US side although American vacationers continued to enjoy southerly access to regional attractions through Ely, Minnesota. With improved highway access from several directions, the tourism sector around the Lake of the Woods expanded before mid-century to reach about sixty commercial camps and resorts, all reliant to an important degree on the district's valuable aquatic amenities.[42]

THE RAINY LAKE REFERENCE

In conjunction with the signing of the Lake of the Woods Convention in February 1925, the governments of Canada and the United States shifted their attention upstream. The new Rainy Lake study derived directly from the 1917 IJC recommendation that, when warranted by demand for additional water power, storage or reservoir capacity might be increased on the upper Rainy watershed.[43]

The 1925 reference presented four questions, commencing with a request to determine whether the levels of Rainy and Namakan Lakes should be raised. If so, new levels were to be recommended, along with advice as to associated costs and an indication concerning what interests in Canada and the United States would benefit, as well as the nature of the benefit.

The governments next asked the IJC to describe feasible methods of control and operation. The final question invited an examination of Canadian and American interests currently benefited by storage on Rainy Lake and on the waters controlled by the dams at Kettle Falls, with a view to identifying how the costs of lake level changes should be apportioned.[44]

Preliminary hearings were held in International Falls from 28 to 30 September 1925 to gather general background information.[45] On behalf of the Minnesota and Ontario Paper Company, E.W. Backus renewed his long-standing call for a vast reservoir to the east of the Lake of the Woods. His plan called for new storage dams at Lac La Croix, Crooked Lake, and Saganaga Lake to raise the headwaters of the river by four feet.[46] Estimating costs at around $425,000, Backus urged that these should initially be covered by the two governments and then assessed against the power sites along the system from the upper lakes and downstream along the Rainy and Winnipeg Rivers.[47] Backus argued further that the IJC should assess and allocate development costs. He bolstered this rather "aggressive" proposal with his insistence that the economic well-being of the region rested essentially on the availability of the water power and his personal enterprise in capturing its benefits.[48]

In further explanation, Backus argued that "public and private advantage" had been conferred upon the industrial, civic, and transportation interests of Fort Frances and International Falls only because of available water power and raw materials used through the addition of capital and enterprise, which he had in large part contributed.[49] Further progress depended upon expansion of the water powers, a development that was in turn entirely contingent upon increased storage. He thus called upon the commission to endorse his plan to render the water power "uniformly dependable through proper storage and regulation."[50]

Backus denied that his proposal would harm the public interest. He dismissed past damage from flooding as an "act of God," going further to suggest that it was only thanks to the dams at Kettle Falls and Koochiching Falls that Rainy Lake levels had not risen even higher in the devastating spring floods of 1916.[51] In Backus's view, the disappearance of a few islands "would not be any loss" for the value of scenic beauty was merely "nominal."[52] While admitting that Lac La Croix, for example, might be beautiful, he asked: "What good does that do if only a hundred people a year can see it?"[53] He went on to predict that after new water levels were established, "you will have just as beautiful a lake as you had before."[54]

Arrayed against Backus, the sole proponent of expanded storage on the upper waters, were towns, municipal organizations, and conservation

groups. Those opposing alterations to lake levels were represented principally by E.C. Oberholtzer, who spoke for American landowners, especially
those from Ranier, Minnesota. Hugh J. McClearn participated on behalf
of the Minnesota Arrowhead Association, alongside George H. Selover
of the Izaak Walton League.[55] Manitoba delegates, reflecting an internal
consensus among provincial hydro interests, opposed Backus's recommendation "because they would have to contribute to the cost of these dams,
although the benefits they would receive would be very doubtful, because
the flow of water in the Winnipeg River might be interfered with."[56]

One of the US commissioners, Porter J. McCumber, a former senator
from North Dakota, struggled to understand "upon what theory the
government should be called in to make the development."[57] Backus
reasoned that navigational improvements would extend from Rainy Lake
to Lake Winnipeg, even though only a few steamers on the Lake of the
Woods plied these waters. Backus also pointed to the advantages of industrial development and higher taxes, advancing the proposition that the
governments involved should contribute financially in accordance with
those benefits. Under questioning, Backus confirmed, however, that his
companies had "not the faintest idea" of building the dams at their own
expense.[58]

Fort Frances feared that higher water levels on Rainy Lake would cause
flood damage to the municipal sewage system, as well as adverse impacts
on regional recreation. The Arrowhead Association, an organization devoted to Minnesota tourism, directly contradicted Backus: "There is no
money that can repay the American people for the desolation of these
beautiful shores."[59] On behalf of the Minnesota branch of the Izaak
Walton League, Selover asserted that the dams would destroy the country
"for all scenic and tourist purposes." Selover pleaded with the IJC to "help
preserve things as they are unless some overweening public necessity ab-
solutely demands their use."[60]

In October 1928, IJC engineers reported that field investigations were
nearing completion. They also advised, however, that further complex
studies were required to support their conclusions. This particular observation represented a vindication for Canada's earlier assertion that information was insufficient to proceed immediately with the Rainy Lake
arrangements.[61]

From an engineering standpoint, many of the proposed projects were
feasible, depending upon the ultimate purpose, financing, and regulation
of the dams and other works. The IJC engineers suggested "maintaining

a dependable flow of water from Lake of the Woods, a maximum flow over the Koochiching Falls dam, and a maximum dependable discharge from the boundary waters," with the exception that Saganaga and Northern Light Lakes should be regulated by dams on the Maligne River in Ontario, with a view to maximum dependable power development at Lac La Croix.[62] This would permit construction of hydro facilities and ancillary works at Upper and Lower Basswood Falls, Curtain Falls, Loon Lake, and Little Vermillion Narrows. Additional dams and canals would allow diversion from Lac La Croix waters to the international boundary.[63]

Oberholtzer and the other conservationists were stunned: the engineers had essentially endorsed "everything that Backus asked for."[64] However, they took comfort from the opinion of Stuart S. Scovill, a Canadian consulting engineer who questioned statements about the per-horsepower cost of the project. As the son of a pioneering Rat Portage doctor who had invested actively in early gold mining activity, Scovill brought deep regional roots to his assignment.

It was Scovill's view that development expenses figured prominently in any power plan and that the commissioners ought to give the actual costs "great weight in any final determination." He also suggested that some engineering opinion might have strayed beyond the commission's current authority, since arrangements for regulation of the Lake of the Woods and the flow of the Winnipeg River had been established by the 1925 treaty and "are not subject matter under the present reference."[65]

Scovill's cautionary remarks reinvigorated the conservationists, who enlisted engineering advice to examine the commission's survey. This initiative resulted in the gratifying conclusion that there was "no immediate need" to develop power from the northern boundary lakes. The engineers added helpfully that even if further power were needed, "it is obvious that most of the possibilities are not now economically sound if developed."[66]

When hearings resumed in Winnipeg, the manufacturers' proposals were prominent: "That various water levels be artificially raised, eliminating some waterfalls, increasing the flow of water in others and thus bringing into existence power sites at present of negligible importance."[67] Critics, however, responded vigorously to assert the adequacy of existing power supplies and to protest that raising water levels "would entirely spoil many natural beauties."[68]

Ontario and Manitoba were agreed that there was no immediate need for increased storage in Rainy and Namakan Lakes. The two provinces also shared the opinion that if upstream power was eventually developed, "neither province should be called upon to share in the cost," with Manitoba even asserting that "no interest in Manitoba should be assessed any portion of the cost of such work."[69]

Manitoba denied "any possible advantage from increasing storage facilities of Rainy and Namakan lakes," either to itself or to power companies operating within it. The province, accordingly, saw no reason to contribute to the costs of storing boundary waters in the Rainy Lake district. Moreover, Manitoba had already invested in storage arrangements along the English River and Lac Seul. As these storage facilities were located entirely within Canada, no international complications were anticipated.[70]

Ontario rejected expanded storage along upper boundary waters on the grounds that only existing power interests would benefit from proposed development that would effectively transfer twenty-two thousand horsepower from within the province to international channels.[71] On behalf of Canada's Department of External Affairs, J.E. Read, a talented government lawyer with an eye on similar issues affecting the Great Lakes, emphasized Ontario's primary jurisdiction over domestic water power rights. Only where boundary waters might be affected by provincial decision making should matters proceed to the IJC for assessment and recommendation.[72]

Declining pulpwood prices and intensified competition in a contracting market had helped to put Backus's pulp operations, along with Abitibi, another major northern producer, into receivership by 1932.[73] As participants in the hearings, the receivers for the Minnesota and Ontario Paper Company were prepared to forego further increases in the levels of Rainy and Namakan Lakes, while calling for a power and navigation dam at the head of Little Vermillion Lake. With a crest of 1,158 feet, the new regulation would make Loon River navigable. This proposal called for clearing some twelve hundred acres along the Loon River, land described as barren, burned-over, rocky terrain. Additional dam construction was proposed with a crest elevation of 1,186 feet on Lac La Croix with the objective of maintaining the levels of Lac La Croix at about ordinary high-water mark during the navigation season. Without advocating them, the receivers mentioned a second group of projects at Basswood, Saganaga, Northern Light, and Crooked Lakes.[74]

As hearings reconvened in Minneapolis, the receivers presented a revised plan that proposed fewer dams whose construction would be financed by industry rather than by the US and Canadian governments.[75]

Representatives of the Minnesota state government, communities, and organizations within northern Minnesota and of state and national conservation and patriotic groups also appeared at the hearings.[76] The essence of criticism from these quarters, as reported by the *Winnipeg Free Press*, was that "the value of the boundary lakes region as a [wilderness] playground, bringing in thousands of visitors who spend millions of dollars annually, far exceeds the value of any water power and industry that could be developed by the building of dams that would raise the lake levels and thus lessen their scenic beauty."[77] Challenging the storage and power development plan directly on economic grounds was a bold move, especially in a time of economic depression and when methodologies for valuing the natural environment were rudimentary at best. Not only were the intrinsic and aesthetic values of nature difficult to quantify in comparison with projections for actual use, exploitation, and development, but recreational activity was hardly flourishing in the mid-1930s.[78] Nevertheless, the conservationist community seemed confident that employment and expenditure records for recreational activity would support their calculations. Witnesses asserted unanimously that dams on Lac La Croix, Saganaga Lake, and other lakes east of Rainy Lake would produce water levels certain to "damage if not ruin the shores of the lakes and thus detract from the beauty and the wilderness isolation that draws tourists from all parts of the country."[79]

On behalf of Minnesota and state departments of conservation, drainage, forestry, and tourist promotion, Matthias N. Orfield, assistant attorney general, spoke against the dam-building proposal.[80] Orfield set out two key objections. First, the proposed dams would unquestionably raise lake levels, contrary to Minnesota's established policy against any permanent increases. Indeed, Minnesota's position reinforced pioneering US wilderness legislation, the Shipstead-Nolan Act of 1930, which had already established shoreline reserves on boundary waters.[81] Second, Orfield pointed to the inadequacy of estimates submitted by plan proponents, which failed to include compensation payments to owners of land and forest properties who would suffer damages from elevated water levels.[82] The Minnesota spokesman also noted that the state owned extensive woodlands around the lakes.[83]

As Backus had done earlier, the receivers responded to conservationists by asserting that the proposed dams "would not harm the border lakes, but on the contrary would make them even finer for recreation and as wild lake sanctuaries by maintaining an orderly in and out flow of water."[84] Joseph P. Meyer, engineer for the receivers, added that the paper company's need for more water power was already acute, as the use of high-cost coal to generate steam power at the two plants "threatens to force their permanent shutdown." He explained that these plants, given their partial dependence

on coal, were at a competitive disadvantage to other facilities that had all
the water power they needed. He suggested that steam power costs of $43
per horsepower of energy a year could be eliminated with hydroelectric
power at or below $20.[85]

Witnesses representing the local governments of International Falls and
Koochiching County, the workers of the Minnesota and Ontario plants,
and other industries in International Falls and Fort Frances supported the
proposed dam-building. They drew particular attention to employment
levels at the paper mills at International Falls, Fort Frances, and Kenora,
suggesting that "more than 3,300 persons of the border district are dependent on the mills and allied industries for their livings."[86] J.J. Hadler, representing Koochiching County, pointedly declared that "these people have the
right to work and earn livings, if people from other regions have the right
to come to the border and play."[87]

In its final report on Rainy Lake, submitted in May 1934, the IJC acknowledged conservationist claims about the incalculable value of the
boundary wilderness.[88] The commission referred to the waters subject to
the reference as "of matchless scenic beauty and of inestimable value from
the recreational and tourist viewpoints" and expressed great sympathy
for those who urged "that nothing should be done that might mar the
beauty or disturb the wild life of this last great wilderness." The conservationist position was largely vindicated in the commission's conclusion "that
it is impossible to over-state the recreational and tourist value of this
matchless playground. Its natural forests, lakes, rivers and waterfalls have
a beauty and appeal beyond description, and nothing should be done to
destroy their charm."[89]

However, community expectations as to continuing operations and
employment opportunities needed to be taken into account. Works for
the production of pulp and paper, among other commodities, had been
established at International Falls and Fort Frances on the basis of considerable investment: "Towns have been built at these points and large sums
of money expended for public utilities and other purposes. Workmen have
built their homes and their future livelihood and happiness depend upon
the continued existence of these works." With this in mind, the commission advised, it was "of the utmost importance that nothing should be
done that would militate against their continued operation on a firm and
sound economic basis."[90]

In the circumstances, deferral represented the most appropriate pathway
to reconciliation. So, while it was neither necessary nor desirable to construct new power works at the time of the report, the commission chose

"to leave the way open for the approval of a reasonable development of storage facilities upon the waters above Namakan Lake if and when economic and other conditions appear to warrant." When eventually undertaken, the new improvements should be carried out so as "to in no way interfere with the vast arc tributary to the headwaters of the water system in question, and to be constructed under such conditions and supervision as to adequately safeguard recreational interests."[91]

The Great Depression strongly influenced the results of the IJC's final report. By 1934, Backus's dream was no longer feasible because of the decline of his pulp and paper business among other setbacks. In the late 1920s, in anticipation of a more profitable outlook, Backus borrowed $5 million to finance expanded operations at the Minnesota and Ontario Paper Company. Even this sum proved insufficient to cover the company's financial obligations. When Backus sought to alleviate financial pressure by shifting funds between subsidiary corporations, the business was further weakened. By the time the final report was released, the company could no longer expand as Backus had once envisaged.[92] Indeed, the Backus mills did not emerge from receivership until 1941, by which time the company's forest concessions had been trimmed back – significantly, in the case of the English River holding.[93]

The IJC specifically addressed each of the four questions previously referred to it, reporting in answer to the first that it was not currently desirable to increase the level of Rainy Lake or Namakan Lake. Conditions applicable to a proposal for increases could be formulated in response to some concrete future application.[94] Having rejected any immediate increase, it was unnecessary to recommend lake levels or to discuss the associated costs or benefits. Nevertheless, arrangements to control levels in exceptional circumstances should be considered. Accordingly, the commission suggested that it would be "wise and in the public interest" for it to "be clothed with power to determine when unusual or extraordinary conditions exist throughout the watershed, whether by reason of high or low water." And, given such a determination, the commission further sought authority "to adopt such measures of control as to it may seem proper with respect to existing dams at Kettle Falls and International Falls, as well as any future dams or works." However, in the existing circumstances, no attempt to determine feasible methods of control and operation should be pursued.[95]

The final issue assigned to the commission called for discussion of any interests that benefited from Rainy Lake and upstream storage and the allocation of the costs of any changes to lake levels among those interests.

In response, the final report firmly concluded: "No interests on either side of the boundary are benefited by the present storage on Rainy Lake or on the waters controlled by the dams at Kettle Falls, other than and except the interests by which the dams and works providing for such storage and control were constructed and are owned and operated."[96] It was thus unnecessary to consider a formula for apportioning costs more widely as Backus had long advocated.

Another four years passed before the signing of the Rainy Lake convention between Canada and the United States on 15 September 1938, with a further two years required for completion of ratification and proclamation procedures. By agreement, the IJC was empowered to regulate the water level of the Rainy Lake watershed in emergency conditions as determined by the commission itself "whether by reason of high or low water." Upon such a determination, the commission could implement "such measures of control as to it may seem proper with respect to existing dams at Kettle Falls and International Falls, as well as with respect to any existing or future dams or works in boundary waters of the Rainy Lake watershed."[97] The International Rainy Lake Board of Control was established in 1941.

In accordance with the new arrangements and following public hearings and engineering analysis, the IJC issued an order on 8 June 1949 requiring that water levels in Rainy Lake be kept, as much as possible, between prescribed elevations on particular dates of the year to avoid "emergency conditions." The commission also ordered the relevant private interests to operate the International Falls Dam so as to maintain Rainy Lake and Namakan Lake at prescribed elevations.[98] As described by the IJC, the objective was "to prevent the occurrence of both extremely high and extremely low levels, and restrict lake fluctuations to a prescribed range, insofar as possible."[99] This order was later amended to direct the companies to operate their discharge facilities at Kettle Falls to keep the level of the lakes between a specific maximum and minimum elevation on particular dates, as authorized by the International Rainy Lake Board of Control.[100]

The orderly administrative process that finally appeared to have resolved a prolonged struggle between industrial water use and wilderness advocates belied a difficult controversy lingering in the aftermath of Treaty 3 and the allocation of Indian reserves. The Lac La Croix Reserve on Quetico's western extremity had absorbed several families from the Sturgeon Lake Reserve in the park's interior when local food supplies failed. The Sturgeon Lake community – whose members travelled extensively during traditional hunting, fishing, and harvesting cycles – found their Reserve 24C cancelled in 1915 on the basis of federal and provincial government decisions suggesting

– wrongly – that it had been abandoned. In fact, remaining residents of Sturgeon Lake ultimately left the park in the 1930s, following years of persistent friction around provincial parks regulation.[101]

MANAGING QUETICO-SUPERIOR

From the time Backus actively began his quest for comprehensive regulatory control of the Rainy-Lake of the Woods water flows early in the twentieth century to the IJC's initial order governing Rainy Lake levels, a half century had elapsed. Yet the landmark accomplishment of the Rainy Lake convention by no means ended negotiations. In May 1951, the cabinet of Prime Minister St. Laurent considered an American proposal for further IJC consultations. After the extensive flood on the Lake of the Woods in the spring of 1950, the US government was calling for a full investigation into the methods of regulation of the lake and its watershed. During deliberations, Canada's secretary of state for External Affairs, Lester B. Pearson, who would see the Rainy-Lake of the Woods file again as prime minister, explained the strategic considerations. The fact that regulatory arrangements under the 1925 and 1938 conventions were "reasonably satisfactory" from a Canadian perspective did not prevent the United States from pursuing the inquiry on a unilateral basis with terms that might be prejudicial to Canadian interests. Accordingly, relevant departments in Ottawa drafted revised terms for a possible further joint reference.[102]

On the American side, the appointment of Chester S. Wilson as Minnesota's commissioner of conservation in 1943 and the work of H.H. Chapman, of the Yale School of Forestry, encouraged reconsideration of the comprehensive Quetico-Superior approach with its aspirations towards an international treaty. From a states' rights perspective, Wilson was apprehensive about increased federal ownership and control of natural resources in a manner broadly consistent with long-standing Ontario concerns.[103] Chapman, for his part, highlighted the distinction between reasonable progress towards wilderness protection and the unlikely prospects of a treaty with widespread application along the entire Rainy system.[104]

Shortly after World War II, Chester Wilson, who was now also chair of Minnesota's Water Pollution Control Commission, visited Ontario to promote acceptance of a more limited vision for safeguarding the Quetico-Superior area. In meetings at Port Arthur, Fort Frances, and Kenora, he reassuringly endorsed a highway north of Quetico linking Port Arthur

with Atikokan and Fort Frances; it would connect with the Heenan Highway between Kenora and Fort Frances that had opened in 1936. Regional
awareness of the commercial potential of the northern Ontario and
Minnesota recreational sector increased significantly in the postwar era,
despite historically low levels of Canadian visitorship to Quetico.[105] The
completion of the highway from Port Arthur in 1954, along with systematic promotional efforts, enhanced appreciation of remarkable attractions
such as Rushing River Provincial Park, opened in 1958, as did a broader
understanding of the multiple contributions of northern woodlands. In
this respect, Ontario's Royal Commission on Forestry, chaired by Howard
Kennedy, was also influential.

The Kennedy report underlined limitations in "the narrow concept of
forestry" – that is, a perspective oriented around growing trees and extract-
ing wood products. Other opportunities for contributions such as controlling stream flow, preventing floods, and providing wildlife habitat were
being lost. For emphasis, Kennedy added that habitat protection "is basic
to the recreational values of our countryside and, if neglected, tourist enterprises which are potentially so valuable to Ontario will never reach their
optimum development."[106] This more comprehensive appreciation of the
environmental and social contributions of forest lands represented an
important step in the evolution in public and political understanding.

The International Sportsmen's Show, a new feature on postwar Ontario's exhibition circuit, launched its third iteration in Toronto in March
1951. The event, sponsored in part by the fourteen hundred members of
the Northern Ontario Outfitters' Association, drew prospective customers
from the urban confines of the Ontario capital. As for the observations
of northern exhibitors, their distinctive perspective was summed up in
the magazine *Saturday Night*: "When a citizen of Northern Ontario visits
Toronto, he gapes at the city's harassed residents folded into streetcars
like sausages into a carton and at the glue-like flow of bumper to bumper
auto traffic." Such conditions were largely beyond the imagination of
northern residents, who took for granted roaming space and "room to live
and breathe and raise a family."[107]

Nevertheless, the efforts of US conservation interests to advance an
international treaty model for wilderness protection were not well received
in Ontario.[108] Indeed, a draft "Treaty for the Establishment of an
International Forest in the Quetico-Superior Area," developed by the US
State Department on the basis of an initial formulation by Oberholtzer,
reached the desk of Ontario premier Leslie Frost in 1949. Reference to
joint management under the direction of a six-member advisory committee

appointed by the two national governments, combined with strong apprehension expressed by the Northwestern Ontario Associated Chambers of Commerce and the Northern Ontario Outfitters' Association, condemned the proposal.

Although joint management of the Quetico-Superior region was unattainable, there were at least welcome, if preliminary, signals that coordination in some form offered shared advantages. An exchange of diplomatic letters in 1960 secured the foundations of cross-border communication concerning wilderness protection of Quetico Park and the Boundary Waters Canoe Area of Minnesota's Superior National Forest, although the substantive challenges posed by the ambitions of forest and power developers were not finally resolved.

Following the extended sequence of conflicts and controversies over the regulation of water levels and flows, and the closely associated contest concerning the delineation and protection of the Quetico and Boundary Waters reserves, mid-century attention shifted more directly to emerging concerns centred on urban and industrial impacts on water quality.

10

We Are All in This Together

Regulation of flows and levels dominated debate over water management across the Rainy-Lake of the Woods basin during the first half of the twentieth century, but additional concerns respecting water quality were also beginning to emerge. Although less visibly transformational than interventions associated with power dams, water quality impacts from resource, industrial, and municipal activity also represented significant alteration of the natural system. After mid-century, more systematic efforts were made to address these impacts in the interests of public health, aquatic life, and general environmental conditions, particularly as these affected recreational users.

IRON MINING, PULP MILLS, AND SEWAGE

In 1920, MP Frank Keefer addressed Parliament enthusiastically on the importance of iron mining in Canada.[1] Although he made no direct reference to Atikokan, Keefer had in mind a promising iron-bearing formation in the vicinity of Steep Rock Lake, north of Quetico.[2] But, as winter drilling from the ice above the lake confirmed in 1938, the major ore bodies lay beneath the lake itself, and the best means of reaching the deposit was highly unconventional: draining or "dewatering" Steep Rock Lake. This massive undertaking required construction of canals, spillways, and other control works that effectively relocated an eight-mile stretch of the Seine River to the West Arm of Steep Rock Lake. A dam then separated the West

Arm from the portion of the lake covering the ore. High-volume pumps capable of moving 300,000 gallons per minute extracted much of the water above the ore and were then used in combination with high pressure jets to remove the overburden, which was pumped to the West Arm.[3]

These unprecedented interventions – draining the lake, diversion, and flooding – required clear authorization. With reference to Canada's *War Measures Act,* cabinet declared that development of the iron deposits was "advantageous to Canada as a protection against the possible shortage of ore to meet war requirements." Accordingly, diversion was deemed "necessary or advisable for the security, defence, peace, order and welfare of Canada." To accelerate decision making, regular procedural requirements were suspended or streamlined.[4] Further preparations, pursuant to the instructions of fisheries officials, involved fishing out Finlayson and Steep Rock Lakes prior to draining. Thus, four crews using 142 nets caught enough fish to fill dozens of hundred-pound boxes for daily shipment to Montreal during the 1943 season.[5]

With further encouragement in the form of the 1943 *Steep Rock Iron Ore Development Act* and extensive US financial support facilitated by Cyrus Eaton, production began. As *Life* magazine reported to its North American readership: "Once a wilderness lake, now the Steep Rock mine is busily producing ore."[6] With open pit operations supplemented by underground mining, annual ore production – overwhelmingly destined for the United States – reached about 3 million tons in the early 1950s, while the 1943 Atikokan population of some three hundred people had multiplied tenfold.[7] Steep Rock involved more dredging and earth moving than any previous Canadian development.[8] In 1949, Inland Steel of Chicago leased rights to explore and develop neighbouring opportunities.[9] Prospects were such that as new investors entered the area, some observers anticipated enormous returns.[10]

As these welcome production accomplishments were celebrated, less public consideration was given to environmental impacts. Mining activity and the reconfiguration of regulatory arrangements previously put in place by Ontario-Minnesota Pulp and Paper (O&M) to produce power at Moose Lake, Calm Lake, and Sturgeon Falls profoundly altered the Seine River system, including Marmion Lake. Between 1942 and the early 1950s, again with further legislative authorization, the Moose Lake power station was closed down, Ontario Hydro assumed responsibility for a series of new control structures, and the entire outflow from Marmion Lake, part of which became a silt basin, was diverted around Steep Rock Lake to rejoin the Seine River downstream.[11]

Steep Rock Iron Mine (Showing Lake Drained)
Nr. Atikokan Ont.

FIGURE 10.1   Steep Rock Iron Mine, n.d. *Courtesy of Thunder Bay Historical Museum Society.*

High levels of turbidity attributable to clay in the overburden accompanied the economic success of the new venture. Given the colloidal size of the particles, turbidity persisted as the Seine River carried it through Steep Rock Lake. By 1950, turbidity was evident in Seine Bay of Rainy Lake. By the following year, evidence of the disruptive impact had reached Fort Frances and International Falls, at the entrance of the Rainy River. Both communities expressed considerable resentment, with Fort Frances officials particularly alarmed by silt only a mile from town that was destroying the feeding grounds of fish and discolouring water used by the paper mill.[12] Governor Youngdahl of Minnesota called for intervention on the part of the IJC.[13]

In 1951, the Canadian Department of National Health and Welfare studied the effects of Steep Rock Iron Mines on Rainy Lake. After this investigation, "lagooning of wastes from stripping operations was effective to the extent that no further complaints of discoloration were received."[14] The situation was sufficiently problematic, however, that Ontario officials identified the colloidal matter transported from Steep Rock operations to the Rainy River and the sulphur dioxide (SO_2) emissions from Sudbury nickel smelters as the only two pollution challenges from the mining sector that called for immediate remedial attention.[15]

In response, Steep Rock Iron Mines extended the Seine River diversion in order to bypass the West Arm of Steep Rock Lake entirely. This work, actually projected by mining officials as part of the overall development plan but intended for a later date, was accelerated to address the excessive turbidity. The diversion opened in May 1952.[16] Subsequent aerial and water-based surveillance revealed significant scouring of the bottom of the Seine River. The company had anticipated the need for remedial measures but was clearly hoping that the situation might stabilize before further expenditures became necessary. Meanwhile, turbidity intensified in Rainy Lake itself, particularly near the centre of the lake.[17]

Other matters – postwar droughts and Hurricane Hazel, together with water supply and control challenges in southern Ontario – engaged public attention in the early 1950s, leading to the creation of the Ontario Water Resources Commission (OWRC).[18] After 1956, the commission's mandate encompassed the entire province, so when northwestern Ontario mayors convened for public hearings at Port Arthur in September of that year, Steep Rock was high on the agenda of local concerns about municipal water supply and pollution.[19]

Kenora, drawing its water from the Lake of the Woods, foresaw no future supply shortages. However, Mayor Fregeau drew attention to risks associated with acute pollution from upstream mining. The town's written brief elaborated the sources of apprehension that had begun to loom on the far horizon: "The question of pollution of this supply ... is one which may in the future cause some concern although presently the expanse of this lake and the virtual lack of populated areas for some sixty miles or more seems to ensure a reasonably pure water supply." To eliminate all doubt, Kenora confirmed that developments around Atikokan were the source of its concerns. The town called for "every precaution" in order "to ensure that the industrial wastes discharged into these upper streams should be controlled so as to eliminate the possibility of pollution either by way of discoloration or any other means."[20]

Fort Frances officials also attributed contamination of the lower Rainy River to Steep Rock iron mining, with conditions expected to worsen as mining activity expanded. Rainy River municipal representatives complained of deterioration in local fishing but specifically blamed pulp mill operations at Fort Frances and International Falls. The Lake of the Woods and Rainy River Anti-pollution Association, a citizens' organization formed to protest the decline in water quality, took legal action against International Falls for discharging raw sewage and against Ontario-Minnesota Pulp and Paper for dumping sulphite and mill refuse. International Falls responded with plans for an $800,000 sewage disposal facility, while the company proposed to reduce bark and sulphite dumping. The legal proceedings in 1953 were, in fact, only one round in escalating concern dating from at least 1948, when industry agreed to address pollution from fibrous materials discharged by groundwood plants. When further proposals offered in response to the litigation again proved inadequate to address chemical contamination alongside the discharge of solids, the water quality conflict escalated.[21]

Of equal concern to the communities were fluctuations in water levels, a subject also introduced during the OWRC's northwestern Ontario hearings when a spokesperson for Rainy River expressed the opinion "that varying water levels were to a large extent responsible for the disappearance of wild rice and other plants which support fish and ducks." A representative of O&M "could not recall any dead fish in the last two years" and advised that neither sulphite nor kraftwood were entering the river from the Canadian plant. The company, he insisted, was "doing everything we know how to do."[22]

What the pulp and paper industry knew how to do and what it was actually doing to alleviate water pollution was of great interest. Litigation elsewhere in Ontario against a major polluter on the Spanish River brought the matter to prominence, culminating in legislation to dissolve a court injunction that threatened to curtail mill operations.[23] A more general provincial statute then seemed to afford the industry considerable leeway, if not outright immunity, on the pollution front. The 1949 enactment authorized a court to refuse to issue an injunction when "the importance of the operation of the mill to the locality in which it operates and the benefit and advantage, direct and consequential, which the operation of the mill confers on the locality and the inhabitants of the locality" outweighed "private injury, damage or interference."[24]

Nevertheless, departmental mandates increasingly encompassed pollution concerns with varying degrees of effectiveness. The Department of Lands and Forests added a chemical engineer specialized in pollution matters to its summer staff in 1946 and, with over twenty mills operating across the province, made the position permanent at the end of the decade.[25] An interdepartmental Pollution Control Board, formed in 1952, initiated annual conferences on industrial waste that were subsequently sponsored by the OWRC. The extensive pulp and paper sector certainly came under scrutiny, but fledgling environmental agencies in Ontario preferred to encourage water quality improvements through general guidance rather than formal requirements, and by means of collaborative efforts rather than prosecutorial coercion.[26]

By 1963, seven major pulp mills, fifteen paper mills, and nineteen integrated facilities were operating across Ontario, producing about 3.2 million tons of pulp, paper, and paper products. In achieving this impressive output, the industry's daily water usage exceeded 280 million gallons, roughly equivalent in terms of biochemical oxygen demand to the sewage of 6.65 million people. Underscoring this observation, officials noted that "the total wastes from the industry exert an oxygen-consuming effect on the receiving waters, greater than would be expected from the untreated sanitary sewage from all municipal and residential sources in the Province."[27] Government engineers noted the potential impact of settleable solids, such as bark and fibre, and pulping wastes known to be toxic to aquatic life, both of which were often "equally as important in a consideration of pollution control."[28]

Environmental concerns in northwestern Ontario (in addition to Port Arthur, Fort William, and Marathon) centred on the kraft pulp and paper mill at Dryden and the Ontario-Minnesota plants at Fort Frances and Kenora.[29] At Fort Frances, where paper production ran around 315 tons per day, bark was recovered for burning, while devices known as "save-alls" captured additional waste. There was no chemical pulping at the Rainy River site. In Kenora, where the operation produced 710 tons of newsprint on a daily basis, bark was screened out for burning, but no attempt was made to recover sulphite liquor, which entered the river "without treatment."[30]

The remedial program contemplated process improvements to reduce waste volumes – notably bark – at the outset of production. Primary treatment procedures were then required to remove remaining solids. Settling basins or lagoons would sometimes be sufficient for this purpose, but larger facilities might require mechanical equipment such as clarifiers. Finally, but over an extended period of time, the OWRC officials called for secondary treatment to be implemented alongside continuing developments in chemical pulping processes.[31] Observers of regulatory oversight would have understood the commission to be proceeding on the basis of objectives or goals rather than clearly formulated and enforceable performance standards.

At Kenora, newsprint production doubled from 105,000 tons in 1950 to 215,000 in 1960. Annual production peaked at around 262,000 tons in 1970, declining modestly by 1980 to 230,000. At Dryden, kraft pulp production increased from 30,000 tons in 1950 to 118,000 in 1970, reaching a high of 195,000 tons in 1980. Other paper production from Dryden was generally level between 1960 and 1980, ranging from 50,000 to 64,000 tons. At Fort Frances, newsprint production declined from about 80,000 tons in 1950, to be replaced by a growing emphasis on kraft paper and other paper products, amounting to 161,000 tons and 195,000 tons, respectively, in 1980.[32]

New construction or refurbishment of mills at Kenora, Fort Frances, and Dryden increased efficiency and capacity but simultaneously accentuated water quality concerns.[33] Those concerns and persistent apprehension about other sources of municipal and industrial contamination, however, were not easily transformed into remedial action and expenditure.

Despite its early criticism of environmental threats from mining around Atikokan, the town of Kenora continued to discharge raw sewage into Laurenson's Creek, the Winnipeg River, and the Lake of the Woods below the municipality's own water intake. A proposal for sewage treatment, beginning with interceptor sewers and eventually involving primary treatment, had been prepared, although the estimated financial burden was "extremely heavy." Kenora's concern about "tremendous" levels of algae in the fall prompted suggestions that experiments with similar situations elsewhere might offer guidance on appropriate treatment arrangements. Fort Frances, where chlorination had been implemented following extended controversy early in the century, expressed apprehension about the lack of sewage treatment for the expanding summer resort sector along the Rainy River. Nevertheless, Fort Frances, like Kenora, was disinclined to treat its own sewage because of substantial costs and the belief that the town's contribution to contamination was modest in comparison with impacts from industrial waste. For its part, the OWRC emphasized the responsibility of local governments for sewage and water supply and sought to cajole some of the less forward-looking communities to obtain professional advice on their requirements.[34]

Cleaning Up Boundary Waters

Alongside any industrial and municipal initiatives, the early stages of international response to the long-standing pollution situation in the Rainy Lake and boundary waters region were underway. These corresponded roughly to arrangements encouraged by the IJC, in its landmark 1918 final report, *On the Pollution of Boundary Waters Reference*, when attention had been directed primarily towards the water quality situation in the Great Lakes.[35]

In April 1954, the American embassy communicated with Lester B. Pearson, Canadian secretary of state for External Affairs, to propose a joint IJC reference on Rainy River pollution. Ottawa consulted Ontario, then in the process of establishing the OWRC and not in a position to reply immediately. Following a reaffirmation of US interest in a broadened pollution reference that included the Lake of the Woods, Ontario premier Leslie Frost indicated that his government would welcome such an inquiry. Frost suggested that the study "should extend to pollution rising on both sides of the International Boundary, including that caused by industrial waste."[36]

In the early years of Diefenbaker's Conservative administration, Canada confirmed its agreement in principle to the proposed reference, including, to echo Premier Frost, "that caused by industrial waste."[37] Almost eighteen months later, the Canadian and American governments asked the IJC to consider four questions. The first, with reference to transboundary pollution as mentioned in the *Boundary Waters Treaty*, was whether the waters of the Rainy River and Lake of the Woods were "polluted on either side of the boundary to the injury of health or property on the other side." Second, some discussion of the extent and causes of such pollution was requested. Third, the two governments called for an inquiry into remedial measures. Finally, the commission was invited to consider in more detail the construction of and financial responsibility for "remedial or preventive works ... necessary to render the waters sanitary and suitable for domestic and other uses."[38] This was, in essence, an increasingly familiar formula: Is there a problem? If so, why? What should we do about it? And who should pay?

Alongside growing awareness of pulp and paper industry impacts, the specific genesis of this IJC investigation was a long-standing concern that the waters of Rainy Lake, Rainy River, and perhaps the Lake of the Woods were increasingly vulnerable to pollution from mining, forestry, agricultural, and recreational activity. As of October 1959, a technical advisory body was in place to assemble data and to oversee field research. By the time this advisory body reported in 1963, earlier concerns surrounding the health impacts of human sewage and bacteria had indeed been joined on the agenda by issues arising from industrial development. Industrial wastes, of secondary consideration from a health perspective to sewage, had deleterious impacts on the physical and chemical properties of water and on its aesthetic qualities and, accordingly, impaired domestic, recreational, and other industrial uses. The IJC, in its 1963 report, stated that "these problems are further aggravated in this area by the demand of large sections of population of both countries for the preservation of these extensive recreational resources."[39]

The mid-century study was inspired by previous transboundary pollution surveys dating back to the IJC's pioneering 1918 report on bacteriological pollution.[40] This investigation of the quality of boundary waters had been "the first serious attempt to establish the extent of pollution in these waters over an extensive area from the St. Lawrence to the Rainy River."[41] But there was other, more recent, research upon which to build.

During the summer months of 1937, Ontario and Minnesota government officials collaborated on a transboundary investigation of stream pollution affecting the Rainy Lake and Lake of the Woods region. Samples were analyzed at a Fort Frances laboratory "to determine to what extent the quality of the water in the river was injured by discharges of sewage and industrial wastes."[42] In the same era, studies carried out for Canada's Department of Mines and Resources indicated that "Rainy River is soft to very soft with an intensity of colour of 40 to 45 parts per million; Wabigoon River, medium hard, with colour from 20 to 40 parts per million; Lake of the Woods, soft to medium hard, with 20 to 40 parts per million colour intensity."[43] The implications of these distinctive characteristics from a pollution perspective remained to be determined.

Minnesota, in 1954, announced "a comprehensive water pollution control program" for the Rainy River Basin. This was based on state and US federal data collected from investigations of the American portions of the boundary waters.[44] The Minnesota program identified paper company operations at International Falls and Fort Frances as the most significant pollution sources. The downstream impact was such that "the water is unsatisfactory for public water supply, commercial and sports fishing, and other recreational use." Wood fibre and solids discharged from the pulp and paper mills were subsequently deposited along the entire downstream portion of the Rainy River, interfering with recreational usage and aesthetic values. It was also thought, though not definitively established, that "fibre and wood solids deposits are harmful to the spawning effectiveness of fish and to the quality of fish food in those areas where the bottom is covered." This 1954 Minnesota initiative underscored the shared nature of regional waters when it reported further that eleven of the thirteen municipalities on the US side had some arrangements for waste treatment, while on the Canadian side, Fort Frances provided no treatment and Rainy River only partially treated municipal wastes.[45]

Although some waste treatment facilities had been constructed, the IJC Advisory Board emphasized that "continuing efforts will be required to insure that these waters will be maintained in a satisfactory state for the use of the people of both nations."[46] The Advisory Board underscored the importance of clean water by noting the "considerable number of people interested in fishing and boating" who spent nearly half a million dollars in the area each year.[47] As the Rainy River commission eventually noted, "the cost is high for correction, but it is higher for continuance of the defilement of these waters."[48]

Personnel from the US Public Health Service, the Canadian Department of National Health and Welfare, the OWRC, and the Minnesota Department of Health carried out field studies between June 1960 and September 1962, supplementing the main chemical laboratory in the International Falls sewage treatment plant with mobile laboratories.[49] Coliform organisms, pH (hydrogen ion concentration), temperature, dissolved oxygen, biochemical oxygen demand, turbidity, solids (total, suspended, and volatile), lignin, chemical oxygen demand, phenol, calcium, alkalinity, conductivity, and hardness all came under scrutiny. To trace the direction of currents, floats were distributed along the channel, while on-site examinations were carried out at the sources of waste.[50]

The IJC's 1965 *Report on Pollution of Rainy River and Lake of the Woods* described economic activity and water quality impacts. Pulp and paper, the predominant industry, was characterized by close connections between operations on the two sides of the border. The degree of integration was such that manufacturing processes in the two plants "operate in effect as one mill." Groundwood, sulphite, and kraft processes were all used, with an average wood consumption in 1961 of approximately 1,530 cords per day. The facilities, employing some twenty-two hundred people at International Falls and nearly seven hundred at Fort Frances, produced 730,000 tons of paper and 710,000 tons of insulite board per year.[51]

Agricultural activity, the second most important industry in the area, was also noteworthy. There were 2,235 farms in the Rainy River drainage basin. Minnesota farmers cultivated more than 210,000 acres, with their Ontario counterparts using about 90,000.[52] The overall population of the Rainy River watershed as of 1960 numbered around forty-seven thousand, with just under 60 percent residing in rural settings. About ninety-five hundred resided in Fort Frances, ninety-three hundred in International Falls and South International Falls, eleven hundred in Rainy River, Ontario, and sixteen hundred in Baudette, Minnesota.[53]

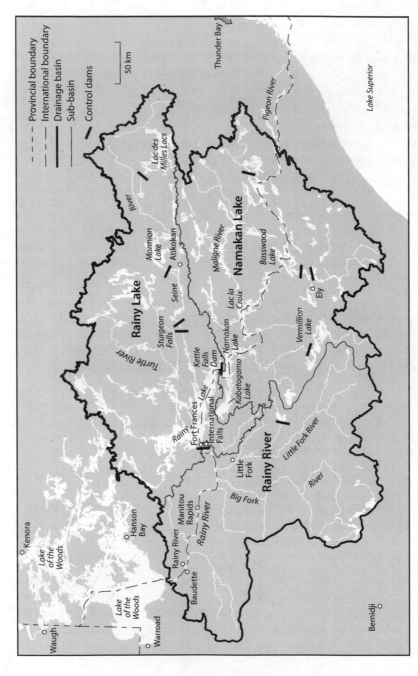

MAP 10.1 Rainy River Drainage Basin. *From International Rainy River Board of Control. Map adapted by Eric Leinberger.*

The Rainy River served a range of uses, from water supply to waste disposal to recreation, the latter being an expanding area of economic activity. By spelling these out, the report not only underlined the diverse and valuable contributions of the waterway but clearly exposed the potential for conflicts among various municipal and industrial demands. International Falls (including South International Falls) and the town of Rainy River obtained their domestic water supply from the river, the former via a purification plant run by Ontario-Minnesota Pulp and Paper Company and the latter via municipal chlorination. Baudette had been forced to abandon the river in favour of a well supplying "hard water" because of the high costs of treating Rainy River water. Four of the five sewered communities along the Rainy River discharged into the river itself for final disposal. Secondary treatment facilities were available at International Falls, while Baudette, the town of Rainy River, and Fort Frances provided only primary treatment. South International Falls discharged civic waste effluent into Rainy Lake.[54]

Industrial users constituted a further category of those reliant on the river, with the pulp and paper mills at Fort Frances and International Falls consuming 83 million US gallons (69 million imperial gallons) per day. Power generation facilities at International Falls had capacity to use up to 10,500 cfs. Industrial waste, including sewage from the pulp and paper mills, was discharged directly into Rainy River at the time of the investigation, although facilities to divert domestic sewage from the paper mills to municipal systems were under construction.[55]

Recreational water users interested in fishing and boating were also noted, especially along that section of Rainy River adjacent to the Lake of the Woods. In 1959, vacationers spent an estimated $480,000 in this area.[56] Boat ramps, navigational improvements, and channel dredging were among initiatives designed to support and encourage recreational activity, although Canada's Department of Public Works was unwilling to create a channel between Sable Island, along the south shore of Big Traverse Bay, and the mainland – largely, it seems, because drifting sand was likely to require frequent or continuous dredging. However, elsewhere along the eastern shore, Public Works removed boulders and dredged Turtle Portage between Whitefish Bay and Sabaskong Bay to facilitate small boat traffic. Vacationers, especially American patrons of about twenty nearby fishing camps, were among the beneficiaries. A hydrographic survey of Rainy Lake – facilitated by Aerodist, an economical new aerial survey technique – offered further support for valuable recreational activity.[57]

To underscore the shared nature of Rainy River waters, the investigation confirmed extensive transboundary flows. Indeed, it could be said that "the currents of Rainy River cross and re-cross the international boundary." The constituents in these waters are thoroughly mixed at Manitou and Long Sault Rapids, about thirty miles downstream from International Falls.[58]

Turning to the issue of pollution, the report confirmed that the water entering Rainy River from Rainy Lake was of "good quality." Marked deterioration occurred immediately below Fort Frances and International Falls, where municipal and industrial waste streams were concentrated along the shoreline. Downstream, at Long Sault Rapids, the wastes were more or less completely mixed. In the lower reaches, "effects of sedimentation and biological stabilization became more evident."[59]

Along the Rainy River, from Fort Frances to the Lake of the Woods, pollution was considered serious. The water quality of the Lake of the Woods was "satisfactory," evidence of "a remarkable recovery when compared to the contaminated condition in the upper reaches of Rainy River."[60] The commission set out its conclusions, confirming the "major source" of pollution as the sewer outlets of Ontario-Minnesota Pulp and Paper Company plants at Fort Frances and International Falls. With the exception of about half of the domestic sewage from the International Falls facility, "all wastes" were released into the Rainy River without treatment.[61]

In elaborate detail, the report explained what was actually meant by the observation that industrial plants were the "major source" of pollution, and that "all wastes," with the exception of some domestic sewage, were discharged "without treatment." The inventory of materials flushed from the plant at International Falls included

> screened overflow from the pulp thickener, waste from the woodroom and bark recovery plant, overflow from the ash pond which receives the main boiler plant ashes, waste water from the sulphite screens and wet room, diluted spent sulphite liquor, bleach plant wastes, kraft mill wastes including lime sludge, wastes from the insulite mill, sewage wastes from the paper mill, backwash from the filtration plant and cooling water from the asphalt rodding mill.

Across the river at Fort Frances, plant wastes included discharges from the rotary bark screens, waste from the Tyler screens, waste from the sulphite deckers, lean white water overflow, and sewage.[62]

The IJC also identified harmful pollution effects. From a human health perspective, the flow of untreated domestic wastes resulted in high counts

of coliform bacteria. Accordingly, without auxiliary pretreatment beyond
conventional purification, the river could not be considered a source of
drinking water. Moreover, health officials deemed Rainy River waters to
be "unsuitable for bathing." Fish populations were also at risk and suffered
especially from wood fibres and associated wastes. These materials impeded
the development of flora and fauna found at the bottom of lakes and
streams, known as benthos or benthic organisms. In normal summer flows,
some of the more desirable fish food organisms were unable to survive.
The river's fish population was noticeably reduced in the upper eleven
miles, including reductions in the expected numbers of younger specimens
of game fish. Overall, witnesses indicated that the fish population "has
been drastically reduced over the past twenty-five years."[63]

The inventory of injury or damage resulting from pollution concluded
with adverse recreational impacts – above and beyond the determination
that swimmers should avoid the river: "Sludge banks and floating islands
of bark, fibre and chips, floating scum from lime sludge wastes, and malodorous conditions caused by bottom deposits [have] adversely affected the
aesthetic value of Rainy River." Deposits of woody materials were known
to be over three feet thick around the outlet in Four Mile Bay. Moreover,
as a consequence of "fibre and slime entanglement on fish lines," sport
fishing was confined to the fast waters of the Sioux and Manitou Rapids
and the lower ten miles of the river. Even outboard motors, according to
witnesses, became so entangled with fibres that they had to be overhauled
regularly. Anglers abandoned the resort facilities in the lower reach of the
river in favour of other locations.[64] During weekends, when power production declined, reduced flows from the dam at International Falls resulted
in still more acute conditions. With weekend flows sometimes falling below
half of the weekday average during periods of low inflow into Rainy Lake,
unsightly banks and portions of the river bed were exposed: "As a result,
bottom animals and fauna on the exposed areas were destroyed and malodorous conditions developed."[65]

Following this indictment, the IJC outlined completed or contemplated
remedial measures. Thanks to the OWRC, Fort Frances – as of 1964 – had
a pollution-control plant equipped to provide primary sewage treatment.
For their part, the pulp and paper companies had nearly completed connections to link their sanitary sewers with municipal treatment facilities.
Additional in-plant work was underway to complete waste segregation
and recovery projects, including arrangements to capture bark and waste
wood for burning in a new steam plant, fibre recovery at the insulite mill,
and re-engineering of the sulphite chemical-cooking plant to utilize half

of the calcium carbonate that was being wasted. These initial measures, welcome and overdue, nevertheless fell well short of a comprehensive solution to the Rainy River's environmental plight.[66]

The IJC responded to each of the questions presented to it for consideration. In answer to the desire of the two neighbouring governments to know whether the waters of the Rainy River and the Lake of the Woods were being polluted to the extent that transboundary damage was occurring, the commission answered yes – "to an extent that is injurious to property and a hazard to health on the other side of the boundary." As indicated by test results, however, Lake of the Woods water quality was assessed as "satisfactory."[67]

In response to the second question concerning the location, extent, and causes of pollution, the commission was clear. Downstream from the Fort Frances-International Falls area, the Rainy River was "a potential menace to health, unfit for bathing, discourages the development of water front property, is unsuitable for the growth of many forms of aquatic life and unattractive for recreation." Nor was there any doubt about the source of pollution in untreated discharges from the pulp and paper plants. Additional pollution was attributed to domestic wastes from Fort Frances and to sewage treatment effluents from Baudette, International Falls, and the town of Rainy River.[68]

As a foundation for further action, the commission called upon the two national governments to adopt "Water Quality Objectives for the Rainy River," with the further recommendation that these should serve as minimum criteria for state and provincial water quality standards in Minnesota and Ontario. Industries and municipalities should then be required to implement necessary abatement measures according to prescribed timelines.[69] Measures recommended for the pulp and paper plants included "an extension of the scheduled in-plant segregation and recovery projects to cover all processes, external treatment of all high-solids wastes, recovery or treatment of spent sulphite liquor, and continuous waste monitoring." In the view of the commission, the pulp and paper company should bear the expense of pollution abatement.

As for the municipalities, Fort Frances, Baudette, and Rainy River were urged to install secondary sewage treatment and to initiate long-term programs for separating domestic sewage from storm water. The municipalities should assume the costs themselves, with assistance from senior governments so far as circumstances allowed. Baudette would require an estimated $200,000 for secondary treatment, while expenditure for the two Canadian communities would run at around $500,000.[70]

On the institutional plain, the commission sought authorization from the two national governments to appoint a board with responsibility to supervise pollution along the Rainy River. For purposes of enforcement where pollution contrary to the objectives was found and persisted beyond "a reasonable time," the commission broadly proposed "action deemed necessary or advisable."[71] The recommendations – extending from proposed national objectives, to standard setting by law at the state or provincial levels, to municipal and industrial performance measures subject to timelines and independent supervision with some ultimate prospect of enforcement action – was a thorough response to the interjurisdictional diffusion of responsibility that had contributed to water quality deterioration for much of the century.

On 23 July 1965, the Canadian cabinet, now presided over by Prime Minister Pearson, already well-acquainted with the Rainy River file, approved the IJC recommendations for pollution control measures. Cabinet also directed the Department of External Affairs to consult with the US Department of State concerning coordinated responses by the two national governments.[72] Nearly fifty years after the initial evaluation of water quality problems along the Rainy River boundary, effective measures of intervention finally appeared to be on the horizon, at least for the transboundary category. The International Rainy River Water Pollution Board was established in January 1965, but the question of implementation lay ahead.

TACKLING PULP AND PAPER POLLUTION: EARLY ROUNDS

Water quality issues not implicating international boundary waters remained to be addressed. But in an era preceding the creation of ministries of the environment and in a context where the transboundary jurisdiction of the IJC would not apply, the question arose: Addressed by whom?

Dorothy Bolton anticipated an answer to that question. When she had had enough of the "s..t" in her river – the Winnipeg – she didn't fool around. On 27 January 1967, she wrote to Ontario premier John Robarts, who had succeeded Leslie Frost. He was not even Dorothy Bolton's premier, since she lived for most of the year in Winnipeg. But as a long-time summer resident of Minaki, which was downstream from the outlets of the Lake of the Woods, she addressed her concern to someone who was in a position to redirect the aforementioned substance to the proverbial fan. Mrs. Bolton spoke frankly of the "deep alarm" experienced by everyone in the area – Indigenous residents, local property owners, tourist camp operators, and private cottagers – as pollution encroached. It was impossible, she lamented, to "sit idly by" as contaminated water ruined the "lovely country" downstream from Kenora to Minaki en route to Manitoba's Whiteshell district.[73]

"How can we possibly reconcile the fantastic expense of the cleaning-up process, as against ever having allowed it to happen in the first place?" she inquired, pursuing the same logic that had emerged from the IJC's Rainy River report. She emphasized further that Ontario tax and tourist dollars were jeopardized by damage to the waterway, whose natural attractions were the foundation of the livelihood of many people, before concluding with a plea for help: "Surely something can be done by your government to initiate a program with the O&M plant and with the town of Kenora that would immediately stop the *increase* in pollution." Indeed, she hoped to see pollution eventually eliminated "before some of your province's most beautiful lake country has been destroyed beyond reclamation."[74]

As a citizen commentator, Dorothy Bolton spelled out several salient considerations. If the deterioration of the Rainy River was worthy of attention, then why not the Winnipeg? Would a preventive response not be preferable to facing a more extensive remedial challenge after further decline? Water pollution threatened public health and was destined to impose significant costs on other resource users, notably the valuable tourism sector. As a first step towards improving water quality, should we not ensure that it does not get worse?

Given a reasonable interlude for delivery of Mrs. Bolton's 27 January letter to the Ontario premier, the 7 February response of the OWRC to an inquiry from the deputy minister of Energy and Resources Management, following up on the premier's behalf, reflects an impressive turnaround rate. The response was no doubt expedited by the fact that John Robarts had lived in Winnipeg as a child, and still more by his primary responsibility in 1958 as a junior member of Leslie Frost's cabinet, which was centred on relations between the province, Ontario municipalities, and the Ontario Water Resources Commission.[75]

In the year after it circulated water quality objectives for the pulp and paper industry, the OWRC reported a disheartening assessment to O&M's Kenora manager: "The waste loadings discharged to the Winnipeg River were the highest ever recorded for your mill."[76] From a production perspective, the mill was producing seven hundred tons of newsprint each day using a combination of groundwood pulp (75 percent) and sulphite pulp (25 percent).[77] Operations used over 30 million imperial gallons of water per day. In-plant control measures and stock recovery efforts had not significantly reduced effluent loads entering the waterway. The OWRC accordingly recommended direct pollution abatement to reduce "excessive discharges of wastes to the Winnipeg River."[78]

The Kenora plant faced several challenges, including a heavy reliance on Jack pine and the resulting pitch accumulation. Pitch degraded the quality of groundwood pulp, a problem that had been accentuated by efforts to reduce water flowing through the paper mill's white water system. But until this flow could be minimized, it was impractical to use conventional primary treatment equipment. Meanwhile, high water levels in the Winnipeg River largely prevented the existing barking screens from working effectively, and none of the proposed improvements in either equipment or design were operational. Other initiatives, such as bark burning and the substitution of magnesium bisulphite for calcium in the pulping process, were under consideration, but any pollution-control benefits were anticipated to be modest. Overall discharges were still not fully sampled and monitored because of the continued flow of sanitary sewage into the main mill sewer.[79]

To alleviate environmental impacts, O&M planned to spend $350,000 on operational changes in 1966. Reusing machine "white water" in the woodroom would reduce consumption, while separating sanitary wastes from the industrial stream would allow diversion for municipal treatment when Kenora's long-deferred sewage treatment arrangements became available. New equipment and renovations were designed to permit full-time screening of bark wastes. Moreover, an initiative to remove as much as 25 percent of bark in the forest would substantially reduce the volume of bark to be handled at the plant. Provincial inspectors generally anticipated that these measures would produce "an appreciable reduction in suspended solids from the woodroom operations, but will leave the pulp and paper mill problems pretty much as they were before."[80]

Perhaps J.P. Erichsen-Brown, an OWRC legal officer, had O&M in mind when, at a public forum on wastes in 1967, he discussed injunctions to prohibit industrial pollution. This powerful legal remedy might be invoked, he suggested, "where companies have been under investigation for years, have been the subject of inspection, reports and recommendations, and where the Commission will already have exercised ... other powers under the Act without having been able to terminate the pollution." These were not emergency situations, but "hard core cases," often of long standing.[81] Whether Erichsen-Brown's remarks drew specifically upon the Kenora file or not, the discouraging results of repeated inspections, combined with the premier's interest in pursuing Dorothy Bolton's plea for intervention, accentuated the need for action and compliance on the part of mill officials.

To initiate proceedings formally, the OWRC's senior solicitor prepared a most business-like resolution in early November 1967: "Resolved that agents and employees of the Ontario Water Resources Commission are hereby authorized to commence and prosecute charges against The Ontario-Minnesota Pulp and Paper Company Limited under the *Ontario Water Resources Commission Act* R.S.O. 1960, c. 281, for its operations in the District of Kenora during the period of six months commencing July 1st, 1967."[82] Hardly business as usual, the proposal to commence prosecution with reference to the one hundredth anniversary of Canadian Confederation was recognized by officials as an important test case: "We can expect that the paper mill is not going to take this lying down."

The decision to prosecute was a departure for OWRC officials, who generally preferred to resolve water quality conflicts through agreement or on the basis of administrative guidance, the latter being the recommended response as late as October 1967.[83] Endorsement of even this moderate enforcement measure followed an extended process of exchange and discussion in which the water resources agency had waited patiently for some indication – any indication – that O&M was finally prepared to tackle pollution with conviction. The commission, however, faced external expectations of its own from public and media attention.[84]

In April 1967, O&M's general manager at Fort Frances "raised the question of the assimilative capacity of the receiving stream and why the Company shouldn't be allowed to utilize this as a form of waste disposal." This, simply put, was a proposal to accept dilution as the solution to pollution.[85]

Although the OWRC was undertaking research on watercourse assimilation of waste effluents, the agency was unlikely to authorize pulp and paper discharges without a great deal of additional information. Officials explored the implications of a hardline response. An injunction issued against the Kenora mill to force closure of the sulphite operation would have far-reaching economic consequences. Instead, the OWRC called for the company to submit a proposal for a continuing program of pollution control, accompanied by engineering specifications and a schedule for completion. Although OWRC officials hoped that "the pulp and paper industry must realize that it will, ultimately, have to face a final waste treatment expenditure," it was still necessary to prepare for a prosecution.[86]

Water resources officials assembled evidence concerning "demonstrable effects of pollution by the pulp and paper mill in the river," including the extent and severity of such pollution. Additional information to support the prosecution called for the identification of downstream users and documentation of complaints they may have made. It was also necessary to ask: "Is there really a severe pollution problem from the point of view of mill benefits to the area versus loss due to damage to the environment?"[87]

The decision to prosecute was hardly precipitous. Annual surveys dating from 1962 recorded regular waste discharges "far in excess of Commission objectives."[88] Moreover, in responding to a January 1965 government "Proposal for Pulp and Paper Waste Pollution Control," the company had missed deadlines, failed to produce promised engineering reports, and, in October 1967, abandoned one possible pollution-control project while seeking a considerable extension of time to explore a new alternative.[89]

In mid-November, inspectors arrived at the Kenora mill to obtain water and biological samples, informing the plant manager that these might be used in a possible prosecution. The unexpected arrival of inspectors signalling the possibility of prosecution engaged corporate attention. The O&M manager inquired what might be done to avert such action but was not offered much solace. The reason given for the prosecution was that "the Commission had been unable to obtain any definite commitment for waste treatment from the Company, and therefore, had little alternative but to resort to legal means to impress upon the Company the seriousness with which the problem is viewed."[90] An OWRC legal officer underscored that assessment by explaining that company officials had never submitted a clear engineering proposal capable of producing major improvements in effluent quality and reminding them "that such a proposal had been requested two and one-half years ago."[91]

Within days, O&M's head office in Portland, Oregon, authorized installation of primary clarification treatment facilities.[92] All plant sewers would be combined to discharge into the clarifier.[93] Then, a week before Christmas 1967, a delegation representing O&M met with OWRC officials in Toronto to follow up on the company's proposal for waste treatment. Further information was clearly required, certainly in relation to board approval of pollution-control measures, but the commission indicated that the prosecution would proceed in any event, since the company had "run out of time."[94]

E.C. Burton, Crown attorney for the Kenora District, took charge of the case. He was aware that a prosecution would not be popular in the local community and urged that some effort be made to bring the pollution problem to public attention prior to the trial.[95] As the year drew to a close, Burton reviewed technical evidence provided by the OWRC and began to assess possible witnesses from the Minaki area.[96] One possibility was H. Rod Carey, the new proprietor of Minaki Lodge, the old railway resort whose occupancy levels were closely tied to the condition of the waterway and the state of the sport fishery.[97] Mill effluent from Kenora was merely a foretaste of environmental threats to the hotel's viability. As for cottagers, they were not only available as witnesses but had independently considered legal proceedings against the company and were prepared to take such action if they failed to obtain satisfaction through government channels.[98]

When charges were laid on 11 January 1968, the company petitioned the minister, whose personal intervention resulted in interim relief. The delay provided three additional months to complete remediation plans that were already two and a half years late. In the legislature, R.S. Smith, MPP for Nipissing, challenged the ministerial intervention: "If the government does not intend to have the law enforced with unco-operative industries, what respect will industry have for the law, and for that matter what respect will anybody in the province have for the OWRC?" More pointedly, Smith inquired: "What special status does this company have with the Minister that they can exert such influence that a charge that has been laid can be withheld?"[99]

Dorothy Bolton's letter to Premier Robarts also had implications for the situation at Fort Frances, where the remedial recommendations of the IJC's Rainy River reference were under consideration. Following up on her correspondence, the deputy minister of Energy and Resources Management asked the OWRC for a briefing on the Fort Frances situation, "so that I can bring this to the attention of the Minister when discussing concessions with the Company."[100] At Fort Frances, at least, progress was underway: "Through a system of pumping wastes to the International Falls plant and the provision of a retention lagoon or basin at the Ontario site, waste control will be accomplished to meet our requirements within reasonable limits."[101]

In addition to these remedial efforts, O&M had proposed significant further investment in the form of a kraft mill at Fort Frances. Waste treatment and waste flows were under discussion between company representatives and the OWRC. Preliminary drawings incorporated proposed arrangements to neutralize wastes from the mill and bleachery, to remove foam, and to promote sedimentation of suspended solids. Commission staff expressed disappointment about the absence of secondary treatment that was required to alleviate taste and odour problems and also assessed company estimates of predicted concentration levels for biological oxygen demand (BOD) and suspended solids in the final effluent as "somewhat optimistic."[102] By 1969, O&M (then owned by Boise Cascade) had spent over $5 million to abate the physical pollution issues and would subsequently invest a great deal more to address chemical contamination.[103]

The IJC, the OWRC, and determined citizens like Dorothy Bolton were gratified by the steps finally being taken during the 1960s to address the long-standing impacts of sewage and pulpwood wastes on oxygen levels in the waters of the Rainy and Winnipeg Rivers. However, the measures underway would by no means resolve pollution of these waters, let alone similar situations across the province.

As the decade drew to a close, industry representatives addressed public and governmental pressure "to clarify the air and the waters." The president of Abitibi Paper, for example, informed those attending the company's 1968 annual general meeting that an additional $25 million in expenditures might be required to meet antipollution goals. He argued that "the cost of this social objective should be shared by all," and accordingly, he called upon governments to provide financial incentives to support investment in environmental protection.[104] An extended public debate on the allocation of environmental costs was soon underway.[105]

Provincial policy makers contemplated opportunities to promote pollution abatement alongside modernization of the pulp and paper industry on the basis of approximately $100 million worth of financial assistance.[106] Funding at the level of one government dollar for every three dollars invested by industry was to be made available upon completion of work related to pollution abatement and plant modernization. It remained a concern, however, that companies, in the interest of competition and profitability, were still more likely to pursue plant upgrades independent of pollution abatement.[107] Other commentators criticized the funding proposal as favouring environmental laggards over industry leaders by "envisaging grants to the companies which had been least cooperative in the past and consequently still needed major investments to meet pollution abatement requirements." Such an approach "would implicitly penalize companies that have already completed their abatement programs."[108]

The legislature's Standing Committee on Resources Development endeavoured to appreciate the investment calculus from an industry perspective. On one hand, given the cost of pollution abatement, "even companies discharging unacceptable (illegal) quantities of pollutants have an interest in avoiding expenditures that do not contribute to revenues," noted the committee. On the other hand, "a significant portion of needed pollution abatement expenditures are in reality also modernization expenditures that do contribute to longer term productivity and efficiency." Counter-vailing pressure, however, arose from the fact that abatement expenditures often offered limited potential for economic return.[109]

Given these circumstances, the committee observed that unless penal-ties for noncompliance were high enough, a company might delay or seek to avoid abatement costs. Accordingly, the government's options required some discussion. One reaction might be "raising the penalties so that they exceed the costs of compliance." As an alternative, various forms of financial aid could be provided to offset expenses. Grants, loans, or tax relief repre-sented potential alternatives in this regard.[110]

With reference to an idea that would only grow in prominence, the legislators examined the significance of financial penalties. Penalties were attractive in the sense that "the polluter pays." In other words, either the costs of compliance or penalties imposed for noncompliance fall on the companies that discharge pollutants and are accordingly included within the overall cost of production. With industry and consumers rather than taxpayers in general paying for environmental investments, this ap-proach differed from the view previously expressed by industry leaders that "the cost of this social objective should be shared by all."[111]

Yet a penalty-based regime was not without weaknesses. In the legislative committee's view, heavy penalties "can force plant closures when companies lack sufficient funds to pay for abatement," while the use of penalties to compel substantial expenditures on abatement "can cause immediate and longer term problems by reducing the amount of money available for other necessary investments in maintenance and modernization." The committee even predicted behaviour that would later be evident in practice in parts of northwestern Ontario: investment constraints in the pulp and paper sector could have adverse impacts on forest management and regeneration.[112]

Regrettably, alongside debate about the most appropriate responses to the most obvious pollution issues, other challenges remained. Wild rice production, contributing $500,000 to regional harvesters in the early 1970s, was vulnerable to continuing water level fluctuations.[113] With wild rice production situated both upstream on Lake of the Woods waters and downstream along the Winnipeg River, it seemed impossible to promote optimum harvests simultaneously at both locations. Particularly in years of high inflow to the system, regulators could not stabilize water levels within a narrow desirable range in one area without subjecting other parts of the watershed to flood damage.[114] Tragically, alongside the severe challenges of conventional pollution and water level fluctuations, a far more acute and devastating water-quality crisis – again associated with the pulp and paper sector but not yet even identified – was already an inevitability.

11

"Slowly to the Rescue as a Community Fails"

Sustained efforts to restore water quality along the Rainy River following the International Joint Commission's (IJC's) inquiry failed to avert far more devastating environmental and social impacts elsewhere. Though not tributary to the Rainy-Lake of the Woods basin, northern waters flowing into the Winnipeg River system were contaminated during the 1960s. Two Aboriginal communities experienced staggering health and environmental impacts from mercury released to the environment, which also severely damaged commercial operations in the surrounding area.

"THE GODS OF PROGRESS HAVE A DARKER SIDE"

In 1977, while introducing legislative amendments to Canada's *Fisheries Act*, Roméo LeBlanc, minister of Fisheries and the Environment, underlined important connections between the protection of fisheries and human well-being. "Our water resists pollution no more than the water in Minamata," LeBlanc remarked, invoking the toxic experience of a Japanese coastal fishing community that had been devastated by mercury. "If our laws can protect the water, if we give the fish a place to live, we can have a better place for man to live. People should be able to see clean water, swim in it, maybe catch a fish."[1] Pointing to the notorious results of mercury discharges, the minister concluded his advocacy of new statutory provisions with a caveat: "We have made of progress a god. But mercury was named for the messenger of the gods, and mercury has warned us clearly that the gods of progress have a darker side."[2] The dark side was no more starkly in evidence than in distant corners of northwestern Ontario.

It had long been understood and acknowledged that certain constituents of pulp and paper production could be toxic to fish and other aquatic life if present in high concentrations. Yet far into the twentieth century, prevailing opinion accepted the formulaic response that contaminants were unlikely to reach harmful concentrations because of the significant volumes of water available for dilution.[3] A rough dilution factor of twenty to one was often presumed sufficient to prevent harmful levels of concentration. One prominent assessment dating from the late 1950s had identified oxygen depletion from the discharge of bark and other mill refuse as a greater culprit than toxicity.[4] In the case of mercury, a process ingredient in some forms of pulp and paper making, limited consideration was given to its potential adverse impacts on aquatic environments until the 1960s.

The *New York Times* announced an abrupt end to complacence on a continent-wide scale. As that paper's editorial page explained in the summer of 1970, even though mercury was a known poison, its toxicity had not previously been linked to waterways: "Until recently neither Government officials nor scientists gave much thought to the possible harmful effects of mercury-containing wastes dumped into sewer systems by industrial plants." It had been widely assumed that mercury was insoluble in water and would, accordingly, "lie forever quietly and inertly at the bottom."[5] That reassuring conclusion was now graphically rebutted: "One tablespoon of mercury in a body of water covering a football field to a depth of fifteen feet is enough to make fish in that water unsafe to eat."[6]

How often that concentration might be reached – and, more pointedly, where – challenged those responsible for measurement and calculation when the risks came to public attention in 1970. Both Japan and Sweden had previously experienced the tragic consequences of mercury poisoning from industrial sources. Indeed, the deeply disturbing experience of "Minamata disease" proclaimed the nature and extent of potential suffering in haunting and irrefutable terms.[7]

Reports of mercury contamination in Ontario waters and wildlife based on the work of Norvald Fimreite, a Norwegian graduate student in zoology at the University of Western Ontario, helped to trigger intense North American examination of the situation in 1971.[8] Fimreite's findings on mercury releases in Ontario stimulated further research at the Ontario Water Resources Commission (OWRC) and precipitated emergency debate in the Ontario legislature. The province soon closed commercial and sport fishing in the St. Clair River and Lake St. Clair, and Canadian officials alerted their counterparts in the United States, where preventive measures were soon widely adopted.[9]

By this point, cumulative twentieth-century use of mercury in the United States was estimated at 163 million pounds, with contemporary annual demand in the range of 4 to 6 million pounds. Widely used in battery cells, bleach production, pharmaceuticals, the electrical industry, and paints, mercury was also extensively used in certain forms of pulp and paper manufacturing, notably in chlor-alkali plants, after it was learned that a process involving mercury electrolytic cells was particularly effective in producing chlorine and a purer grade of caustic soda, the industry's key bleaching agents.[10] By 1970, fifteen chlor-alkali plants operated in Canada using a total of roughly 110,000 kilograms of mercury each year. Sixty-two percent of this was discharged in liquid effluent, while the remainder was disbursed to the air or found its way into manufactured products or solid wastes.[11]

In the United States, chlor-alkali plants discharged fourteen hundred pounds of mercury daily to the waterways, with roughly 10 percent of that amount attributable to ten facilities. The most serious offenders discharged into the Puget Sound in Washington State, the Niagara River in New York State, and the Androscoggin River in Maine.[12] Those companies initially faced charges under the United States' 1899 *Refuse Act,* but the prosecutions were soon withdrawn in exchange for remedial commitments.[13] New production techniques rapidly achieved substantial decreases across the United States.[14] Canadian mercury users, including chlor-alkali plants, were equally – and encouragingly – successful in reducing mercury losses dramatically once the problem had been identified.[15] Nevertheless, the extent of damage already caused and what might be done about it remained to be determined.

When mercury contamination forced suspension of commercial fishing in parts of Manitoba, the provincial government distributed approximately $2 million in compensation to roughly sixteen hundred people whose economic circumstances were adversely affected. The province also obtained the right to sue those responsible for injuries to the fishing operations it had compensated. Manitoba then applied, in December 1970, for an injunction against further discharges and attempted to recover its financial loss from the polluting industries. Among these companies, Dryden Chemicals Limited, in northwestern Ontario, and Interprovincial Co-operatives Limited (IPCO), in Saskatchewan, had been discharging industrial mercury from their chlor-alkali plants on the basis of permits from their respective provincial governments. The receiving waterways, the Wabigoon in northwestern Ontario and the South Saskatchewan, both drained through connecting watercourses into Manitoba, where mercury damage to the fisheries had occurred. Manitoba, residents of the province have often remarked, is "downstream from everywhere."[16]

Manitoba's claim against out-of-province polluters rested on provincial legislation – the *Fishermen's Assistance and Polluters' Liability Act.*[17] The statute sought to impose liability on any person who discharged a contaminant "into waters in the province or into any waters whereby it is carried into waters in the province."[18] Manitoba went further, declaring that a permit from a regulatory authority with responsibility at the location of the discharge provided no lawful excuse for damage to the fishery outside that authority's own jurisdiction.[19] This provision, among other features of the *Fishermen's Assistance and Polluters' Liability Act,* was directly challenged in legal proceedings that eventually reached the Supreme Court of Canada.[20]

In March 1975, Canada's highest court struck down Manitoba's initiative in a complicated decision.[21] Some members of the court asserted that Manitoba's legislative authority did not extend beyond the province's boundaries. Manitoba legislation, accordingly, could not undermine the statutory arrangements of neighbouring jurisdictions, even in an effort to safeguard the interests of its own residents and even in the context of a "truly interprovincial" pollution problem. Another judge, also rejecting the Manitoba legislation, expressed the opinion that if Dryden Chemicals and IPCO had valid authorizations from Ontario and Saskatchewan, then "the acts were authorized by licence and therefore justifiable in the places where they were done, [therefore] they were not civil wrongs and [could] form no basis for a damage action."[22] This reasoning, in its subordination of ecological realities to boundary lines, offered a generous dose of immunity to anyone with enough foresight to ensure that damage to water quality occurred outside the jurisdiction from which they had secured official authorization to discharge contaminants.

Only Chief Justice Bora Laskin and two fellow dissenters appreciated the legal situation from Manitoba's downstream perspective. It is "plain enough," Laskin wrote with characteristic clarity, that a province is entitled to protect its property rights against injury. Equally, provinces are entitled to protect the interests that others might have in such property.[23] Turning his attention to Manitoba's contested legislation, Laskin explained that it did indeed make Manitoba law applicable to the activities of IPCO and Dryden Chemicals, originating in their respective provinces, but only because these operations had damaged a Manitoba fishery by discharging a contaminant into waters flowing into Manitoba.[24]

While Manitoba pursued mercury dischargers for compensation, other governments took steps to forestall further contamination. In the short term, working agreements with chlor-alkali operators initiated marked reductions in mercury releases. Guidelines were in place shortly thereafter, followed by statutory amendments accompanied and reinforced by increased penalties. As of June 1972, federal Chlor-Alkali Mercury Regulations were in effect under the *Fisheries Act*.[25] In the assessment of a respected legal observer, control of mercury discharges from chlor-alkali plants "appears to represent a major success for regulatory agencies."[26] By that time, however, an uncertain legacy of contamination was embedded in river sediments. Once again, compensation and remediation of the consequences of discharging wastes to waterways would prove singularly difficult.[27]

MERCURY CONTAMINATION
OF THE ENGLISH-WABIGOON RIVER SYSTEM

When pulp and paper operations began on the Wabigoon River at Dryden in 1913, environmental deterioration – completely unrelated to mercury contamination – was immediately apparent.[28] The facilities, which were substantially expanded during the 1940s and 1950s, were subsequently acquired by Reed Paper Limited, owner of Dryden Chemicals, one of the defendants in Manitoba's failed fisheries compensation claim.[29]

When Dryden Chemicals and Reed Paper began to discharge mercury into the English-Wabigoon river system in 1962, Ontario officials remained focused on suspended solids and biological oxygen demand (BOD), the issues that had initially absorbed regulatory attention along the Rainy River and elsewhere, rather than on mercury.[30] A biological investigation conducted in September 1968 concluded that the Wabigoon River was severely polluted by an average daily discharge of seventy-one thousand pounds of suspended solids consisting primarily of wood fibre and bark, together with thirty-three thousand pounds of BODs, a measure of the amount of biodegradeable organic matter in the water. As they settled out, the suspended solids blanketed the stream bed and formed "unsightly and malodorous islands and banks for the first five miles along

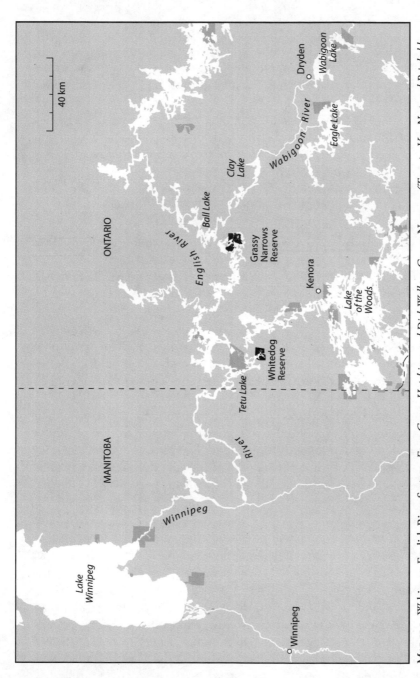

Map 11.1 Wabigoon English River System. *From George Hutchison and Dick Wallace, Grassy Narrows (Toronto: Van Nostrand Reinhold, 1977). Map adapted by Eric Leinberger.*

the river." As far away as Clay Lake, fifty-four miles downstream, foam, unnatural colour, and odours were noticeable.[31]

The level of dissolved oxygen was depressed for significant distances downstream from the Dryden mill; for twenty-eight miles down to the confluence of the Eagle River, the only organisms found in the stream bed were those that were highly tolerant of pollution.[32] Observers reported that "little or no use is made of the Wabigoon River aside from the over-utilization of its capacity to translocate and assimilate wastes."[33] Although this assessment acknowledged the collapse of fishing and agricultural utilization along the river, it disregarded the contribution of Wabigoon River waters to downstream power facilities.

Substantial increases in hydroelectric power production resulted from generating stations at Whitedog Falls, on the Winnipeg River, and at Caribou Falls, on the English River, during the mid-1950s. The capacity of the Caribou Falls facility was augmented by the diversion of Albany River flows from Lake St. Joseph to Lac Seul for release at Ear Falls into the English River. Variants of the two schemes had been under examination by Manitoba and Ontario survey agencies for over a quarter of a century before development approval for Whitedog was granted in 1955 and for Caribou Falls the next year. As part of Ontario Hydro's northwestern system, the two power stations were interconnected with Manitoba's power network rather than with the Ontario grid. Continuous coordination of water flows along the Winnipeg River system was managed by remote control from Kenora.

Road building preceded construction, which had important implications not only for water regulation but for the forest sector. In particular, preparations for a headpond on the English River at Caribou Falls, roughly fifty miles north of Kenora, employed nearly four hundred men clearing over eighteen thousand acres and salvaging roughly twenty-seven thousand cords of pulpwood prior to flooding. The completed headpond, extending approximately thirty miles along the river and connected lakes, had an overall shoreline of roughly five hundred miles.[34]

Water level increases resulting from the Caribou Falls facility had further consequences for Indigenous residents. In 1958, flooding displaced local communities, including a small settlement at One Man Lake; the trapping and fishing sectors were also severely damaged, along with Ojibwa grave-sites. Compensation for losses to the fishery and wild rice harvesters were not readily forthcoming and the two communities – Grassy Narrows and Whitedog (Islington) – waited years for electricity service.[35] Power did not reach Whitedog until 1968, while Grassy Narrows waited a further half decade.[36] Compensation in the form of seventeen hectares of land and a payment of $1.5 million, together with substantial accumulated interest from Ontario Hydro, finally arrived three decades after the flooding.[37]

The lengthy delay and limitations in the delivery of compensation were attributable, at least in part, to uncertainty respecting the legal status of claims for losses that occurred outside reserve boundaries and in part to disagreements between public agencies over responsibility. Ontario Hydro, for example, insisted that some flooding resulted from operations conducted by the Lake of the Woods Control Board rather than from its own dam construction and power production at Caribou Falls.[38]

By the time mercury contamination attracted an urgent regulatory response in 1970, prompting installation of effluent treatment processes to isolate and recapture the heavy metal, an estimated twenty thousand pounds of mercury had entered the English-Wabigoon system.[39] After 1970, mercury discharges to the river declined significantly, although airborne emissions continued until the mercury-cell technology in the Dryden chlor-alkali plant was finally eliminated in 1975.[40] The elimination of industrial mercury discharges and emissions into the river was not, however, synonymous with the elimination of mercury from the river.[41]

Inorganic mercury that settles in rivers, lakes, and streams is converted, through the action of aquatic organisms, to a particular form of mercury called methylmercury.[42] Methylmercury, a neurotoxin, is harmful to the central nervous system – the brain and spinal cord. It is capable of crossing the blood-brain barrier in both children and adults and may also cause neuro-developmental effects by crossing the placental barrier during pregnancy.[43] Through bacteria and contaminated aquatic organisms that were eaten by fish, methylmercury entered the food chain, leading to animal and human consumption.[44]

Symptoms of methylmercury poisoning, including a sensation of numbness or "pins and needles" in the hands and feet or around the mouth, may take years to appear. Speech, peripheral vision, and mobility may be impaired, and victims may experience mental disturbances.[45] During the late 1970s, medical observers recorded and analyzed the human health impacts of consumption of mercury-contaminated fish by members of the Whitedog and Grassy Narrows communities.[46] These findings, in turn, became the basis of a neuro-assessment protocol or guidelines that – years later – came to serve as a framework for compensation awards determined by a uniquely designed Mercury Disability Board.[47]

In Sylvia Cosway's 2001 historical report of events leading up to federal and provincial legislation on mercury contamination settlements, medical researchers describe seven categories of neurological abnormalities: tremor, ataxia, incoordination, dysarthria, absent reflexes, sensory abnormality, and visual field constriction.[48] For each of these, a scale of deficit or impairment is suggested, ranging from none to mild, moderate, and severe. For each level of impairment, these innovative guidelines contemplate cultural implications of the disability that might be experienced by Indigenous people.[49] The analysis thus takes into account the most common forms of employment for residents of Grassy Narrows and Whitedog during the 1960s, including guiding for hunters and fishermen, other tourism sector employment, and commercial fishing.[50]

An illustration of the assessment process indicates how the signs of impairment might be applied. If symptoms in the category of coordination appeared, consideration would be given to the degree of impairment. Some interference with fine manual skills such as threading a fish hook or needle would constitute a mild impact within this category; even at this level of impairment, such tasks as net mending or guiding might be very challenging. An individual who experienced difficulty doing up buttons would fall within the moderate zone. For community members facing this degree of impairment, certain everyday tasks associated with hunting, trapping, or guiding might be difficult, possibly even dangerous. A person who experienced significant interference when using utensils to eat would represent a severe example of incoordination and might be completely disabled from undertaking physical work.[51]

Symptoms associated with developmental impacts from exposure to methylmercury were also examined and analyzed in order to formulate a framework for assessing compensation on behalf of pediatric claimants.[52] A public inquiry later reflected on the anguish that might arise if unborn children were also vulnerable to historical mercury contamination: "Perhaps most frightening for the members of the two bands," the commissioners wrote, "is the possibility of congenital mercury poisoning, whereby an unborn child can develop mercury poisoning from mercury in the mother's circulatory system."[53]

Signs of illness associated with mercury poisoning were endemic. Tests conducted during the 1970s identified sixty-one people whose blood contained over one hundred parts per million (ppm) of mercury, the limit considered safe according to Canadian government studies. More than two dozen people had mercury blood levels above two hundred ppm.[54] Native representatives described consequences of mercury exposure extending beyond direct health impacts: "Mercury has robbed us of our health, and our psychological well-being, our lifestyles, our jobs and our food."[55]

The social, economic, and cultural impacts of mercury contamination on Aboriginal residents of the downstream Grassy Narrows area were also enormous. The commercial fishery, a key source of daily food and income for residents, was destroyed. Moreover, communal existence was severely undermined for members of the Whitedog and Grassy Narrows bands, as institutions and traditions were lost. Dr. Peter Newberry, a retired Canadian Forces physician employed by the National Indian Brotherhood to examine the situation, spoke of "social disintegration" and, following nearly a year on the reserve, reported that "there has been a violent death every month I have been at Grassy Narrows."[56]

Grassy Narrows chief Andy Keewatin, a former head guide at the popular Ball Lake Lodge, lamented the transformation of his community from a place with employment at 95 percent to one with unemployment at the same remarkable level. "Once there was pride. You went out, caught fish, brought it home," he explained. "But when people weren't making their own livings and started to get handouts, it changed their whole lives." The tragic consequences were overwhelming: "It takes the pride out of a man to go up there and ask for welfare. There was nothing to do ... Then the drinking came."[57]

Native leaders pressed for an alternative source of protein to replace fish, while calling for compensation for the loss of fishing activity, along with alternative employment opportunities.[58] They campaigned as well for closure of the sport fishery because of the continuing threat that fish consumption posed to members of their communities who were still engaged in guiding.[59] Roy McDonald of the Whitedog Reserve neatly summed up the failure of health warnings to alter long-standing dietary preferences: "Suppose you lived here with your family and there was no meat on your table, and the government came and told you not to eat the fish from the river. You can see the American tourists out your window. They're catching fish and they're eating them. What would you think?"[60] This concern was partially addressed in late 1975 when the provincial government undertook to provide free fish for consumption to replace contaminated stocks. Job creation initiatives were announced simultaneously.[61] By this point, however, conditions at Whitedog and Grassy Narrows had already contributed to political action and protest – notably the 1974 occupation of Anicinabe Park – in conjunction with the broader American Indian Movement.[62]

Undetectable by human senses, the perilous presence of mercury in a dietary staple raised a deeply alarming prospect: "It was part of everyone's growing dread that not until cases of extreme deformity turned up on the reserves ... would the government and the Canadian public take the problem seriously."[63] Against this backdrop, questions arose about the continued operation of the recreational fishery, where guides remained exposed to the contaminated catch.

The substantial costs of a sport fishing ban for the northwestern Ontario tourism sector, for Aboriginal employment, and for the province generally were expected to reach $40 million.[64] The Whitedog and Grassy Narrows communities eventually abandoned their call for complete closure and accepted new arrangements. With financial support from Ontario, the Kenora District Campowners Association agreed to hire fifty additional guides from each reserve and to provide shore lunches so that guides would no longer be expected to partake of the morning's catch with visiting anglers, whose very limited personal consumption did not put their health at risk.[65]

INCOMPENSABLE LOSS

The tragic experience of these two reserve communities compellingly illustrates how insidious and pervasive damage may arise where natural waterways have been overwhelmed by industrial wastes. Disasters, as sociologist Kai Erikson observes, have the potential to inflict two types of damage: injury to individuals and the destruction of community institutions. Community loss, though generally less obvious than personal injury, can irreparably harm the fabric of society, the cultural bonds connecting people to each other, and their sense of communality. "We ... are better equipped to repair the kinds of damage inflicted on *persons* than the kinds of damage inflicted on *communities*," writes Erikson. Our capacity "to restore a sense of community to people who have lost it" is much more limited than our experience in providing shelter and provisions, largely because "we do not generally think of that loss as an injury requiring treatment."[66] Remarkably, as subsequent resistance to further resource development would show, mercury contamination shifted the community sense of the balance of environmental responsibility: "The natural world came to be seen as more in need of human protection than ever before."[67]

In 1977, the Whitedog and Grassy Narrows communities initiated litigation against corporate owners of the Dryden operations claiming substantial damages for injuries from the release of mercury into the English Wabigoon River System.[68] Yet, despite the toll of personal and collective injury, it was far from clear whether these victims of a degraded northwestern Ontario river system would fare any better than Manitoba in securing compensation.

Generally assumed was the question of the lawfulness of the mercury discharge inside the boundaries of Ontario and Saskatchewan – a question that had not been conclusively answered when Manitoba had sought to recover compensation for its damaged fisheries. If residents of the jurisdictions that had licensed – and thereby approved – the operations that resulted in mercury contamination experienced some injury or loss, would they be deprived of a claim for compensation on the grounds that mercury had been released lawfully into the waterways?

In their search for a key to unlock the compensation vault, the bands consulted Robert Sharpe, an experienced litigator and respected academic lawyer. Sharpe surveyed the available options, outlining the possible application of legal doctrines such as riparian rights, negligence, and nuisance to the known facts of the situation – and to its uncertainties. He explored potential claims not only against the polluting companies but also against the provincial government for its role in the devastation. There was doubt about whether any of the legal alternatives would work – a guaranteed winner was very hard to find – but also some question about the extent and amount of compensation that might be secured even if liability could be established.

Sharpe cautioned about important restrictions on recovery of damages. Losses associated with personal injury would have to be proven rather than simply asserted, and purely economic losses might be problematic. Social losses accompanying the devastation of the community were even more so. The legal analysis emphasized that such losses would probably not be compensated under principles of law existing at the time because they were not legally recognized as harms.[69]

Sharpe's thoughtful and balanced assessment took account of the complexity of the overall claim. Yet the legal position of the bands was far from hopeless. Sharpe estimated the prospects of success at about 50 percent, citing both the capacity of the common law to adapt in novel circumstances and his personal inclination that "a court would be very sympathetic to the Bands and their members if it [could] be shown that their overwhelming loss and plight was caused by the discharges from the Dryden mill."[70]

Public impatience over the plight of two isolated native communities intensified dramatically in conjunction with more general concerns about Ontario's northlands. This spawned the Royal Commission on the Northern Environment. In an interim report, Justice E. Patrick Hartt, who initially headed up the inquiry, conveyed a deep sense of frustration in describing a situation he regarded as "intolerable." Epidemiological studies and debate about the presence of Minamata disease were no doubt valid, yet Hartt pleaded, "surely we must not await absolute scientific proof to recognize that there is a serious problem which must be rectified." Hartt called on governments to help restore the confidence of the communities: "They must feel that Governments are interested in, and will seriously consider, their proposals for resolving the impasse." In order to facilitate progress and to overcome jurisdictional and bureaucratic hurdles, Hartt proposed tripartite discussions where the wishes and needs of Whitedog and Grassy Narrows could be expressed.[71]

In 1978, the provincial government, led by Premier Bill Davis, agreed to try to move forward. Before the year's end, a memorandum of understanding confirmed the appointment of Edward B. Jolliffe as mediator. Terms of reference, accepted by the federal and provincial governments as well as the Grassy Narrows and Whitedog bands, identified issues related to adverse effects on the economic, social, physical (health), cultural, and environmental well-being of the two bands that could be attributed, directly or indirectly, to the following:

- the artificial raising and lowering of water levels affecting the reserves
- the flooding of reserve and non-reserve land
- the relocation of the reserves and/or the residents thereof
- the pollution of the environment affecting the reserves.[72]

This initial foray into the realm of alternative dispute resolution had limited impact on the disputed matter of legal responsibility. In March 1982, however, Canada's federal government concluded a settlement with the Whitedog community that provided $2.3 million towards compensation.[73]

In early 1985, the distinguished jurist Emmett Hall accepted an assignment from David Crombie, then Canada's minister of Indian and Northern Affairs, to examine prospects for settlement in the English-Wabigoon mercury pollution litigation. Hall's investigation led him to conclude that a negotiated agreement would be in the best interests of the two communities collectively and of their members. Given the costs, complexities, and uncertainties of a lawsuit, it was "impracticable, unaffordable, and inadvisable to attempt to resolve the issues in the litigious context."[74]

Hall's view of the litigation corresponded in many ways with Robert Sharpe's earlier analysis. Hall noted, for example, that the river pollution had occurred off-reserve and it would therefore be challenging for either the bands or individual members to demonstrate a sufficient legal interest in the river system to ground a claim. Even if they could surmount that obstacle by establishing some proprietary interest in the waterway and the life it supports, Hall was concerned about the difficulty of successfully asserting the liability of Reed Paper, Dryden Chemicals, and Dryden Paper, especially in relation to social and economic losses. Again, even assuming success on basic liability, Hall questioned the sufficiency of available evidence to demonstrate the extent of the actual social and economic losses that the community and its members had suffered since the closure of the commercial fishery fifteen years earlier.[75]

Turning to the matter of injury to the health of band members, Hall confirmed severe limitations at the heart of the litigation approach. Medical reports and expert opinions were "very cautious" and "stopped short of stating definitely that the conditions were caused by mercury poisoning." The most that could be taken from the available medical advice was that "while the symptoms in question were not incompatible with mercury poisoning, they were also compatible with other diagnoses." Expert evidence was equally indecisive, if not more so, in relation to children and to the assertion that mercury poisoning represented a threat to the health of the unborn resulting from genetic damage.[76]

Hall reiterated concerns about whether a link between mercury pollution and health damages could be established in court, given that certain symptoms of mercury poisoning, such as tremors and sensory abnormalities, were also symptomatic of other conditions, including alcoholism. Accordingly, Hall advised that "it is medically speaking extremely difficult to pinpoint the exact cause of the conditions that are compatible with the diagnosis of mercury poisoning since they are as likely to be compatible with alternative diagnoses."[77]

In early July 1985, the *Globe and Mail* examined the continuing struggle of Whitedog and Grassy Narrows to find a pathway out of a state of desperate dependency. Two decades of dislocation, environmental degradation, and social disintegration "would make a saint despair." Above and beyond human and economic tragedy, band members "felt betrayed by the river which had nurtured them spiritually and materially." "It will take much," concluded a rare two-part editorial, "for Grassy Narrows to find a future when it barely had a present and has lost its past."[78] This dismaying summation was written more than a decade after the same newspaper had called urgently for "a program of highest priority to assist the Ojibways in rebuilding their lives."[79]

By November 1985, following extensive deliberations, the negotiating parties concluded a Memorandum of Agreement to establish the foundations for settlement of the claims.[80] Hall advised the supervising court that the proposal, "although not a perfect agreement, was the best possible agreement achievable after so many years of frustration." He hoped it would encourage satisfactory resolution for the two communities affected by mercury contamination along the English-Wabigoon River system.[81]

In financial terms, the settlement agreement provided for the White-dog and Grassy Narrows bands to receive $5,451,500 and $6,208,500, respectively, from Great Lakes Paper and Reed Paper Limited. In addition, each band would receive $1,083,500 from the Government of Ontario and $1,375,000 from the Government of Canada. From the government payments, each band agreed to use $1 million plus interest to establish a Mercury Disability Fund. Payments received by the bands were otherwise to be directed to social and economic development within the communities.[82]

Decisive ratification votes by the two communities, Grassy Narrows with 92 percent in favour and Islington/Whitedog with 97 percent support, together with legislation at the federal and provincial levels completed settlement arrangements and led to the creation of the Grassy Narrows and Islington Bands Mercury Disability Board in 1986.[83] The board began to assess individual claims and to make payments to victims of mercury contamination.[84] Over one thousand applications have since been processed, while representatives of Whitedog and Grassy Narrows continue to seek compensation for their communities and to advocate for environmental restoration of the waterways affected by mercury contamination.[85]

Continuing Consequences

While compensation arrangements afforded basic assistance to the individual victims of mercury contamination, questions remained about general responsibility for pulp and paper pollution, preventive measures to reduce future harm, and a wider range of consequences flowing from environmental damage. In terms of environmental prosecutions, the Ontario record was limited, consisting of a mere twelve convictions in the pulp and paper sector between 1968 and 1976. In 1974, for example, both Canadian International Paper and the Ontario-Minnesota Pulp and Paper Company were convicted and fined $2,000. Significantly more charges were initiated around mid-decade. In 1977, Reed Paper – the source of the English-Wabigoon mercury crisis – received a modest fine upon conviction for pollution offences involving suspended solids and organic wastes, while American Can of Canada, convicted on several counts under federal legislation, received a fine of $64,000.[86] Fines were generally inconsequential in comparison with abatement costs. In Reed's case, the fine was a mere $5,000, whereas the recommended environmental expenditures amounted to several million.

The costs of modernization and antipollution measures aroused significant resistance. For example, when Reed Paper was asked during a legislative inquiry whether it might close and abandon the mill if its request to implement an abatement program over an extended period was refused, a spokesperson replied: "If ... the control order we receive is of sufficient financial burden, and burdensome in other ways without government assistance ... I believe the answer to that is yes."[87] A municipal official from Dryden even downplayed the impact of contamination of the English-Wabigoon waters. Community residents, he observed, "will never be able to visit and fish all the rivers near us in a lifetime ... and there is no reason why anybody has to worry about the Wabigoon River being polluted."[88] Members of the legislative committee gently intimated that "the socio-economic seriousness of the evident and extensive pollution of the Wabigoon River was minimized in some testimony."[89]

The "socio-economic seriousness" of the situation was evident in many ways beyond the suffering and loss experienced directly by Aboriginal communities. Barney Lamm, whose sport fishing lodge at Ball Lake was another casualty of the river pollution, eventually sold the property and discontinued his claims.[90] Minaki Lodge also descended irretrievably as mercury contamination undermined the sport fishery, forcing a new owner, Rod Carey, to announce closure in 1971. The 1972 reopening was immediately contentious, with Carey insisting that the decision to carry on despite ongoing losses was only made on the basis of government offers of financial support. As losses mounted further and receivership loomed ahead, Carey sold Minaki Lodge to the Ontario Development Corporation on the understanding that this agency would assume responsibility for all accumulated indebtedness, apart from shareholder loans.[91]

Seeking to enforce government commitments – and to reduce his personal losses – Carey initiated legal proceedings in 1976. Ontario immediately responded that cabinet documents he was trying to obtain to support his claim were protected by an absolute evidentiary privilege and thus not subject to disclosure.[92] Ten years after Carey's suit began, Canada's Supreme Court concluded that the contested documents should have been presented to the trial judge for inspection and for a determination of whether they should be included in the evidentiary record.[93]

As for Minaki Lodge itself, despite a vote of confidence in 1974 from Claude Bennett, the minister of Industry and Tourism, who anticipated that it might become "a jewel in the necklace of tourist facilities that threads throughout Ontario," the resort, under public ownership, was at best a tarnished gem and publicly disparaged as "that great northwestern Ontario money-eater."[94] An Ontario legislative committee concluded in 1986 that the government "made a mistake in its decision to commit public funds for the redevelopment of the Minaki resort." To no one's surprise, the committee observed that "the Ontario Government should not be in the hotel business."[95] By this point, provincial expenditures exceeded $50 million on a property that was appraised for insurance purposes at one fifth of that amount.[96] An opposition party MLA condemned the Minaki proceedings with reference to Leo Bernier, the influential provincial cabinet minister for Mines and Northern Affairs: "The member for Kenora turned this into his own private sinkhole, and the public of this province has been paying for it ever since."[97]

In 1986, looking back upon "the mystery of Minaki," the *Globe and Mail* reflected that financial retreat might have been wise long before, "beginning, we suppose, at the beginning, when Minaki Lodge, along with other lodges on the mercury-polluted Winnipeg-English-Wabigoon River system, suffered losses."[98] To avert further losses arising from the original environmental harm, the province sought an alternative future for the Minaki facility.

Many uses for Minaki Lodge had been contemplated over the years, and Orland French, an award-winning columnist, mischievously solicited additional suggestions: official residence of the leader of the opposition; detention centre for cabinet ministers found to be in conflict of interest; or bush camp for young offenders.[99] French further speculated that two problems could be solved simultaneously by offering the money-losing resort to Baby Doc Duvalier in exchange for 20 percent of whatever the notorious Haitian leader could extract from the property.[100]

The first of a lengthy list of owners after 1986 was the Four Seasons chain of hotels. Four Seasons, focusing on the expectations of resident guests, made significant efforts to restore the appeal of Minaki as a destination resort.[101] But enhanced services and accommodations, on-site entertainment, and even direct flights from Toronto to Kenora failed to reverse the decline. In 1994, the Whitedog First Nation acquired the resort facility, using funds from the mercury compensation settlement. This investment also foundered and the property continued to change hands every few years.[102]

Contamination of the English-Wabigoon river systems by mercury in the 1960s and the continuing consequences of that experience have been prominent, among similar influences, in the evolution of environmental and resource policy. Awareness of toxic substances has increased greatly, contributing to more elaborate regulatory intervention and, later, endorsement of precautionary action. The innovative compensation arrangements implemented at Grassy Narrows and Whitedog underscore the extent of human injury associated with environmental damage and the particularly disruptive impact on Indigenous communities. Native residents were in no position to "fish for fun" or "catch and release" when those slogans gained prominence across Canada and the United States as one popular response to widespread recognition that the quality of many North American waterways had been severely compromised by decades of waste discharges.

More fundamentally, just as Fisheries and Environment Minister LeBlanc had sought increased security against the dark side of progress, others wondered whether steps might usefully be taken to anticipate and prevent the further degradation of waterways before indications of contamination appeared in fish populations. While sport fishing guides proclaimed the virtues of "fishing for fun," this instruction was a frank acknowledgment that the long-standing practice of discharging industrial wastes had condemned many waterways to receive effluents whose long-term consequences were essentially unknown to regulators.

Across the broader Rainy-Lake of the Woods watershed – as in many other settings – a new array of water, resource, and environmental issues surfaced in the 1970s and 1980s. These had implications for the fishing, forestry, energy, and recreation sectors, as well as for Aboriginal communities. For guidance with respect to such challenges and environmental management, policy makers engaged in widespread consultations and discussion.

Ontario's Ministry of Natural Resources examined prospects for land-use planning in the Lake of the Woods area. The planning goal was "to provide a place where the highly desirable characteristics of the lake are maintained in a state not less than is presently being experienced while still providing acceptable levels of development for quality recreation experiences, community life and resource extraction."[103] Comparable aspirations were being voiced on the other side of the Canada-US boundary. Shortly thereafter, a broader perspective began to emerge from transformational international deliberations launched by the United Nations. The new paradigm, one that is still gaining ground, took the form of sustainability, or sustainable development. In the same way that the environmental consequences of early mineral development, water regulation, and pulp and paper mill operations extended over many years, the incorporation of sustainability into aspects of the forest resource sector and water management represents long-term commitment to protection and recovery.

12

Lumbering towards Sustainability

In the mid-1980s, the United Nations invited a high-level panel to examine "shared perceptions of long-term environmental issues and the appropriate efforts needed to deal successfully with the problems of protecting and enhancing the environment, a long-term agenda for action during the coming decades, and aspirational goals for the world community."[1] Sustainable development, a principle intended to capture the relationship between economic activity and its essential environmental foundations, emerged from this initiative. The new concept initially took shape from the invaluable work of the United Nations under the leadership of Norwegian prime minister Gro Harlem Brundtland. *Our Common Future*, the report of the Brundtland Commission, provided general guidance towards sustainable development.[2]

Reflections on the sustainability of ecosystems and economies subsequently resonated in countless settings around the planet, including the Lake of the Woods, as they continue to do. Indeed, thanks in part to environmental and community devastation along the English and Wabigoon Rivers as well as mounting controversy over water quality generally, acid rain, and northern forest industry practices, policy makers in Ontario were pressed to explore more sustainable approaches to development.

EXPERIMENTAL LAKES AND THE NORTHERN FOREST

Blooms of blue-green algae in Lake Erie – colourfully featured on magazine covers – provoked public alarm and widespread calls for effective countermeasures. Anxiety was heightened by the understanding that through bacterial decomposition, algal blooms depleted dissolved oxygen, with severe adverse effects on commercial and sport fish species. A request from the International Joint Commission (IJC) in 1965 for additional resources to study water pollution – including eutrophication, as this process of nutrient enrichment was known – helped to stimulate a remarkable scientific venture in northwestern Ontario.[3]

With complex ecosystems under threat, far-sighted researchers recognized an urgent need for sustained experimental inquiry into the causes and control of water pollution. Canada's federal Fisheries Research Board, in association with the Canada Centre for Inland Waters in Burlington, Ontario, and the new Freshwater Institute at the University of Manitoba in Winnipeg, set up institutional arrangements for landmark experimental initiatives where northwestern Ontario lakes replaced laboratory test tubes.

Dr. W.E. (Wally) Johnson conceived the idea of an area devoted to water quality experimentation on a lake-wide level by extension from lake-based research that he had observed as a student in Wisconsin. In collaboration with J.R. (Jack) Vallentyne, the scientific head of eutrophication research at the Freshwater Institute, Johnson surveyed potential sites during 1966 and 1967. Numerous small lakes would be required, but they needed to be of sufficient depth to experience thermal layering or stratification characteristic of the large deep lakes whose protection was the ultimate research objective. For pollution experiments to be controlled and free from human disturbance, the research area would have to be sufficiently removed from population or development. To permit long-term experiments, the selected site would need to be available for an extended period of time.[4]

Jack Vallentyne, also known through his contributions to environmental education as "Johnny Biosphere," explained the significance of lake-wide research. The "residence time" of water in lakes was the central consideration and could be determined from an analysis of a lake's volume relative to the outflow. Using an arithmetic formula whose complexities he described, researchers could theoretically determine the time required for a lake to be replenished and, on that foundation, assess "removal times" for various pollutants.[5] Lake-wide research would allow scientists to test these calculations under controlled experimental conditions.

The search for a suitable outdoor laboratory narrowed to a dense concentration of headwater lakes in an unsettled region lying east of Kenora and south of Highway 17, the TransCanada Highway. In 1968, Ontario's Ministry of Natural Resources, Dryden Pulp and Paper Company, and the Ontario-Minnesota Pulp and Paper Company agreed to set aside forty-six small lakes in seventeen localized drainage basins. All of these waters drained to the Winnipeg River, either through the Lake of the Woods or by way of the English River. Unromantically identified by number, the lakes ranged in size from about five to twenty hectares, with maximum depths of about twenty metres.

The first whole-lake enrichment experiment was underway by June 1969. Dozens of researchers – including international specialists from Japan, Sweden, and Norway, among other countries – were soon head-quartered at a permanent field station at the Experimental Lakes Area (ELA) and engaged in carefully managed studies designed to evaluate the impact of selected substances on water and to identify effective pollution controls.

Even as international research to safeguard water quality was getting underway at the ELA, regional waters faced new environmental threats. With Steep Rock and other iron mines around Atikokan anticipating closure and significant employment losses in the mid-1970s, a billion-dollar proposal by Ontario Hydro to establish an eight hundred-megawatt generating station on a nearby site at Marmion Lake increased in attractiveness – at least for some in the area. Planning for the new facility, a fossil-fuelled operation that would, at full capacity, consume roughly four hundred tons per hour of subbituminous coal from Alberta, was underway in 1974.

The Marmion Lake site was about seven miles northeast of Atikokan and roughly twice that distance north of Quetico Park. The appeal of the location – ultimately selected with regard to environmental, engineering, and economic considerations – involved rail access by means of a modest extension of the existing track serving mining sites and the availability of substantial supplies of water for cooling and other requirements. Three small lakes – Snow, Abie, and Icy – were to be dedicated to cooling purposes. Parts of Marmion Lake would be dewatered to serve as an ash disposal area. Apparently without irony, the design and development division of Ontario Hydro explained: "Due to its low elevation, the use of this site would considerably reduce the chances of water pollution due to leaching of contaminants from the ash."[6]

Native people and other residents expressed apprehension about environmental impacts. In addition to water concerns in the immediate vicinity of the proposed facilities, works at the Marmion Lake site potentially had wider implications, since Marmion Lake is on the Seine River system, previously re-engineered pursuant to legislation that facilitated developments by Ontario-Minnesota Pulp and Paper, the Steep Rock Iron Mine, and the Caland Ore Company.[7] The Seine waters flowed, via Rainy

Lake and the Lake of the Woods, to the Winnipeg River en route to Hudson Bay. Important migratory bird habitat was located in Marmion Lake's upper basin and in a region known as the Marmion Lake Flats, while fur-bearing animals were abundant.

The air quality implications of a large-scale generating facility using fossil fuel were also controversial. The presence of sulphur – somewhat under 1 percent – in the Alberta coal that would serve as fuel triggered concerns about impacts of acid rain on vegetation and waterways.[8] Despite assurances that SO_2 emissions from the Atikokan generating station would meet existing Canadian standards, questions remained, particularly as more stringent restrictions had been established in neighbouring Minnesota. The US Environmental Protection Agency began to inquire into the possible effects of the plant after Canada declined to join the United States in a proposed submission of the Marmion Lake project to the IJC for review. For its part, the Ontario government decided to exempt the Atikokan power project from evaluation under the province's new environmental assessment legislation on the grounds that matters were so far advanced by the time the legislation became operative in October 1976 that it would be impractical to do so. Clearing work began at Marmion Lake in January 1978, as a significantly more contentious resource conflict unfolded.[9]

In October 1976, Ontario's Ministry of Natural Resources (MNR) and Reed Paper Limited, then owners of the Dryden pulp and paper complex, signed an agreement on timber-cutting rights in a large tract of northwestern Ontario forest. The agreement authorized Reed to cut conifers on 49,200 square kilometres of virgin forest, the largest continuous cutting area ever allocated to one company in the province. This extensive grant was intended to support an industrial facility with a daily pulp capacity of nine hundred to one thousand tonnes as well as a sawmill capable of producing 180 million board feet of lumber each year, which Reed was expected to establish.[10] Significant employment was anticipated in connection with cutting operations and a new mill to be constructed at Ear Falls.

The proposal intensified the public anxiety that had already been aroused by the alarming consequences of mercury contamination in northern waters.[11] Grand Council of Treaty #9 (later known as Nishnawbe Aski Nation), along with Stephen Lewis of the New Democratic Party, figured prominently in the intense protest against the Reed plan. Andrew Rickard, Treaty 9 president and grand chief, questioned apparent inconsistencies between the guidance of foresters and land-use planners, on one hand, and the terms proposed for development, on the other. He forecast, yet hoped to forestall, severe social and environmental disruption.[12] Rickard referred to "secret plans to invade our lands and rape them of their life" in "the sellout of the century." The overall scheme, he declared, "means genocide."[13] Treaty 9 insisted upon an independent investigation or an impartial inquiry or royal commission into development "north of 50."[14]

The provincial response to mounting criticism of the Reed proposal and the call for further study and consultation initially took the form of an agreement with Reed for public hearings under general environmental legislation, further inventory of the forest resources in question, and reduction of the original development tract to remove some of the least productive areas. While the latter concession appeared to safeguard some Indigenous communities, the government's October 1976 statement failed to satisfy critics.[15] Ontario subsequently agreed to designate the Reed proposal under new environmental assessment legislation as the first undertaking by a forest products company to be subject to that review process.[16] Chief Rickard, still largely unmoved by procedural gestures, declared that reliance on the good faith of government was akin to "asking Col. Saunders to babysit your chickens."[17] In the somewhat understated assessment of journalist Stan Oziewicz: "Reed's record in the north has not enthralled the Indians."[18]

Pressure mounted from other quarters following critical reports on the limitations of current forest industry practices.[19] With the thought that Ontario might be "lost in the woods," a *Globe and Mail* editorial weighed in: "What is at stake is the rights of native peoples, the timber wealth of the area, the degree of environmental health that can be preserved in a large forestry development, and the economic return to the Province."[20] That agenda, less concisely expressed, soon became the mandate of the Royal Commission on the Northern Environment (RCNE).[21]

As the RCNE pursued its inquiry, the pulp and paper sector still employed nearly 5 percent of Canadian production workers and accounted for 7.6 percent of value added in manufacturing. In Ontario, the industry ranked just behind motor vehicle parts, iron and steel, motor vehicles, and the general category of "other machinery and equipment," but it employed 2.8 percent of the manufacturing workforce and produced 3.5 percent of the total value added by production workers.[22] Yet critical assessment of the forest industry overall was underway in the context of widespread concern and eventual endorsement of sustainable development as a long-term economic, environmental, and social objective.

J.E.J. Fahlgren, a northerner with direct experience in mining, transportation, and resources, presided over the completion of the RCNE assignment following the resignation of the original commissioner. Reflecting his own conviction that fundamental considerations had been disregarded, Fahlgren set out the consequences: "If you cut down a tree and don't make certain another grows in its place, the forest disappears." The fate of the boreal forest was, in Fahlgren's estimation, "the heart of the matter."[23] Much of the water supply and "the very air we breathe" are affected by the condition of the boreal. The warning was unmistakable: "Unless we begin acting as if we believed, once and for all, that the forest, like any other living thing, is finite and fragile, we will destroy it."[24] Pioneering federal conservation officials, early twentieth-century border lakes conservationists, and Aboriginal communities, among others who had previously expressed the same views, might have taken some comfort from the opinion of their late-twentieth-century ally.

Past practices and entrenched assumptions about the potential of the northern forest to meet demand for wood supply were inconsistent with evidence of its vulnerability – even fragility – that strongly influenced the outlook of the RCNE. One prominent concern was the lingering assumption that "it is not only economically foolish but somehow ecologically wasteful, not to cut the 'overmature forest.'" This misconception was attributed to the long-standing tendency of the provincial government to administer forest resources from the perspective of exploitation and public revenue.[25]

In contrast, witnesses such as Wilf Wingenroth, a Sioux Lookout trapper, conveyed a different perspective. Wingenroth objected to a local bumper sticker that declared: "Trees are a renewable resource." In his own more nuanced view, trees might be a renewable resource, but that was untrue of their context: "You can regrow trees anywhere if you have enough time, but you can never build up a wilderness again."[26]

The commission sharply criticized assumptions supporting determination of "the annual allowable cut" (AAC) – that is, "the portion of the growing stock that the Ministry considers can be cut each year without harm to the forest's regenerative capacity." The AAC might be expressed as "the constant area in hectares that may be harvested annually, assuming that new growth in the forest equals the volume of wood cut" – all well in theory, but in the words of the RCNE, "patently wrong."[27]

Missing from the official analysis of the AAC was appropriate adjustment for areas that cannot, or should not, be cut for reasons such as inaccessibility or limited prospects for regeneration. Nor did the conventional formula acknowledge profound inefficiencies in utilization: low levels of hardwood usage in the north – despite some signs of improvement – were "disquieting ... truly shocking," while reluctance to cut and process timber exposed to budworm resulted in further losses.[28] There were indications, too, that AAC calculations had not been suitably adjusted to take into account failures, shortfalls, or backlogs in the regeneration effort. Readers for whom this analytical commentary was excessively subtle or obscure were given an example: "The presumed growth rate of trees used in setting the AAC includes trees that are non-existent."[29]

Ontario still failed to recognize forest renewal as "the first charge against all of the revenues derived from cutting the forest by government and industry." And, in a remark that resonated with emerging concern for a broader valuation of natural resources and the environment, the RCNE described the backlog in forest regeneration as "an as-yet-undeclared part of the province's long-term debt which we must now begin to repay."[30] This was more or less the silvicultural equivalent of the message Dorothy Bolton had delivered to Premier Robarts about water pollution along the Winnipeg River: pay to fix it now or pay more to fix it later. Others questioned the effectiveness of existing measures to account for and maintain the productive capacity of the resource base or to preserve "natural capital."[31]

In 1979, forest management agreements (FMAs) were implemented through changes in Ontario's *Crown Timber Act*. The new arrangements offered greater long-term security of forest tenure in exchange for regeneration.[32] FMAs were expected to provide "within the context of a sustained-yield approach ... a continuous supply of wood ... for a mill or mills to meet market requirements." To the RCNE, however, this objective embodied internal contradictions between sustained-yield management and meeting market requirements. The problem of priorities was unavoidable: "Which goal takes precedence if mill capacity and market demand outpace sustained-yield, which, in essence is a commitment to cutting no more than can be regenerated?"[33] Regeneration, in the commission's view, was in need of serious attention, particularly in light of evidence that natural regeneration was often unsuccessful and northern conifers tended not to recover after cutting.[34]

THE FOREST SUSTAINABILITY FRAMEWORK

Reservations expressed by the RCNE about shortcomings in the existing sustained-yield approach to Ontario forest production and calls for further examination of the concept stimulated a comprehensive environmental assessment of forest management. This subsequent inquiry, carried out between 1987 and 1994, produced valuable insights into limitations of current arrangements and suggested helpful, if challenging, new directions.[35]

Landmark provincial legislation contributed significantly to a reorientation towards the evolving objective of forest sustainability as a more appropriate replacement for the production-oriented standard of sustained yield. The *Crown Forest Sustainability Act* (*CFSA*) was enacted "to provide for the sustainability of Crown forests and ... to manage Crown forests to meet social, economic and environmental needs of present and future generations."[36] Although sometimes elusive in detail, the adoption of forest sustainability as a statutory benchmark underpinned an array of transformative initiatives.

The *CFSA* articulated core principles for operational guidance. First, "large, healthy, diverse and productive Crown forests and their associated ecological processes and biological diversity should be conserved." But one might reasonably ask how this would be done, given potential contradictions between forest health and productivity similar to the challenge that the RCNE had previously highlighted. A second principle suggested an approach, if not a prescription, to promote "the long term health and vigour of Crown forests." Within the limits of silvicultural requirements, forest practices were expected to "emulate natural disturbances and landscape patterns while minimizing adverse effects on plant life, animal life, water, soil, air and social and economic values, including recreational values and heritage values."[37] The core principles, notably forest health, were elaborated in a forest management planning manual.[38]

The forest manual initially set out five measureable criteria for use as benchmarks of forest sustainability at the management unit level: biodiversity; forest condition and ecosystem productivity; soil and water conservation; multiple benefits to society; and social acceptance of responsibility for sustainability.[39] Numerous associated indicators provided further refinement and facilitated monitoring and accountability.

Sustainable forest licences are subject to independent performance audits at five-year intervals.[40] The audit process, combining documentary review with field sampling, assesses forest management as actually performed on the ground against forest management as originally planned, proposed, and approved.[41]

AUDITING THE KENORA FOREST

The Rainy Lake and Lake of the Woods basins are included within the Ontario MNR's Northwest Region and are divided, for administrative purposes, into designated "Forests." The Kenora Forest extends from the international boundary northwards beyond the English River and includes some of the eastern shoreline of the Lake of the Woods, around Nestor Falls and Sioux Narrows and Kenora, as well as the Aulneau Peninsula across the central portion of the lake. The Kenora Forest management unit covers 1,225,536 hectares, 93 percent of which is Crown land, including 468,743 hectares described as productive forest area.[42] The Kenora Forest notably incorporates portions of three major river systems – the English, Wabigoon, and Winnipeg Rivers – and over seventeen hundred lakes.

Northern sections of the Kenora Forest unit are boreal in nature, while the most southerly parts are representative of the Great Lakes-St. Lawrence forest region. Poplar and Jack pine, together with white and black spruce, dominate the forest composition of the boreal sections. Great Lakes-St. Lawrence trees such as balsam fir, eastern white cedar, red and white pine, maple, ash, and other hardwoods are more prevalent to the south.[43] Twelve First Nations live within or adjacent to the Kenora Forest boundaries, the highest concentration within any provincial forest management unit.[44] The neighbouring Whiskey Jack Forest covers 964,000 hectares in two large blocks, the more northerly of which is roughly centred on Grassy Narrows.[45] The Dryden, Wabigoon, Crossroute, and Sapawe Forests cover much of the remainder of the Rainy-Lake of the Woods watershed.

An independent audit of the Kenora Forest examined the forest management activities of Weyerhaeuser Company Ltd. and its Trus Joist operations at Kenora, as well as the MNR district office for the 2003–08 period.[46] Operations were assessed against objectives previously established in connection with the licence. One objective was related to forest diversity characteristics, including natural landscape patterns or the diversity of tree age and diameter features. Socioeconomic objectives included provision of a sustainable wood supply for industrial needs and the availability of agreed volumes to one of the First Nations – Whitedog or Wabaseemoong – within the management unit. Forest cover objectives were also assessed, specifically habitat requirements for caribou, deer, moose, and marten, among other species.[47]

Of the five sustainability criteria, three – biodiversity, forest condition and ecological productivity, and soil and water conservation – were judged satisfactory in the Kenora Forest. Two others – multiple benefits to society and social acceptance of responsibility for sustainability – were partially met. In regard to the former, low levels of harvest activity reduced economic benefits, while in relation to the latter, limited First Nations participation in forest management planning contributed to continuing dissatisfaction.[48]

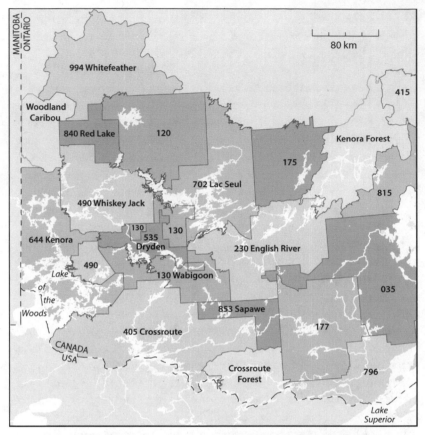

MAP 12.1 Northwestern Ontario Forest Management Units. *Ontario, Management Units in Ontario – April 2014. Map adapted by Eric Leinberger.*

In keeping with the reorientation of management objectives away from timber production or yield towards the multidimensional goals of sustainability, several features of the Kenora Forest merit consideration. For example, the area has "an unusually complex diversity of wildlife and fisheries values" when considered from the perspective of tourism, First Nations communities, cottagers, and other resource users.[49] That natural diversity now includes the largest nesting concentration of bald eagles in Ontario, together with the province's largest colony of white pelicans. These have returned to the area after several decades of displacement in the mid-twentieth century.[50] Significant water-based recreational opportunities further highlight the importance of nontimber values, for the audit identified more than 130 tourism establishments and roughly eight thousand cottage properties within the Kenora Forest, but outside municipal boundaries.[51]

The prevalence of tourism and recreational activity throughout Ontario, including the Kenora Forest, has widespread implications for forest operations and has therefore increasingly influenced environmental aspects of forest planning.[52] After decades of friction, the tourism and forestry sectors reached agreement on a proposal for forest management plans to acknowledge and accommodate some of tourism's distinctive land-use requirements.[53] One specific mechanism for addressing the relationship between tourism and forest operations is a resource stewardship agreement (RSA).[54] Operationally, elements of an agreement negotiated between a holder of a sustainable forest licence and a resource-based tourism establishment (RBT) licensee can be incorporated directly into the management plan.

The possibility of developing RSAs within the Kenora Forest was presented to 116 licensed tourist operations during the 2006 forest management plan (FMP) planning process. Tourist operators appeared to be "happy with initial contacts and follow-up, and felt that their values had been protected."[55] More than two dozen expressed initial interest in an RSA, but only one agreement was concluded at the time the FMP was submitted, and only a handful were completed subsequently. This limited response to the RSA option may be attributed to a perception that few direct impacts on tourist operators' activities would result from the 2006 plan. There were indications, however, that tourist operators were reluctant to participate "in a quasi-legal, formal process with either the government or the forest industry," although it is also possible that they were satisfied by other environmental planning mechanisms.[56]

Environmental values are also accommodated through the designation of areas of concern (AOCs), roughly grouped around such broad categories as wildlife, water, and cultural heritage. Prescribed management guidelines that have been developed at the provincial level to promote relevant safeguards are then applied.[57] More broadly, a conservation reserve was established in 2006 within the framework of Ontario's Living Legacy, a province-wide initiative to enhance protection for significant portions of provincial public lands.[58] The Lake of the Woods Conservation Reserve includes most of the islands on the lake, along with portions of the Eastern and Western Peninsulas, totalling over forty-five thousand hectares. The planning process seeks to identify natural and cultural heritage values and to develop guidelines to protect those features.[59]

Increased consideration of ecological and social values within the region has by no means displaced the objective of resource production, and,
ironically, a decline in timber production can even complicate efforts to
achieve sustainability. In an assessment that might appear counterintuitive
to observers unfamiliar with the overall forest management framework,
the auditors expressed concerns about shortfalls in projected harvest
activity.[60]

Within the forest management framework, production shortfalls represent a range of potentially adverse implications. Strikingly, the Kenora
audit declared that "the continued inability to achieve planned harvest
levels is the single largest contributing factor to the non-achievement of
the long term management direction on the Forest." The "under-harvest"
was significant because "it represents a lost economic opportunity and
will affect the long term productivity and structure of the Forest over
time." The expected age-class imbalance would be exacerbated by the
failure (attributable to harvest decline) to renew younger age classes.[61]

When confronted with the prospect of continuing decline in the Kenora
Forest, the parties principally concerned with the industry in this district
successfully formulated a new working arrangement in 2010. Weyerhaeuser
and the Wabaseemoong community agreed to a cooperative venture fea-
turing shared management of the sustainable forest licence for the Kenora
Forest.[62] In the neighbouring Whiskey Jack Forest, however, it proved
impossible to conclude a comparable agreement, at least in part because
of firm and continuing opposition to the use of chemical treatments to
promote forest renewal.[63]

CONTROVERSY AND CONFRONTATION
IN THE WHISKEY JACK FOREST

Whiskey Jack Forest operations were also generally complying with applicable legislation, regulation, and policies at the time of an independent
review in 2009.[64] However, Whiskey Jack received a significantly more
critical sustainability assessment from its auditors, particularly in connection with a projected decline in conifer coverage in favour of hardwood
forest.[65] A continuation of this trend would run counter to the intended
goal of maintaining Whiskey Jack as a conifer-dominated forest. The
decline of conifers – especially spruce – would have further implications
for wildlife species that depend on conifer-based habitat.

Regrettably, the forest transformation was easier to describe than to reverse. A number of issues were involved: a decline in industrial wood consumption, including both softwood and hardwood supplies; inadequate vegetation control; limitations in site preparation and slash management; and tension between MNR and one of the First Nations over management arrangements.[66] Viewed either sequentially or in isolation, these concerns might appear to be susceptible to discrete and independent resolution, but – cumulatively and in combination – because of their interconnections and historical context, they represented an immensely challenging and problematic situation.

The decline in industrial wood consumption already had clear local manifestations, notably the permanent closure of Abitibi-Consolidated Company of Canada's (ACCC) Kenora paper mill in 2005 and declining operations at the Kenora Forest Products sawmill, compounded by Boise Cascade's decision to avoid wood products originating in the Whiskey Jack Forest. More broadly, an overall downturn in the prospects of Canada's forest products industry reduced softwood harvest levels in comparison with forecasts. As a corollary to the reduced softwood harvest, the hardwood supply commitment for Weyerhaeuser's Trus Joist engineered wood products facility was not being met, because hardwood production from Whiskey Jack is incidental to softwood cutting rather than a primary objective in itself.[67]

Also problematic were the forest regeneration issues – that is, shortcomings in the implementation of procedures or treatments intended to promote renewal. In many blocks logged after 2006, logging slash had not been appropriately piled and burned. As a consequence, otherwise productive areas were not being regenerated. Moreover, in areas that were seeded to Jack pine, inadequate site preparation reduced the likelihood of successful conifer recovery. "Fill" planting appeared to be required. In addition, where vegetation control had been inadequate or neglected, aspen and other competitor species had already begun to displace conifers, leading towards a forest composition that was inconsistent with long-term management objectives. The failures and limitations in these various aspects of the regeneration effort were not free-standing: that is, these failures and the long-term impacts on forest composition that had been set in train were connected to other issues.

First, lower harvest levels exacerbated financial constraints at ACCC; this situation, in turn, encouraged the company to reduce expenditure on renewal. The company, for example, abandoned intensive renewal treatments involving advance site preparation, with tree planting accompanied by follow-up tending, and turned instead towards basic planting: "Reducing silviculture costs, rather than adjusting operations according to actual field conditions, was the main reason for changing from preferred to alternate prescriptions."[68] Reduced investment in regeneration in such circumstances was precisely the consequence forecast when the Ontario legislature had considered the challenge of appropriate incentives a quarter of a century before.

The preference for less extensive and less costly options had further implications for forest regeneration. By lowering expenditures, a surplus could be generated in the Forest Renewal Trust (FRT) Fund. In turn, the existence of a surplus could be used to request a reduction in contribution rates to the renewal fund during the term of the management agreement. The auditors reported requests for decreases to the contribution rate for spruce, pine, and fir. Despite some awareness of shortcomings in the renewal program, MNR approved two reductions in the FRT Fund contribution rate for those species.[69]

ACCC's scaling back on forest regeneration may be attributed to escalating conflict between MNR and the Grassy Narrows First Nation over management of traditional lands within the Whiskey Jack Forest, as well as to the company's deteriorating financial circumstances.[70] Conflict with regulatory authorities was long-standing, traceable perhaps to the advent of commercial logging on traditional lands in the 1920s; it was certainly heightened by the introduction of controls on hunting, trapping, fishing, and wild rice harvesting later in the century and coloured by the aftermath of flooding, dislocation, and the impacts of mercury contamination.[71]

Thus, in response to historical and contemporary grievances, members of the Grassy Narrows community began a blockade at Slant Lake in December 2002. Attracting widespread attention and support from such organizations as Christian Peacemakers and Amnesty International, along with environmentalist allies, the blockade soon came to be appreciated as "a site of cultural revitalization and renewal."[72] Sustained over more than a decade, the Slant Lake blockade helped bring logging to a standstill within the traditional lands of the Grassy Narrows community. If they were successful in these terms, however, the protesters also constituted something of a challenge to established decision-making arrangements within Grassy Narrows; ultimately, it proved impossible during negotiations for the community to advance and sustain an internally agreed position.[73]

Herbicide spraying was effectively suspended across the Whiskey Jack Forest. Chemical tending had been planned for 2004–05 and 2005–06, but the proposed spray program was cancelled over "concerns about the use of herbicides from stakeholders."[74] ACCC's decision to suspend herbicide spraying was based in large part on the desire "to avoid the anticipated political backlash from Grassy Narrows First Nation."[75] Political backlash was not merely anticipated. In widely circulated open letters, leaders of the Grassy Narrows community had provided Abitibi and Weyerhaeuser – as well as customers, bankers, and investors – with "official notice that you are taking part in the destruction of our homeland against our will" and had indicated that a failure to cease logging and resource extraction would result in "a fierce campaign against you on all fronts – in the woods, in the streets, in the market place, in your board-rooms, and in the media."[76] These circumstances, including repeated calls for a moratorium on resource development, contributed to the eventual closure of Whiskey Jack operations.

Abitibi had already redirected investment – notably in the form of a new biomass boiler – to Fort Frances when it abandoned the Whiskey Jack Forest entirely in June 2008. The decision, welcomed in Grassy Narrows and by community supporters, produced further employment losses for regional contractors and left the status of the existing forest management plan to be resolved through future negotiations.[77]

Members of the Grassy Narrows community had long been critical of forest management planning and had generally declined to participate formally. In 2008, Frank Iacobucci, retired from the Supreme Court of Canada, undertook the difficult task of mediation, which led to agreement between the community and the province on a process to advance col-laborative management, protection, and use of the Whiskey Jack Forest.[78] But the status of the overall long-term relationship remained unresolved amidst frustration and lingering dissatisfaction.

Grassy Narrows representatives viewed MNR as intransigent and un-willing to accept change or compromise. They argued, for example, that it does not make ecological sense to set buffer widths where slopes are involved and that thirty-metre-wide buffers are largely ineffective in safe-guarding wildlife habitat. Underlying specific criticisms of this nature was a persistent desire for direct participation in decision making with respect to traditional lands.[79]

The fundamental nature of the different perspectives separating MNR and the Grassy Narrows community compelled the independent auditors to conclude that there would be no resolution of the differences unless Ontario set aside several statutory management requirements and elements of the forest planning manual. The province might have to relinquish "significant authority to the First Nation to manage portions of the Whiskey Jack Forest according to the desires of the GNFN community." Overall, forest management planning neither anticipated nor was designed to resolve the kind of conflict illustrated by the Whiskey Jack Forest experience.[80]

ABORIGINAL RIGHTS AND FOREST MANAGEMENT

As a formal requirement, and as a matter of good practice, numerous attempts to solicit Aboriginal participation were made in the 2004–06 period of forest management planning. In addition to notification of opportunities provided through a distinct Forest Management Native Consultation Program and invitations to information workshops, community representatatives, including the Kenora Métis Council, were invited to join the Forest Management Planning Team.[81]

The Anishinaabeg of Kabapikotawangag Resource Council Inc., headquartered at Sioux Narrows, assumed responsibility for representing six First Nation communities in consultations. The Bimose Tribal Council participated on behalf of its member communities. The Wabaseemoong Independent First Nation (representing several small communities, including Whitedog) participated in planning team meetings directly on behalf of its interests in a defined Traditional Land Use Area resulting from the 1983 Ontario Islington Band Agreement, which provided for an annual wood supply allocation of about seven thousand cubic metres.[82]

Wabaseemoong's principal interests were initially associated with the Kenora Forest but soon extended to Whiskey Jack. The community expressed interest in participating in a new cooperative sustainable forestry licence that anticipated the merger of the Kenora and Whiskey Jack Forests. Wabaseemoong embarked on a traditional ecological knowledge project to identify values such as gravesites and traplines and set up its own geographic information system (GIS) for this purpose, as well as to monitor environmental values contained in MNR's database. Some community members operate logging equipment while others have undertaken tree planting. A partnership was also formed with a local company to build modular homes designed for northern conditions.[83]

This level of Aboriginal engagement nevertheless fell short. Describing efforts to promote First Nations' participation as "disappointing," "largely ineffective," or representing "peripheral involvement," and noting the "poor uptake" in response to an array of invitations, the Kenora Forest auditors

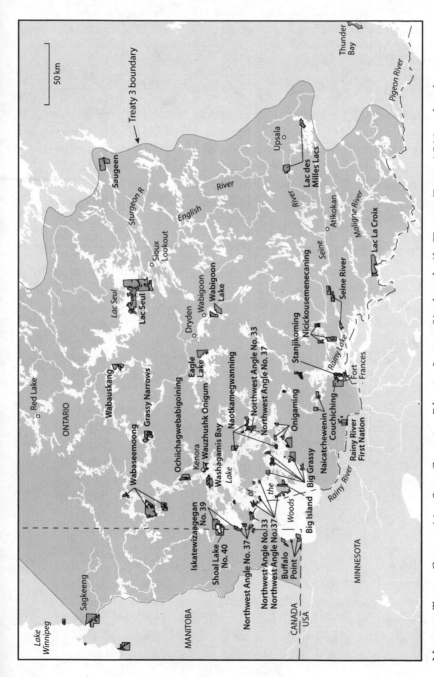

MAP 12.2 Treaty 3 Communities. *Seven Generations Education Institute, "Anishinaabe Aki (Treaty #3 Territory)." Map adapted by Eric Leinberger.*

reviewed the experience.[84] Despite being initially represented on the planning team, the First Nation participants generally withdrew as the process
continued, with the result that few communities actually contributed to
the development of values information or participated in the review of
planning documents.

Lack of involvement on the part of First Nations was not to be equated
with lack of concern for the forest or associated economic opportunities.
Furthermore, given the widely shared objective of enhanced Indigenous
involvement in all aspects of forestry operations, "minimal" participation
called for some explanation.[85] Most communities appeared to be lacking
in administrative capacity and were clearly challenged by the prospect of
managing the volume of information available or of responding to invitations to participate in a vast array of federal and provincial initiatives. In
the context of forest planning, structural limitations are partly responsible.
For example, community office holders may turn over at a high rate, with
the result that leaders with limited understanding of forestry matters are
reluctant to participate. Even First Nation forestry staff may suffer from
lack of experience when uncertainties in the annual budget process result
in contract discontinuities. Futhermore, participating Aboriginal representatives were rarely authorized to make commitments on behalf of their
communities or to sign off on relevant documentation. As a result, the
auditors concluded that "Aboriginal members are reluctant to indicate
acceptance of milestone documents and become upset when the other
members of the group proceed without their acceptance."[86]

More fundamental concerns reflected divergent expectations regarding forest management planning in comparison with assumptions about
other possible avenues of participation in public affairs. As noted by the
Kenora Forest audit team, the forest planning process has "become a surrogate for larger grievances related to land ownership, access, competing
non-Aboriginal interests, aspects of self-government, etc.," at least for some
potential participants. Since such grievances lie well beyond the intended
scope of the forest management planning process, First Nations are "continually disappointed with the results of their participation."[87] To certain
First Nation leaders, forest management was completely incapable of addressing community concerns for "*lightening of the logging footprint*" with
extended buffers, more protected areas, and so on. From this perspective,
participation would simply lend legitimacy to a process that was believed
to be "fundamentally flawed."[88] Criticism of forest management arrangements thus reflected broader concerns expressed at the Treaty 3 level.

Meeting in the spring and summer of 1997, Anishinaabe elders formulated a law to be known as Manito Aki Inakonigaawin (MAI). The MAI, or Great Earth Law, adopted in September and announced early the next month, contemplated authorization requirements and regular levies for activities having potential to affect the environment within the territory of Treaty 3. In keeping with the perspective and outlook of Aboriginal communities, the environment was broadly conceived to include "the entire environment of the Anishinaabe as it affects them and the exercise of their rights and responsibilities, and includes the spiritual, social, physical, ecological and economic environment."[89]

Consultation forms a central element of the MAI. Thus, proponents of development on Treaty 3 lands are called upon to consult prior to detailed planning and to seek the consent of the Grand Council. Through consultation, potential effects would be better understood, conditions of authorization would be identified, and the basis of a "mutually beneficial continuing relationship" could be explored. With consent, proponents acting in good faith were authorized to proceed. A failure, "without honest reason," to respect the MAI or a failure to comply with a condition set out in an authorization is considered to be a moral offence against the Anishinaabe Nation in Treaty 3.[90]

Against this backdrop, and with the renewed assistance of Frank Iacobucci as mediator, the Province of Ontario and the Grassy Narrows community concluded an accord in the spring of 2011.[91] Both parties reaffirmed their commitment to continuing negotiations and accepted a process that would allow progress with respect to interim forest harvesting. Pilot project areas that had been identified in conjunction with the 2008 agreement on process were to be managed so as to integrate traditional uses and culturally significant sites with forest operations. The 2011 agreement also addressed questions of future governance, funding, and accountability.

Chief Simon Fobister, anxious to demonstrate that his community was not opposed to logging, insisted that "we are against bad logging."[92] The community thus severely condemned clear-cutting and sought to identify opportunities to harvest logs in a responsible manner. This affirmation was important in the context of the ongoing dispute with Grassy Narrows as well as Abitibi's closure of its Kenora newsprint mill and the surrender of its sustainable forest licence.[93]

Before Abitibi surrendered its Whiskey Jack timber-cutting licence, the company's forest management arrangements and their authorization were the subject of court action as well as community protest. In 2005, following an initially unsuccessful attempt to overturn the province's approval of Abitibi's forest operations in administrative proceedings, three community representatives challenged the validity of Ontario's forest management framework and the timber licences that were granted to permit cutting on lands that have been within the province's boundaries since the northward extension of 1912. Willie Keewatin, Andrew Keewatin Jr., and Joseph William Fobister were members of the Grassy Narrows First Nation as well as the Grassy Narrows Trapping Council. Each held a registered trapline near the English River, north of Kenora. They alleged various forms of economic and cultural damage attributed to the activities of Abitibi Consolidated Ltd. operating under a 1997 licence from MNR in the Whiskey Jack Forest.

In a preliminary phase of the legal challenge, Justice Spies of the Ontario Superior Court of Justice recapped the background circumstances. The Whiskey Jack Forest, Spies observed, had been administered according to forest management plans developed on a twenty-year cycle under the authority of the *Crown Forest Sustainability Act* in conformity with the Forest Management Planning Manual and other applicable policies or guidelines. The current FMP, covering the period 2004–24, authorized logging on the traditional lands of the Grassy Narrows community, including areas where traplines were located. As the judge further explained, the plan included approvals for clear-cutting and forest access roads. Culverts were installed to extend road life, and beaver dams were removed to prevent road flooding. In addition to work camps in the cutting area, other related activities such as brush burning, tree planting, and herbicide application were carried out.[94]

The legal challenge took direct aim at Ontario's authority to permit this range of activity on the traditional lands of the Grassy Narrows community. As representatives of the Grassy Narrows Trappers Council, Andrew Keewatin Jr., Joseph William Fobister, and Willie Keewatin insisted that any governmental "taking up" of lands within Treaty 3 required prior approval by federal authorities representing Canada, or the Dominion of Canada, the phrase that was used in the text of the North-West Angle Treaty of 1873 (Treaty 3).[95] The plaintiffs did not deny that section 109 of Canada's *Constitution Act, 1867* conferred upon Ontario the jurisdiction or authority to issue forestry licences affecting its own lands within the province. They insisted, though, that this could not be done in violation of their treaty harvesting rights because those rights were historically within the realm of federal government responsibilities – and remained so. They argued that nothing in the 1873 treaty and no subsequent occurrence (including legislation and agreements dating from the 1890s and the northward extension of the provincial boundary in 1912) had altered that situation.[96] The harvesting clause, it may be recalled, stated:

> They, the said Indians, shall have the right to pursue their avocations of hunting and fishing throughout the said tract surrendered as hereinbefore described ... and saving and excepting such tracts as may, from time to time, be required or taken up for settlement, mining, lumbering or other purposes by Her said Government of the Dominion of Canada, or by any of the subjects thereof, duly authorized therefor by the said Government.[97]

For its part, Ontario understood itself to be the owner of the lands under dispute and, as such, fully entitled to "take up" these lands for a variety of purposes. Controversy over interpretation of the harvesting clause stemmed, in the view of the province, from a misconception on the part of the treaty commissioners in thinking that Canada – that is, the federal government – would own Treaty 3 lands. But the lands that Ontario now licensed to Abitibi for timber purposes were annexed to the province in 1912, joining the southerly two-thirds of Treaty 3 lands that were recognized to lie within provincial boundaries following the *St. Catharines Milling* decision of 1888.

On 16 August 2011, Justice M.A. Sanderson of the Ontario Superior Court of Justice accepted the view advanced on behalf of the three Aboriginal litigants. In doing so, she outlined an intellectual roadmap through the quagmire – or muskeg – of legal argument. She suggested that there were two essential questions. Boiled down, the court was initially required to determine whether Ontario had the authority to "take up" for forestry purposes Treaty 3 lands added to the province in 1912 so as to limit the rights of members of the Grassy Narrows First Nation to hunt or fish, as otherwise provided for in the treaty. Justice Sanderson reasoned that this inquiry involved three central elements: first, principles of treaty interpretation as established by Canadian courts needed to be applied; second, it was necessary to consider Ontario's argument that the claim against the province should be rejected because it was not consistent with constitutional realities; and third, the significance of the 1912 annexation of the Keewatin district to Ontario needed to be addressed.[98] If analysis along the foregoing lines supported the conclusion that Ontario was not authorized to employ the "taking up" clause in the treaty itself, it would then be necessary to ask whether the province nevertheless had constitutional authority to significantly infringe the treaty harvesting rights of the Grassy

Narrows community. This investigation would seek to determine whether the infringement took place in a manner that was consistent with constitutionally required procedures as set out by the Supreme Court of Canada.[99]

According to Canadian principles of treaty interpretation, it is essential to appreciate the perspective and expectations of the Ojibwa participants in the negotiations. Sanderson carefully explained her understanding of the rationale for this requirement: "Different circumstances may lead treaty signatories to have different understandings ... The actual treaty terms may be found to differ from the formal written treaty terms. Identical formal treaty terms may be interpreted differently from treaty to treaty, depending on the contextual evidence and findings about actual mutual intention and understanding."[100]

Certainly, Commissioner Morris and his associates in the 1870s found the negotiations challenging, for a number of Ojibwa appeared unpersuaded of the necessity for any treaty that would acknowledge a permanent Canadian presence within their lands. "Obstinate" and "careless" are among the words used to record their outlook and demeanour.[101] Crooked Neck, a principal chief, was particularly blunt in 1870: "We will let the pale-faces pass through our country, but we will sell them none of our land, nor have any of them live amongst us."[102] That early rejection of a proposed treaty was echoed intermittently before growing awareness of treaty benefits and improved payment terms encouraged acceptance of the agreement.[103]

With respect to the Rainy River chiefs being "careless about entering into a treaty," Justice Sanderson concluded that "they were in no rush to make a deal." Facing no immediate threat and experiencing no lack of resources, "they did not believe they needed to enter into a treaty, or that they should accept the best deal they could make whatever it might be." As the judge further explained, Indigenous residents at a distance from the Dawson route were not exposed to an influx of settlement and were quite capable of rejecting any treaty proposal.[104] Ultimately, however, they were prepared to reach an agreement. As Justice Sanderson concluded, "all the Chiefs understood and intended to give up exclusive use and share the use of the *whole* Treaty area, on certain conditions, which by October 3 they understood the Commissioners had agreed to meet."[105] And, most forthrightly, she remarked: "Had they perceived that a treaty would bring serious detriments to or seriously interfere with their way of life, they would have refused to sign."[106]

The Ojibwa, Justice Sanderson eventually concluded, recognized that some interference with their lands was to be expected, especially along the Dawson route and the proposed railway line, but otherwise they resisted limitations on resource harvesting. It was also expected that resource use and the sharing of benefits would be largely reciprocal. In this regard, one of the expert witnesses offered an account of the Ojibwa concept of lending and borrowing of resources, which she characterized as "reciprocal altruism": in other words, "the Ojibway were willing to share their resources and certainly parts of their territory, as long as they also had reciprocal access to the benefits of whatever was being introduced by outsiders."[107] In summarizing the mutual understanding, Justice Sanderson concluded that both the Ojibwa and the commissioners expected that Canadian land uses would be compatible with traditional harvesting, carried out on a subsistence basis rather than to maximize returns.[108]

Justice Sanderson signalled her view early in the three hundred-page decision that much depended on the status of the 1891 legislation in the relevant territory: "The lands in issue in this litigation are **not** in the Disputed Territory but in Keewatin, which at the time was unaffected by the 1891 Legislation. If the 1912 annexation did not affect it, the 1873 Treaty Harvesting Rights continue in respect of Keewatin to this day."[109]

Sanderson considered with great care why the Dominion was mentioned in the "harvesting clause," before concluding that the reference was intentional and significant.[110] "In 1873," she wrote, "I find Canada recognized its obligation to protect the Indians, its wards, a vulnerable minority – against exploitation by the majority."[111] Moreover, she attributed to Commissioner Morris an insightful appreciation of the potential dynamics of the federal-provincial conflict that was beginning to unfold.[112] Morris's language and analysis were carefully dissected. He might, for example, "have made it clear in the Treaty that an owner could authorize uses inconsistent with Harvesting Rights." If Morris had done so, "after Ontario was held to be the owner, Canada would not have been able to do anything to protect harvesting on those lands once the use was authorized." Instead, in Justice Sanderson's opinion, Morris selected wording "that would protect Indian interests (and indirectly Canadian strategic interests) regardless of whether Canada won or lost the Boundary Dispute." Justice Sanderson concluded that by specifically referring to the Dominion in the harvesting clause, "Morris made it clear that if Ontario purported to 'take up'/authorize land uses that would significantly interfere with Harvesting Rights, an authorization from Canada would be needed under the Treaty."[113]

Sanderson credited Morris with a prescient understanding of the emerging Ontario Boundary Dispute and of the possibility that Canada might ultimately be found not to own the lands in the disputed territory.

Accordingly, "Morris had good legal, Constitutional, political and strategic reasons for specifically mentioning Canada in the Harvesting Clause."[114]

According to Sanderson, Morris recognized that Canada would be in a position to avert or manage threats to harvesting rights under the treaty if it won the boundary dispute with Ontario. However, if Ontario were to be victorious in its boundary claim, Morris "understood that while the federal government would not be able to patent Ontario's land or authorize forestry operations or forestry uses on provincial Crown lands, his mention in the Harvesting Clause of authorizing of taking up by the Dominion meant that land uses threatening interference with Treaty Harvesting Rights would require two authorizations." Initially, Ontario would exercise its proprietary rights concerning use of the lands under section 109. Then, Canada, pursuant to the treaty and section 91(24), would be required to authorize the interference.[115]

In summarizing her findings as to the meaning of the harvesting clause, Sanderson concluded that Indian Affairs officials did not regard their mandate as confined to reserves. Federal authorities took several initiatives to protect Indigenous fisheries, and, in the context of negotiations following the *St. Catharines Milling* decision, they "extracted an agreement in principle from Ontario that Ontario would confirm the Treaty 3 reserves already allotted to the Ojibwa, absent strong reasons to do otherwise and that the Ojibwa would have exclusive fishing rights in the waters between the headlands."[116] After the death of Sir John A. Macdonald and with the passage of time, "Canada's firm resolve was increasingly diluted."[117]

Justice Sanderson's elaborate argument in favour of a continuing twenty-first-century responsibility and participation on the part of the Government of Canada in resource management within the former Keewatin district lands that had been transferred to Ontario in 1912 did not survive scrutiny in the Ontario Court of Appeal. There, nearly two years after the trial judgment, a unanimous three-judge panel systematically unravelled the fabric of the original decision. The keystone of its analysis was one central observation: "The Ojibway's Treaty partner is the Crown, not Canada."[118] This point of departure did not alter the significance of Treaty 3, but it did serve to clarify the remedial context: "The Ojibway may look to the Crown to keep the Treaty promises, but they must do so within the framework of the division of powers under the constitution."[119] Thus, given Ontario's constitutional jurisdiction as owner and manager of Crown lands within the province, by virtue of the legal decisions associated with the boundary dispute, and on the basis of legislation and intergovernmental agreements of the 1890s, followed by the 1912 northward boundary extension, the "taking up" of lands was within provincial authority, now subject to requirements for consultation where impacts on Aboriginal rights may be involved. In addition to the constitutional conclusion, the suggestion that a two-step procedure involving both federal and provincial governments was ever even contemplated was largely put to rest by the acknowledgment "that there was no evidence to suggest that Morris communicated to the Ojibway an intention to require Canada's approval of taking-up by Ontario."[120] In July 2014, the Supreme Court of Canada – also citing Canada's constitutional provisions, federal and provincial legislation dealing with Treaty 3 lands, and principles of treaty interpretation – dismissed an appeal brought by Grassy Narrows, stating, "Ontario and only Ontario has the power to take up lands under Treaty 3."[121]

The extent of authority implied in such a conclusion may appear highly satisfying for the constitutional clarity and order it suggests. In the context of many contemporary resource management questions, however, the sense of autonomy conveyed by neatly circumscribed categories of decision-making is deceptive. Consultation, collaboration, cooperation, institutional development, and joint planning are widespread – and welcome. The formulation of agreed "visions" may be used to capture common purposes and aspirations, but even express commitments to sustainability will leave many potentially contentious questions unresolved. Fish and watersheds, as the following chapters indicate, offer some guidance and insight into the more challenging aspects of occupying shared places and common ground.

13
Fishing Contests

Cultural, commercial, and constitutional dimensions of the fishery continued to influence aquatic resources management in the late twentieth century. Aboriginal resource users asserted their claims, on both traditional cultural and subsistence grounds and for commercial objectives. Other regional users were equally insistent about access to food and livelihoods. The popular sport fishery remained controversial, with transboundary skirmishing that reached the heights (or depths) of Canada-US diplomacy, if the spectre of hand-to-hand physical combat between the elected political leaders of Minnesota and Ontario qualifies for inclusion in the international dispute resolution tool kit. Cross-border traffic and conflict over North American free trade affected the fishery in previously unimaginable ways, while simultaneously stimulating consideration about opportunities for resource conservation and collaboration within a shared watershed.

NEGOTIATING THE PICKEREL MARKET

Northwestern Ontario, along with the western Canadian inland commercial fishery, faced difficult mid-century economic circumstances. Some lakes suffered from overexploitation, while marketing challenges and weak prices limited returns to primary producers. A 1966 federal inquiry reported that western inland and northern Ontario fishermen were in a "particularly appalling" state. Participants in these fisheries, mostly Ojibwa or Métis, lacked both training and alternative employment opportunities. In consequence, "during the fishing season, they must fish or remain idle." Those harvesters operating on small, remote lakes often had only one buyer for their fish, a situation that further undermined their prospects. Lacking capital, small operators depended for equipment on buyers who furnished boat, motor, nets, and fuel in anticipation of an assured supply of fish. But after one catch came another – the Catch-22: "At the end of the fishing season, the buyer indicates whether the value of the catch was sufficient to pay for the rental of the equipment and the cost of the supplies. Often it is not, and the fisherman remains in debt until the coming season."[1]

In 1966, a federal commission of inquiry into freshwater fish marketing proposed a new public agency that would take delivery of the catch and make all sales arrangements. After allowing for marketing expenses, the suppliers would receive their respective share of pooled sales revenue. The Freshwater Fish Marketing Corporation, as the institution was constituted in 1969, derived its status and authority from complementary federal and provincial legislation.[2] In the Ontario context, Hon. René Brunelle, minister of Lands and Forests, explained that "it is the Fishermen who decide by a majority vote if they want to come under this Act." On that basis, he confirmed that the new arrangements would only apply in northwestern Ontario, including the districts of Sioux Lookout, Kenora, and Fort Frances, but excluding Rainy and Namakan Lakes.[3]

Implementation was problematic in several respects. Some commercial operators remained opposed to participation, while uncertainty also arose over the relationship between marketing, on the one hand, and processing, refrigeration, packaging, transportation, and related services, on the other. The Kenora Fish Market, operating from before World War I as a wholesale purchaser for Lake of the Woods suppliers and smaller operations on northern lakes, was among a number of enterprises that did not survive the marketing transition that required all commercial sales to be made to the new public agency.[4] After a brief period of reliance on local retail sales, the market closed in 1976.[5]

For the primary producers in northwestern Ontario, early results under the Freshwater Fish Marketing Corporation regime fell short of expectations. As a consequence, part of northwestern Ontario was withdrawn from the jurisdiction of the government agency in the spring of 1973 and returned to a free enterprise system.[6]

Apart from, and indeed prior to, the fish marketing process were fundamental questions of fisheries management and allocation. A particularly acute controversy arose in Shoal Lake, where over 500,000 pounds of pickerel were harvested in 1977. This was the highest level in nearly three decades, during which the pickerel catch had rarely exceeded 150,000 pounds.[7] In large part as a consequence of the fishery (including several other species), the First Nations of Shoal Lake enjoyed favourable economic circumstances in comparison with neighbouring Indigenous communities.

Among Shoal Lake's more successful commercial fishers was Herb Redsky, who, in the spring of 1978, anticipated a gross income of $18,000, mostly from fishing, with wild rice and trapping each contributing about $1,000.[8] But revenues soon proved to be vulnerable, engendering intense conflict over control of the Aboriginal fishing sector.

Spring fishing in 1978 was indeed exceptional. With pickerel selling for $1.25 per pound and jackfish at $0.35, Herb Redsky averaged $300 to $400 per day, on one occasion earning $567 for the day's catch. It was widely understood that by the end of April, fifteen fishermen from each of two Shoal Lake bands had already exceeded the limit proposed for the entire year.[9] Yet the future was far from certain, because in August 1977, the Ministry of Natural Resources (MNR) announced reduced commercial quotas in order to conserve fish stocks following an extended period of decline. There were five commercial licences on Shoal Lake, two held by the bands and three by non-Native owners. Quotas per licensee were scheduled for progressive reductions, from twenty-nine thousand pounds in 1979 to twenty-four thousand in 1980, with sharp further decreases to thirteen thousand in 1981.[10]

The reduced quotas, in Herb Redsky's view, would "destroy our way of life" and amounted to "legislating us onto welfare." Some band members saw no choice but to disregard them, and band leaders took the position that the provincially established quotas were actually inapplicable to waters lying between headlands within the reserves.[11]

The fishing controversy extended more broadly across the region. Ominous general warnings were in circulation from at least 1972, when the ethnologist E.S. Rogers forecast the collapse of a viable commercial fishery in northwestern Ontario.[12] But ten years earlier, the Department of Lands and Forests had endeavoured to scale back the Shoal Lake harvest, particularly within the sensitive Snowshoe Bay spawning area.[13] Ontario's MNR now expressed concern about fluctuating catch levels and overfishing throughout the entire Lake of the Woods area, while Indigenous resource users insisted that fish populations were healthy when assessed against their long-term experience of good years and bad. As Michael Moore summarized the situation for the *Globe and Mail:* "There is no way an outsider can judge between the claims." It seemed, however, that anglers enjoyed favourable allocations, since their economic contribution to the region significantly exceeded that of the commercial fishery. According to government calculations, anglers contributed $50 to the regional economy around the Lake of the Woods for every $1 associated with commercial fishing. Furthermore, Moore reported, "angling gives jobs to 20 people for every commercial licence-holder."[14]

Facing sharp criticism of the quota reductions, MNR agreed to postpone implementation to 1 January 1979. The delay was intended to permit a biologist hired by the bands to review government data and to allow those involved in the Shoal Lake commercial fishery to investigate alternative opportunities for employment. The delay also allowed time for tripartite talks involving the federal and provincial governments and the communities as a further means of resolving controversy.[15]

Members of Shoal Lake Band No. 39, whose reserve straddled the Ontario-Manitoba border, took legal action. Justice Peter Cory, then of the Ontario High Court, acknowledged the urgency of the dispute about quotas when it came before him in the summer of 1979. Before tackling the legal and constitutional questions, Cory ventured a frank personal assessment, calling upon both sides to address the "difficult subject" of quotas with "reason and goodwill." He urged the province "to approach the situation with a sense of sympathy and understanding," since commercial fishing represented a major source of income for band members. Sympathetically, Cory remarked: "The loss of a right to fish as they see fit, is contrary to the history and tradition of countless generations of their people."[16]

Yet Cory simultaneously counselled band members that quotas "may now be essential" as a result of changing circumstances. More efficient methods of fishing inevitably contributed to the decline of the fish population. Demand for the commercial fisher's product was also increasing with population growth. He cautioned accordingly that "the resource may soon be so depleted that it will be impossible to restore it and the livelihood of the bands will thus be forever destroyed." That possibility underscored the judge's suggestion that in the interests of its future well-being, the band "must approach the problem of quotas with the realization that they are a necessity and will continue to be a necessity for the foreseeable future."[17]

Ultimately, the band's legal challenge only partially succeeded on one issue. Justice Cory determined that the Ontario Fishery Regulations "do not apply to those waters of Shoal Lake lying within the Province of

Manitoba." He dismissed the wider constitutional arguments that were made against the proposed quotas before concluding, not without hesitation, that the ministry had proceeded fairly in hearing and responding to criticisms and objections. In so doing, however, he imposed a further delay on the introduction of quotas until 15 August 1979, adding his expectation that the ministry could use the interval to reassess the quotas and their allocation and "demonstrate its goodwill, its interest in the people, [and] its concern for their awesome problems."[18]

For guidance respecting allocation of the overall Lake of the Woods fishery among competing users whose collective consumption exceeded sustainable levels, MNR commissioned a comprehensive economic and social assessment in 1980–82. Estimates indicated that the total actual harvest amounted to around 1.3 million kilograms per year, in comparison with a maximum sustainable yield of just over 1 million. The total harvest included 480,000 kilograms of walleye, with 310,000 kilograms going to anglers, predominantly US visitors to tourist camps and facilities. Local operations engaged in commercial fishing sold 565,000 kilograms, including 150,000 of walleye, mostly to the United States. Aboriginals operating under commercial licences, mainly using gill nets but also fishing for domestic consumption, accounted for 55,000 kilograms of the harvest, with walleye constituting 20,000 kilograms.[19]

As explained by Anthony Usher, an experienced consultant who directed the research, some user groups would experience a decline in social and economic benefits following harvest reductions. Since "livelihoods were at stake," any reduction or reallocation would be closely watched.[20]

For purposes of allocation, seven user groups were identified. The "commercial fishermen" class, sometimes subdivided between Indian and non-Indian commercial fishermen, included all commercial fishing carried out under the authority of a commercial licence. The "Indian fishermen" class included treaty Indians fishing under commercial licence for either commercial or domestic purposes, a category whose problematic character, due to the intermingling of domestic and commercial activity, was acknowledged: "The same Indian fisherman can harvest both domestic and commercial fish with the same gear at the same time and gain the same social benefits from so doing, whatever the ultimate economic use of the fish being caught at the moment."[21] Aboriginal commercial operations, generally considered to be band fisheries, held fifteen of the forty-eight licensed commercial lots around the lake.[22] The remaining thirty-three lots on the Ontario side were held by twenty-eight non-Indian commercial operators. Fifteen commercial operations were active on the Minnesota side, although commercial walleye fishing was scheduled to be phased out by 1992.[23] Other user categories included resident anglers, resort guests, non-resident cottage anglers, and "Minnesota-based boater anglers."[24] The latter designation applied to anglers who travelled on a day-use basis from Minnesota to fish in Ontario waters. This group would later become a flashpoint in its own right.

Using survey techniques, researchers examined the significance of the fishery for each constituency, a task that was – and remains – exceptionally sensitive, for "'worth' is in the eye of the beholder."[25] While various measures or indicators applicable to commercial fishing may be obtained from business records and government accounts, the problem of valuation is particularly complex in relation to recreational fishing, where "the primary units of production are angler-days rather than kilograms of fish."[26]

To provide insight into how they might respond to alternative allocation scenarios, recreational anglers were invited to tell fish stories. Specifically, anglers were surveyed to determine how their level of fishing activity might change if they could imagine catching more or fewer fish of the same size without alteration in the time or expenditure allocated to the pastime. Another inquiry asked for anglers' thoughts on catching the same number of smaller or larger fish. Such research seeks to identify "catch per unit of effort," or CUE, sometimes presented as fish caught per hour or, alternatively, as hours per fish caught: "With information on the hypothetical relationship between individual user harvest and behaviour, it was then possible to estimate total angler-days and harvests for each user group at 0.5 and 1.5 times current CUE."[27]

From an economic perspective, results might well have suggested that the problem of overfishing would take care of itself since there was no good economic rationale for persisting in the activity; once net operating revenues were analyzed, "tourist operations and commercial and domestic fisheries all operated at a loss."[28] The study, however, identified other considerations, notably the dominance of tourism from the perspective of direct economic returns from the Lake of the Woods fishery. In the base year of the study, 1979, tourism accounted for over 80 percent of total overall returns. However, considering profitability, the commercial and domestic fisheries out-performed the tourist fishery, and more revenues remained in the region.[29] The Lake of the Woods fishery was also regionally significant, given the direct contribution of about a thousand jobs. Relative to revenue, the commercial and domestic fishery created more employment than the tourist fishery, although the positions were overwhelmingly seasonal.

Above and beyond the economic contribution, the fishery produced intangible social benefits. Commercial fishers and employees of tourist operations often lacked alternative local employment. People in this situation might thus regard seasonal employment in the fishery as a preferable pathway to unemployment insurance rather than welfare. It also appeared that seasonal engagement in fishing complemented other resource production activities, with revenue derived from one activity then used to purchase supplies or equipment required to pursue the next. Benefits from the fishery – and especially from its relative autonomy – also encompassed considerations relating to quality of working life. Native fishers found commercial fishing "particularly congenial." Distinctive benefits enjoyed by Ojibwa from the commercial and domestic fishery "may be categorized into quality-of-life values, security values, identity values, and status values."[30]

The fishery was regarded as "an integral component in the total socio-economic and cultural situation of the Ojibwa-Cree." Describing commercial fishing as "an inseparable or constituent part of their holistic outlook on life," researchers argued that "to neglect this one aspect of this philosophy would create a vacuum effect (or a sense of emptiness)." By way of overall assessment, a consensus emerged in favour of retaining commercial fishing for a variety of reasons. First, without it, most reserves had a very limited economic base and faced severe youth unemployment. The deep emotional attachment to the land and natural resources was a further important consideration. A commercial fisheries task force, acknowledging that few people fished full-time, with many deriving only casual employment, considered the resulting income to be "very important" at the individual, family, and community level. In sum, "commercial fishing ... offers relief to the unemployed and at the same time provides meaningful employment ... in a social and economic system that is relative to their unique attitudes, thoughts and values."[31]

By the 1970s, a number of lakes that Indigenous fishers had traditionally harvested were experiencing closure, some, apparently, as a result of a government preference to promote tourist camp operations and some as a result of mercury contamination. Native fishers advanced numerous recommendations to improve conditions, including assistance in the form of training and grub staking for those new to the industry, funding to support the ice harvest, and help with repairs to motorized equipment. Other proposals called for enhanced facilities such as docks and more convenient receiving points to reduce high air transportation costs. From an organizational perspective, other suggestions centred on operations of the Freshwater Fish Marketing Corporation, or strengthened control of the industry, including rationalization through reductions in the number of active participants. Additional suggestions included licensing un-exploited lakes or reopening lakes that had previously been licensed to Indigenous fishers.[32]

Negotiations failed to resolve fisheries controversies during the mid-1970s, but the discussions, combined with judicial decisions on fishing rights, encouraged policy adjustments. In a set of general enforcement guidelines, MNR acknowledged that certain provisions of the Game and Fish Act were superseded by treaty hunting and fishing rights. Conserva-tion officers were directed to "exercise leniency when dealing with native people" who were otherwise in violation of the Fisheries Act and the Ontario Fishery Regulations for taking fish "for their own personal con-sumption" on unoccupied Crown land, particularly in Ontario's northern regions.[33] As fishing controversies proliferated before and after constitu-tional amendments concerning Aboriginal and treaty rights, great debate ensued on the nature of "leniency" as opposed to rights or entitlements and on the scope of "personal consumption."

Ongoing analysis by the Royal Commission on the Northern Environ-ment (RCNE) placed resource conflicts and controversies in a broader context. Thus, in 1978, Justice E.P. Hartt, the commission's original chair, described the post-Confederation treaties as "agreements of a special nature; they gave access to the land to the Euro-Canadian interests wishing de-velopment while at the same time guaranteeing the Indians continued hunting, fishing and trapping rights, plus exclusive use of reserve lands."[34]

Following his resignation from the RCNE to assume leadership of the newly created Indian Commission of Ontario, Hartt observed that Ontario introduced band licensing on the assumption that Aboriginals who wished to fish commercially could not all be accommodated by the resource. The band-based licensing arrangements allowed anyone in the band to fish while simultaneously managing the volume of fish caught. At the same time, these arrangements allowed traditional fishing methods to continue and were generally consistent with the established pattern of collective ownership.[35] Others were less confident that commercial limits were ac-tually being respected by Indigenous and non-Native resource users.[36]

With the encouragement of the Indian Commission of Ontario, federal, provincial, and First Nations representatives discussed fisheries matters. By December 1982, the parties had concluded the Ontario Native Fishing Agreement (ONFA).[37] As of this date, 58 of 117 Ontario bands held commercial fishing licences. These were predominantly in northwestern

Ontario, where many communities held multiple licences, some as many as ten, such that they were entitled to fish in different lakes or sections of lakes.[38] The ONFA set out a definition of "harvest fishing," the entitlement to fish for personal or family use or for use by band members, including by sale or barter between bands. "Harvest fishing" could be carried out without a licence anywhere other than in fish sanctuaries and using any means that was not banned or injurious to the fishery. In addition, the agreement classified a number of Ontario lakes that were considered to be significant to Indigenous people into five zones, ranging from areas open to anyone to restricted waters over and above reserve lakes. Further terms of the ONFA provided for the involvement of Indigenous communities in fisheries management and for the appointment of Indian conservation officers.[39]

Early assessments were cautiously optimistic that the ONFA might simultaneously satisfy the ministry's goal of establishing a legal framework for managing Indigenous fishing and the objectives of the communities: safeguarding traditional practices, modifying fisheries regulations for greater consistency with treaty provisions, and supporting economic development.[40] Yet dissatisfaction was evident in several quarters.

Once again, the Shoal Lake situation provoked controversy when MNR – within about six months of the ONFA – finally closed the commercial pickerel fishery to encourage rehabilitation of the depleted population.[41] Grand Council Treaty #3 responded to the closure by withdrawing support from the province-wide agreement. Native representatives again questioned the credibility of MNR's forecast of a collapse of the Shoal Lake pickerel stock, not the first time such an outcome had been predicted. Moreover, Indigenous representatives felt that the ministry's failure to consult before closing the fishery had breached the spirit of the agreed relationship.[42] Others, however, felt that the province had not appropriately respected the range of affected interests and expectations in the negotiations.

As assessed by experienced observers of Indigenous resource usage, the agreement "appears to lack the mechanisms to implement 'harvest fishing' rights without upsetting other user-groups, or to implement the conservation clause in a manner which is mutually acceptable."[43] Indeed, critical reaction to the proposed fishing agreement represented "one of the hottest political issues" of Premier William Davis's career and produced an acknowledgment from the Natural Resources minister that he had "goofed" in limiting consultations to brief public sessions.[44] The collapse of the Ontario Native Fishing Agreement in 1983 was ultimately attributed to the exclusion of other constituencies from the deliberations. The *Globe and Mail* later placed blame for the "political storm" on secret negotiations and ambiguous language: "The recognition of (native) fishing rights depends on judicious accommodation: it has to balance the traditional fishing rights of Indians against the livelihood of non-native operators in northern Ontario."[45] Instead, however, with public deliberations in abeyance, a full buyout of existing licences was initiated in anticipation of preferential allocation to commercial operators from Treaty 3.

In June 1986, Treaty 3 representatives proposed a framework for renewing the lapsed discussions. They called for treaty fishing rights to be given precedence in a new system of fisheries management. Acknowledging that "the overall concern will be preservation and renewal of the fish populations," the proposal insisted that "governments must halt pollution and poaching" and echoed a widespread call for "unbiased scientific information" that would include "information from Indian experts." Four ranked priorities were then set out:

> Indian requirements will be the first priority of the permitted fish catch ... This includes fish for sale and barter, and exclusive Indian fishing areas. Indian government will be solely responsible for managing this aspect.
>
> The second priority for the fish catch will be the needs of local non-Indian residents, subject to adjustment according to Indian requirements.
>
> The third priority will be local non-Indian commercial fishermen.
>
> The fourth priority for permitted fish catch would be the wants of non-Indian non-residents. The only claim these people have on the resource is their ability to pay for it. To the extent that fish stock is available, and they are able to pay so that Indians and local residents gain the benefit, they should not be denied.[46]

To facilitate implementation, the chiefs of Treaty 3 advocated an intergovernmental mechanism that would involve Canada, Ontario, and First Nations.[47]

In a renewed attempt to reach agreement, once again under the auspices of the Indian Commission of Ontario, the ministry initiated a broader consultative process in the fall of 1986, alongside a commitment to "the principles of Indian rights to fish, sound conservation practices and proper fisheries management."[48] Native participants, for their part, now favoured regional frameworks oriented around treaty areas. Band-based subagreements could then be formulated within this context.[49]

Conservation represented a crucial consideration for all parties. Indeed, the concept was being explored in judicial commentary on the tension between Aboriginal claims and long-term resource management goals. Canada's Supreme Court, for example, noted in one West Coast salmon dispute that "conservation is a valid legislative concern," as all parties agreed. Aboriginal communities "do not claim the right to pursue the last living salmon until it is caught." Their focus, rather, was the allocation of fisheries resources following the application of reasonable conservation measures. The court summarized the ranking of priorities, after conservation, as Indian fishing followed by non-Indian commercial fishing and, finally, non-Indian sport fishing, before adding that "the burden of conservation measures should not fall primarily upon the Indian fishery."[50]

This still left many contentious matters, such as restrictions on the manner of fishing, the application and design of quotas or limits, and licensing or authorization arrangements to be resolved. And the interests of non-Indian resource users also had to be respectfully accommodated. But when Ontario discussions resumed, non-Native fishing interests remained particularly critical of the ability of a provincial negotiator to act on their behalf.[51] To see their concerns addressed, non-Aboriginal resource users constituted their own independent advisory committee.[52]

The advisory committee process sought to be responsive both to the exclusion of non-Native communities from the negotiations overseen by the Indian Commission of Ontario leading up to the stillborn Ontario Native Fishing Agreement drafts of 1982 and to the position later taken by Grand Council Treaty #3. The latter, as noted, asserted that "Indian requirements will be the first priority of the permitted fish catch, as guaranteed by the Treaty," and insisted that Indigenous governments would manage "exclusive Indian fishing areas."[53]

The advisory committee placed great emphasis on the significance of the fishery to many residents of the North for whom fishing "is much more than recreation – it is an integral part of our lifestyle, whether for social reasons, or because our livelihood depends on it."[54] To underscore this observation, the report repudiated the impression that fishing was merely a holiday pastime.[55]

This perspective grounded the committee's insistence that "no group or organization be given rights if the effect of such is to diminish the rights of other groups or organizations." Accordingly, it was clearly stressed that "any position or recommendation ... that suggests that natives ought *not* to have something, such as priority rights, is made to impress upon Government that with respect to the natural resources of this Province, *all* people must have the same rights, and share the resources fairly and equitably."[56] Thus, while acknowledging rights claimed under treaty, the report noted the position of other users:

> residents claim rights by virtue of a variety of natural rights – by birth place of themselves or their parents, by virtue of having selected residency in this Province, by virtue of having paid a prescribed fee to enable them to earn a livelihood, or by virtue of having invested significant capital into the establishment of businesses centred around this major resource.[57]

As its own first priority, the advisory committee championed conservation, anchoring that objective on firm foundations: "If conservation does not remain as the single most important principle, there will undoubtedly be a time when ... the resource will effectively disappear."[58] To the advisory committee, notwithstanding express commitment to the principle of conservation, the Treaty 3 proposal appeared problematic in operational terms. It was difficult to determine the nature and extent of the Indigenous harvest: "Without any requirement to report how many fish are being taken or might actually be required to be taken it seems virtually impossible to carry out truly effective conservation measures."[59]

Commentators acknowledged the legitimacy of some forms of flexibility – perhaps licences issued by bands or the waiver of fees – but there was a bottom line: "In order to know with a much greater degree of certainty what type of pressure the resource is under, the managing authority must have an accurate number of users and the number of fish taken." Given a shared interest in preserving the fishery, "conservation requires respect of all fishermen and there must be a realization that every group must lose a little so that all may gain."[60] From a management perspective, even the subsistence fishery was problematic, since "it does not allow any determination of how much of the resource is actually being used." That information gap severely impeded conservation planning, and the report was clear in its assertion that any right to fish "must include also a responsibility to contribute to the conservation and also the management of the resource."[61]

In the view of the advisory committee, the distinctive historical position of Indigenous communities would be recognized in relation to reserve lands. "To be effective," the committee observed, "any management system must recognize that in view of the historical position of the natives with respect to the fisheries resource, native people have a unique role to play." The implications of that uniqueness then had to be addressed, something best done – in the committee's opinion – with reference to "the fact that reserve lands are devoted uniquely to their use." The committee urged that "the same principles of management should apply and the same spirit of cooperation by comanagement should exist," notwithstanding "obvious legal differences in the treatment of reserve lands." While it might be necessary to address different considerations, "the basis of management should not change." This conclusion derived from the underlying, presumably shared, goal: "We are attempting to manage a resource, not a band, or its people."[62]

Distinctive opportunities for economic development assistance, including enhancement of the resource, were also noted: a Native aquaculture industry, fish hatcheries, habitat enhancement, removal of coarse fish, tourism development, and Native conservation officers.[63] Whether this range of initiatives would be sufficient to accommodate the aspirations of Indigenous resource users remained to be determined.

By this point, however, charges under the *Fisheries Act* were increasing across Canada and had produced "a history of varied and almost uniformly unsuccessful strategies which attempt to insulate native people from prosecution."[64] More significantly, when Aboriginal rights, including fishing rights, were recognized in 1982 constitutional amendments, a further series of controversies entered the reconceived legal system. Among these, the 1990 *Sparrow* decision provided an opportunity for Canada's Supreme Court to discuss the role of conservation in cases of conflict between governmental regulation of the resource and Aboriginal or treaty claims to the fishery.[65] In situations where Aboriginal or treaty rights were subject to regulatory interference, or even extinction, the Crown would henceforth assume the legal duty or onus to justify that interference according to tests and standards established by the court. *Sparrow*'s significance soon became apparent in northwestern Ontario, when members of the Rainy River Band who had been charged with fishing out of season at Manitou Rapids, fishing with a prohibited net, and selling fish out of season successfully appealed their conviction.[66]

In Shoal Lake, commercial fishing continued, with increased production of whitefish and northern pike. Pickerel or walleye were harvested on a subsistence basis at a rate estimated at around 18 percent of levels associated with a healthy fishery, although no reports or monitoring records are available to verify the assessment.[67] A detailed review of the Shoal Lake situation conducted under the auspices of the Anishinabek/Ontario Fisheries Resource Centre two decades after the 1983 commercial and recreational closure offered very limited prospects for short-term optimism.[68]

The walleye stock had not recovered from overfishing in the period leading up to commercial restrictions in 1979 and remained "severely depressed." A moratorium on subsistence fishing was contemplated as possibly "the most effective strategy in order to increase adult biomass."[69]

Shoal Lake watershed planners remarked that overexploitation had severely undermined fish populations, resulting in depletion of "the very resource that fishers depend on for their livelihood."[70] Coming the better part of a century after the destruction of the sturgeon fishery in the Lake of the Woods – which was, in 1910, declared "the greatest sturgeon pond in the world" – this was a remarkably limited and disheartening insight.[71] But in a further echo of the competitive environment that contributed to the earlier sturgeon decline, new transboundary differences arose between fishing interests on the Canadian and US sides of Lake of the Woods waters.

Walleye Wars

Minnesota tourist facility and resort owners, operating as the Border Waters Coalition against Discrimination in Services Trade, put the Lake of the Woods on the radar screen in Washington, DC, in March 1999 with allegations concerning violations of the North American Free Trade Agreement (NAFTA), involving Canada, the United States, and Mexico.[72] NAFTA Article 1202 requires each party to accord service suppliers from the other countries such treatment as is no less favourable than the treatment accorded to its own service suppliers in like circumstances.[73] The coalition's petition, presented to the US trade representative, Charlene Barshefsky, bluntly accused Ontario of imposing "blatantly discriminatory" rules to undermine the resort, guiding, and sport fishing industries in northern Minnesota. The surprisingly controversial pickerel thus joined softwood lumber and other major irritants on the Canada-US trade agenda in 1999.

The American petitioners specifically objected to an Ontario practice that allowed a nonresident of Canada to keep game fish caught on the Ontario side of the border only if the angler stayed overnight in an Ontario commercial establishment or otherwise consumed local tourist services in the province. A nonresident angler who returned from Canadian waters to accommodation in Minnesota was not permitted to keep the day's catch.[74] The objective, Ontario insisted, was conservation.

Minneapolis lawyer James D. Southwick recognized fishing as "very close to an official state religion" in Minnesota. He offered to spearhead the petition process using his Washington experience as legal adviser to the US trade representative on NAFTA issues.[75] By way of a remedy under section 301 of the US Trade Act, the Border Waters Coalition felt that the imposition of fees on about forty miles of Canadian National Railway line traversing Minnesota's border lakes region and carrying about fifteen trains daily would be appropriate. Minnesota state legislators went so far as to introduce a number of bills along these lines.[76]

The degree of upset among Minnesotan resort and tourist operators affected by Ontario's sleepover rule was unmistakable and particularly acute around the Northwest Angle, the "geographical orphan" that "juts like a thumb into the smooth Canadian underbelly at the 49th parallel."[77] To Gary Dietzler of Northwest Angle Resort, where business had plummeted, the situation had produced "an atmosphere like you're going fishing in Bosnia." Celeste Colson, whose lodge, Jake's, had also suffered a falling off in business, condemned the provincial regulation as "bedroom economics."[78]

Minnesota governor Jesse ("The Body") Ventura vigorously championed state interests, at one point offering to wrestle his Ontario counterpart, Premier Mike Harris, to settle the matter. The premier reportedly proposed golf as an alternative dispute-resolution procedure.[79] The walleye conflict coincided with another source of cross-border friction: an announcement by the Ontario Ministry of Natural Resources of the cancellation of the spring bear hunt, thereby outraging rock musician and wildlife aficionado Ted Nugent, whose biodiverse repertoire includes "Cat Scratch Fever" and "Great White Buffalo." Nugent called on US tourists to boycott Ontario.[80] Representatives of Ontario hunting and tourist outfitting organizations also challenged the cancellation of the hunt, but court proceedings failed.[81]

The US trade representative dismissed Ontario's suggestion that the walleye protection measures were motivated by conservation, concluding instead that they "simply redirect capital toward Ontario resorts and away from Minnesota resorts." To US officials, the main issue was "differential and discriminatory treatment based on whether U.S. anglers stay overnight in Ontario or otherwise use or purchase Ontario services or goods."[82]

The controversial Ontario initiative had emerged within the context of cross-border relations and differences concerning the Lake of the Woods and Rainy Lake fisheries. In response to a decline in Lake of the Woods pickerel stocks during the 1970s, Minnesota took firm steps to phase out the commercial harvest in favour of the sport fishery. Ontario, in contrast, pursued general quota reductions, not vigorously attempting full closure of the commercial fishery in favour of the Indigenous harvest and sport sector until the late 1990s.[83]

Regulations imposing conditions and limitations on access to Ontario fish – not just pickerel – by US recreational fishermen dated back to 1994, a time when Ontario's minister of Natural Resources, Howard Hampton, was the elected representative of this northwestern Ontario region. Hampton, a native of Fort Frances, was a vigorous advocate for northern tourism. He reported childhood experiences of seeing cars from the United States lined up for three or four miles to cross the border at Fort Frances for summer recreation and fishing, and he worked with determination to promote the tourism sector.[84]

Ontario restrictions on Rainy Lake emerged following Minnesota's failure to implement conservation recommendations from an International Citizens Task Force in 1993.[85] In January 1998, the more elaborate control regime for the Lake of the Woods triggered vigorous reaction. Minnesota retaliated with state legislation intended to restrict the importation of fish from Ontario. This was expected to discourage fishing in the first place and to undermine whatever economic advantage Ontario might have anticipated.[86]

The escalating trade controversy and the resolute determination of American participants to discount the conservation issue presented severe challenges. As John Ibbitson, an experienced political commentator, outlined the dilemma facing Ontario: "Was the province really prepared to court US sanctions for the sake of some fish? Were we ready to risk the proverbial tariffs on Hamilton steel simply because we had upset some Minnesota resort owners? Were we prepared to pit our out-of-shape Premier against a governor formerly known as 'The Body'?"[87] The section 301 investigation was ultimately terminated on 5 November 1999, when Ontario removed the overnight stay requirement and simultaneously lowered catch and retention limits for all nonresident anglers.[88] *New York Times* columnist James Brooke characterized Charlene Barshefsky's news release as a "victory statement."[89] While the United States welcomed cancellation of the objectionable provincial regulations, a corresponding reduction in the Minnesota summer catch limit to eight fish from the previous limit of fourteen was responsive to Ontario's long-standing concerns about the long-term well-being of the resource.

Around the Lake of the Woods, apprehension indeed centred on the fate of the resource rather than on the state of international trade relations. Mal Tygesson, a former president of the Kenora District Camp Owners

Association and the owner of Evergreen Lodge on Eagle Lake, some fifty miles north of the border, voiced the underlying fear: "A trade deal on tourism gives them unfettered access to a resource." He was speaking from experience; Evergreen Lodge – located on a domestic Canadian lake – was vulnerable. The new ruling would allow Minnesotans to arrive by the busload, catch the local limit, and return home at the end of the day: "If one country has the right to do that with the resources of another country, then they have the right to do that with the water, with the trees." This alarming prospect was magnified by the mammoth scale of the United States: "It's hungry, and it's looking for resources all around the world."[90]

Some faint glimmer of a reconceived approach to the watershed and its resources could be found in the musings of walleye war veterans. Clarence Larson, holding forth in Grumpy's Bar in Angle Inlet, Minnesota, remarked that the Lake of the Woods was the biggest body of walleye fishing in the world, adding: "There's plenty here for everyone." He continued: "I don't figure that the fish belong to any one country; they belong to the lake. Both of our countries are pretty well off. I don't understand why we can't work this thing out."[91] On the Canadian side, Erick Bennett of the Maple Leaf Motel in Sioux Narrows mused pointedly on a possible outcome: "I would like one day to see equal rules – one lake, one rule."[92]

The "one lake, one rule" ideal seems like a distant vision, both for the contested fishery and in connection with other water-related issues. Interjurisdictional rivalries, jealousies, and advantages are rarely abandoned for mere ecological imperatives, although a remarkable international treaty under the auspices of the United Nations now seeks to nudge nation states sharing transboundary waters in that direction.[93] Around the Rainy-Lake of the Woods region, there has already been some movement – at least towards common principles – and increasing effort to imagine institutional arrangements that would support cooperation within and around historical legal and political boundaries that fragment this vast and vulnerable watershed.

14
"For Water Knows No Borders"

Throughout the Rainy-Lake of the Woods region, concerns associated with water quality, lake levels, fisheries, and even the potential effects of climate change prompted late-twentieth- century reflection about more suitable frameworks for the long-term well-being of northern waters. Ongoing deliberations had wide-ranging, interjurisdictional implications for a variety of institutions and stakeholders as the frameworks being explored increasingly acknowledged interrelationships between and among activities in a watershed, encouraging enhanced communication and collaborative initiatives.

POURING GOLD INTO WATER

As the twentieth century drew to a close, proposals to exploit valuable gold mining properties triggered anxiety over protection of Winnipeg's Shoal Lake water supply and highlighted continuing uncertainty over responsibility for water quality. The Consolidated Professor venture, after spending from $10 to $15 million on surface and underground exploration on Stevens Island in Shoal Lake, turned its attention to development approvals and production opportunities.[1] By some estimates, the project represented 175 jobs and a $25 million annual contribution to the regional economy flowing from an initial $50 million investment.[2]

Concerned Manitobans urged Ontario to undertake environmental assessment, prompting the *Winnipeg Free Press* to address the question of "protecting our water."[3] Dissatisfaction with Ontario's apparent willingness to approve a gold mine in the middle of a drinking-water supply source even prompted calls for Manitoba to revisit the historical boundary decision by annexing the Shoal Lake watershed, much of which "was swindled from us by a bunch of smooth talkers from Upper Canada," according to an irate letter writer. Now, by "pushing the development of a mine that would poison our drinking water," he wrote, Ontario politicians, including Premier David Peterson, "have relinquished any moral claim they may once have had to the area." A bold – if fanciful – proposal to annex all of Shoal Lake might "wake up just enough people in the Ontario legislature to understand the stupidity of their actions."[4]

On the national stage, the Consolidated Professor proposal was featured in parliamentary debate over federal legislation to establish more stringent Canadian drinking water safeguards. Bill Blaikie, MP for Winnipeg-Transcona, felt that such legislation "will make this type of madness, having a mine that produces arsenic right in the middle of our water supply, impossible."[5]

In August 1989, with no indication that public controversy was likely to abate, Ontario announced that Consolidated Professor would be subject to scrutiny through environmental assessment, a public review process considerably more elaborate and demanding than standard permit approvals under water protection legislation. This was the first such designation of a private mining development under a provincial regime that ordinarily applied to undertakings initiated by the public sector.[6]

The environmental assessment exercise was expected to encourage consideration of technologies that might mitigate adverse environmental effects on Winnipeg's water supply, on recreational activity around Shoal Lake, and on First Nations' traditional land uses. Risks associated with potential spills and accidents and the challenges of rehabilitating the landscape at the end of the mine's life would also probably be examined.

Following the election that saw Bob Rae replace David Peterson as Ontario premier, Rae's counterpart in Manitoba, Gary Filmon, contemplated a neighbourly "courtesy call," with Shoal Lake on the conversational agenda.[7] Despite assurances from Rae, observers in Manitoba remained apprehensive about mining development.[8] Indeed, early in 1991, one citizens' organization, the Winnipeg Water Protection Group (WWPG) – based on their own meeting with the Ontario premier – understood that Premier Filmon was prepared to accept the Shoal Lake mine development if it obtained approvals from Ontario.[9] The group pressed vigorously for clarification.[10]

The WWPG, whose membership rose to over fifteen hundred, success-fully parlayed its summer advocacy into a substantial municipal grant to finance preparation for the environmental assessment inquiry into the Consolidated Professor proposal.[11] As a spokesperson proclaimed, "what is needed on Shoal Lake development issues is a very strong message ... that when a development is going to occur that may pollute Shoal Lake, the City of Winnipeg is going to take every action that's in its capacity to protect its water."[12] In submissions to Ontario's environmental assessment process, the WWPG set out its expectations: "If they want to build a mine in Winnipeg's drinking water, then we want them to prove that they can do it with no discharge."[13]

The WWPG raised the stakes further with a call for preventive legisla-tion. Citing the rumoured release of known carcinogens – arsenic and nickel – into Winnipeg's Shoal Lake water supply, the WWPG echoed the call for a national initiative on safe drinking water.[14] Criticism of the federal government's limited engagement with drinking-water quality continued as the WWPG charged that "the failure of the federal govern-ment to exercise its legal and jurisdictional responsibilities on Shoal Lake ... is a reflection of the Mulroney government's failure to provide the leadership role on environmental issues."[15] With environmental assessment hearings still expected in late 1990, however, the WWPG's financial position remained insecure.[16]

For its part, Consolidated Professor vigorously denounced critics for "a torrent of inaccurate reports intended to raise a panic about environmental concerns."[17] The company's president specifically rebutted concerns about arsenic and nickel. "This company," G.R. Cunningham-Dunlop asserted, "does not propose to release anything to the waters of Shoal Lake that does not meet the strict requirements of the Ontario Ministry of the Environ-ment for receiving waters and protection of aquatic life." To make the point still more firmly, Cunningham-Dunlop affirmed that "all metal levels in water released will be well below regulatory requirements. As a result, there will be no impact on existing water quality within Shoal Lake."[18] This re-assurance, like many similar assertions, took no account of the potential gaps between regulatory requirements and actual impacts that had been revealed all too frequently. Coincidentally, although of no immediate ap-plication in the region, the environmental "precautionary principle" was just coming to prominence in international policy-making circles as a valuable procedural response to uncertainty concerning risks of this kind.[19]

Consolidated Professor subsequently abandoned plans to process and mill rock on the Stevens Island site and withdrew the original application,

thereby terminating the environmental assessment. A modified development plan later called for chemical processing operations to be relocated
outside the watershed.[20]

At about the same time as public discussion of the Consolidated
Professor proposal was getting underway, WWPG representatives reported
"extreme concentrations of cyanide" at another Shoal Lake property, a site
at Bag Bay where Kenora Prospectors and Miners Ltd. had reactivated the
historical Mikado Mine to recover gold from tailings. The revelation
surprised Ontario officials, whose own monitoring had found substantially lower levels.[21] Manitoba's Environment minister, Glen Cummings,
expressed a strong preference against development at Shoal Lake, although
during negotiations with his Ontario counterpart over the Consolidated
Professor mine, he declined to specify how this goal might be achieved.[22]

The situation soon took a turn, when Sue Dobson, president of the Kenora
Prospectors and Miners operation and a Shoal Lake resident, confirmed
that there had been no activity on the mine site for two years. Thus, according to scientific advice, residual cyanide should have been eliminated
through interaction with chlorine that the company had introduced for
this purpose, as well as through the effect of sunlight. Believing that some
intruder had spiked the pond with cyanide, Dobson called for a police investigation.[23] Further tests confirmed high, but declining, levels of cyanide in only one of five ponds. While consideration was still being given
to the most effective means of neutralizing the contamination, the results
were consistent with the spiking hypothesis.[24] Subsequent analysis pointed
to leaching from accumulated tailings in the pond and significant ice cover
that would have delayed decomposition of cyanide as possible explanations
for the high residual levels.[25]

Amidst accolades for the WWPG, one zealous city resident called for
a broader inquiry into "why we need Ontario water anyway, and why
we are not using our own ground water and water from the Red,
Assiniboine and Seine rivers."[26] Gary Doer, Manitoba's opposition leader,
entered the fray intermittently to denounce the Environment minister's
apparent willingness to accommodate a variety of threats to Manitoba
waters.[27] On a number of occasions, he pressed for stronger provincial
restrictions on mining activity in the Shoal Lake watershed.[28]

The significance of preventive and precautionary measures had very
practical dimensions. In exercising historical constitutional responsibilities over navigation, the federal coast guard advised Ontario's environmental officials that its resources in the Kenora area were "extremely

limited." Still more explicitly, the coast guard acknowledged that it "would not be possible" for personnel from Kenora to respond to a spill of hazardous materials in the Lake of the Woods watershed. The deficiency in emergency response capacity could not have been more clearly exposed than when officials contemplated an accident involving the transportation of fuel, chemicals, and ore over remote winter ice-roads. "I have been unable to determine any agency responsible for transportation over ice roads made on the lake during the winter period," a Kenora-based environment official reported.[29]

In January 1989, a spill of about twenty-two thousand litres of fluorosidic acid from a holding tank leading to measurable levels of fluoride in Shoal Lake's Falcon Bay, and delayed disclosure by Winnipeg officials, disturbed critics and afforded Gary Doer a further opportunity to challenge Manitoba's overall performance on the water quality file. Doer argued that as a result of the inadequate civic and provincial responses to the acid spill, Manitoba had surrendered the moral high ground to Ontario.[30] But whether Ontario or any other government had firm footing on the environmental incline was an intriguing question only a few years after the April 1985 spill of four hundred litres of PCBs from a leaking electrical transformer being shipped through the region along the Trans-Canada Highway.[31] The moral high ground – not infrequently surrounded by slippery slopes – became still more challenging for Manitoba to secure when the "human error" dimension of the Falcon Bay spill was attributed to alcohol consumption at the work site.[32]

Dr. Eva Pip, a biologist at the University of Winnipeg, began to sample Shoal Lake water in 1975, continuing to do so – winter and summer – for many years. Her findings highlighted emerging threats to water quality as shoreline cottage development expanded, as winter ice-roads transformed the surface into a potentially toxic corridor, and as enthusiastic duck hunters peppered Indian Bay with lead shot.[33] Accordingly, Dr. Pip directed her calls for controls on development against all forms of activity that threatened drinking water quality. "Mining is just one of the aspects of the pollution problem in Shoal Lake," she said. "You've got to restrict public access and human and commercial activities there."[34] Such isolated proposals as this call for more vigorous protection of municipal water supply sources were later endorsed by the influential Walkerton inquiry in the commission's 2002 report.[35]

Ontario, following testing of all of the 120 cottages on its side of the lake, reported no indications of sewage discharges into Shoal Lake.[36] The

Manitoba Medical Association eventually entered the debate, calling for mining to be prohibited until it could be shown that the activity would not place Winnipeg's water supply at risk.[37]

WWPG condemned Manitoba's provincial regulation of Sensitive Areas, which was designed to curtail development in the vicinity of Winnipeg's water supply, as a 20 percent solution, for it covered only that much of the drainage basin within Manitoba. The group insisted that tougher restrictions should be embedded in the provincial *Environment Act* and made subject to the scrutiny of legislators, rather than left in a legal instrument that could be amended by the minister alone.[38] Following a surveyor's assessment, the regulation was rhetorically downgraded to an 11 percent solution.[39]

Then, alongside an increase in the price of gold, development pressure again mounted from the Ontario side. Kenora-based mining interests and engineers lamented that billions of dollars in potential economic activity was tied up in ill-defined approvals procedures. George Miller, president of the Mining Association of Canada, expressed concern about the precedent being set at Shoal Lake, where, in his view, political rather than scientific and technical considerations were dominant. In a manner entirely reminiscent of doubts surrounding Lake of the Woods mining ventures a century before, Miller cautioned that international investors were aware of projects like the venture proposed by Kenora Prospectors and Miners. "People watch for signs," he said. "And investors are a little bit nervous about Canada today."[40] Yet assessment of shoreline mineral development was only one of the governance controversies surrounding the quality of Winnipeg's water supply: while some lamented the threat that gold mining posed for Shoal Lake water, others explored ways to turn that water into gold.

TURNING WATER INTO GOLD

Jean Chrétien, newly returned to legal practice during an interlude away from politics, was particularly appreciative of the opportunity to represent First Nations. As he recorded in his autobiography, after "staring at the telephone and wondering if it would ever ring," Chrétien welcomed his first call from representatives of a Shoal Lake band who had remembered his earlier work as minister of Indian Affairs.[41] Shoal Lake Indian Band #40 was a community of about 150 people embroiled in an unfolding clash over the security of the Winnipeg water supply.

In its quest for economic self-sufficiency, Shoal Lake Band #40 proposed to build and lease some 350 cottages, together with condominiums and a marina, along the lakeshore.[42] As explained by Chief Herb Redsky, the venture was a direct response to the impact of Ontario's decision to close the commercial fishery to preserve the lake for tourists. "Tourism, they told us is where it's at," he said. "So we looked and saw that, yes, we had land, why not go into tourism."[43] The cottage venture proposed at Shoal Lake triggered pollution concerns and raised the possibility that Winnipeg might incur significant expenditures for water treatment. The city's refusal to permit road access across a dike to the development site provoked the band to seek compensation for lost income and employment.[44]

In a lunchtime address, Chrétien insisted that the city's rights to Shoal Lake water were subject to a fundamental limitation: "The rights obtained by the City were to draw water, not necessarily to draw clean water." Winnipeg's problem was simple enough, he suggested: "The land around the water intake is not the property of the City. It is occupied by other people." The fact that these other people "happen to be Indians," observed the folksy advocate, "surely does not mean that they have less rights than if they were non-Indians." Chrétien went on to explain that his clients could pursue development "as they see fit subject only to normal restrictions" and then insisted that "that there are no restrictions that can be imposed upon them legally by the City of Winnipeg other than with the consent of the Band."[45]

While Winnipeg wanted to protect the quality of its water supply and avoid the expense of treatment, it was Chrétien's objective to highlight the virtues of negotiating for the band's consent to restrict shoreline cottage development. Speaking plainly from the perspective of his clients, Chrétien declared: "If you want us to restrict our rights to develop as we see fit on our own land, you will have to pay us."[46] This was a fairly rudimentary, and characteristically direct, version of what has become the more widely recognized concept of payments for ecosystem services, whereby landowners are paid to forego development opportunities that could undermine or destroy such natural functions as air and water purification, wildlife habitat, migration corridors, or, in the era of climate change, carbon storage to forestall greenhouse gas emissions.[47]

In exchange for agreed compensation, the band was prepared to accept reasonable limitations on a range of activities – cottage, recreational, commercial, and industrial development – along with controls on forestry, mining, waste, and the use of chemicals on reserve lands. Chrétien cautioned, however, that perfection was not on offer: "If the City, in order to achieve complete theoretical protection, wants to impose conditions on the Band that strike at the pride of the people by eliminating virtually all potential productive employment, then no agreement is possible and instead of perfect protection there will be no protection whatsoever."[48] Chrétien suggested that the matter could be resolved for the cost of about a dollar a year for each of Winnipeg's 600,000 residents. Other observers were more inclined to remark on the total compensation of $36 million over the sixty-year span of the proposed arrangement. To Gary Doer, then NDP minister of Urban Affairs for Manitoba, much of the Chrétien speech "borders on blackmail."[49]

Facilitated in part by the success of Winnipeg mayor Bill Norrie in securing contributions from other levels of government, a tripartite agreement resolved outstanding matters in 1989.[50] The agreement acknowledged the importance of both economic development to the band and the city's interest in maintaining water quality in Indian Bay. In conjunction with a trust fund to generate long-term income for the band and in anticipation of a parallel agreement involving the federal government, the agreement among Shoal Lake Band #40, the Province of Manitoba, and the City of Winnipeg incorporated a number of water quality safeguards.[51] In addition to abandoning cottage development, the band undertook to prohibit other designated activities, including mining and heavy industry on reserve lands, and to avoid the use of toxic chemicals such as pesticides.[52]

The 1989 agreement also provided for an environmental management plan to regulate land use with a view to "effective control over the preservation and enhancement of the natural environment, especially as it relates to the preservation of the water quality of Indian Bay."[53] The reserve was also to receive waste management facilities, for which Manitoba and Winnipeg agreed to contribute technical and other services.[54] Subject to certain oversight arrangements, the band's regulatory authority over land use was confirmed.

These arrangements fell well short of a comprehensive resolution of land use and water quality issues in Shoal Lake, but the experience demonstrated the potential of collective deliberations involving a range of stakeholders around the watershed. Even if not congruent, interests might be complementary and subject to reconciliation. As interconnections between land use and water quality became better understood, this insight was gaining acceptance in the form of watershed planning and associated institutions.

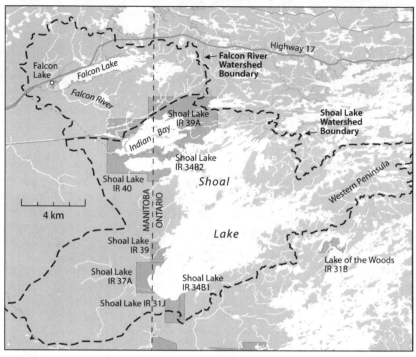

MAP 14.1   Shoal Lake Watershed. *Manitoba, Water Stewardship Division, "Shoal Lake Watershed Management Plan." Map adapted by Eric Leinberger.*

MAKING WATERSHEDS WORK

Political and administrative boundaries rarely coincide with watersheds; these natural – but not necessarily convenient – frameworks have had few organizational champions. Yet as the twentieth century drew to a close, a watershed orientation such as that illustrated in the evolving Shoal Lake experiment began to enjoy a broader measure of support, especially in conjunction with important initiatives unfolding under the auspices of the International Joint Commission.

Within the context of its International Watersheds Initiative (IWI), the IJC set out a general framework within which watershed boards might pursue watershed-specific responses along boundary waters. The IJC's proposal took the form of guiding principles for international watersheds, with an emphasis on the contribution of local capacity and scientific knowledge to promote an integrated ecosystem approach to issues arising in transboundary waters.[55] These ideas had been discussed and refined over more than a decade through a series of IJC studies, workshops, and reports.[56]

Growing concern over the long-term prospects for water quality in the Rainy-Lake of the Woods basin, highlighted through the efforts of dedicated grassroots organizations, ultimately persuaded the governments of Canada and the United States to re-engage the International Joint Commission. Letters dated 17 June 2010 called for review of aspects of the binational management of the Rainy-Lake of the Woods watershed, a request echoing the IJC's own earlier proposal to explore watershed-management challenges along the Canada-US border. Indeed, the Namakan-Rainy Lake system had been highlighted as an early example of promising collaboration in the aftermath of severe flooding (2001–02) and then drought conditions (2003) that challenged existing arrangements.[57]

When, following intergovernmental discussions, a task force assumed specific responsibility for investigating options in the Rainy-Lake of the Woods basin, a vast inventory of issues cried out for attention. Blooms of blue-green algae (sometimes toxic) were attributed to various sources of nutrient enrichment; aquatic and terrestrial invasive species such as rusty crayfish and the ash borer were increasingly widespread; fluctuating water levels adversely affected traditional uses including the sturgeon catch; and shoreline erosion along the south shore was worrisome. Added to these concerns were the continuing effects and potential future impacts of mining and hydro-power operations on water quality and the uncertain impacts of climate change, including the consequences of a longer ice-free season resulting from milder winters.[58] A century of gold mining, hydroelectric power development, and resource and industrial production, accompanied by centres of population growth and recreational activity, had left their cumulative mark.

Task Force members were struck by the range of initiatives within the watershed. Since 2004, an annual Lake of the Woods Water Quality Forum had allowed researchers to share their findings and to identify emerging concerns. The Lake of the Woods Water Sustainability Foundation, also dating from 2004, was promoting awareness of water quality issues and actively pursuing research funding to strengthen the database. An array of local governments and organizations endorsed the effort to engage the IJC in Lake of the Woods water quality questions. These included the City of Kenora, the Koochiching County Board of Commissioners, the Lake of the Woods Water Sustainability Foundation, and the Lake of the Woods County Soil and Water Conservation District.

Aboriginal organizations had also demonstrated interest in watershed issues, a prominent example being efforts by the Rainy River First Nation to establish a fish hatchery to restore sturgeon. Increasingly, public health concerns and their relationship to water quality and supply gained attention.[59] Government initiatives with regional responsibilities included the Lake of the Woods International Multi-agency Working Arrangement, created in 2009 by nine separate entities to collaborate for the purpose of restoring water quality. This innovative body included seven agencies in Canada and the United States, one nongovernmental organization, and one US tribe.

Resource management agencies and other organizations were also pursuing research and exchanging information to determine the sources and pathways of nutrients finding their way into the water system. In association with the existing Rainy Lake regulatory boards, dam operators and representatives of provincial, state, and federal government agencies sought to minimize environmental impacts through a voluntary "hydro peaking agreement." Agreement to avoid peak power production during the spring spawning season would moderate fluctuations in water flows resulting from variations in demand for electricity from the Fort Frances-International Falls hydro-power facilities.[60] Dishearteningly for regional residents, even as the IJC Task Force was at work, the Fort Frances pulp and paper facility staggered towards closure in the face of the global financial crisis, a strong Canadian dollar, and an accelerating shift of readers from print to the internet.[61]

All of the water management activity was being carried out alongside or within the framework of national, state, provincial, and intergovernmental resource and environmental programs. The scope of contemporary activity around the watershed was indeed impressive and rested on an extensive history of consultation and coordination. That background included, of course, hearings associated with IJC deliberations dating back to 1912 and the institutions resulting from IJC reports as well as any number of memorandums of understanding (MOUs) and comparable working arrangements involving government agencies and, occasionally, First Nations and tribes. There is also some history of municipal and other domestic decision-making bodies in each country inviting participation from their counterparts or other affected parties across the border. "Many of these arrangements have evolved over time to address changing needs," the task force dryly remarked about the largely ad hoc nature of institutional evolution. More hopefully, however, the task force commented that varied approaches "contribute to bi-national governance to some degree and provide opportunities to reflect and incorporate the shared interests in these waters."[62]

Shared interests ultimately underpin the potential for successful watershed management, assuming they are recognized and acknowledged. Watersheds have been identified as "catalytic entry points" both for analyzing substantive policy challenges around resource use and sustainability and for fostering responses that are able to account for ecological and social dimensions, including human health and well-being.[63] Moreover, from a practical perspective, watershed-based frameworks are also considered to offer promising opportunities to alleviate some of the notorious problems of fragmented water governance in interjurisdictional settings.[64] Backsliding remains a constant challenge, however, as established agencies not infrequently submit to the inclination to favour institutional interests over collaborative missions.

Although not a watershed governance issue as such, the Experimental Lakes Area (ELA) experience of institutional discontinuity merits reference. Despite an unparalleled list of early and continuing research accomplishments involving control of eutrophication, acid rain, and impacts of hydro-power reservoirs and aquaculture, as well as contributions to the ecosystem approach to environmental management, the ELA project suffered from repeated alteration of its governance framework.[65] The Fisheries Research Board was first relieved of direct control of this and other research programs and then dissolved in 1979. Overall supervision of the ELA shifted to the new federal Department of the Environment in 1972 and then to Fisheries and Oceans in 1979. Federal-provincial agreements, negotiated and renegotiated at intervals during the 1980s and 1990s, led eventually to a joint management board.

In conjunction with severe financial constraints introduced by Canada's Finance minister Paul Martin during the mid-1990s, spending on freshwater research was sharply cut back. The Freshwater Institute faced a staff reduction from fifty-four to sixteen in the context of cuts amounting to 70 percent of established long-term funding. The impacts were widely regarded as a catastrophic dismantling of the world-renowned initiative.[66]

A further round of financial restraint accompanying the 2012 Canadian federal budget signalled the ELA's impending closure. Supporters – local, national, and international – were vocal in their endorsement of the ELA and its contribution, with many suggesting that in the context of adaptation to climate change, the greatest benefits from research still lay ahead. Federal funding for other water-related programs across Canada, including a substantial allocation for restoration work on Lake Winnipeg, was widely welcomed. However, as one indication of his government's limited support for climate change initiatives, Prime Minister Harper – with reference to the ELA – affirmed that "obviously we are not intending to continue that other project."[67] In response, the *Winnipeg Free Press* described the budget cut as "short-sighted and counterproductive." The ELA, the editorial proclaimed, should be regarded as a core responsibility for the Fisheries and Oceans Department. ELA research was necessary "to establish the security of Canada's water, which is still the best argument for funding its work."[68] Water security, broadly conceived, is indeed an underlying objective of enhanced governance arrangements at the watershed level, including international watersheds such as the Rainy-Lake of the Woods system.

The fragmented nature of water governance typically results in poor alignment among efforts that should be reinforcing. As the IJC Task Force remarked, "significant gaps exist in the governance structure and greater synergy could be attained if these gaps were to be addressed."[69] An early challenge also existed in the form of uncertainty about the exact location of watershed boundaries. This problem had caused Robert Bell of the Canadian Geological Survey to remark in 1880 that "water soaks through the moss and swamps and one cannot tell on which side of the watershed he may be," and it was finally addressed by means of a sophisticated cross-border initiative to harmonize data and definitions using GIS technology.[70]

The entry point to institutional complexity is easy enough to grasp: many different bodies are involved in decision making and more attention has historically been devoted to their creation than to their operations, coordination, and integration. Given the transboundary character of the Lake of the Woods, "there are multiple layers of government agencies and organizations, some with over-lapping jurisdictions and some with no jurisdictional overlap that play similar roles on opposite sides of the border."[71] As the IJC Task Force noted, it is not easy to understand the complicated roles, responsibilities, and interactions of these organizations that affect water. It is nevertheless essential.

The range of responsibilities extends through sewage and industrial discharges, environmental assessment procedures, municipal land-use planning, objectives for water quality, flooding, and best practices in such sectors as agriculture and resource extraction.[72] Selected examples illustrate ways in which citizens and governments are pursuing water-related initiatives along the lengthy chain of waterways.

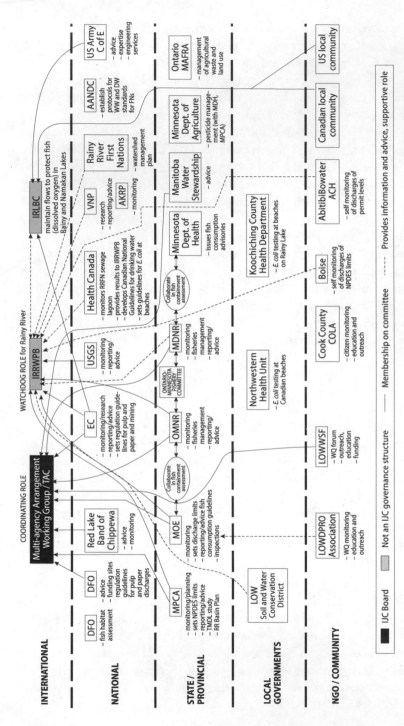

FIGURE 14.1 Water Quality Management, 2012. International Joint Commission, International Lake of the Woods and Rainy River Watershed Task Force.

One effective management initiative involving local participation emerged from work associated with the boards established pursuant to IJC recommendations to address issues in the upper lakes and Rainy River. Historically, perhaps the most significant demonstration of successful environmental remediation in the region is the long-term recovery of the Rainy River from a state of devastation in the 1950s. A single statistic highlights the measure of the achievement: biological oxygen demand (BOD) levels have fallen from seventy-four metric tons per day to just under four metric tons per day in 2009.[73] In the aftermath of the initial Rainy River clean-up program, the involvement of the IJC and the International Rainy River Water Pollution Board declined, although regional groups and organizations continued to seek guidance and support from the International Rainy Lake Board of Control (IRLBC) respecting water level management. The IJC and the IRLBC responded with efforts to promote compromise among relevant interest groups in the general interest of the watershed.

Gatherings sponsored by the IRLBC in the 1980s fostered appreciation of the watershed concept, contributing, according to some observers, to "the birth of the international watershed initiative in the watershed."[74] By 1991, interest in communication, cooperation, and collaboration were such that a binational steering committee was formed. This body, the Rainy Lake/Namakan Chain International Water Level Steering Committee, consulted across the watershed about adjustments to guidelines for managing water levels within the Rainy Lake and Namakan reservoirs that would favour more natural flows such as in Lac La Croix, an unregulated border lake. Described as rule curves or reservoir rule curves, these guidelines evolved following the original 1949 order to prescribe a range or baseline governing the operation of dams and reservoirs over the long term. For its part, the IJC commissioned further studies and eventually established new rule curves in 2000, accompanied by a commitment to conduct further review.[75]

Efforts on the fisheries front – walleye wars notwithstanding – also demonstrate the potential of collaborative action to deal with issues affecting or influenced by multiple jurisdictions and agencies. First published in 1984, the *Ontario-Minnesota Boundary Waters Fisheries Atlas* provides background information to support border fisheries management. In technical terms, the exercise has encouraged disparate agencies to address inconsistencies in data reporting and thereby to facilitate joint efforts to assess and manage fisheries resources.[76]

The administrative framework for management of the regional fishery deserves some explanation. From the Canadian perspective, the Lake of the Woods Fisheries Assessment Unit, based in Kenora, is associated administratively with the Northwest Science and Information office in Thunder Bay. For purposes of assessment, the Ontario waters of the Lake of the Woods have been classified into seven sectors according to physical and chemical characteristics, the composition of the fish community, and the behaviour and activities of user groups.[77] On the US side are two key fisheries-management centres. The Baudette station oversees fisheries management on the Minnesota portion of the Lake of the Woods and the lower Rainy River, while an International Falls office is responsible for work on Rainy, Namakan, and Sand Point Lakes as well as the upper Rainy River.[78]

To suggest that fisheries are under the jurisdiction of designated officials is all well and good, but opportunities for control do not actually extend to the fish themselves. These elusive creatures are significantly more difficult to count than sheep in a pasture and possess a disconcerting inclination to move about, to some extent according to their own peculiar preferences.[79] Fisheries managers are therefore constantly engaged in an inquiry into the whereabouts – and provenance – of the resource over which they preside.

Monitoring procedures are exceptionally sophisticated at one end of the spectrum, but much less so on the other. Movement patterns may be identified by tagging fish for release at designated locations and noting the location of their subsequent recapture. Tagging operations provide indications of the impacts of angling and commercial harvesting on overall populations. These insights, in turn, permit officials to assess the effectiveness of existing management interventions and to propose adjustments accordingly. On an ongoing basis, it is also possible to track fish that have been surgically implanted with miniaturized radio transmitters. The results help to identify areas of critical habitat – spawning grounds, for example. Such information has obvious implications for potentially harmful land-use activity, including land-use activity that may affect fish stocks that are shared between Ontario and Minnesota.[80] Sometimes fish are tested (as in the case of some small-mouth bass), radio-tagged, and released to see if they can find their way home.[81] Fisheries specialists frankly acknowledge the difficulties of interpreting information on the movement of fish, particularly where issues of partitioning stocks between jurisdictions may arise.

The fate of sturgeon remained a question of particular interest within the watershed, where lake and river sturgeon populations are distinguished and where governance arrangements differ across the international border.[82] Despite premature announcements of recovery, the twenty-first-century status of the sturgeon population remains affected by overfishing in the early 1900s and the limiting effect of Rainy River pollution and water level fluctuations for much of the remainder of the last century.[83]

The prospect of rehabilitating the Rainy River and Lake of the Woods stocks now animates the efforts of managers who observed a modest recovery of sturgeon following water quality improvements brought about by the Rainy River clean-up. However, stream flow, especially in the crucial spawning season, as well as water quality remain important considerations. As a consequence of licensing arrangements that authorized daily "peaking" of stream flows to maximize efficiencies at the hydro-power dam as operated by Boise Cascade and Abitibi Consolidated, "documented cases of de-watering lake sturgeon spawning sites have caused the loss of eggs, fry, and habitat."[84] Government agencies have also carefully examined conditions upstream in the South Arm of Rainy Lake, where sturgeon were once abundant, as well as in Lac La Croix, Namakan, and Sand Point Lakes.[85] The movement of Seine River sturgeon is monitored in detail via transmitters. Further efforts have been undertaken to encourage downstream populations along the Winnipeg River below Norman Dam.[86]

In 1993, the Rainy River First Nation, supported by Ontario Hydro, established the Manitou Fish Hatchery, a further crucial element in efforts to restore the lake sturgeon. The facility first released fingerlings in 1996.[87] In 2003, the operation was privatized and continued as Sustainable Sturgeon Culture. Between 150,000 and 400,000 fry are released annually into the Rainy River, and eggs are shipped to the Dalles First Nation, on the Winnipeg River near Kenora; to the Red Lake and White Earth Tribes in Minnesota; and to places as far away as China.[88]

Biologists working for Ontario, Minnesota, and the Rainy River First Nation collaborated in the development of a sturgeon management plan. This is intended to re-establish and sustain sturgeon in suitable habitats within Ontario-Minnesota border waters, and a Border Waters Lake Sturgeon Committee has drafted goals for shared lake sturgeon stocks.[89]

Over the longer term extending out two to three decades, the stated objective is "to maintain healthy, self-sustaining stocks of lake sturgeon that will provide subsistence, along with limited recreational and commercial harvests." Criteria for assessment or evaluation are again somewhat more ambitious than in the shorter term.[90]

Key areas for sturgeon are found in the southern portion of the Lake of the Woods on both the Ontario and Minnesota sides. In Ontario, attention focuses on South Sector 5, an area of roughly 72,000 hectares (180,000 acres) extending south of the Aulneau Peninsula, from Miles Bay to the mouth of the Rainy River.[91] Since all non-First Nations commercial fishing licences were retired in 1995, and with a voluntary suspension of commercial fishing by the Rainy River First Nation, the current Canadian sturgeon catch consists entirely of the subsistence fishery. Options to regulate angling for sturgeon have been under consideration, since a modest level of interest is again evident.[92]

On the Minnesota side, the sturgeon fishery of Big Traverse Bay is notable. Minnesota closed the commercial lake sturgeon fishery in 1930 but has recently experienced a significant increase in angler interest. Indeed, on the basis of creel surveys, state officials noted a surge in catch levels during the 1997–2002 period, with an average of 5,100 kilograms (11,300 lbs.) on an annual basis. That level closely approximates the potential lake sturgeon yield from Minnesota waters of the Lake of the Woods and Rainy River and exceeds the target annual harvest of 3,500 kilograms (7600 lbs.), a level set with a view to increasing "the likelihood and rate of population recovery." Despite an attempt to reduce the sturgeon take with new regulations in 2001, the catch continued to exceed target levels and indeed reached 6,800 kilograms (15,000 lbs.) in the two week season from 15 to 30 April 2003. Regulatory controls were further tightened in 2004 for close evaluation, but preliminary confidence in the recovery process was accompanied by continued expansion of the lake sturgeon recreational fishery on the US side.[93] Meanwhile, under new Ontario legislation to protect endangered species, the status of lake sturgeon shifted from "special concern" to "threatened," and a recovery plan for stock in northwestern Ontario was introduced.[94] Thus, despite genuine efforts aimed at collaboration, arrangements respecting sturgeon were not fully harmonized.

CLIMBING THE LEARNING CURVE

The Shoal Lake area, where conflicts over resource use intensified during the 1980s, became an important setting for efforts to implement comprehensive land-use planning. In fact, preliminary interest on the part of Manitoba officials in a basin-wide approach emerged in response to Ontario's support for exploratory mineral work by Kenora Prospectors and Miners Ltd. in the Bag Bay area.[95] Although Ontario ultimately decided against an environmental assessment of the new Bag Bay venture, the province also expressed sympathy for basin-wide planning.[96]

There was little initial indication of what such an innovation might entail. Even in September 1994, when Ontario and five Native bands signed an agreement to consult on development within the Shoal Lake watershed, details were scarce, and arrangements concerning participation by the Province of Manitoba and the City of Winnipeg were yet to be resolved.[97] The 1994 agreement led to the creation of a supervisory committee and an intergovernmental working group on the watershed. In due course, a plan emerged for Shoal Lake to guide future watershed development with a view to maintaining environmental quality and sustaining communities in the watershed.[98] Although endorsed by both provincial governments, the watershed plan failed to secure approval from the two First Nations communities who participated in its preparation.

The overall goals are reflected in a proposed "Watershed Vision," which outlines a commitment to ecosystem health and excellent water quality in combination with sustainable economic activity that respects traditional and cultural values. With that in mind, the 2002 plan endorses guiding principles. It is the stated expectation, for example, that development decisions will be the shared responsibility of all participating jurisdictions and will be consistent with the integrity of the watershed ecosystem, while seeking to balance the distribution of socioeconomic benefits. First Nations, along with the populations of Ontario and Manitoba, should continue to benefit from the quality and adequacy of water resources. Renewable resources are to be used on a sustainable basis, with development decisions for these, and for nonrenewable resources, to follow best management practices to ensure ecological and environmentally responsible usage. Operationally, all stakeholders are expected to cooperate and to share information, including traditional First Nations' knowledge. Overall, the Shoal Lake Watershed Management Plan is to be "viewed not only as a product, but also as part of an ongoing process." It might be revisited and refined according to new information.[99]

One of the participating communities, Shoal Lake First Nation #40, proposed an alternative decision-making process to involve a wider range of watershed stakeholders. Despite attempts over a period of years to recruit participants from government, industry, and cottager and recreational associations, the forum foundered – among other reasons, because of the unwillingness of four other Shoal Lake First Nations to engage in the process.[100] Shoal Lake #40 has continued to suffer drinking water quality issues, since the community was separated from mainland at the time of the Shoal Lake diversion: lack of road access has prevented construction of a water treatment plant with the result that residents – subject to a long-term boil water advisory – have relied heavily on bottled water deliveries.[101]

Far to the east, the heavily transformed Seine River system, flowing into Rainy Lake, also presents continuing challenges. It was impossible to restore Steep Rock Lake and to re-establish the Seine in its original channel following the closure of iron mining operations in 1979, partly because accumulated sediments – high in sulphate content – would have been disturbed, with severe consequences on downstream fish habitat. In addition, various control works, including dams and drainage channels, were incorporated into the control system of the Atikokan Electrical Generating Station when it began operations in 1985. The Seine could not be restored to its original course, so long-term control structures were put in place.[102] Following further extensive studies and consultation, a water management plan was developed. Accompanied by operational requirements and compliance measures, the plan addresses water levels and flows with social, economic, and environmental considerations in mind. In light of spawning requirements, for example, the plan incorporates guidance to stabilize or limit spring fluctuation in several lakes.[103] Biological and physical indicators have been selected as a means of assessing ecosystem response. Despite these elaborate arrangements, water levels in the open-pit iron mines have continued to rise, forcing renewed consideration of rehabilitation options in anticipation of an eventual toxic overflow.[104]

The Lake of the Woods has also benefited significantly from initiatives on the US side, where governments, agencies, and citizens in Minnesota have pursued long-term protection of water quality. At the state level, the Clean Water, Land, and Legacy Amendment is most striking. As explained by the Minnesota Environmental Quality Board, this 2008 measure demonstrated "the importance of water resources, habitat and environmental health to the state's citizens, and represents the opportunity to bring all participants and stakeholders together to achieve what is best for nurturing Minnesota's economy, communities, human health, recreation and environment."[105] Building on the *Clean Water Legacy Act* of 2006, the 2008 initiative took the form of a constitutional amendment. This led, in turn, to a state sales tax of three-eighths of 1 percent dedicated to priority expenditures, including the protection of freshwater. Early estimates suggest that roughly $85 million per year may be directed to the Clean Water Fund to support surface and groundwater initiatives. Guidance on the most appropriate allocation process was presented to the state legislature on 5 January 2011 in the form of a proposal for a twenty-five-year Minnesota Water Sustainability Framework, prepared by the Water Resources Center at the University of Minnesota.[106]

The state constitutional amendment reinforced adoption of a watershed-oriented approach within Minnesota. In the Rainy-Lake of the Woods basin, this entails a rotating ten-year cycle of comprehensive investigation of each of nine separate watersheds.[107] The main state agencies responsible for this work include the Minnesota Pollution Control Agency, Minnesota Department of Natural Resources, and Minnesota Board of Water and Soil Resources. Within each watershed, the program involves monitoring and assessment (chemical, physical, biological, flow), watershed modelling, watershed planning and total maximum daily load (TMDL) development, implementation of restoration and protection measures, data management, and evaluation and reporting, as well as civic engagement, outreach, and education. State agencies are expected to spend between $3.3 million and $5.3 million in the Rainy Basin over a ten-year period, with additional resources provided in subsequent cycles to "reassess, adapt strategies, and implement."[108]

Prior to new measures stimulated by the 2008 Clean Water, Land, and Legacy Amendment, water quality received less comprehensive attention. For example, monitoring data from International Falls and Baudette are available from the 1950s to 2006.[109] More recently, pursuant to a declaration of impairment under national legislation, the US *Clean Water Act*, a TMDL study for phosphorous and algae in the Minnesota portion of the Lake of the Woods was undertaken.[110] Prior to this, the Minnesota Pollution Control Agency completed work on Rainy River basin planning in 2004.

The IJC Task Force identified "other accomplishments worthy of celebration," a list that includes several monitoring and sampling initiatives that were providing valuable information on aquatic wildlife and water quality.[111] At the county level, governments have also adopted water management plans to address land-use issues, soil erosion and sedimentation, sewage treatment, and public education.[112]

Principles and strategies articulated in the context of the 2010 Minnesota Water Plan are directed overwhelmingly at areas of domestic responsibility. They are naturally suggestive, however, of opportunities extending into the transboundary or binational context. The principles emphasize, for example, the importance of optimized coordination among entities operating at the local, state, and federal levels and the need to prioritize resource allocation. The call for a holistic approach to land and water resources is firmly stated, while the contribution of adaptive management to informed decision making and improvements in future management is also highlighted. Targets and timetables are essential to assess progress and to further accountability for the overall achievement of a shared long-term vision. From the perspective of strategy, the state plan urges increased protection efforts over rearguard restoration. Information gathering and access to available data are viewed as further contributors to effective action, with an emphasis on strengthened local capacity to manage water resources at appropriate levels of governance. Additional operational principles include the importance of targeting protection and restoration initiatives and of updating management tools to do so. Finally, the state plan exhorts decision makers to respond to emerging threats on a systematic basis.[113]

The IJC Task Force celebrated the "passion for environmental protection within this watershed that its citizens take very seriously."[114] The overall track record of accomplishment in the watershed was an impressive demonstration of past commitment and future potential for problem solving.

Yet the task force reported that water governance remains fragmented; efforts that should have been reinforcing were often poorly aligned.[115] Most significantly, perhaps, "there is no one entity that has the role of overall coordination and reporting for the entire watershed, and there is not presently an international governance mechanism in place to manage water quality throughout the watershed."[116] The challenge, therefore, was to redress current institutional shortcomings in order to strengthen still further the potential for effective watershed management in this large, remote, and culturally diverse basin.

Institutional design criteria were clearly spelled out. First, any new mechanisms would need to fill existing gaps and "streamline water management" so as to avoid duplication. Yet the new arrangements would have to draw upon past accomplishments and incorporate appropriate levels of governance "to deal with issues at the proper scale." Simultaneously, decision making would require local involvement alongside commitment at the highest levels to ensure continuity and to enhance prospects for long-term success. Ultimately, any new watershed framework "must promote bi-national cooperation, for water knows no borders."[117]

The task force formulated a thoughtful reform agenda that combined a proposal for a shared watershed vision with detailed institutional recommendations. The program revolved around five key themes.

First, by consolidating the two existing Rainy River boards into an International Watershed Board with enhanced responsibilities for water quality, the basin would benefit from an agency that was well-positioned to encourage joint action by participating governments.[118] The new board could, for example, promote integration of potentially complementary watershed initiatives. In addition to offering an ongoing binational forum where issues of transboundary concern might be raised and discussed, the new board could encourage cross-border collaboration.[119]

A second theme on the reform agenda revolved around matters where collaborative scientific and technical research represent essential elements of broader planning and decision making, such as nutrient loading to the water system and south shore erosion. The task force was anxious to see the work of the International Multi-agency Working Arrangement group continue and, indeed, to ensure the availability of the resources necessary to complete the present tasks and to provide interim updates to state-of-the-basin reporting.[120]

Local and citizen participation was a third theme of the recommendations, with the result that trees are being planted for conservation purposes, individuals are engaged in water sampling, and bass have been recruited in the battle against rusty crayfish upstream in the boundary waters. Echoing a request from Grand Council Treaty #3, Aboriginal participation and traditional knowledge were also identified as critical elements of enhanced community engagement.[121]

Each of the foregoing would, in some respects, contribute to the fourth element of the proposed agenda – a watershed summit to take stock of critical issues and to map directions for future collaboration.[122] The task force anticipated that outcomes might include "a common vision and objectives along with agreement on how to proceed in the future." Options beyond this point, all with precedents of some form, included a binational MOU, or new legislation oriented around the basin, or various forms of federal-provincial collaboration – even a binational watershed management plan.[123]

Finally, the task force called for a review of regulation on the Lake of the Woods to assess the appropriateness of the current range of water levels in light of past experience and potential future developments, including climate change and a phenomenon known as isostatic or postglacial rebound.

To complete the process leading to recommendations to governments, the IJC itself reported in January 2012, with a call to combine the two existing boards into a new International Watershed Initiatives Board and to increase support in order to develop a Lake of the Woods/Rainy River water quality plan of study. Simultaneously, further attention would be given to water levels on the Lake of the Woods, with the ultimate goal of formulating a comprehensive binational water management plan.[124] While such an ambition might seem intrusive or unnecessary in a region where boundary lines have been so firmly contested and drawn, the IJC outlined a rationale for binational water management: "An issue which affects the quality or quantity of the surface water runoff or groundwater in the watershed, which eventually flows downstream to significantly affect a boundary water, could potentially be considered an issue of bi-national concern."[125]

From the deck of the *Grace Anne II*, an elegant vessel once owned by the 3M corporation, Canada's minster of Foreign Affairs announced Canada's positive response to the proposed reconfiguration of the Rainy boards on 4 August 2012. John Baird referred to the water quality of the Rainy-Lake of the Woods system as a "tremendous priority." And so it should be. To remain a "tremendous priority" in the absence of a crisis, however, is always a policy challenge, one that now rests in many hands around the watershed.

CONCLUSION

Finding the Watershed

Completed in December 2014 and endorsed by the International Joint Commission (IJC) in January 2015, the *Water Quality Plan of Study for the Lake of the Woods Basin* is a pioneering venture, the first such undertaking initiated with the IJC's encouragement in response to a complex array of transboundary water management concerns. The plan calls upon Canada and the United States to support roughly thirty specific projects and activities at a total cost of around $10 million.[1]

The inventory of urgent and essential assignments is clustered around five general challenges. Monitoring to provide consistent, long-term data is a precondition for understanding nutrient flows, the impact of contaminants, and the introduction of invasive aquatic species. A second focus of attention is algal blooms, a long-standing concern but now more commonly recognized as an occasional source of harmful toxins. The importance of this issue derives from the potential for algal blooms to generate adverse effects on recreational use, fish populations, water treatment facilities, and even human health. Several specific measures are also proposed to respond to aquatic invasive species: alas, some keen angler with $50,000 worth of boat, motor, trailer, and equipment but not enough time, apparently, to clean the vessel properly or to scrub the bait pail may have given zebra mussels a free ride into new territory. The possible contamination of groundwater, either from legacy pollution attributable to historical and established mining ventures or from new operations or transportation accidents, makes risk and vulnerability assessment a fourth field for research and analysis. Finally, the complexities of coordinating management efforts across national, subnational, and local contexts and including Indigenous governments underscore the significance of capacity building as an independent need. Similar institutional questions are also at the heart of transboundary water governance deliberations being pursued in many other settings around the world.[2]

The *Water Quality Plan of Study* notes a recent shift in attention towards the ecosystem health of the basin and towards cooperative, binational responses to water quality challenges.[3] The shared interest in such water-related ecosystem services as habitat, the fishery, flood control, and recreation, alongside human health, clearly encourages and supports collaborative basin-wide processes of consultation and exchange as these continue to evolve.[4] Yet despite the considerable scope of recommendations in the plan, a still broader agenda encompassing water level regulation, resource development impacts, and the consequences of climate change is already on the near horizon.[5] Even water transfers out of the basin have come under consideration.[6]

In this volume on the resource and environmental experience of the Rainy-Lake of the Woods region, I have not proposed immediate practical guidance to those charged with identifying and now actively pursuing effective responses to water management challenges, whether they are local or external to the region or even global, such as climate change.[7] What this book confirms, however, and what the IJC's *Water Quality Plan of Study* also acknowledges, is that the profound commitment to environmental protection and restoration that has been demonstrated over the past decade or so does not represent the first effort to underscore the fundamental importance of water quality and ecological integrity in this part of the continent. Some awareness of the historical record may even assist in strengthening responses to today's challenges.

Over roughly a hundred and fifty years, the Lake of the Woods watershed has been subject to ever increasing human intervention entailing extensive environmental impacts. An inventory of modern resource and industrial activity might stretch from the establishment of Fowler's Mills along the Rainy River, through timber harvesting and transport by log boom across the watershed, to widespread precious metal mining and the massive effluent discharges accompanying pulp and paper production beginning in the early years of the twentieth century. Simultaneously, spillways, storage dams, and power production facilities altered water flows and regulated lake levels in a manner designed to reduce the natural range of fluctuation, both long term and seasonal. Massive overharvesting had already devastated the fishery in various portions of the system before flow controls at power dams transformed fish habitats and breeding grounds. Shoreline agriculture, including wild rice, was often disrupted or dislocated. Population expansion in the region, though never achieving the most fanciful forecasts of 2 million residents, brought new forms of water quality impact through alterations in runoff that accompanied agricultural clearing. Municipal sewage discharges later added to the mix. Alongside these continuing processes, mid-twentieth-century mineral developments, most notably the Steep Rock iron mining operation, brought about an unprecedented dispersal of sedimentary material and tailings over vast stretches of the Rainy River watershed, eventually reaching the Lake of the Woods. The devastating health impacts of mercury discharges from the 1960s and 1970s fell tragically on Aboriginal communities to the north of the Rainy-Lake of the Woods system; adverse economic consequences extended more broadly.[8]

Each stage of environmental disruption and transformation stimulated critical attention and sometimes outraged response. Fisheries inspectors, public health officials, conservation pioneers, researchers engaged under the auspices of the IJC, and First Nations representatives who observed the deterioration of fishing or wild rice harvesting voiced protests and concerns in the half-century following Treaty 3 and the interprovincial boundary conflict. Their later counterparts, again including IJC officials or researchers and First Nations and their advisors – as well as concerned individuals, citizens' organizations, and community groups – have continued to express disappointment, apprehension, and alarm over environmental deterioration within the watershed. This is an important legacy that has sheltered and defended, if not fully protected, valuable dimensions of the natural heritage.

In anticipation of the challenges of the twenty-first century, questions inevitably arise: What is different now? Can we do better? Can this watershed (or any other) be effectively stewarded short of a crisis? These basic questions arise because determined inaction plants remarkably deep roots in the generally infertile environmental policy field that lies somewhere between "not as bad as it might get" and "not as good as we would like." Here, platitudes on the level of "let's see how it goes" or "if it ain't broke, don't fix it" pass for sage counsel, when they are often just camouflaged variations on "not my problem" or "I've got other things to do." Understandable? Yes, but not good enough for the long haul.

Among significant differences that are now increasingly incorporated into decision making respecting watersheds, a growing understanding of the values of ecosystem services is prominent. Particularly important contributions have been made at the international level through the Millennium Ecosystem Assessment and related work.[9] In addition, the significance of the watershed framework is more widely appreciated, with watersheds now more frequently viewed as appropriate settings where interaction between social systems, ecosystems, and health can be effectively understood and managed.[10] The motivation to safeguard water systems is somewhat strengthened accordingly.

Indications that such opportunities are being embraced are evident in several settings, with the IJC's watershed initiative representing a promising opportunity for sustaining appropriate and necessary actions. The International Watersheds Initiative of the IJC describes its fundamental aim as "to facilitate watershed-level solutions to transboundary environmental challenges by promoting communication, collaboration and coordination among the various stakeholders and interests, using an integrated, ecosystem approach."[11] For a variety of reasons, watershed-level arrangements do not represent a panacea: for example, as climate change so dramatically demonstrates, watersheds will not always correspond with the scale of the problem to be addressed, and the authority and resources of existing jurisdictions cannot readily be channelled so as to achieve common ends.[12] Nevertheless, watershed-based arrangements offer valuable opportunities to advance public understanding of the interrelationships linking community well-being – both social and economic – and its essential foundations in the integrity of the natural environment.

Yet how, one may reasonably ask, can an appreciation of the watershed and the importance of collaborative initiatives be nurtured within the jurisdictionally and sectorally fragmented transboundary institutional hodgepodge where decisions are currently made? Thoughtful researchers have offered varying accounts of recent transformation of water-governance arrangements to facilitate broader mechanisms of participation and engagement as a means of designing and implementing effective management interventions. Some have analyzed social processes involved in incorporating the perspectives and values of diverse participants or actors in the formulation of strategies to pursue in response to particular issues or situations as these emerge.[13]

Recent experience around the Rainy-Lake of the Woods basin is instructive and generally encouraging. Some long-standing internationally constituted institutions have been reconfigured with an enhanced mandate.

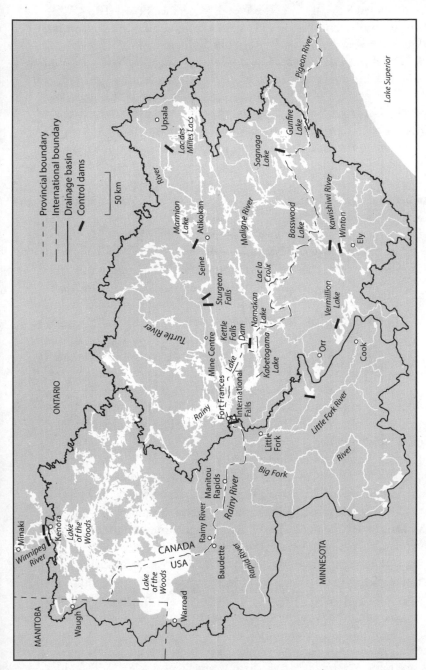

MAP C.1 Regional Sub-basins per International Joint Commission. *Environment Canada,* "*Lake of the Woods Science Initiative, 2008–2011.*" *Map adapted by Eric Leinberger.*

The International Rainy-Lake of the Woods Watershed Board (IRLWWB), for example, was established in 2013 with a general mandate concerning water quality, levels, and flows. The board's duties include recommending appropriate objectives for water quality and/or aquatic ecosystems and maintaining continuous surveillance, with a particular focus on "water quality, alien aquatic invasive species, climate change indicators and adaptation, and ground and surface water contamination."[14] Although it does not function as the direct regulatory authority, the IRLWWB works with responsible authorities and management agencies to pursue shared objectives. Opportunities for the participation of First Nations, Métis, US tribal personnel, and community representatives, together with advisory mechanisms involving industry and residents, enhance communication and exchange around the basin.[15] Moreover, relevant agencies on both sides of the border at the national and state/provincial levels, as well as local, tribal, and civil society organizations have entered into an agreement for the broad purpose of coordinating and sharing research.[16]

Beyond these developments, numerous additional localized measures have been identified and acknowledged as valuable contributors to enhanced understanding and management of resource and water quality issues within the basin. Among notable activities of this nature are the Rainy River First Nation Watershed Program, a water sampling program undertaken by the Red Lake Band of Chippewa that encompasses educational, survey, and resource stewardship elements, and an annual Lake of the Woods Water Quality Forum, hosted by the Lake of the Woods Water Sustainability Foundation in partnership with government agencies and educational institutions.[17]

Important concerns about water security underlie collaborative arrangements at the watershed level as broadly encouraged through the IJC's International Watershed Initiative. These concerns emphasize the environmental dimension of security, including resultant advantages – generally widely shared – for the dependent human population. As Jutta Brunnée and Stephen Toope, both experienced observers, write, "the security referred to is the maintenance or re-establishment of ecological balance."[18] Adopting ecological integrity as an objective may be expected simultaneously to highlight the advantages of cooperation and to diminish inclinations towards conflict. But Brunnée and Toope note that "with an ecosystem orientation, negotiations will not so easily resolve into debates over competing national uses or equitable shares. Protection of the freshwater resource for humanity today and in the future will take on an independent value."[19] Otherwise expressed, new environmental norms are gradually emerging through a more collaborative approach to water management.[20] This is indeed the promise of the watershed framework as now being explored and elaborated within the Rainy-Lake of the Woods system. It took a long time to find the watershed; let's try not to lose it.

Notes

FOREWORD

1 Jamie Benidickson, *Environmental Law*, 4th ed. (Toronto: Irwin Law, 2013). For Benidickson's academic CV see: https://commonlaw.uottawa.ca/en/people/benidickson-jamie; Jamie Benidickson, *The Culture of Flushing: A Social and Legal History of Sewage* (Vancouver: UBC Press, 2007).

2 Jamie Benidickson, *Idleness, Water, and A Canoe: Reflections on Paddling for Pleasure* (Toronto: University of Toronto Press, 1997).

3 Benidickson, *Idleness*, 244.

4 *Pushpanathan v Canada* (Minister of Citizenship and Immigration), [1998] 1 S.C.R. 982, citing P. Cane, *An Introduction to Administrative Law* (3rd ed. 1996), 35 for "interlocking" phrase.

5 S. St. George, "Hydrological Dynamics in the Winnipeg River Basin, Manitoba," in *Report of Activities 2006*, Manitoba Science, Technology, Energy and Mines, Manitoba Geological Survey (Winnipeg: Queen's Printer for Manitoba, 2006), 226–30. Available at: http://manitoba.ca/iem/geo/field/roa06pdfs/GS-20.pdf.

6 http://www.wilderness.net/NWPS/wildView?WID=70.

7 R. Newell Searle, *Saving Quetico-Superior, A Land Set Apart* (Saint Paul, MN: Minnesota Historical Society Press, 1977).

8 David Lowenthal, "The American Scene," *The Geographical Review* 58, 1 (January 1968): 61–88.

9 Anthony Giddens, *The Constitution of Society* (Cambridge: Polity Press, 1984), 181.

10 Marwyn S. Samuels, "The Biography of Landscape: Cause and Culpability," in *The Interpretation of Ordinary Landscapes: Geographical Essays*, ed. D.W. Meinig (New York: Oxford University Press, 1979), 65–66; Marwyn S. Samuels, "Individual and Landscape: Thoughts on China and the Tao of Mao," in *Humanistic Geography: Prospects and Problems*, ed. David Ley and Marwyn Samuels (Chicago: Maaroufa Press, 1978), 283–96.

11 Samuels, "The Biography of Landscape," 65–66.

12 Jane Brown, *The Omnipotent Magician: Lancelot 'Capability' Brown, 1716–1783* (London: Chatto, 2011); John Phibbs, *Capability Brown: Designing the English Landscape* (New York: Rizzoli, 2016); John Phibbs, *Place-Making: The Art of Capability Brown* (London: Historic England, 2017); Keith N. Morgan, Elizabeth Hope Cushing, and Roger G. Reed, *Community by Design: The Olmsted Firm and the Development of Brookline, Massachusetts, Frederick Law Olmsted's Firm and the Coming of Age of Suburban Development* (Amherst, MA: University of Massachusetts Press, 2013); Nathaniel Rich, "When Parks Were Radical: More Than 150 Years Ago, Frederick Law Olmsted Changed How Americans Think about Public Space," *The Atlantic* (September 2016); Larry McCann, *Imagining Uplands: John Olmsted's Masterpiece of Residential Design* (Victoria, BC: Brighton Press, 2016); Carl Smith, *The Plan of Chicago: Daniel Burnham and the Remaking of the American City* (Chicago: University of Chicago Press, 2006).

13 This discussion draws on Jan Kolen and Johannes Renes, "Landscape Biographies: Key Issues," in *Landscape Biographies: Geographical, Historical and Archeological Perspectives on the Production and Transmission of Landscapes,* ed. Jan Kolen, Hans Renes, and Rita Hermans (Amsterdam: Amsterdam University Press, 2015), 21–47 (and especially 32–35). See also Michel de Certeau, *The Practice of Everyday Life* (Berkeley: University of California Press, 1984).

14 Meinig, *Interpretation, 44.*

15 This discussion rests for the most part on "The Era of E.W. Backus," Koochiching County, Minnesota, available at: http://www.co.koochiching.mn.us/222/The-Era-of-EW-Backus.

16 Rainy Lake Conservancy, *A Century of Wilderness Preservation in the Rainy Lake Watershed* (Fort Frances: Rainy Lake Conservancy, n.d.), available at: http://www.rainylake conservancy.org/Resources/Documents/century.pdf.

17 USDA Forest Service, "History of the BWCAW," available at: https://www.fs.usda.gov/detail/superior/specialplaces/?cid=stelprdb5127455; Stephen Wilbers, "Boundary Waters Chronology," available at: http://www.wilbers.com/BoundaryWatersCanoeAreaWilderness ChronologyLong.htm.

18 Brant Short, "Giving Voice to the Wild: The Rhetorical Legacy of Sigurd Olson and *The Singing Wilderness,*" *Speaker & Gavel* 44, 1 (2007): 45–61.

19 Sigurd F. Olson, *Reflections From the North Country* (Minneapolis: University of Minnesota Press, 1998; originally published in New York: Alfred A. Knopf, 1976), 35.

20 David Backes, "The Land Beyond the Rim: Sigurd Olson's Wilderness Theology," *Forest and Conservation History* 39, 2 (April 1995): 56–65; David Backes, *A Wilderness Within: The Life of Sigurd F. Olson* (Minneapolis: University of Minnesota Press, 1999).

21 Tim Ingold, *The Perception of the Environment: Essays on Livelihood, Dwelling and Skill* (London: Routledge 2000), 189 and 199, cited by Kolen and Renes, "Landscape Biographies," 39–40.

22 Anastasia Shkilnyk, *A Poison Stronger than Love: The Destruction of an Ojibwa Community* (New Haven, CT: Yale University Press, 1985); Warner Troyer, *No Safe Place* (Toronto: Clarke, Irwin, 1977); Anna J. Willow, *Strong Hearts, Native Lands: Anti-Clearcutting Activism at Grassy Narrows First Nation* (Winnipeg: University of Manitoba Press, 2012).

23 "free Grassy Narrows," available at: http://freegrassy.net/learn-more/the-boreal-forest/.

24 David Bruser, Robert Benzie, and Jayme Poisson, "Province and Ottawa Criticized for Handling of Grassy Narrows Mercury Poisoning," *Toronto Star,* 16 November 2017.

25 Adele Perry, *Aqueduct: Colonialism, Resources, and the Histories We Remember* (Winnipeg, ARP, 2016); Adele Perry, "Water and the Infrastructure of Colonialism," available at: http://www.niche-canada.org.

26   Erwin Redsky, and Cathy Merrick, "For Our First Nations, New Museum a Monument to Hypocrisy," *Globe and Mail*, 25 September 2014.

27   See "Statement by Chief Erwin Redsky on the Occasion of the Visit of Prime Minister Justin Trudeau to Shoal Lake 40 First Nation, April 28, 2016" and other material available at: http://www.sl40.ca/. I benefited from hearing a compelling presentation by Daryl Redsky and Cuyler Cotton, "Shoal Lake 40 First Nation, Strategies and Tactics That Work Now," delivered at a symposium organized by the Art Museum of the University of Toronto and the Canadian Centre for Architecture, held at the art museum, 8 July 2017: *Have We Won Yet? Conversations on Recent Pasts and Possible Futures for Environmental Activism.*

Introduction

1   Tim O'Brien, *In the Lake of the Woods* (Penguin Books, 1995), 129.

2   Some highlights from this literature include Inger Weibust and James Meadowcroft, *Multilevel Environmental Governance* (Edward Elgar, 2014); Tun Myint, *Governing International Rivers* (Edward Elgar, 2012); Grethel Aguilar and Alejandro Iza, *Governance of Shared Waters: Legal and Institutional Issues* (IUCN Environmental Policy and Law Paper, No. 58, 2011); Lee Botts and Paul Muldoon, *Evolution of the Great Lakes Water Quality Agreement* (Michigan State University Press, 2005); Alistair Rieu-Clarke, Ruby Moynihan and Bjorn-Oliver Magsig, *UN Watercourses Convention: User's Guide* (IHP-HELP Centre for Water Law, Policy and Science, University of Dundee, 2012); Juan Carolos Sanchez and Joshua Roberts, eds., *Transboundary Water Governance: Adaptation to Climate Change* (IUCN Environmental Policy and Law Paper No. 75, 2014).

3   Lon L. Fuller, "The Forms and Limits of Adjudication" *Harvard Law Review* 92 (1978): 395.

4   The concept of watershed is not without controversy. While the idea of watershed as an area draining into a common body of water seems straightforward enough, precise application may be elusive because of poorly defined boundaries, uncertainty associated with groundwater flows, the notion of nested watersheds – one forming part of another – among other factors. Researchers appropriately distinguish watersheds from other natural systems such as airsheds or ecosystems/regions. See, for example, J.M. Omernik and R.G. Bailey, "Distinguishing between Watersheds and Ecoregions," *Journal of the American Water Resources Association* 33 (1997): 935.

5   John E. Carroll, *Environmental Diplomacy: An Examination and a Prospective of Canadian-U.S. Transboundary Environmental Relations* (University of Michigan Press, 1983), 310.

6   For other examples of basin or watershed-oriented studies, see Christopher Armstrong, Matthew Evenden, and H.V. Nelles, *The River Returns: An Environmental History of the Bow* (McGill-Queen's University Press, 2009); Margaret Beattie Bogue, *Fishing the Great Lakes: An Environmental History, 1783–1933* (University of Wisconsin Press, 2000); Susan L. Flader, ed., *The Great Lakes: An Environmental and Social History* (University of Minnesota Press, 1983); Daniel Macfarlane, *Negotiating a River: Canada, the US and the Creation of the St. Lawrence Seaway* (UBC Press, 2014).

7   Recently water specialists have drawn attention to the potential significance of variable depths and circulation patterns across and among bays and sub-basins within the Lake of the Woods. See Environment Canada, "Environment Canada's Lake of the Woods Science Initiative, 2008–2011 – Summary," available at: https://ec.gc.ca/eaudouce-freshwater/default.asp?lang=en&n=8c50c138-1.

8 Hans Christian Bugge and Christina Voigt, *Sustainable Development in International and National Law* (Europa, 2008); Robert T. Lackey, "Seven Pillars of Ecosystem Management," *Landscape and Urban Planning* 40 (1998): 21–30.

9 Institutional dimensions of water governance have recently been examined in considerable detail. See, for example, Ralph Pentland and Adele Hurley, "Thirsty Neighbours: A Century of Canada-U.S. Transboundary Water Governance," Ch. 8 in *Eau Canada: The Future of Canada's Water,* ed. Karen Bakker, 163–83 (UBC Press, 2007); Timothy Heinmiller, Carolyn Johns, and Mark Sproule-Jones, "Institutions and Water Governance in Canada," Conclusion in *Canadian Water Politics: Conflicts and Institutions,* ed. Mark Sproule-Jones, Carolyn Johns, and Timothy Heinmiller, 308–31 (McGill-Queen's University Press, 2008); Jamie Linton and Noah Hall, "The Great Lakes: A Model of Transboundary Co-operation" Ch. 11 in *Water Without Borders: Canada, the United States, and Shared Waters,* ed. Emma S. Norman, Alice Cohen and Karen Bakker, 221–43 (University of Toronto Press, 2013); Laurence Boisson de Chazournes, Christina Leb, and Mara Tignino, eds. *International Law and Freshwater: The Multiple Challenges* (Edward Elgar, 2013).

CHAPTER 1: BUILDING BOUNDARIES

1 G.E. Cartier and W. McDougall to the Colonial Under-Secretary, 16 January 1869, in *Correspondence, Papers and Documents Relating to the Northerly and Westerly Boundaries of Ontario* (Toronto, 1882), 149–50.

2 Deputy Governor of the HBC to the Colonial Under-Secretary, 22 December 1868, in *Correspondence, Papers and Documents,* 148.

3 Cartier and McDougall to the Colonial Under-Secretary, 16 January 1869, in *Correspondence, Papers and Documents,* 151.

4 Ibid., 150.

5 Ibid.

6 Ibid.

7 Ibid.

8 Governor of Rupert's Land to the Provincial Secretary, 16 April 1862, in *Correspondence, Papers and Documents,* 90.

9 Quoted in Francis M. Carroll, *A Good and Wise Measure: The Search for the Canadian-American Boundary, 1783–1842* (Toronto: University of Toronto Press, 2001), 117.

10 Ibid., 127–44. The northwesternmost corner of the Lake of the Woods was ultimately situated in a manner consistent with British strategic and commercial interests, and the focus of international boundary debate shifted elsewhere. See also Theodore C. Blegen, *Minnesota: A History of the State* (Minneapolis: University of Minnesota Press, 1963), 121–23.

11 S.J. Dawson, *Report on the Exploration of the Country between Lake Superior and the Red River Settlement, and between the Latter Place and the Assiniboine and Saskatchewan* (Toronto, 1859).

12 Elizabeth Arthur, "Dawson, Simon James," *Dictionary of Canadian Biography,* vol. 13 (1901–10); see also Elizabeth Arthur, *Simon J. Dawson, C.E.* (Thunder Bay, ON: Singing Shield Productions, 1987). Dawson, a member of the legislative assembly (1875–78) and a member of Parliament (1878–91), advocated on behalf of a separate northern province and remained sympathetic to Ojibwa interests.

13 Janet E. Chute and Alan Knight, "Simon J. Dawson and the Upper Great Lakes Native Resource Campaign of the 1860s and 1870s," in *With Good Intentions: Euro-Canadian and*

Aboriginal Relations in Colonial Canada, ed. Celia Haig-Brown and David A. Nock (Vancouver: UBC Press, 2006), 106–31.

14 As indicated in Dawson's *Report on the Line of Route between Lake Superior and the Red River Settlement*, the meeting took place on 20 April 1868. See *Keewatin v Minister of Natural Resources* 2011 O.N.S.C. 4801, Exhibit 45, 261.

15 Quoted in *Keewatin v Minister of Natural Resources* 2011 O.N.S.C. 4801 (hereafter *Keewatin*), para. 164.

16 Ibid.

17 *Keewatin*, ex. 1, vol. 4, tab. 53.

18 Quoted in *Keewatin*, para. 165.

19 "Indian Demands as Terms of Treaty, January 22, 1869," quoted in *Keewatin*, para. 167.

20 Indian Treaty Negotiation Proceedings, 3 October 1873, shorthand reporter's notes as published in *The Manitoban*, 18 October 1873, quoted in *Keewatin*, para. 368.

21 Adams G. Archibald to Joseph Howe, 12 November 1870, quoted in *Keewatin*, para. 195.

22 W.F. Butler, *The Great Lone Land: A Narrative of Travel and Adventure in the Great North-West of America* (London: Sampson Low, Marston, Low, and Searle, 1875), 159.

23 Ibid., 170–72.

24 W. Robert Wightman and Nancy M. Wightman, *The Land Between: Northwestern Ontario Resource Development, 1800 to the 1990s* (Toronto: University of Toronto Press, 1997), 60–61, 91.

25 *The Manitoban*, 31 May 1873, quoted in *Keewatin*, para. 290.

26 Wightman and Wightman, *Land Between*, 61.

27 "A Letter from Fort Frances," 11 July 1872, quoted in *Keewatin*, para. 639. George M. Grant described the North-West Angle as "the dirtiest, most desolate-looking, mosquito-haunted of all our camping grounds." George M. Grant, *Ocean to Ocean: Sandford Fleming's Expedition through Canada in 1872*, rev. ed. (Toronto: Radisson Society, 1925), 67.

28 Wightman and Wightman, *Land Between*, 61.

29 For further discussion of such activities, see the work of Leo G. Waisberg and Tim E. Holzkamm, including "'Their Country Is Tolerably Rich in Furs': The Ojibwa Fur Trade in the Boundary Waters Region 1821–71," in *Papers of the Algonquian Conference* 25 (1994): 493–513, and Tim E. Holzkamm, Victor P. Lytwyn, and Leo G. Waisberg, "Rainy River Sturgeon: An Ojibway Resource in the Fur Trade Economy," *Canadian Geographer* 32 (1988): 194–205.

30 Wightman and Wightman, *Land Between*, 53.

31 S. Barry Cottam, "Federal/Provincial Disputes, Natural Resources and the Treaty #3 Ojibway, 1867–1924" (PhD diss., University of Ottawa, 1994), 244–47.

32 *Keewatin*, paras. 335, 340, 341.

33 Chute and Knight, "Simon J. Dawson," 127n63.

34 *Keewatin*, para. 344. For a somewhat more complex analysis of the exchange over forest resources, see Chute and Knight, "Simon J. Dawson," 115n70.

35 Joseph Howe to Pither, 11 March 1870, quoted in *Keewatin*, para. 179.

36 Chute and Knight, "Simon J. Dawson," 113.

37 Dawson joined the negotiation team after the resignation of Lindsay Russell. Chute and Knight, "Simon J. Dawson," 115. Several accounts of the negotiations have survived, including notes of the proceedings published in *The Manitoban*, 11 and 18 October 1873; a longhand report prepared by Simon Dawson; and a transcript written by Joseph Nolin, a Métis employed by the Ojibwa chiefs for this purpose. The documentation is described in *Keewatin*, paras. 308–25.

38 Leo Waisberg and Tim Holzkamm, "'We Have One Mind and One Mouth. It Is the Decision of All of Us': Traditional Anishinaabe Governance of Treaty #3," Working Paper for Grand Council Treaty #3, Kenora, October 2001, 6.

39 From *The Manitoban* version of treaty negotiations, quoted in *Keewatin*, para. 340.

40 Quoted in *Keewatin*, para. 366.

41 Wightman and Wightman, *Land Between*, 53. Further extensive literature on treaty making in western Canada includes Sarah Carter, *Aboriginal People and Colonizers of Western Canada to 1900* (Toronto: University of Toronto Press, 1999); James R. Miller, *Compact, Contract, Covenant: Aboriginal Treaty-Making in Canada* (Toronto: University of Toronto Press, 2009); Brian Titley, *The Indian Commissioners: Agents of the State and Indian Policy in Canada's Prairie West, 1873–1932* (Edmonton: University of Alberta Press, 2009); and Treaty 7 Elders and Tribal Council, *The True Spirit and Original Intent of Treaty 7* (Montreal and Kingston: McGill-Queen's University Press, 1996).

42 Donald B. Smith, "Aboriginal Rights a Century Ago," *The Beaver* (February-March 1987): 8. As expressed by James R. Miller: "Indians thought that they had concluded treaties of friendship and mutual assistance, while agreeing to the entry into their lands at some future date of agricultural settlement. The government in Ottawa believed that the treaties secured the Indians' surrender of whatever claim they had to the vast lands of western Canada." J.R. Miller, *Skyscrapers Hide the Heavens: A History of Indian-White Relations in Canada* (Toronto: University of Toronto Press, 1989), 168–69.

43 *Keewatin*, paras. 31, 35.

44 Ibid., para. 802.

45 Ibid., para. 747.

46 Ibid., para. 760.

47 Commissioner Morris, Official Report, 14 October 1873, quoted in *Keewatin*, para. 928.

48 Chute and Knight quote an Order-in-Council of 8 July 1874 stating that reserves "should not include any lands known to the Commissioners to be mineral lands or any lands for which mineral lands bona fide applications have been filed with either the Dominion or Ontario Governments." Chute and Knight, "Simon J. Dawson," 128n79. For Dawson's report, see Library and Archives Canada (hereafter LAC), "Dawson to the Minister of the Interior," 29 January 1875, RG 10, vol. 1918, file 2790D.

49 In 1872, the HBC elected to extend its land base from 50 to 640 acres. Cottam, "Federal/Provincial Disputes," 91. The Fuller lease covering 38,400 acres had been issued on 17 February 1873. Canada, House of Commons, *Debates*, 4 May 1886, 1051. Some fifty to sixty patents were issued northwest of Lake Shebandowan in 1870–71. Cottam, "Federal/Provincial Disputes," 198. Chute and Knight cite Archives of Ontario (hereafter OA), RG3, Executive Council Office, Ontario, Department of the Prime Minister, Orders-in-Council, "Staying Issues of Patents and Mining Licenses in the Neighbourhood of Lake Shebandowan and Head of Lake Superior," Order-in-Council, 28 December 1871. Cited in Chute and Knight, "Simon J. Dawson," 127n50.

50 *Keewatin*, paras. 936–42. In 2005, the Rainy River First Nations settled a land claim allowing them to buy back lands they had lost when reserves were consolidated nearly a century before.

51 Grant, *Ocean to Ocean*, 60.

52 "A Sketch of the Resources of the Lake of the Woods Country," *Weekly Herald and Algoma Miner*, 1 May 1896; Canada, Crown Lands Department, *Our Northern Districts* (Toronto, 1894), 65.

53 Morris Zaslow, *The Opening of the Canadian North, 1870–1914* (Toronto: McClelland and Stewart, 1971), 149–51. Wightman and Wightman, *Land Between*, 54, citing Morris Zaslow, "The Ontario Boundary Question," in *Profiles of a Province: Studies in the History of Ontario* (Toronto: Ontario Historical Society, 1967).

54 "Report of Col. Dennis, Dominion Surveyor-General, Prepared at the Request of Sir John A. Macdonald," 1 October 1871, in *Correspondence, Papers and Documents*, 210.

55 "Report of Col. Dennis, Dominion Surveyor-General, Prepared at the Request of Sir John A. Macdonald," 1 October 1871, in *Correspondence, Papers and Documents*, 210.

56 Smith, "Aboriginal Rights," 6.

57 S. Barry Cottam, "Indian Title as a 'Celestial Institution': David Mills and the *St. Catherine's Milling* Case," in *Aboriginal Resource Use in Canada: Historical and Legal Aspects*, ed. Kerry Abel and Jean Friesen (Winnipeg: University of Manitoba Press, 1991), 251.

58 OA, Irving Papers, 42/42/02, memorandum, 26 June 1874.

59 Canada, House of Commons, Select Committee on Boundaries of Ontario, Report, 42, quoted as "Testimony of Robert Bell Before the Select Committee on Boundaries, 1880," in *Thunder Bay District 1821–1892: A Collection of Documents*, ed. Elizabeth Arthur, Champlain Society Ontario Series No. 9 (Toronto: Champlain Society, 1973), 27.

60 Norman L. Nicholson, *The Boundaries of the Canadian Federation* (Toronto: Macmillan, 1979), 97.

61 *An Act respecting the Northerly and Westerly Boundaries of the Province of Ontario*, S.O. 1874, (2d Sess.) c. 6; A.F.N. Poole, "The Boundaries of Canada," *Canadian Bar Review* 42 (1964): 130.

62 Nicholson, *Boundaries of the Canadian Federation*, 97. Poole refers to S.M. 1880, (2d Sess.) c. 1, An Act to Provide for the Extension of the Boundaries of the Province of Manitoba. Poole, "Boundaries of Canada."

63 An Act to Provide for the Extension of the Boundaries of the Province of Manitoba, 1880–81, SC 44 Victoria c. 14, s. 1; consolidated in SC 1886, c. 47.

64 "Toronto's Interest," *The Globe*, 27 February 1883, quoted in Kenneth A. MacKirdy, "National vs. Provincial Loyalty: The Ontario Western Boundary Dispute, 1883–1884," *Ontario History* 51 (1959): 194.

65 "Petition for the Establishment of a Division Court at Rat Portage," in *Correspondence, Papers and Documents*, 401–2.

66 OA, Irving Papers, "Squatters' Claims, Rat Portage, July 1883."

67 A. Begg, *A History of the North-West* (Toronto: Hunter Rose, 1895), 3:82.

68 Ibid., 81–82.

69 Ibid., 83, 84.

70 Quoted in Kenneth A. MacKirdy, "National vs. Provincial Loyalty: the Ontario Western Boundary Dispute, 1883-1884," *Ontario History* 51 (1959): 196; "Judgment When Delivered Will Be in Favour of Ontario," *The Globe*, 23 July 1883.

71 Quoted in Anthony J. Hall, "*The St. Catherine's Milling and Lumber Company versus the Queen*: Indian Rights as a Factor in Federal-Provincial Relations in Nineteenth-Century Canada," in Abel and Friesen, *Aboriginal Resource Use in Canada*, 271–72. Hall cites a May 1882 speech reported in *Toronto Mail*, 1 June 1882, cited in C.R.W. Biggar, *Sir Oliver Mowat: A Biographical Sketch* (Toronto, 1905), 2:459–61.

72 OA, Irving Papers, 25 August 1883. See, for example, "The Argus," *Winnipeg Times*, 14 September 1883.

73 Joseph Schull, *Ontario Since 1867* (Toronto: McClelland and Stewart, 1978), 99.

74 The quotations are, respectively, from Barry S. Cottam "The Twentieth Century Legacy of the St. Catharine's Case: Thoughts on Aboriginal Title in Common Law," in *Co-Existence? Studies in Ontario-First Nations Relations*, ed. Bruce W. Hodgins, Shawn Heard, and John S. Milloy (Peterborough, ON: Frost Centre for Canadian Heritage and Development Studies, 1992), 120; Mr. Cameron (Huron), Canada, House of Commons, *Debates*, 4 May 1886, 1047.

75 Canada, House of Commons, *Debates*, 4 May 1886, 1048.

76 Rhonda Mae Telford, "The Sound of the Rustling of the Gold Is under My Feet Where I Stand" (PhD diss., University of Toronto, 1996), 245–50.

77 For description of the St. Catherine's Milling and Lumber Company litigation as it progressed through four courts, see Sidney L. Harring, *White Man's Law: Native People in Nineteenth-Century Canadian Jurisprudence* (Toronto: University of Toronto Press/Osgoode Society, 1998), 136–43.

78 Cottam, "Indian Title," 248.

79 Ibid., 249–51. OA, Irving Papers, David Mills to T.B. Pardee, 5 September 1883.

80 Cottam, "Indian Title," 253–54.

81 Ibid., 248.

82 Harring, *White Man's Law*, 125.

83 Smith, "Aboriginal Rights," 5.

84 Quoted in ibid., 10–11.

85 Quoted in Cottam, "Indian Title," 257.

86 *St. Catharines Milling and Lumber Company v The Queen* (1887), 13 S.C.R. 577, 608.

87 Morris' report of the statement of Chief Mawedopenais quoted in Smith, "Aboriginal Rights," 13.

88 *St. Catharines Milling and Lumber Company v The Queen* 14 Appeal Cases, 49.

89 Cottam, "Indian Title," 261.

90 Canada (Ontario Boundary) Act, 1889, UK 52–53 Victoria c. 28.

91 See, for example, David T. McNab, "The Administration of Treaty 3: The Location of the Boundaries of Treaty 3 Indian Reserves in Ontario 1873–1915," in *As Long as the Sun Shines and the Water Flows*, ed. Ian A.L. Getty and Antoine S. Lussier (Vancouver: UBC Press, 1983), 145–57.

92 *Keewatin*, para. 951. Chute and Knight state that Dawson left reserve allocation to Dennis, who was less accommodating to Native interests. Chute and Knight, "Simon J. Dawson," 117.

93 *Keewatin*, para. 948.

94 McNab, "Administration of Treaty 3"; Cottam, "Federal/Provincial Disputes."

95 Cottam, "Federal/Provincial Disputes," 208.

96 *Keewatin*, para. 1014.

97 LAC, Oliver Mowat to Edgar Dewdney, Superintendant General of Indian Affairs, 1 January 1889, RG 10, vol. 2313, file 62509–2, quoted in Cottam, "Federal/Provincial Disputes," 200.

98 For the legislation, see Ontario 54 Victoria c. 3; An Act for the Settlement of Certain Questions between the Governments of Canada and Ontario Respecting Indian Lands, Canada 54–55 Victoria, c. 5. For the ratification, see LAC, RG 10, Black Series, vol. 3883, file 95, 6 April 1894, 721.

99 Justice Sanderson assessed the impact of these arrangements on harvesting rights in *Keewatin*, para. 1242:

the 1891 Legislation that came into effect in 1894 took away Harvesting Rights from the Ojibway on lands taken up that they otherwise would have had under the Treaty ... the 1891 Legislation amended the Treaty by allowing Ontario to 'take up' lands in a manner visibly incompatible with Treaty Harvesting Rights. As a result, the federal interest could not have engaged after 1894 to protect Harvesting Rights on those lands.

For Sanderson's further discussion, see generally *Keewatin*, paras. 1028–47.

100 McNab, "Administration of Treaty 3," 149. For further discussion of the 1891 and 1894 arrangements, see Cottam, "Federal/Provincial Disputes," 202–10.

101 OA, Irving Papers, 30/36/6 (2), E.B. Borron, "Report on Indian Claims Arising out of the North-West Angle Treaty, No. 3," 30 December 1893, cited in McNab, "Administration of Treaty 3," note 20; Cottam, "Federal/Provincial Disputes," 203–10.

102 Cottam, "Federal/Provincial Disputes," 203–10.

103 Having lost the land ownership contest with Ontario, the federal government unsuccessfully pursued a claim against the province to recover a range of expenditures associated with the treaty and its subsequent administration. *Dominion of Canada v Province of Ontario*, [1910] AC 637 PC.

104 *Keewatin*, para. 62.

105 For theoretical discussion of the social and political underpinnings of boundaries as illustrated more specifically in this chapter, see Alice Cohen and Seanna Davidson, "The Watershed Approach: Challenges, Antecedents, and the Transition from Technical Tool to Governance Unit," *Water Alternatives* 4, 1 (2011): 8.

CHAPTER 2: CULTURAL, COMMERCIAL, AND CONSTITUTIONAL FISHING

1 "The greatest sturgeon pond in the world" is from Barton Warren Evermann and Homer Barker Latimer, "The Fishes of the Lake of the Woods and Connecting Waters," *Proceedings of the United States National Museum* 39, 1778 (1910): 126; "almost to the vanishing point" is from Kelly Evans, quoted in John J. Van West, "Ojibwa Fisheries, Commercial Fisheries Development and Fisheries Administration, 1873–1915: An Examination of Conflicting Interests in the Collapse of the Sturgeon Fisheries of the Lake of the Woods," *Native Studies Review* 6, 1 (1990): 43.

2 For early discussion of the impact of water level regulation on fisheries, see International Joint Commission (IJC), *Final Report of the International Joint Commission on the Lake of the Woods Reference* (hereafter *Lake of the Woods Reference*) (Washington, DC: Government Print Office, 1917), 186–89.

3 Tim Holzkamm and Michael McCarthy, "Potential Fishery for Lake Sturgeon (*Acipenser fulvescens*) as Indicated by the Returns of the Hudson's Bay Company Lac la Pluie District," *Canadian Journal of Fisheries and Aquatic Sciences* 45, 5 (1988): 921–23.

4 "North-West Correspondence," *The Globe*, 15 July 1859, 2, quoted in Van West, "Ojibwa Fisheries," 51n15.

5 Holzkamm and McCarthy, "Potential Fishery."

6 Dawson to Minister of Public Works, 19 December 1870, is quoted extensively in *Keewatin v Minister of Natural Resources* 2011 O.N.S.C. 4801 (hereafter *Keewatin*), para. 230.

7 W.F. Butler, *The Great Lone Land: A Narrative of Travel and Adventure in the Great North-West of America* (London: Sampson Low, Marston, Low, and Searle, 1875), 166.

8   Dawson to Minister of Public Works, 19 December 1870, quoted in *Keewatin*, para. 230.

9   Ibid.

10 For discussion of blueberry harvests within the overall Indigenous resource system, see Iain J. Davidson-Hunt, "Indigenous Land Management, Cultural Landscapes and Anishinaabe People of Shoal Lake, Northwestern Ontario, Canada," *Environments* 31, 1 (2003): 21.

11 Archives of Ontario (hereafter OA), Mather Diary, 21 September 1895. One hundred and sixty tons of Lake of the Woods blueberries were shipped in 1901. Payments to pickers – Indians and "town boys" – and dealers' revenues generated $22,400 in Rat Portage, although only a quarter of the crop was harvested because of the limited availability of pickers. See *Rat Portage Miner and Semi-Weekly News*, 26 August 1901.

12 From the shorthand reporter's account of the 3 October 1873 proceedings as published in *The Manitoban*, 18 October 1873, and quoted in *Keewatin*, para. 366.

13 Quotations are from an annotation to the Rainy River Reserve Agreement, 1 October 1875, in para. 950 of *Keewatin*. For discussion of fishing along the Rainy River reserves, see *Keewatin*, paras. 950–53.

14 David T. McNab, "The Administration of Treaty 3: The Location of the Boundaries of Treaty 3 Indian Reserves in Ontario, 1973–1915," in *As Long as the Sun Shines and the Water Flows*, ed. Ian A.L. Getty and Antoine S. Lussier (Vancouver: UBC Press, 1983), 145–57.

15 Van West, "Ojibwa Fisheries," 38; Canada, Department of Fisheries, Annual Report 1890, *Sessional Papers*, 1891, No. 8, lxii–lxiii.

16 An Act for the Settlement of Certain Questions between the Governments of Canada and Ontario, Respecting Indian Lands, 1891, 54–55 Victoria c. 5.

17 Quoted in Leo G. Waisberg and Tim E. Holzkamm, "The Ojibway Understanding of Fishing Rights under Treaty 3," *Native Studies Review* 8, 1 (1992): 49.

18 J.P. Chartrand, cited in *Keewatin*, para. 1035; G.F. Adams and D.P. Kolenosky, *Out of the Water: Ontario's Freshwater Fish Industry* (Toronto: Fisheries Branch, Ontario Ministry of Natural Resources, 1979), 8.

19 For examples from the prosecutorial record, see Sidney L. Harring, "'The Liberal Treatment of Indians': Native People in Nineteenth Century Ontario Law," *Saskatchewan Law Review* 56, 2 (1992): 326–27.

20 Petition to Frank Oliver, Minister of the Interior and Superintendent of Indian Affairs, 9 April 1909, quoted in *Keewatin*, para. 1053.

21 Petition, 29 September 1909, quoted in *Keewatin*, para. 1053.

22 Van West, "Ojibwa Fisheries," 34 and 55n38.

23 Details on the Reid operations may be found in "Records of the Joint Committee Relative to the Preservation of Fisheries in Waters Contiguous to Canada and the United States, Interviews and Field Notes, 1893–1894," US National Archives, College Park, MD.

24 OA, Irving Papers, "List of Licences Issued in Lake of the Woods, Ont. 1892, '93, '94 and 1895," box 31, pkg. 37, item 12. The figures include some licences on Dryberry Lake.

25 John Dobie, "Commercial Fishing on Lake of the Woods," *Minnesota History* 35 (1957): 275.

26 Van West, "Ojibwa Fisheries," 36 and 55n40. Railway services from Warroad on the US side became available in 1908 via the Great Northern.

27 "The Commercial," Toledo, 14 April 1894, as quoted in "Records of the Joint Committee Relative to the Preservation of the Fisheries."

28 *Rat Portage Semi-Weekly Record*, 19 February 1896.

29 Evermann and Latimer, "Fishes of the Lake of the Woods," 125.

30 OA, Irving Papers, box 32, pkg. 37, item 20. Alan B. McCullough provides a more comprehensive account of fishing techniques in *The Commercial Fishery of the Canadian Great Lakes* (Ottawa: National Historic Parks and Sites, Canadian Parks Service, Environment Canada, 1989), 28–30.

31 OA, Irving Papers, Margach to Irving, 2 May 1896, box 32, pkg. 37, item 20.

32 Evermann and Latimer suggest that gill nets were used exclusively on the Canadian side and pound nets on both sides of the border. "Fishes of the Lake of the Woods," 122. W. Robert Wightman and Nancy M. Wightman report 14 pound nets on the Canadian side in 1895, with at least 250 in the United States. *The Land Between: Northwestern Ontario Resource Development, 1800 to the 1990s* (Toronto: University of Toronto Press, 1997), 116. The 1894 Joint International Commission on Fisheries also recorded extensive use of pound nets on the US side. See "Records of the Joint Committee Relative to the Preservation of Fisheries."

33 "Records of the Joint Committee Relative to the Preservation of the Fisheries."

34 Evermann and Latimer, "Fishes of the Lake of the Woods," 183.

35 G. Barnes, "Rat Portage," in *The Canadian Album: Encyclopedic Canada*, ed. J. Castell Hopkins (Toronto: Bradley-Garretson, 1896), 440.

36 Ibid.

37 "A History of Kenora Forest District" (Toronto: Ontario, Department of Lands and Forests, 1963), 8.

38 Canada, Department of Fisheries, Annual Report 1890, Canada, *Sessional Papers*, 1891, No. 8, lxiii.

39 E.E. Prince, "The Canadian Sturgeon and Caviare Industries," Canada, *Sessional Papers*, 1905, No. 22 (Special Appended Report I), lvi.

40 Prince, "Canadian Sturgeon," lvii.

41 Ibid., lxvi. The prevalence of shipments to Germany was noted by other observers. See H.E. Pearson, "Commercial Fishing, Rainy River District," *The Colonist*, May 1890.

42 Prince, "Canadian Sturgeon," lxvi.

43 IJC, *Lake of the Woods Reference*, 184–85. Even the Canada-US allocations may be misleading, for in other contexts, fish caught in American nets or even nets owned by Americans were classified as American and entered the United States on a duty-free basis even if the catch came from Canadian waters. See McCullough, *Commercial Fishery*, 55.

44 "Records of the Joint Committee Relative to the Preservation of Fisheries."

45 Ibid. F.A. Rice, Interview, 10 August 1894.

46 For information on the Canadian catch out of Kenora for the 1914 season, see IJC, *Lake of the Woods Reference*, 237.

47 OA, Irving Papers, Margach to Irving, 18 February 1896; Margach to Aubrey White, 9 May 1896, box 32, pkg. 37, item 20.

48 IJC, *Lake of the Woods Reference*, 184–85.

49 Evermann and Latimer, "Fishes of the Lake of the Woods," 126, quoted in IJC, *Lake of the Woods Reference*, 185.

50 IJC, *Lake of the Woods Reference*, 185.

51 Holzkamm and McCarthy, "Potential Fishery."

52 Canada, Department of Fisheries, Annual Report 1890, Canada, *Sessional Papers*, 1891, No. 8, lxiii.

53 *Fifth Report of the Ontario Bureau of Mines, 1895*, 167, quoted in IJC, *Lake of the Woods Reference*, 186.

54 OA, Irving Papers, Margach to Irving, 2 May 1896, box 32, pkg. 37, item 20.
55 OA, Mather Diary, 30 April–3 May 1887; 7 July 1894.
56 McNab, "Administration of Treaty 3," 148; Janet E. Chute and Alan Knight, "Simon J. Dawson and the Upper Great Lakes Native Resource Campaign of the 1860s and 1870s," in *With Good Intentions: Euro-Canadian and Aboriginal Relations in Colonial Canada*, ed. Celia Haig-Brown and David A. Nock (Vancouver: UBC Press, 2006), 121–22.
57 *Hansard*, 19 May 1888, quoted in *Keewatin*, para. 547.
58 *Hansard*, 28 May 1888, quoted in *Keewatin*, para. 548.
59 *Keewatin*, paras. 550 and 1047.
60 Vankoughnet to Pither, McCracken, and McIntyre, 13 November 1889, quoted in Van West, "Ojibwa Fisheries," 36.
61 Chief Conducumewininie, as quoted in Manitoba Superintendancy, Office of the Inspector (E. McColl), 18 November 1890, Canada, *Sessional Papers*, 1891, No. 18, 198.
62 *Keewatin*, para. 1012.
63 Lawrence Vankoughnet to Edgar Dewdney, 17 December 1890, quoted in *Keewatin*, para. 1018.
64 Van West, "Ojibwa Fisheries," 38. McNab says that Powassan and Flat-Mouth led the August 1890 raid. Reid sold to Baltimore Packing in 1891. See "Records of the Joint Committee Relative to the Preservation of Fisheries."
65 Van West, "Ojibwa Fisheries," 38; Order-in-Council PC no. 2002.
66 Vankoughnet to Tilton, 23 June 1890, quoted in Van West, "Ojibwa Fisheries," 38.
67 Quoted in *Keewatin*, para. 1087; B.W. Muirhead also indicates that federal officials intended to reserve commercial fishing in the Lake of the Woods to the Indians and to ban the use of pound nets. "Between Scylla and Charybdis: The Ontario Boundary Dispute and Treaty 3, 1873–1915" (Thunder Bay, ON: Lakehead University, Department of History, 1994), 11.
68 See chap. 15, "To Save the Fish," in Margaret Beattie Bogue, *Fishing the Great Lakes: An Environmental History 1783–1933* (Madison: University of Wisconsin Press, 2000).
69 See, for example, Douglas Harris, *Fish, Law and Colonialism: The Legal Capture of Salmon in British Columbia* (Vancouver: UBC Press, 2001); Library and Archives Canada, "Correspondence Relating to Fishing Rights on Indian Reserves throughout Canada, 1897–1898," RG 10, vol. 3908, file 107, 297, part 1.
70 Prince, "Canadian Sturgeon," lv.
71 Ibid., lix.
72 Ibid., lxx.
73 Evermann and Latimer, "Fishes of the Lake of the Woods," 129, 120.
74 "The Vexed Question of Riparian Rights," *The Globe*, 2 May 1882.
75 Ibid.
76 Ontario Fisheries Act, SO 1885, c. 9, s. 2.
77 Ibid., s. 14 (1).
78 Enforcement limitations were widespread in the late nineteenth century. See McCullough, *Commercial Fishery*, 83–86.
79 OA, Irving Papers, box 32, pkg. 37, item 20.
80 "Records of the Joint Committee Relative to the Preservation of the Fisheries."
81 Van West, "Ojibwa Fisheries," 44–46.
82 Lise C. Hansen, "Treaty Fishing Rights and the Development of Fisheries Legislation in Ontario: A Primer," *Native Studies Review* 7, 1 (1991): 13–15. For further discussion see, Harring, "Liberal Treatment of Indians," 305.

83 OA, Irving Papers, Irving to Hogg, 2 May 1895.
84 OA, Irving Papers, Irving to Margach, 18 April 1896.
85 *Keewatin*, para. 1012.
86 *In Re Provincial Fisheries*, (1896) 26 SCR 444.
87 *The Globe*, 14 October 1896.
88 *The Globe*, 15 October 1896.
89 J.A. Corry, "The Growth of Government Activities Since Confederation," paper prepared for the Royal Commission on Dominion-Provincial Relations, Ottawa, 1939, 147. For discussion of continued skirmishing over matters of legislative authority and enforcement action, see McCullough, *Commercial Fishery*, 94–97.
90 Adam Shortt and Arthur George Doughty, eds., *Canada and Its Provinces: A History of the Canadian People and Their Institutions* (Toronto: Glasgow, Brook, 1914), 9:251, quoted in Peter Gossage, "Water in Canadian History: An Overview," Inquiry on Federal Water Policy, Research Paper 11 (Montreal: Université du Québec à Montréal, Département d'histoire, 1985), 121. The report of the Canadian-American Fisheries Conference in 1918 addressed sturgeon fisheries generally, commending Canada's decision in March 1918 to impose a four-year ban on sturgeon fishing in Lake Erie and calling for a five-year suspension of all sturgeon fishing in contiguous waters. See LAC, Keefer Papers, MG 26, Vol. 98, F.H. Keefer, "Memorandum Respecting the Report of the Canadian-American Fisheries Conference," 30 December 1918; John J. Van West, "Formation and Rescision of Headland to Headland Boundaries," Ontario Native Affairs Directorate, Toronto, 12 October 1989.

CHAPTER 3: THIS LAND IS MY LAND – IT CAN'T BE YOUR LAND

1 "Return re Timber Limits in the North-West Territories and Keewatin," 22 February 1881, Canada, *Sessional Papers*, 1881, No. 86, 1–5.
2 To reduce the possibility of later confusion, I note here that under new ownership, the Keewatin Lumbering and Manufacturing would later become the Keewatin Lumber Company.
3 As of 1882, the forty shares of Keewatin Lumbering and Manufacturing Company were owned by Mather (15), W.H. Browse (5), John Dennis (2), S.J. Dennis (5), and Richard Fuller (13). Archives of Ontario (hereafter OA), Mather Diary, 26 February 1882.
4 OA, Irving Papers, John Mather to Oliver Mowat, 20 October 1885; OA, Lake of the Woods Milling Company Papers, Mather to T.B. Pardee, 17 February 1888. For a detailed company narrative, see D. McLeod, "Memorandum re Keewatin Lumbering and Manufacturing Company Limited and Their Operations at Keewatin, Ontario 1879 to 1906," in the records of the Lake of the Woods Museum. The supply chain is described in Allan Shaw, *The Days Between* (1973, privately published).
5 *The Colonist*, Supplementary Number, August 1893, 16; "Rat Portage and Rainy River District," *The News*, 1888, 18. Production levels ranged from 1,497,777 feet in 1880 to 18,758,554 in 1903.
6 OA, Irving Papers, Mather to Mowat, 20 October 1885.
7 OA, Irving Papers, Aubrey White to T.B. Pardee, 8 September 1883.
8 Ontario, *Journals of the Executive Council* 62, 322 (6 May 1909). A copy of the agreement, dated 24 November 1891, is in the John E. Read Papers at Library and Archives Canada (hereafter LAC).

9 Following the 1894 federal-provincial agreement, Ontario continued to question KLM's rights in parts of the region. Samuel Price, of St. Thomas, was later appointed commissioner to look into charges that KLM cut pine from islands in 1902–3 without making proper returns or paying dues.

10 Agnes M. Larsen, *The White Pine Industry in Minnesota: A History* (Minneapolis: University of Minnesota Press, 1949), 307–8. See also Bergit I. Anderson, *The Last Frontier*, (St. Paul, MN: Bruce Publishing, 1941) and the commentary on this work by D. McLeod in the Lake of the Woods Museum, Kenora, ON.

11 See International Boundary Commssion, *Joint Report upon the Survey and Demarcation of the Boundary between the United States and Canada from the Gulf of Georgia to the Northwesternmost Point of Lake of the Woods* (Washington, DC: Government Printing Office, 1937).

12 Arthur R.M. Lower, *The North American Assault on the Canadian Forest: A History of the Lumber Trade between Canada and the United States* (Toronto, 1938), 182.

13 OA, Lake of the Woods Milling Company Papers, David Mills, "Memorandum," Department of the Interior, 16 April 1878.

14 OA, Lake of the Woods Milling Company Papers, Macauley (sometimes Macaulay) to John A. Macdonald, 3 May 1882 and 10 October 1883.

15 OA, Lake of the Woods Milling Company Papers, Macauley to John White MP, 23 April 1884; Dick and Banning to Ontario Commissioner of Crown Lands, 23 January 1885.

16 "Rat Portage and Rainy River District."

17 OA, Irving Papers, J.P. Macdonell to Attorney General, "Re Bulmer," 30 June 1887; S. Barry Cottam, "Federal/Provincial Disputes, Natural Resources and the Treaty #3 Ojibway, 1867–1924" (PhD diss., University of Ottawa, 1994), 117–19. Macdonell's memo indicates that six licences covering over 310 square miles were issued to a group represented by Henry Bulmer Jr. of Montreal. Access to timber was specifically granted by virtue of the federal government's Indian title claim rather than pursuant to arrangements under the Provisional Boundary agreement. The Bulmer interests were the only federal licence holder to construct a substantial mill in connection with their timber berth. In 1896, they were awarded $15,000 for business and investment losses flowing from the invalidity of the federal timber permit. See LAC, "Report of the Sub-committee of the Privy Council on the Henry Bulmer Case," Privy Council Minutes, 21 April–28 April 1896, RG 2, series I, vol. 685.

18 *The Colonist*, May 1890.

19 *The Colonist*, Sept. 1889.

20 Lower, *North American Assault*, 182.

21 Rat Portage Lumber, headquartered in Winnipeg, operated mills in that city and in Kenora, as well as in Banning, Vancouver, and Harrison, BC. See the Canadian Manufacturers' Association magazine, *Industrial Canada*, October 1912, 469. In this era, the Rat Portage operation employed 300 to 400 men in the Lake of the Woods district and an additional 350 in the Rainy Lake region. See International Joint Commission (IJC), *Final Report of the International Joint Commission on the Lake of the Woods Reference* (hereafter *Lake of the Woods Reference*) (Washington, DC: Government Print Office, 1917), 170–71.

22 OA, Ontario Lumberman's Association, Minutebooks, 172; Minutebooks, 151–52, letter to Sir Wilfrid Laurier from lumbermen of Northwestern Ontario, the West etc., 21 March 1898.

23 "Statement of Licenses Granted by the Dominion Government in North-Western Ontario," Canada, House of Commons, *Debates*, 4 May 1886, 1051. Fowler's operation was taken over by Hugh Sutherland. See Cottam, "Federal/Provincial Disputes," 108–11.

24 OA, Lyons Letterbooks, Lyons to Oliver Mowat, 27 July 1879.
25 R.S. Lambert and Paul Pross, *Renewing Nature's Wealth: A Centennial History of the Public Management of Lands, Forests, and Wildlife in Ontario, 1763–1967* (Toronto: Ontario Department of Lands and Forests, 1967), 252–54. See also H.V. Nelles, *The Politics of Development: Forests, Mines, and Hydro-electric Power in Ontario, 1849–1941* (Toronto: Macmillan, 1974), 73–74.
26 Mark Kuhlberg, "'Eyes Wide Open': E.W. Backus and the Pitfalls of Investing in Ontario's Pulp and Paper Industry, 1902–1932," *Journal of the Canadian Historical Association*, n.s., 16, 1 (2005): 201–33.
27 IJC, *Lake of the Woods Reference*, 171. For a detailed company narrative of Backus's forest operations in Canada, see D. McLeod, "Memorandum re Keewatin Lumber Company Limited, Kenora Paper Mills Limited and Allied Companies and Their Operations at Kenora and Hudson, Ontario & St. Boniface, Manitoba, 1906 to 1943 & 1945," in the records of the Lake of the Woods Museum.
28 See Chapters 5, 7, and 8 in this volume.
29 OA, Lyons Letterbooks I, no. 83, Lyons to Mowat, 23 February 1881.
30 Ibid.
31 Greg Clark, *Sultana Memoirs* (Winnipeg: D.T. Publishing, 1994), 7. For a comprehensive survey of mining prospects and properties in the region, see J.C. Davies and P.M. Smith, *The Geological Setting of Gold Occurrences in the Lake of the Woods Area* (Toronto: Ontario Geological Survey, Open File Report 5695, 1988). Patrick Chapin provides a detailed account of local mining operations and governmental oversight in "The Roots of a Shady Tree: Provincial Regulation of the Northwestern Ontario Speculative Gold Mining Boom, 1890–1902" (unpublished manuscript).
32 W. Robert Wightman and Nancy M. Wightman, *The Land Between: Northwestern Ontario Resource Development, 1800 to the 1990s* (Toronto: University of Toronto Press, 1997), 84.
33 Ontario Bureau of Mines (OBM), *Annual Report*, 1893, 20; 1896, 98.
34 OBM, 1893, 27.
35 Ibid., 11–13.
36 OBM, 1894, 7, 8.
37 OBM, 1896, 108.
38 Ibid., 47 and 105. For an informative discussion of the Engledue leases, see Chapin, "Roots of a Shady Tree."
39 Ibid., 256–57. One English syndicate acquired two tracts totalling forty-six thousand acres under a three-year licence of occupation. One area covered the west side of the Lake of the Woods, while the other was north of Rainy Lake. OBM, 1896, 8. Block B of the Engledue concession consisted of fifteen thousand acres in the western peninsula lying south of Carl Bay in Shoal Lake. OBM, 1898, 55 to 56.
40 OBM, 1896, 257.
41 OBM, 1900, 52.
42 See Chapter 14 in this volume.
43 *New York Engineering and Mining Journal*, 1900, quoted in Cottam, "Federal/Provincial Disputes," 148.
44 OBM, 1899, I, 49.
45 OBM 1892, 234–35; 1895, 187–88; 1896, 50, 259; 1898, I, 37.
46 OBM, 1900, 88.
47 OBM, 1896, 53. See also OBM, 1898, 59–61.

48 *New York Engineering and Mining Journal*, 1900, quoted in Cottam, "Federal/Provincial Disputes," 148.

49 Ibid.

50 OBM, 1895, 210.

51 OBM, 1899, I, 50.

52 OBM, 1898, 143.

53 OBM, 1900, 69.

54 Regarding Mikado, see OBM, 1900, 76. Regarding Sultana Island and Indian Reserve 38B, see LAC, Indian Affairs, Black Series, 1872–1956, RG 10, vol. 3895, file 97971, part 0, microfilm, reel C-10156. For correspondence regarding the Keewatin Lumber claim to islands, including Sultana, see LAC, Indian Affairs, Black Series, 1872–1956, RG 10, vol. 3824, file 60008, part 0, microfilm, reel C-10144.

55 For claims about land value associated with gold, see *Keewatin v Minister of Natural Resources* 2011 O.N.S.C. 4801 (hereafter *Keewatin*), paras. 348–49. For Nolin's notes on what was said about gold found on and off reserve, see ibid., para. 370. See also Janet E. Chute and Alan Knight, "Simon J. Dawson and the Upper Great Lakes Native Resource Campaign of the 1860s and 1870s," in *With Good Intentions: Euro-Canadian and Aboriginal Relations in Colonial Canada*, ed. Celia Haig-Brown and David A. Nock (Vancouver: UBC Press, 2006), 116.

56 *Keewatin*, para. 366.

57 Ibid.

58 *Ontario Mining v Seybold* (1899) 31 OR 386 at 387.

59 Greg Clark speculates that when winter surveying was being carried out in 1881, the swamp may have appeared to be a clearing on the mainland – that is, it was not supposed to be included in the reserve. Clark, *Sultana Memoirs*, 5. Patrick Chapin concludes that Sultana was a peninsula until dam construction. Chapin, "Roots of a Shady Tree," note 47.

60 The Matheson reference is in Metropolitan Toronto Reference Library (hereafter MTRL), Matheson Papers, file 1884–1886, Hugh J. Macdonald to A. Matheson, 6 August 1886. See also Cottam, "Federal/Provincial Disputes," 158–60.

61 In 2009, members of the band accepted an agreement to provide financial compensation associated with gold production from Sultana mining operations.

62 Cottam, "Federal/Provincial Disputes," 132–37; Clark, *Sultana Memoirs*, 18–19. See also Chapin, "Roots of a Shady Tree," for a discussion of the terms of timber leases excluding other occupants of the land, ostensibly because of fire risk. The 1891 KLM agreement with Ontario concerning Tunnel Island and the Fuller Lease from the Government of Canada states: "It is hereby agreed by and between the said parties hereto that the island known as Sultana Island is in no way to be affected by the terms of this agreement or by the surrender aforesaid." Ontario, *Journals of the Executive Council* 62, 322.

63 OBM, 1893, 14.

64 Detailed maps of the situation are found in Burley Smith's report in the *Canadian Mining Journal* 18, 3 (March 1899): 68.

65 Following successful assays in Detroit, American backing became available for mineral development at Sultana Island. See Wightman and Wightman, *Land Between*, 83, citing *The Globe*, 13 April and 9 August 1882.

66 Cottam says that Caldwell paid $135.35 for patents held by these four in April 1890. Cottam, "Federal/Provincial Disputes," 166.

67 Clark, *Sultana Memoirs*, 20. Clark describes Ophir as A20 and says that it was owned by
    the Ontario Mining Company (32). For Sultana Mine development under Caldwell, see
    Cottam, "Federal/Provincial Disputes," 150–56. Caldwell took over all but 1/16th in April
    1890 and finally bought out Henesy in the fall of 1892. For a contemporary description
    and map of the approach to Sultana and the 38B Reserve issue, see OBM, 1893, 13–14.
68 *Ontario Mining v Seybold*, (1901) 32 SCC, 18. Indian Affairs issued patents for 42X and
    43X (roughly 180 acres) to Ontario Mining Co. in 1889, the year of the company's incor-
    poration. See Cottam, "Federal/Provincial Disputes," 132n90 and 91.
69 *Ontario Mining v Seybold* (1899) 31 OR 386 at 387–88.
70 *Weekly Herald and Algoma Miner*, 15 November 1890. Benjamin E. Chaffey faithfully re-
    ported to Alexander Matheson on the sluggish early progress of Sultana. MTRL, Matheson
    Papers, 27 February 1890; 3 May 1890.
71 MTRL, Matheson Papers, Chaffey to Matheson, 22 June 1891.
72 For the beginning of mining, see OBM, 1893, 16; 1892, 231, 235; 1893, 18. For $2,000, see
    Weekly Herald and Algoma Miner, 1 May 1896. For the value of gold produced in Ontario,
    see OBM, 1896, 47. For $3,000, see OBM, 1896, 249–50.
73 OBM, 1900, 38.
74 "The 'Sultana Mine Ltd.,'" *Canadian Mining Review* 18, 1 (1899): 1.
75 Caldwell received his provincial patents to X42 and X43 in March 1897, subject to Fraser's
    patent of November 1896. See Rhonda Mae Telford, "The Sound of the Rustling of the
    Gold Is under My Feet Where I Stand" (PhD diss., University of Toronto, 1996), 267.
76 J. Burley Smith, "Description of the Sultana Quartz Lode, and the Sinking of the Burley
    Shaft in Bald Indian Bay, Lake of the Woods," *Canadian Mining Review* 18, 3 (1899): 64–71.
77 Smith, "Description of the Sultana Quartz Lode," 71.
78 Greg Clark explains the conflict between Burley and Caldwell over the water lots in Bald
    Indian Bay, citing the *Rat Portage Miner and Rainy Lake Journal*, 13 January 1898, as well
    as *The Colonist*, November 1898, for details. Clark, *Sultana Memoirs*, 37–38.
79 A sequential account of grants is provided in Telford, "Sound of the Rustling," 276n133:

    > Ontario issued patents on Sultana Island for the following locations: D193 on 18
    > November 1896 to A.W. Fraser; X 42 and X43 on 5 March 1897, to J.F. Caldwell
    > (subject to the limits of Fraser's patent); (two patents issued for) A20 on 16 and 24
    > January 1899 to Seybold, et. al.; and D193 on 26 May 1899 to the Bald Indian Bay
    > Mining and Investment Co. Ltd. Personal Communication. Vic Prasaud, MNR,
    > CLR, 13 June 1994.

    Fraser held D193A from Ontario. This can be seen in the map in ibid., 281.
80 The Matheson Papers indicate that the case opened in Barrie on 24 November. Judgment
    was reserved in the Caldwell case. MTRL, Matheson Papers, Bulmer to Matheson, 14
    December 1897. Justice Rose's decision in *Fraser v Caldwell*, released 31 January 1898, is
    reproduced in W. David McPherson and John Murray Clark *The Law of Mines in Canada*
    (Toronto: Carswell, 1898) from which quotations below have been taken.
81 J. Rose. quoted in McPherson and Clark, *The Law of Mines in Canada*, 17.
82 Ibid.
83 Ibid.
84 McPherson and Clark, *The Law of Mines in Canada*, 20–23. See also Cottam "Federal/
    Provincial Disputes," 217–18.

85 See Telford, "Sound of the Rustling," 282–83.

86 LAC, Indian Affairs, Black Series, RG 10, vol. 3799, file 48508.

87 For Gwynne's discussion of Ontario letters patent, 9 January 1899, see *Ontario Mining v Seybold*, (1901) 32 SCC 1 at 19.

88 *Ontario Mining v Seybold* (1899) 31 OR 386 at 388.

89 OA, Irving Papers, Memorandum, 19 February 1899 (research document 30, part V).

90 The proceedings took place in Toronto on 26 and 27 October and 10 November 1899. *Ontario Mining v Seybold* (1899) 31 OR 386 at 396.

91 Ibid., 395–96.

92 Ibid., 396.

93 Ibid., 398. Boyd's reasoning in *Seybold* was recently revisited in *Keewatin*, para. 434.

94 For Boyd's discussion of the treaty, see *Ontario Mining v Seybold* (1899) 31 OR 386 at 400.

95 *Ontario Mining v Seybold*, (1900) 32 OR 301 at 304.

96 *Ontario Mining Co. v Seybold*, 1903 AC 73. With *Seybold* as a prime example, Snell and Vaughan condemned Chief Justice Strong as "sometimes ... intellectually lazy and frequently irresponsible." James G. Snell and Frederick Vaughan, *The Supreme Court of Canada: History of the Institution* (Toronto: Osgoode Society, 1985), 78.

97 Paul Romney, "John Wellington Gwynne," in *Dictionary of Canadian Biography*, ed. Ramsay Cook and Jean Hamelin, vol. 13 (Toronto: University of Toronto Press, 1994).

98 *Ontario Mining v Seybold* (1901) 32 SCC 1at 5.

99 Ibid., 9.

100 Ibid., 22.

101 *Ontario Mining v Seybold*, 1903 AC 73. Decades later, Gwynne's forthright, if isolated, invocation of the "honour of the sovereign" might be recognized in a foundational principle of post-Charter Canadian treaty interpretation, "the honour of the Crown."

102 Cottam, "Federal/Provincial Disputes," 225. An agreement respecting the administration of Indian reserves in Ontario, including minerals and water resources, was concluded on 24 March 1924 and incorporated in parallel federal and provincial legislation. An Act for the settlement of certain questions between the Governments of Canada and Ontario respecting Indian Reserve Lands, SC 1924 c. 48 and The Indian Lands Act, SO 1924 c. 15. For subsequent criticism, see Richard H. Bartlett, "Mineral Rights on Indian Reserves in Ontario," *Canadian Journal of Native Studies* 3 (1983): 245–73, and David T. McNab, *Circles of Time: Aboriginal Land Rights and Resistance in Ontario* (Waterloo, ON: Wilfrid Laurier University Press, 1999), 124.

103 MTRL, Matheson Papers, Bulmer to Matheson, 24, 25, 26 November 1897.

104 MTRL, Matheson Papers, Bulmer to Matheson, 25 November 1897. Cottam, "Federal/Provincial Disputes," 211–12, says that the Sabaskong Gold Mining Company got a surrender from the Ojibwa in 1888 for otherwise unclaimed mining lands on Sultana but could not get federal mining licences because Indian Affairs policy – on advice from the Justice department – was to not deal with "reserve" lands in Treaty 3 until confirmation had been received by Ontario. Approximately forty investors were involved. See LAC, RG 10, vol. 3803, file 50358.

105 The Matheson Papers contain correspondence from Henry Bulmer, Charles W. Chadwick, Alexander Matheson, George F. Hartt, Benjamin E. Chaffey, Caldwell, George Heenan, John Flett, Stephen M. Mathews, and James Conmee. Most of these, but not Conmee, were originals in Sabaskong.

106 MTRL, Matheson Papers, Conmee to Matheson, 17 July 1897.

107 Ibid.
108 MTRL, Matheson Papers, Conmee to Matheson, 30 August 1897.
109 MTRL, Matheson Papers, Dewart to Matheson, 27 September 1897. An Act to Further
     Improve the Mining Act, S.O. 60 Victoria, 1897, c. 8, was enacted on 13 April 1897.
110 MTRL, Matheson Papers, Dewart to Matheson, 27 September 1897.
111 MTRL, Matheson Papers, Dewart to Matheson, 27 September 1897.
112 MTRL, Matheson Papers, Bulmer to Matheson, 29 September 1897.
113 MTRL, Matheson Papers, Bulmer to Matheson, 24 November 1897. Angus William Fraser,
     an Ottawa lawyer, was one of the original incorporators (1897) of the Ottawa Gold Milling
     and Mining Company.
114 MTRL, Matheson Papers, Bulmer to Matheson, 24 November 1897.
115 MTRL, Matheson Papers, Gibson to Atwater, as quoted in Bulmer to Matheson, 26
     November 1897.
116 MTRL, Matheson Papers, Bulmer to Matheson, 15 February 1898.
117 MTRL, Matheson Papers, Bulmer to Matheson, 16 April 1898.
118 MTRL, Matheson Papers, Drewry to Matheson, 21 July 1898.

CHAPTER 4: WATER RIGHTS AND WATER POWERS

  1 H.V. Nelles, "Public Ownership of Electrical Utilities in Manitoba and Ontario, 1906–1930,"
     Canadian Historical Review 57 (1976): 461–84.
  2 Archives of Ontario (hereafter OA), Irving Papers, "Re Rainy River Boom Slide and
     Navigation Company," Mather to William Edwards, 12 February 1890.
  3 OA, Irving Papers, "Re Rainy River Boom Slide and Navigation Company."
  4 Ibid.
  5 Ibid.
  6 *International Boom Co. v Rainy Lake River Boom Corp.* (1906), 107 N.W. 735; *Rainy Lake
     River Boom Corp. v Rainy River Lumber Co. Ltd.* (1908), 162 F. 287; *Namakan Lumber Co.
     v Rainy Lake River Boom Corp.* (1911), 132 N.W. 259; *Rainy Lake River Boom Corporation
     v Rainy River Lumber Co.* (1912), 27 O.L.R. 131, 6 D.L.R. 401. Border country disputes
     about booming rights were among the first matters coming to the attention of the Inter-
     national Joint Commission: see IJC Docket No. 1 A, "Rainy River Improvement Company"
     (1912), and IJC Docket No. 2 A, "Watrous Island Boom Company" (1912).
  7 OA, Lake of the Woods Milling Company Papers, "Certified Copy of a Report of the
     Committee of the Privy Council 5 April 1887."
  8 Navigable Waters Protection Act, Revised Statutes of Canada 1886 Ch. 92.
  9 Library and Archives Canada (heafter LAC), John E. Read Papers, "Memorandum: A Brief
     Sketch of the History of the Outlets of Lake of the Woods," 5 November 1931. Blasting
     removed the vestiges of the Rollerway Dam in 1899.
 10 The Lake of the Woods outlets, both natural and artificial, are surveyed in International
     Joint Commission (IJC), *Final Report of the International Joint Commission on the Lake of
     the Woods Reference* (hereafter *Lake of the Woods Reference*) (Washington, DC: Government
     Print Office, 1917), 214–16.
 11 A. Ernest Epp, "The Lake of the Woods Milling Company: An Early Western Industry,"
     in *The Canadian West: Social Change and Economic Development*, ed. Henry C. Klassen
     (Calgary: Comprint, 1977), 147; OA, Lake of the Woods Milling Company Papers, Mather
     to Pardee, 3 May 1887.

12 Walpole Roland, *Algoma West: Its Mines, Scenery, and Industrial Resources* (Toronto: Warwick and Sons, 1887), 138. See also LAC, Sandford Fleming, "Memorandum in re Grants of Land with Water Privilege at Keewatin," 14 January 1879, RB 12, vol. 1962, file 3454.

13 OA, Mather Diary, 5 August 1887.

14 OA, Lake of the Woods Milling Company Papers, Mather to White, 30 May 1887.

15 OA, Lake of the Woods Milling Company Papers, Mather to White, 30 May 1887; White to Mitchell, 28 June 1887; Mather to Mitchell, 11 January 1888.

16 OA, Lake of the Woods Milling Company Papers, George B. Kirkpatrick, "Report," 23 November 1889.

17 OA, Lake of the Woods Milling Company Papers, Mather to Mitchell, 6 July 1887.

18 OA, Lake of the Woods Milling Company Papers, Dick and Banning to James Conmee, 20 February 1890.

19 OA, Lake of the Woods Milling Company Papers, W. Whyte, CPR Western Branch General Superintendent, to Hon. J.M. Gibson, Crown Lands Commissioner, 2 February 1897.

20 OA, Lake of the Woods Milling Company Papers, Mather to Mitchell, 25 May 1887.

21 OA, Irving Papers, Mather to Mowat, 20 October 1885; Lake of the Woods Milling Company Papers, Mather to Pardee, 17 February 1888.

22 A copy of the agreement is in the Read Papers (LAC) as an attachment to the 5 November 1931 memorandum on Lake of the Woods outlets.

23 OA, Lake of the Woods Milling Company Papers, "Tunnel Island Agreement," 24 November 1891.

24 OA, Lake of the Woods Milling Company Papers, Transfer of Keewatin Lumber and Manufacturing Company Tunnel Island Rights to Keewatin Power Company, 22 September 1893; "Letters Patent Incorporating the Keewatin Power Company (Limited)," 3 June 1893.

25 OA, Lake of the Woods Milling Company Papers, Transfer of Keewatin Lumber and Manufacturing Company Tunnel Island Rights to Keewatin Power Company, 22 September 1893; "Letters Patent Incorporating the Keewatin Power Company (Limited)," 3 June 1893.

26 Downstream interests, including the Dalles First Nation on the Winnipeg River, experienced significant disruption as a result of water level regulation on the Lake of the Woods originating with the Norman Dam.

27 "Power from the Keewatin Dam," *Rat Portage Miner*, 23 July 1901.

28 Mather and Fuller had contemplated a paper manufacturing facility as early as 1882. See OA, Mather Diary, 28 April 1882.

29 *Rat Portage Miner and Rainy Lake Journal*, 27 July 1899. The pulpwood agreement was subsequently cancelled by a newly elected provincial government. Mark Kuhlberg, "'Eyes Wide Open': E.W. Backus and the Pitfalls of Investing in Ontario's Pulp and Paper Industry, 1902–1932," *Journal of the Canadian Historical Association*, n.s., 16, 1 (2005): 212.

30 Alan F.J. Artibise, *Winnipeg: A Social History of Urban Growth, 1874–1914* (Montreal and Kingston: McGill-Queen's University Press, 1975), 94–95; OA, Lake of the Woods Milling Company Papers, Reports of the Vice-President, Keewatin Power Company, 27 October 1896, 24 January 1900, 9 January 1901, and 31 December 1902; extracts from the Minute Book of the Keewatin Power Company Limited, entry for 28 June 1905.

31 At the time of the 1869 surrender, the HBC proposed to retain thirteen hundred acres in the Lake La Pluie District. These lands comprised property at Fort Alexander (500 acres), Fort Frances (500 acres), Lake of the Woods (50 acres), and Rat Portage (50 acres), along with 20 acres at each of the following locations: Eagle's Nest, Big Island, Lac du Bonnet, Shoal Lake, Whitefish Lake, English River, Hungry Hall, Trout Lake, Clear Water Lake,

and Sandy Point. G.E. Cartier and W. McDougall to the Colonial Under-Secretary, 16 January 1869, in *Correspondence, Papers and Documents Relating to the Northerly and Westerly Boundaries of Ontario* (Toronto, 1882), 189. See also E.E. Rich, *Hudson's Bay Company, 1670–1870*, vol. 2 (*1763–1870*) (London: Hudson's Bay Record Society, 1959), 880–90.

32 Ernest Voorhis, "Historic Forts and Trading Posts of the French Regime and the English Fur Trading Companies" (Ottawa: Department of the Interior, 1930), 144.

33 *The Letters of Charles John Brydges, 1879–1882* (London: Hudson's Bay Record Society, 1977), lxxviii.

34 Archives of Manitoba (hereafter AM), HBC Archives (hereafter HBCA), Chipman to Ware, 18 April 1902, and "Inspection Report, Rat Portage Sales Shop," 15 April 1902.

35 AM, HBCA, "Inspection Report on Kenora Saleshop," 13 January 1906; 18–20 March 1907; 14–17 January 1910.

36 AM, HBCA, H.E. Burbidge to the Governor and Committee, 31 May 1918.

37 AM, HBCA, Chipman to Ware, 12 February 1897.

38 AM, HBCA, Chipman to Ware, 25 June 1907.

39 AM, HBCA, Thomson to Ingrams, 5 June 1912.

40 Rich, *Hudson's Bay Company*, 850–90; *Keewatin Power Company v Town of Kenora* (1907), 13 O.L.R. 245; LAC, RG 12, vol. 1929, 17 September 1887.

41 *Keewatin Power Company and Hudson's Bay Company v Town of Kenora* (1907), 13 O.L.R. 245.

42 E.B. Borron, *Report on the Lakes and Rivers: Water and Water-Powers of the Province of Ontario*, Ontario, *Sessional Papers*, No. 3, 35.

43 An Act Respecting Water Powers, 61 Victoria (1898), c. 8.

44 For details on the regulations, see Jamie Benidickson, "Private Rights and Public Purposes in the Lakes, Rivers and Streams of Ontario," in *Essays in the History of Canadian Law*, ed. David H. Flaherty, 387–88.

45 AM, HBCA, Ware to Chipman, 12 October 1897.

46 AM, HBCA, Ware to Chipman, 27 November 1897.

47 AM, HBCA, Chipman to Ware, 5 August 1898.

48 AM, H.N. Ruttan Papers, "Clippings."

49 AM, HBCA, Chipman to Ware, 18 July 1902, enclosing H.N. Ruttan, Report on "Water Power, the Property of the Hudson's Bay Company at the Eastern Outlet of the Lake of the Woods."

50 See Bill No. 98, 1903 (Private Bill), An Act Respecting the Town of Rat Portage and reports of debate in 1903 correspondence.

51 AM, HBCA, Chipman to Ware, 2 June 1903. An Act Respecting the Town of Rat Portage was passed by the Ontario legislature on 12 June 1903. 3 Edw. VII c. 77.

52 AM, HBCA, Chipman to Ware, 5 July 1904.

53 AM, HBCA, Chipman to Ware, 24 January 1905.

54 OA, Whitney Papers, Adam Beck to Minister of Lands and Mines, 31 August 1905, enclosing "Memorandum of Conditions at Rat Portage." The existing power plant was dilapidated and actually "put out of business" for about two weeks just as the HEPC inspectors arrived in Kenora. See "No Electric Power," *Rat Portage Miner and Semi-Weekly News*, 11 August 1905.

55 OA, Whitney Papers, Adam Beck to Minister of Lands and Mines, 31 August 1905, enclosing "Memorandum of Conditions at Rat Portage."

56 *An Act Respecting the Town of Rat Portage*, 3 Edw. VII c. 77, SO 1903, Section 19.

57 OA, Premiers' Papers, Whitney Papers, RG 3, box 9, "Water Power Dispute."
58 Ibid.
59 "The Water Power Case," *Miner and News,* 13 July 1906.
60 *Miner and News,* 17 July 1906.
61 *Keewatin Power Company v Town of Kenora,* 263.
62 OA, "Return of Correspondence re Kenora Power Case," Ontario, *Sessional Papers,* 1914, No. 70 (NP), RG 8, I-7-B2.
63 Ibid.
64 Ibid.
65 *Keewatin Power Company and Hudson's Bay Company v Town of Kenora* (1908), 16 O.L.R. 184 (CA) per Moss, 189–90, and per Meredith, 196.
66 "Minister's Views on the New Bill," *Mail and Empire* (Toronto), 17 March 1911; An Act for the Protection of the Public Interest in the Beds of Navigable Waters, 1 Geo. V (1911) c. 11.
67 AM, HBCA, Chipman to Ware, 24 January 1908; 31 March 1908.
68 AM, HBCA, Aylesworth, Wright, Moss, and Thomson to Chipman, 17 March 1908.
69 AM, HBCA, Chipman to Ware, 16 February 1910; Chipman to Ingrams, 11 September 1911.
70 AM, HBCA, Currie to McCarthy, 28 January 1911.
71 LAC, Sifton Papers, Amelius Jarvis to Clifford Sifton, 10 February 1909.
72 Quoted in Epp, "Lake of the Woods Milling Company," 149. See Frederick Philip Grove, *The Master of the Mill* (Toronto: Macmillan, 1946).
73 OA, Mather Diary, 2 August 1890.
74 "A Loaf of Bread," *The Colonist,* May 1890.
75 Epp, "Lake of the Woods Milling Company," 152; OA, Lyons Letterbooks, Lyons to Mowat, 23 February 1881.
76 *Globe* report reprinted in *Thunder Bay Sentinel,* 20 May 1881, 1, and quoted in Epp, "Lake of the Woods Milling Company," 152.
77 A contemporary shift from millstones to roller-milling using porcelain rollers promised significant production improvements with reduced power requirements. Ian M. Drummond, *Progress without Planning: The Economic History of Ontario from Confederation to the Second World War* (Toronto: University of Toronto Press, 1987), 121–22.
78 UBC Special Collections, Mather Papers.
79 Mather's diary records that the name of the milling company was chosen 9 March 1887. OA, Mather Diary, 9 March 1887.
80 Epp, "Lake of the Woods Milling Company," 154. Mather was well known to Stephen at least. They also met in Rat Portage. Mather had held repeated discussions with senior CPR officials concerning water power and a grain elevator. OA, Mather Diary, 4 January 1882; 11 August 1882, etc.; 9 July 1885, 20 January 1886.
81 Epp, "Lake of the Woods Milling Company," 159.
82 Ibid., 161.
83 OA, Mather Diary, 12–13 November 1902; 7, 19–20 May 1903.
84 Phil Eyler, "John Mather and Lake of the Woods Milling" (1994), 30.
85 An Act Respecting the Lake of the Woods Milling Company, Limited, and the Keewatin Flour Mills Company, Limited (1906), 6 Ed.VII, S.C. c. 120.
86 Eyler, "John Mather and Lake of the Woods Milling," 31n82, cites the *Rat Portage Miner and Semi-Weekly News,* 18 July 1905, 1, for the narrative.

CHAPTER 5: PULP AND PAPER

1   Mark Kuhlberg, "'Eyes Wide Open': E.W. Backus and the Pitfalls of Investing in Ontario's
    Pulp and Paper Industry, 1902–1932," *Journal of the Canadian Historical Association* 16, 1
    (2005): 207–8.

2   Lambert and Pross remark that "when it came to charming governments, E.W. Backus
    was the master." R.S. Lambert and P. Pross, *Renewing Nature's Wealth: A Centennial History
    of the Public Management of Lands, Forests and Wildlife in Ontario, 1763–1967* (Toronto:
    Ontario Department of Lands and Forests, 1967), 272. Searle describes Backus as "com-
    bative" for his willingness to engage in litigation regarding almost any issue. R. Newell
    Searle, *Saving Quetico-Superior: A Land Set Apart* (St. Paul, MN: Minnesota Historical
    Society Press, 1977), 40.

3   For a summary of Backus's background and experience, see J.P. Bertrand, *Timber Wolves:
    Greed and Corruption in Northwestern Ontario's Timber Industry, 1875–1960* (Thunder Bay,
    ON: Thunder Bay Historical Museum Society, 1997), 102–4.

4   Searle, *Saving Quetico-Superior*, 34–35.

5   Archives of Ontario (hereafter OA), Whitney Papers, Fort Frances to Governor in Council,
    "Answer to Application of Ontario and Minnesota Power Company for License to Export
    Power," 1 February 1910.

6   On the 1905 legislation, see An Act Respecting the Ontario and Minnesota Power Company,
    Canada 4&5 Edw.VII (1905) c. 139. On Backus's industrial endeavours, see C. Armstrong,
    The Politics of Federalism (Toronto: University of Toronto Press, 1981), 92; Lambert and
    Pross, *Renewing Nature's Wealth*, 270.

7   OA, Whitney Papers, Williams to Whitney, 25 May 1910, enclosing brief "A Fight for a
    Fortune."

8   An Act Respecting the Ontario and Minnesota Power Company Limited, 6 Edw. VII
    (1906), c. 132 (Ont.). Federal legislation had addressed the same export issue as follows:
    "There shall not be less of the said power or electrical energy available for use on the
    Canadian side of the international boundary line than on the American side and, subject
    to the provisions of this Act, such power or electrical energy shall be delivered on the
    Canadian side as and when demanded." An Act Respecting the Ontario and Minnesota
    Power Company Limited, 4 & 5 Edw. VII (1905), c. 139, s. 2.

9   OA, Whitney Papers, "Answer to Application of Ontario and Minnesota Power Company
    for License to export power," 1 February 1910.

10 OA, Whitney Papers, Telegram, Fort Frances District Board of Trade to Adam Beck, 11
    May 1910.

11 OA, Whitney Papers, H. Williams to James P. Whitney, 25 May 1910, enclosing "A Fight
    for a Fortune." Over the long term, Fort Frances enjoyed significant financial benefits from
    a fixed rate contract for a growing level of power consumption provided by Ontario and
    Minnesota under terms agreed in 1905. See *Boise Cascade Canada Ltd. v The Queen* (1979),
    9 B.L.R. 20 (O.S.C.) and further appeals from this decision.

12 International Joint Commission (IJC), *Final Report of the International Joint Commission
    on the Lake of the Woods Reference* (hereafter *Lake of the Woods Reference*) (Washington, DC:
    Government Print Office, 1917), 173. Minnesota and Ontario first shipped paper in 1910,
    while the Canadian plant began operations in 1914. Searle, *Saving Quetico-Superior*, 38.

13 L.M. Bloomfield and G.F. Fitzgerald, *Boundary Waters Problems of Canada and the United
    States* (Toronto: Carswell, 1958), 69–70; IJC, "Opinion in the Matter of the Application

of the Rainy River Improvement Company for Approval of Plans for a Dam at Kettle Falls," filed under Article III of the Treaty between the United States and Great Britain, 5 May 1910 (opinion filed April 18, 1913, at Washington and Ottawa). For the IJC's original rules of procedure, see Bloomfield and Fitzgerald, *Boundary Waters Problems*, Appendix 3.

14 See, for example, *Ontario and Minnesota Power Co. and Fort Frances (Town) (Re)* [1914] O.J. No. 136; 32 O.L.R. 235; 22 D.L.R. 701 (Ont. CA).

15 *Isherwood v Ontario and Minnesota Power Co.*, [1911] O.J. No. 773, 2 O.W.N. 651, 18 O.W.R. 459; *Smith v Ontario and Minnesota Power Co. Limited*, [1918] O.J. No. 7, 44 O.L.R. 43, 45 D.L.R. 266.

16 *Smith v Ontario and Minnesota Power*.

17 This operation, originally a saw and paper mill dating from 1908, was further reorganized to become the Dryden Pulp and Paper Company in 1918. See Sylvia Cosway, *The Grassy Narrows and Islington Band Mercury Disability Board: A Historical Report, 1986–2001* (October 2001), 1:19; W. Robert Wightman and Nancy M. Wightman, *The Land Between: Northwestern Ontario Resource Development, 1800 to the 1990s* (Toronto: University of Toronto Press, 1997), 133.

18 OA, Provincial Board of Health, Robert E. Wodehouse to J.W.S. McCullough, 25 April 1913, RG 62 B-2-a, box 458.1.

19 Ibid.

20 Ibid.

21 Ibid. For discussion of continuing pollution from the Dryden mill, see OA, Provincial Board of Health, G.L. Sparks to PBH re "Dryden," 6 September 1921; Sparks to PBH re "Dryden," 4 July 1923.

22 Chapeskie, Andrew J. "Indigenous Law, State Law and the Management of Natural Resources: Wild Rice and the Wabigoon Lake Ojibway Nation," *Law and Anthropology* 5 (1990): 135.

23 Leo G. Denis and Arthur V. White, *Water Powers of Canada* (Ottawa: Mortimer, 1911), 1.

24 Ibid., 3.

25 For background, see Bruce W. Hodgins and Jamie Benidickson, *The Temagami Experience: Recreation, Resources and Aboriginal Rights in the Northern Ontario Wilderness* (Toronto: University of Toronto Press, 1989), 106.

26 See R.C. Brown, "For the Purposes of the Dominion," in *Canadian Public Land Use in Perspective*, ed. J.G. Nelson, R.C. Scace, and A. Coval (Ottawa: Social Science Research Council of Canada, 1973), 5–15.

27 See IJC, *Lake of the Woods Reference*, 209–13.

28 J.B. Challies, "Necessity for a Forest Reserve at the Lake of the Woods District of Ontario," in *Canadian Commission of Conservation Report* 5 (1914): 205.

29 Ibid.

30 "Necessity for a Forest Reserve."

31 OA, Whitney Papers, Kenora Board of Trade to Whitney, 24 February 1910. See also Edith Brown Weiss, *In Fairness to Future Generations: International Law, Common Patrimony and Intergenerational Equity* (New York: Transnational, 1989).

32 LAC, Meighen Papers, Series 2 (M.G. 26, I, Vol. 40) F.H. Keefer, 18 November 1918, 4–5.

33 Ibid., 9.

34 Ibid., 17–18.

35 LAC, Meighen Papers, Series 2 M.G. 26, I, vol. 40, Keefer to Meighen, 13 December 1920, enclosing "Memo Re Natural Resources," 10 December 1920.

36 Aubrey White, Memorandum, 15 December 1914, quoted in *Keewatin v Minister of Natural Resources*, 2011 O.N.S.C. 4801 (hereafter *Keewatin*), para. 1111, citing ex. 1, vol. 17, tab. 799.

37 An Act to Confirm the Title of the Government of Canada to Certain Lands and Indian Lands, 1915 (Ont.), c. 12.

38 Ibid.

39 According to Rhonda Mae Telford, in February 1895, Margach recommended moving Indian communities inland from Rainy River to avoid conflict with settlement. Rhonda Mae Telford, "The Sound of the Rustling of the Gold Is under My Feet Where I Stand" (PhD diss., University of Toronto, 1996), 273. Local interest in opening up the Rainy valley to settlement is illustrated in "Rainy River Indians," *Rat Portage Miner and Rainy Lake Journal*, 27 July 1899, where it is noted that settlers' access to sixty-four thousand acres is intertwined with the status of thirteen reservations occupied by 843 Indian residents of the area.

40 Bernard McEvoy, *From the Great Lakes to the Wide West* (Toronto: William Briggs, 1902), 56.

41 Ibid., 61.

42 *Keewatin*, para. 1205. An agreement reached in 2009 provides the Indigenous communities of the Rainy River with preferential purchasing power to acquire historical lands.

43 The unreported Supreme Court of Canada decision of 16 April 1924 is available from the court library (hereafter *Ontario and Minnesota Power*, SCC, unreported).

44 Ibid., 8. On the Sultana Island litigation, see *Ontario Mining v Seybold*, 32 OR 303–4.

45 *Ontario and Minnesota Power*, SCC, unreported.

46 Ibid.

47 *Ontario and Minnesota Power*, SCC, unreported, 9. According to Justice Idington, section 17 of the development clearly limited the power company's interests to property under Ontario's control.

48 Ibid., 11.

49 Ibid., 14.

50 Ibid., 18.

51 *R. v Ontario and Minnesota Power Co.*, [1924] J.C.J. No 5 (QL).

52 War Measures Act, 1914, S.C. 5 Geo. V, c. 2.

53 Without differentiating between Canadian and US customers, the IJC stated that Backus's International Falls/Fort Frances operations supplied paper to sixty-five newspapers in the northwest. IJC, *Lake of the Woods Reference*, 73.

54 Library and Archives Canada, Blake and Redden Papers.

55 *Fort Frances Pulp and Power Co. v Manitoba Free Press*, [1923] 3 D.L.R. 629 at 633.

56 Ibid., 633.

57 Ibid., 634.

58 Ibid., 636.

CHAPTER 6: BACTERIAL WATERWAYS

1 *Rod and Gun in Canada*, December 1899, 33.

2 G. Barnes, "Rat Portage," in *The Canadian Album: Encyclopedic Canada*, ed. J. Castell Hopkins (Toronto: Bradley-Garretson, 1896), 439.

3 Ibid., 440.

4   W.F. Butler, *The Great Lone Land: A Narrative of Travel and Adventure in the Great North-West of America* (London: Sampson Low, Marston, Low, and Searle, 1875), 156.

5   Marchioness of Dufferin and Ava, *My Canadian Journal, 1872–8: Extracts from My Letters Home Written While Lord Dufferin Was Governor-General* (London: J. Murray, 1891), 30 August 1877, 342.

6   Paula Harper, "Rat Portage: Summer Home of the Winnipeg Elite, 1894–1914," unpublished paper (1974), citing Joyce Kennedy, "History of Kenora," unpublished file at Lake of the Woods Museum, 1974, 21 and 81.

7   W.L. Morton, *Manitoba: A History* (Toronto: University of Toronto Press, 1967), 266.

8   *The Colonist,* May 1896, 517, quoted in Harper, "Rat Portage," 11.

9   Harper, "Rat Portage," 15.

10 *Rat Portage Miner and Semi-Weekly News*, 19 July 1904, 27 August 1904, quoted in Harper, "Rat Portage," 16.

11 Archives of Manitoba (hereafter AM), Keewatin Lumbering and Manufacturing Company Papers, Robert A. Mather to T.J.E. Scones, 13 July 1885.

12 Archives of Ontario (hereafter OA), Mather Diary, 4 July 1895.

13 Harper, "Rat Portage," 19; *Rat Portage Miner*, 27 August 1901.

14 *Rat Portage Miner*, 27 April 1894.

15 OA, Matheson Papers, George Heenan to A. Matheson, 11 March 1897.

16 Harper, "Rat Portage," 29–30, citing *The Colonist*, May 1896, 517.

17 Harper, "Rat Portage," 6.

18 *Semi-Weekly Record,* 11 December 1895, quoted in John Ryan, "The Kenora-Keewatin Urban Area: A Geographic Study" (master's thesis, University of Manitoba, 1964), 95.

19 Author's interview with George Beattie, 18 August 1986.

20 W.G. Rankin, "Moose Hunting in North Western Ontario," *Rod and Gun*, November 1911; R.E. Schubart, "A Moose Hunt at Wabigoon, Ontario," *Rod and Gun*, August 1911; Jack Walker, "A Successful Moose Hunt in North Western Ontario," *Rod and Gun*, July 1911, 198–200.

21 "Town Topics," *Rat Portage Miner*, 29 July 1899, quoted in Harper, "Rat Portage," 22.

22 "Towns against Gaudaur," *Rat Portage Miner*, 27 August 1901. Bernard McEvoy, *From the Great Lakes to the Wide West* (Toronto: William Briggs, 1902), 53–54; "Towns Has Sailed," *Rat Portage Miner*, 26 July 1901; "Big Race Postponed," *Rat Portage Miner*, 6 September 1901.

23 "CPR Opens Devils Gap Bungalow Camp," *Miner and News*, 4 July 1923.

24 "In the Playgrounds of Canada," *Railway Review* 8 (November 1924): 721.

25 Butler, *Great Lone Land*, 175.

26 "A History of Kenora Forest District" (Toronto: Ontario Department of Lands and Forests, 1963), 9.

27 Sandford Fleming, *England and Canada: A Summer Tour between Old and New Westminster* (London: Sampson Low, Marston, Searle, and Rivington, 1884), 175.

28 To what extent the local community later benefited from the presence of a substantial warehouse owned and stocked by distillery interests is impossible to estimate. Peter C. Newman, *Bronfman Dynasty: The Rothschilds of the New World* (Toronto: McClelland and Stewart, 1978), 85.

29 Alan F.J. Artibise, *Winnipeg: A Social History of Urban Growth, 1874–1914* (Montreal and Kingston: McGill-Queen's University Press, 1975), chap. 12. See also Adele Perry, *Aqueduct: Colonialism, Resources, and the Histories We Remember* (Winnipeg: Arp Books, 2016), chap. 3.

30 Robson (H.A.) Report, Fire, Water and Light Committee Correspondence, No. 435, quoted in Artibise, *Winnipeg*, 351n37.

31 Slichter's report, dated 6 September 1912, is quoted in Shoal Lake Watershed Working Group (SLWWG), *Shoal Lake Watershed Management Plan*, April 2002, 22, http://www.gov.mb.ca/waterstewardship/water_quality/quality/shoal_lk_report_index.html.

32 "Cyanide Plant for Cameron Island," *Miner and News,* 24 August 1912.

33 OA, Whitney Papers, Kenora Board of Trade to Sir James Pliny Whitney, 16 April 1913, enclosing a memorial approved 15 April 1913.

34 Ibid.

35 An Act to Enable the City of Winnipeg to Get Water Outside the Province of Manitoba, assented to 6 June 1913, 3–4 Geo. V c. 208.

36 Canada, House of Commons, *Debates*, 23 May 1913, 10752.

37 Perry, *Aqueduct.*

38 David T. McNab, "The Administration of Treaty 3: The Location of the Boundaries of Treaty 3 Indian Reserves in Ontario, 1873–1915," in *As Long as the Sun Shines and Water Flows*, ed. Ian A.L. Getty and Antoine S. Lussier (Vancouver: UBC Press, 1983), 152–53, citing White to D.C. Scott, 15 December 1915.

39 Ibid., 153.

40 The Greater Winnipeg Water District Act (Ontario), 1916, S.O. 6 Geo.V c.17

41 Ibid., Schedule A.

42 L.M. Bloomfield and Gerald F. Fitzgerald, *Boundary Waters Problems of Canada and the United States* (Toronto: Carswell, 1958), 22–23, 85–86. Section 10 of the Shoal Lake legislation confirms the need for IJC approval in relevant circumstances.

43 *International Joint Commission Hearings and Arguments in the Matter of the Application of the Greater Winnipeg Water District for Approval of the Diversion of the Waters of the Lake of the Woods and Shoal Lake for Sanitary and Domestic Purposes* (Washington, DC: Government Printing Office, 1914), 29, evidence of Arthur Meyer.

44 International Joint Commission (IJC), *Final Report of the International Joint Commission on the Lake of the Woods Reference* (hereafter *Lake of the Woods Reference*) (Washington, DC: Government Print Office, 1917), 156.

45 See Chapter 7 in this volume.

46 IJC, *Lake of the Woods Reference*, 156.

47 Ibid., 157.

48 Ibid., 158.

49 Ibid., 157.

50 Ibid.

51 OA, Mather Diary, 16 April 1898.

52 1913 engineers' material quoted in SLWWG, *Shoal Lake Watershed Management Plan*, 22–23.

53 Perry, *Aqueduct*, 63–68, 71–73.

54 Shoal Lake Watershed Working Group, "Shoal Lake Watershed Management Plan: A Report to Governments," (April 2002), 18.

55 See Chapter 14 in this volume.

56 "Municipal Sanitation in Ontario during the Past Twenty Years," chap. 4 in Provincial Board of Health, Annual Report 1901, Ontario, *Sessional Papers*, 1902, No. 36, 46.

57 Dr. Charles A. Hodgetts, "Rat Portage Sewerage Extensions," Report No. 15, 1904, of the Committee on Sewerage, Ontario Provincial Board of Health, *Annual Report, 1904*, 162–63.

58 Drs. Hodgetts and Amyot, "Report on Inspection of Muskoka Lakes," Ontario Provincial Board of Health, *Annual Report, 1905.*

59 Ontario Provincial Board of Health, *Annual Report, 1905,* 123.

60 OA, Provincial Board of Health, District 7 Reports, RG 62-B-2-a, box 457.

61 OA, Provincial Board of Health, District 7 Reports, Robert E. Wodehouse, "Fort Frances," 21 November 1912.

62 Ibid.

63 OA, Bryce to resort operators, Provincial Board of Health (PBH), Scrapbooks, 4 April 1899, item 121, RG 62, series B4.

64 OA, PBH Scrapbooks, 4 May 1911, item 224.

65 OA, Sparks to PBH, "Minaki," 10 May 1923.

66 OA, Hodgetts and Amyot, "Report on the Sanitary Conditions of the Muskoka and Kawartha Districts," PBH Sanitary Reports 1904, 143.

67 OA, Provincial Board of Health, District 7 Reports, Robert E. Wodehouse, "Keewatin," 11 February 1913.

68 OA, Provincial Board of Health, G.L. Sparks to Dallyn, 16 February 1922.

69 "Report of Provincial Sanitary Inspector," *Miner and News,* 28 August 1912.

70 OA, Robert E. Wodehouse, "Sanitary Survey: Town of Kenora, February 1913," RG 62 B-2-a, box 457.

71 Ibid.

72 Ibid.

73 OA, G.L. Sparks, "Visit to 'Kenora,' August 28/21 to August 31/21 (Kenora District)," RG 62 B-2-a, box 459.2.

74 OA, Provincial Board of Health, G.L. Sparks to Dr. J.W.S. McCullough, "Re Sanitary Inspection: Kenora, Ontario," 2 September 1920.

75 OA, G.L. Sparks to J.W.S. McCullough, "Re Sioux Lookout," 5 November 1920, RG 62 B-2-a, box 458.4 #26; OA, Wallace & Tiernan, Limited, to Dr. D.G. Dingwall, 30 July 1926, RG 62 G-1, file 489.10.

76 National Archives, College Park, MD, "Records of the Joint Committee Relative to the Preservation of the Fisheries in Waters Contiguous to Canada & U.S., 1893–1895," Interviews 1893–1894, Lake of the Woods, Gloucester, MA, 3, 64–65, 67.

77 IJC, *Final Report of the IJC on the Pollution of Boundary Waters Reference* (hereafter *Pollution of Boundary Waters Reference*) (Ottawa and Washington, DC, 1918), 5.

78 IJC, "Progress Report of the IJC on the Reference by the United States and Canada," 16 January 1914, 24–26.

79 IJC, *Pollution of Boundary Waters Reference,* 10; OA, John Galt, C.E. and M.E., to the Mayor and Council of Fort Frances, 20 October 1905, in PBH, *Annual Report, 1905,* 206.

80 IJC, *Pollution of Boundary Waters Reference,* 18.

81 Ibid., 18.

82 Ibid., 19.

83 Ibid., 24.

84 Ibid., 19.

85 Ibid., 19.

86 Ibid., 23.

87 Ibid., 23.

88 Ibid., 26.

89 Ibid., 34.

90　OA, "Report on a Plan for the Disposal of Sewage and also for the Water Supply of the Town of Rainy River," PBH, *Annual Report, 1906*, 28.

91　OA, Provincial Board of Health, Dr. George to W.R. Worthington, Acting Provincial Sanitary Engineer, 21 Nov 1918.

92　OA, Provincial Board of Health, Dr. Sparks to PBH re "Rainy River," 5 May 1922.

93　Dr. Sparks to PBH, 22 April 1921.

94　Dr. Sparks to PBH, re "Fort Frances," 4 October 1921.

95　G.L. Sparks to McCullough, 1 February 1922.

96　OA, PBH, *Annual Report, 1906*, 8–9.

97　OA, Provincial Board of Health, G.L. Sparks to PBH, 26 October 1922.

98　OA, Provincial Board of Health, G.L. Sparks to PBH, 14 October 1928.

99　OA, Provincial Board of Health, G.L. Sparks to McCullough, 25 October 1924.

CHAPTER 7: LEVELLING THE LAKE

1　In a pioneering proceeding for the new institution, the commissioners showed determination to consider "all matters," despite arguments from Canadian counsel that the Norman Dam was not subject to the inquiry because its construction preceded the 1909 treaty. International Joint Commission (IJC), *Final Report of the International Joint Commission on the Lake of the Woods Reference* (hereafter *Lake of the Woods Reference*) (Washington, DC: Government Print Office, 1917), 102–9.

2　Ibid., 11.

3　Ibid., 12.

4　Ibid., 16.

5　Ibid., 18.

6　Ibid., 19.

7　Ibid., 17–23.

8　Harriet Whitney, "Sir George Gibbons, Canadian Diplomat, and Canadian-American Boundary Water Resources 1905–1910," *American Review of Canadian Studies* 3 (1973): 65; IJC, *Lake of the Woods Reference*, part 3, Supplement, chap. 13, "Diversions from the Watershed," 224–27.

9　Chandler P. Anderson, Opinion dated September 1907: In the Matter of the Application of Minnesota Canal and Power Company (State Department File No. 1718/27, National Archives), quoted in *International Water Law: Selected Writings of Professor Charles B. Bourne*, ed. Patricia Wouters (London: Kluwer Law International, 1997), 293. For discussion of the Harmon doctrine, see Stephen C. McCaffrey, *The Law of International Watercourses* (Oxford: Oxford University Press, 2007), chap. 5, "Theoretical Bases of International Watercourse Law."

10　IJC, *Lake of the Woods Reference*, part 3, Supplement, chap. 13, "Diversions from the Watershed."

11　IJC, *Lake of the Woods Reference*, 24.

12　Ibid., 25.

13　Ibid., 13.

14　Ibid., 26.

15　Ibid., 37.

16　Ibid., 30.

17　Ibid., 50.

18 Ibid., 41.
19 Ibid.
20 Ibid.
21 Lon L. Fuller, "The Forms and Limits of Adjudication," *Harvard Law Review* 92 (1978): 353.
22 IJC, *Lake of the Woods Reference*, 41.
23 See, for example, *Progress Report on the International Joint Commission on the Reference by the United States and Canada, in re Levels of the Lake of the Woods and its Tributary Waters and Their Future Regulation and Control: Including Public Hearings at International Falls and Warroad, Minn., and Kenora, Ontario* (Washington, DC: Government Printing Office, 1914), 65–70, statement of Mr. E.D. George.
24 IJC, *Lake of the Woods Reference*, 47.
25 Ibid., 59.
26 Ibid., 41.
27 Ibid., 34.
28 Ibid., 35.
29 Ibid., 36–37. The commission also considered opportunities for integration along the broader system, noting, for example, that increased Rainy Lake storage and management of the discharge through the Rainy River could both reduce fluctuation in lake levels on the Lake of the Woods and increase the dependable flow of water for power production through the Winnipeg River. Ibid., 67.
30 Ibid., 37.
31 Ibid., 30–31. For the commission's valuation of different categories of lands, see p. 60.
32 Ibid., 31.
33 Ibid., 42–48. In supplementary chapters to the report, the IJC discussed each of these interests in greater detail.
34 Ibid., 49.
35 Ibid., 65–66.
36 Ecosystem services, as described by the 2005 Millennium Ecosystem Assessment, encompass four broad categories: provisioning services, regulating services, supporting services, and cultural services. Millennium Ecosystem Assessment, *Ecosystems and Human Well-Being: Our Human Planet*, 5 vols. (Washington, DC: Island Press, 2005).
37 IJC, *Lake of the Woods Reference*, 54.
38 Ibid., 53. Thus natural has always been normal, although normal, while not necessarily natural, was more likely to be so when highly natural! Twenty-first century water planning in the region involves model-based comparisons with a "hypothetical State of Nature." See International Rainy and Namakan Lakes Rule Curves Study Board, *Managing Water Levels and Flows in the Rainy River Basin: A Report to the International Joint Commission* (June 2017).
39 IJC, *Lake of the Woods Reference*, 55.
40 On the difficulty of determining "ordinary high water mark" and the legal significance of this concept, see ibid., 57. As noted in the report, "the maintenance of the Lake of the Woods at a relatively uniform level of 1,061.25 will aggravate the erosion of exposed high lands not subject to actual flooding until a new beach is formed upon which the waves can beat" (61).
41 Ibid., 64.
42 Ibid., 75–76.

43 Ibid., 79. Two other US members, Obadiah Gardner and Robert B. Glenn, concurred with Tawney's supplemental conclusions and recommendations. Ibid., 109.

44 R. Newell Searle, *Saving Quetico-Superior: A Land Set Apart* (St. Paul, MN: Minnesota Historical Society Press, 1977), 44.

45 See IJC, *Lake of the Woods Reference*, 80. Under article 2, the parties retained, "exclusive jurisdiction and control over the use and diversion, whether temporary or permanent, of all waters on its own side of the line which in their natural channels would flow across the boundary or into boundary waters" subject to navigational interests and claims for compensation.

46 Ibid., 81.

47 Library and Archives Canada (hereafter LAC), Meighen Papers, Keefer to Arthur Meighen, 27 November 1920.

48 LAC, Meighen Papers, Meighen to Keefer, 2 December 1920.

49 Canada, House of Commons, *Debates*, Meighen, 20 April 1921, 2349.

50 LAC, Meighen Papers, Keefer to Lougheed, 11 March 1921.

51 LAC, Meighen Papers, Keefer to Meighen, 14 March 1921.

52 Senate of Canada, *Debates*, 9 March, 1921, 151–52; LAC, Meighen Papers, J.B.Challies, memorandum and enclosures, 22 March 1921.

53 LAC, Meighen Papers, "Bill D, An Act Respecting the Lake of the Woods Control Board," 1 March 1921.

54 LAC, Meighen Papers, Sir James A. Lougheed to Meighen, 1 March 1921.

55 Senate of Canada, *Debates*, 3 and 9 March 1921, 140.

56 Senate of Canada, *Debates*, 3 March 1921, 140.

57 Canada, House of Commons, *Debates*, 20 April 1921, 2346.

58 Ibid., 2347.

59 LAC, Meighen Papers, Keefer to Meighen, 14 March 1921.

60 LAC, Meighen Papers, Keefer to Meighen, 17 March 1921.

61 Canada, House of Commons, *Debates*, 20 April 1921, 2347.

62 Ibid., 2350.

63 Canada, House of Commons, *Debates*, 31 May 1921, 4187.

64 Canada, House of Commons, *Debates*, 20 April 1921, 2347.

65 LAC, Meighen Papers, Keefer to Meighen, 4 April 1921.

66 LAC, Meighen Papers, Keefer to Meighen, 19 April 1921.

67 Canada, House of Commons, *Debates*, 31 May 1921, 4190.

68 Canada, House of Commons, *Debates*, 31 May 1921, 4191. In a telegram to Keefer, 19–20 March 1921, G.E. Farlinger asked that "in interests of this town that no authority be granted in bill to raise Lac Seul waters to a level affecting powers in this vicinity."

69 Canada, House of Commons, *Debates*, 20 April 1921, 2348.

70 Ibid., 2348–49.

71 Ibid., 2349.

72 Ibid., 2349.

73 Ibid., 2349.

74 Ibid., 2352.

75 Ibid.

76 LAC, Meighen Papers, Keefer to Meighen, 25 May 1921.

77 LAC, Keefer Papers, Keefer to Borden, 26 May 1921.

78 LAC, Keefer Papers, Borden to Keefer, 28 May 1921.

79 Canada, House of Commons, *Debates*, 20 April 1921, 2353.
80 Ibid.
81 "Open Letter to the Right Hon. Arthur Meighen, M.P. P.C., and to the Hon Members of Parliament for Ontario Constituencies," *Mail and Empire* (Toronto), 25 April 1921, quoted in Canada, House of Commons, *Debates*, 31 May 1921, 4185.
82 Canada, House of Commons, *Debates*, 31 May 1921, 4186, (Meighen) 4196.
83 Canada, House of Commons, *Debates*, (Keefer) 31 May 1921, 4189. Keefer's remarks echo concerns about administering the water-level control regime in IJC, *Lake of the Woods Reference*, 71.
84 Canada, House of Commons, *Debates*, (Keefer) 31 May 1921, 4189.
85 Ibid.
86 Ibid., 4192.
87 Ibid., 4190.
88 Ibid., 4195.
89 Meighen, Ibid., 4197.
90 Ibid., 4197–98.
91 Canada, House of Commons, *Debates*, (Meighen) 31 May 1921, 4198.
92 LAC, Keefer Papers, George Toole to Keefer, 11 May 1921.
93 LAC, Keefer Papers, George Toole to Keefer, 4 August 1921.
94 LAC, Keefer Papers, George Toole to Keefer, 11 May 1921.
95 LAC, Keefer Papers, Keefer to Meighen, 15 September 1921.

Chapter 8: Power Struggles

 1 Archives of Ontario (hereafter OA), Drury Papers, file re "Lake of the Woods – Control," First Norman Dam Agreement – 1898. The same agreement, also a copy but dated 22 June 1896, is found in the Read Papers, Library and Archives Canada (hereafter LAC), as an appendix to a memorandum, 5 November 1931, providing "A Brief Sketch of the Outlets of the Lake of the Woods."
 2 R. Newell Searle, *Saving Quetico-Superior: A Land Set Apart* (St. Paul, MN: Minnesota Historical Society Press, 1977), 45–46.
 3 H.V. Nelles, *Politics of Development: Forests, Mines and Hydro-electric Power in Ontario, 1849–1941* (Toronto: Macmillan, 1974), 391–93; OA, Drury Papers, Memorandum of Agreement Between the Town of Kenora and E.W. Backus et al., 7 July 1920.
 4 Mark Kuhlberg, "'Eyes Wide Open': E.W. Backus and the Pitfalls of Investing in Ontario's Pulp and Paper Industry, 1902–1932," *Journal of the Canadian Historical Association*, n.s., 16, 1 (2005): 201.
 5 J. Castell Hopkins, *The Canadian Annual Review of Public Affairs*, 1921 (Toronto: Canadian Review Company, 1922), 630.
 6 OA, Drury Papers, Memorandum of Agreement between the Province of Ontario and E.W. Backus et al., 13 September 1920.
 7 Chris Armstrong adds: "Repeated complaints from Minnesota residents about flooding due to high water led in 1919 to the decision to take the Norman Dam, which was owned by E.W. Backus, out of private hands." Chris Armstrong, *The Politics of Federalism: Ontario's Relations with the Federal Government, 1867–1942* (Toronto: University of Toronto Press, 1981), 162.

8 Peter Oliver, *G. Howard Ferguson: Ontario Tory* (Toronto: University of Toronto Press, 1977), 110–11. Kuhlberg reports that Frank Anson of Abitibi Pulp and Paper had also expressed some interest in the English River concession during wartime and was looking for water power. Kuhlberg, "Eyes Wide Open," 214–15.

9 OA, Drury Papers, file re "Lake of the Woods – Control," extract from a statement signed by George A. Toole, mayor of Kenora 1919 and 1920, and J.P. Earngey, mayor of Kenora 1915–18.

10 OA, Heenan Papers, George Toole to Heenan, telegram, 20 December 1920; Toole to Drury, telegram, 18 December 1920; A.T. Fife to H.H. Dewart, telegram, 21 December 1920; Toole to Dewart and Ferguson, 22 December 1920.

11 OA, Heenan Papers, W. Greenwood (President, Kenora Agricultural Society) to Beniah Bowman, telegram, 20 December 1920.

12 OA, Heenan Papers, George Toole to Backus, 23 December 1920.

13 Canada, Dominion Bureau of Statistics, *The Flour and Grist Milling Industry in Canada 1921* (Ottawa: F.A. Acland, 1923).

14 OA, Lake of the Woods Milling Company, C.C. Robinson to E.C. Drury, 1 October and 16 November 1920, RG 3, box 24.

15 OA, Drury Papers, file re "Lake of the Woods Milling Company." See also Kuhlberg, "Eyes Wide Open," 213, and Mark Kuhlberg, *In the Power of the Government: The Rise and Fall of Newsprint in Ontario* (Toronto: University of Toronto Press, 2015), 98.

16 H.E. Willmot, *The Backus Deal* (Toronto, 1923), 3.

17 Ibid., 6.

18 For contending views, see Nelles, *Politics of Development*, 391–93; Kuhlberg, "Eyes Wide Open," 216–17.

19 Transcript of Ferguson speech at Pine Grove, 1921, quoted in Peter Oliver, *G. Howard Ferguson*, 111.

20 LAC, Meighen Papers, R.H. Mulock to Meighen, file 116, pp. 018711–13.

21 LAC, Meighen Papers, Edward Anderson to Meighen, 11 December 1920.

22 LAC, Meighen Papers, J.B. Challies to Buskard, memo, 18 December 1920. See also J.B. Challies to W.W. Cory, Deputy Minister of the Interior, 11 March 1921.

23 See Chapter 7 in this volume.

24 OA, Drury Papers, Drury to Meighen, 25 May 1921.

25 LAC, Meighen Papers, C.J. Rockwood to The Hon. Ministers of the Crown, n.d., but received in the Prime Minister's Office 23 March 1921.

26 LAC, Meighen Papers, J.B. Challies, memoranda, "Points Raised by Judge Rockwood against Lake of the Woods Control Board Bill" and "Criticisms of Lake of the Woods Control Board Bill," 22 March 1921.

27 Quoted in Armstrong, *Politics of Federalism*, 162.

28 *Mail and Empire* (Toronto), 28 April, 1921; OA, Drury Papers, file re "Lake of the Woods – Control," Drury to Meighen, 28 April 1921, and Drury to King, 4 May 1922.

29 OA, Drury Papers, file re "Lake of the Woods – Control," telegram, Meighen to Drury, 29 April 1921 (copy).

30 LAC, Meighen Papers, Meighen to Edward Parnell, 9 May, 1921; George A. Toole to F.H. Keefer, 11 May 1921; H.D. de Maissac to Meighen, 16 May 1921.

31 "The King versus Backus," *Ottawa Journal*, 19 April 1921. See also the *Mail and Empire* (Toronto), 30 May 1921, quoted in J. Castell Hopkins, *Canadian Annual Review of Public Affairs, 1921* (Toronto: Canadian Review Company, 1922), 633.

32 Senate of Canada, *Debates*, 24 May 1921, 587–92.

33 OA, Drury Papers, file re "Lake of the Woods – Control," Drury to Meighen, 25 May 1921.

34 OA, Drury Papers, file re "Lake of the Woods – Control," Drury to Meighen, 25 May 1921; Drury to Backus, 27 May 1921; Backus to Drury, 27 May 1921; Drury to Meighen, 27 May 1922 [sic; 1921].

35 OA, Drury Papers, file re "Lake of the Woods – Control," Meighen to Drury, 28 May 1921.

36 OA, Drury Papers, file re "Lake of the Woods – Control," N.W. Rowell to Attorney General W.E. Raney, 30 June 1921.

37 LAC, J.W. Walker, Town Clerk of Fort Frances, on behalf of A. McTaggart, Mayor, to Prime Minister Mackenzie King, 2 August 1922, MG 26-J1.

38 Searle, *Saving Quetico-Superior*, 36.

39 Ibid., 46.

40 OA, Drury Papers, file re "Lake of the Woods – Control," Memorandum of Conference re Lake of the Woods Reference Matter, 20 September 1922, 4.

41 OA, Drury Papers, file re "Lake of the Woods – Control," Notes of general conference in Prime Minister's office adjourned from 20 September 1922, 15 November 1922.

42 OA, Drury Papers, Memorandum of agreement between the three governments for a settlement of domestic problems (Ottawa, 15 November 1922).

43 Archives of Manitoba (hereafter AM), Jules Prudhomme, "Re Lake of the Woods," 18 October 1924, para. 32.

44 AM, J. Prudhomme, "Memorandum re Conference on Lake of the Woods at Ottawa, September 12–22, 1924."

45 *Kenora Examiner*, "editorial," 15 October 1924.

46 "United We Stand," advertisement, *Manitoba Free Press*, 18 October 1924.

47 The legislation was repealed in 1928.

48 OA, Drury Papers, file re "Lake of the Woods – Control," box 42(2), George A. Toole to Hon. Beniah Bowman, Minister of Lands and Forests, 29 September 1922. The adequacy or possible excess of the quantity of pulpwood made available to Backus in the English River limit had been one of the principal features of the controversy at the time. See J. Castell Hopkins, *The Canadian Annual Review of Public Affairs, 1921* (Toronto: Canadian Review Company, 1922), 630.

49 "Convention and Protocol between His Britannic Majesty in Respect of the Dominion of Canada and the United States for Regulating the Level of the Lake of the Woods, and of Identical Letters of Reference Submitting to the International Joint Commission Certain Questions as to the Regulation of the Levels of Rainy Lake and other Upper Waters" (hereafter "1925 Convention and Protocol"), 15 George V., Sessional Paper No. 98, signed 24 February 1925, Article 2.

50 Ibid., Article 4.

51 William R. Willoughby comments on the work of the IJC: "It has also successfully resolved such highly controversial issues as the Lake of the Woods water levels and the apportionment of the waters of the Souris River, which on other continents would have led to the sending of ultimatums and the marching of troops." William R. Willoughby, *The Joint Organizations of Canada and the United States* (Toronto: University of Toronto Press, 1979), 53.

52 "1925 Convention and Protocol," Article 7.

53 Ibid., Article 11.

54 Ibid., Article 1.

55 The "1925 Convention and Protocol" came into force in Canada on 17 July 1925 and was
    approved by the US Congress on 22 May 1926.
56 LAC, Read Papers, "Statement as to Benefit to Power Plants as a Result of Regulation of
    Lake of the Woods by Dams at the Outlets." This is an attachment to the 5 November 1931
    memorandum.
57 "Lake of the Woods Levels Treaty Signed," *Kenora Daily Miner and News*, 25 February
    1925, 1.
58 "1925 Convention and Protocol," Articles 8, 9, 10.
59 "1925 Convention and Protocol"; LAC, copy of a Code Telegram to the Secretary of State
    for the Colonies from the Governor General of Canada, 20 February 1925, MG 26-J1.
60 LAC, John E. Read Papers, MG 30, E 148, vol. 4, file 26a.
61 *Olson v United States*, 292 US 246 (1934).
62 *Olson*, 248–49.
63 Ibid., 250.
64 Ibid., 256.
65 Ibid.
66 Ibid., 260.
67 Backus had lost flooding compensation claims, including *Erickson v Ontario and Minnesota
    Power* (1916), and he expected that inclusion of upstream waters within an extended regula-
    tory framework established through the IJC reference would limit his exposure to further
    liability. Searle, *Saving Quetico-Superior*, 47. In a protocol supplementing the 1925 agree-
    ment, the two countries elaborated upon procedures applicable to upcoming decisions.
    In conjunction with that protocol, Canada and the United States formulated a new reference
    to the IJC calling for consideration of lake level regulation for Rainy Lake, Namakan Lake,
    and other upper waters.
68 OA, Lake of the Woods Milling Company Papers.
69 *Keewatin Power Company v Keewatin Flour Mills Ltd.*, [1929] D.L.R. 32.
70 *Keewatin Power Company v Keewatin Flour Mills Ltd.*, [1929] 3 D.L.R. 199.
71 Ibid., 200.
72 Ibid.
73 *Keewatin Power Company v Lake of the Woods Milling Co.*, [1930] AC 640.
74 Ibid., 657–58.

CHAPTER 9: ECONOMY AND ECOLOGY

1 See Bruce W. Hodgins and Jamie Benidickson, *The Temagami Experience: Recreation,
    Resources and Aboriginal Rights in the Northern Ontario Wilderness* (Toronto: University of
    Toronto Press, 1989); Gerald Killan, *Protected Places: A History of Ontario's Provincial Parks
    System* (Toronto: Dundurn Press, 1993); Patricia Jasen, *Wild Things: Nature, Culture and
    Tourism in Ontario, 1790–1914* (Toronto: University of Toronto Press, 1995); and Claire
    Elizabeth Campbell, *Shaped by the West Wind: Nature and History in Georgian Bay* (Van-
    couver: UBC Press, 2005).
2 Report of the Ontario Game and Fish Commissioners, 1892, Ontario, *Sessional Papers*, 1893,
    No. 76. The exemption was in section 12 of the Game Protection Amendment Act, S.O.
    1892, c. 58, s. 12. Ontario Game Protection Act, S.O. 1893, c. 49, s. 27(1).
3 Archives of Ontario (hereafter OA), "Fishing Industry," Walter Davidson and John Mossop
    to Howard Ferguson, 25 February 1926, RG 3, box 85.

4   Jean Teillet, *The Role of the Natural Resources Regulatory Regime in Aboriginal Rights Disputes in Ontario*, Final Report for the Ipperwash Inquiry, 31 March 2005, http://www.attorney general.jus.gov.on.ca/inquiries/ipperwash/policy_part/research/pdf/Teillet.pdf. Sidney L. Harring, "'The Liberal Treatment of Indians': Native People in Nineteenth Century Ontario Law," *Saskatchewan Law Review* 56, 2 (1992): 326–28.

5   Teillet, *Role of the Natural Resources Regulatory Regime*, 26–33. Teillet cites, in particular, LAC, 29 December 1909, 15 January 1910, 15 September 1909, 22 March 1911, RG 10, vol. 6743, file 420–28, pt 1. See also Frank Tough, "Ontario's Appropriation of Indian Hunting: Provincial Conservation Policies vs. Aboriginal and Treaty Rights, ca. 1892–1930," Ontario Native Affairs Secretariat, Research Report, 1991.

6   Chief Land's letter of 3 January 1924 to Kenora Solicitor James Robinson was printed in the *Miner and News* (Kenora), 26 March 1924, quoted in *Keewatin v Minister of Natural Resources* 2011 ONSC 4801 (hereafter *Keewatin*), para. 1139. The Islington Band is now known as Wabaseemoong.

7   Jim Netamequon to Indian Affairs, 10 October 1927, quoted in *Keewatin*, para. 1141.

8   J.H. Bury, Superintendent of Indian Timberlands to Deputy Minister of Indian Affairs, 17 September 1929, quoted in *Keewatin*, para. 1142.

9   Ibid. For discussion of historical berry picking and sales practices, see Charles Wagamese, "We Found Our Thrills on Minaan Hills," in *Common Ground: Stories of Lake of the Woods II – Celebrating Another Five Years of Storytelling, Common Ground, 2011–2015* (Kenora: Lake of the Woods Museum, 2015), 245.

10 Hodgins and Benidickson, *Temagami Experience*, 144–47; Jamie Benidickson, "From Empire Ontario to California North," in *Canada's Legal Inheritances*, ed. DeLloyd J. Guth and W. Wesley Pue (Winnipeg: University of Manitoba, 2001), 627; Sidney L. Harring, "'The Liberal Treatment of Indians': Native People in Nineteenth Century Ontario Law," *Saskatchewan Law Review* 56, 2 (1992): 326–28.

11 A. Spencer, 27 September 1938, quoted in *Keewatin*, para. 1145.

12 Frank Edwards to M. Christianson, 15 April 1939, quoted in *Keewatin*, para. 1148.

13 Canada, Special Joint Committee of the Senate and the House of Commons, "Minutes of Proceedings and Evidence No. 26," 1428–31, 23 May 1947, Appendix FP, Submission by Lac Seul Band, 16 September 1946, quoted in Leo G. Waisberg and Tim E. Holzkamm, "The Ojibway Understanding of Fishing Rights under Treaty 3," *Native Studies Review* 8, 1 (1992): 49.

14 *Keewatin*, para. 1152.

15 Among its incidental findings, the Kennedy inquiry lamented the lack of data on fish and wildlife. Howard Kennedy, *Report of the Royal Commission on Forestry* (Toronto: Baptist Johnston, 1947), 135.

16 Anastasia M. Shkylnik, *A Poison Stronger Than Love: The Destruction of an Ojibwa Community* (New Haven: Yale University Press, 1985), 68, 115.

17 Andrew J. Chapeskie, "Indigenous Law, State Law and the Management of Natural Resources: Wild Rice and the Wabigoon Lake Ojibway Nation," *Law and Anthropology* 5 (1990): 129–66; Louise Erdrich, *Books and Islands in Ojibwe Country* (New York: Harper Perennial, 2003), 40–43.

18 Tim E. Holzkamm and Leo G. Waisberg, "'Our Land Here Is Not As on the Plain': The Development and Decline of Ojibway Agriculture in Northwestern Ontario, 1805–1915," presentation at meetings of the American Society for Ethnohistory, Chicago, 2–5 November 1989, notes 115–18.

19 Lac Seul Conservation Act, SC 1928, c. 32.

20 Joseph Anthony Radocchia, "Resource Development and First Nations in Ontario North of 50: The Right to Participate in Self-Determination" (PhD diss., Faculty of Environmental Studies, York University, 1993), 87–94. See Peter Usher, Patricia Cobb, and Gordon Spafford, "Hydro-electric Development and the English River Anishinabe: Ontario Hydro's Past Record and Present Approaches to Treaty and Aboriginal Rights, Social Impact Assessment, and Mitigation and Compensation," report prepared for Nishnawbe-Aski Nation, Grand Council Treaty #3, and Teme-Augama Anishnabai, Ontario Hydro's Demand/Supply Plan Hearing, Intervenor Panel 3D.

21 *Brodie v King*, [1946] 4 D.L.R. 161 (Ex. Ct.). See also "Local Member Advised of Possibility of Survey to Determine Flood Damage," *Kenora Miner and News*, 20 July 1951.

22 R.S. Lambert and Paul Pross, *Renewing Nature's Wealth: A Centennial History of the Public Management of Lands, Forests, and Wildlife in Ontario, 1763–1967* (Toronto: Ontario Department of Lands and Forests, 1967), 284–85; Killan, *Protected Places*, 22–24; R. Newell Searle, *Saving Quetico-Superior: A Land Set Apart* (St. Paul, MN: Minnesota Historical Society Press, 1977), 15 .

23 W. Robert Wightman and Nancy M. Wightman, *The Land Between: Northwestern Ontario Resource Development, 1800 to the 1990s* (Toronto: University of Toronto Press, 1997), 202.

24 Carhart, "Memorandum," quoted in Curt D. Meine, *Aldo Leopold: His Life and Work* (Madison: University of Wisconsin Press, 2010), 178.

25 Gerald Killan and George Warecki, "The Battle for Wilderness in Ontario: Saving Quetico-Superior, 1927–1960," in *Patterns of the Past: Interpreting Ontario's History*, ed. Roger Hall, William Westfall, and Laurel Sefton MacDowell (Toronto: Dundurn Press, 1988), 330.

26 Aldo Leopold, "The Last Stand of the Wilderness," *American Forests and Forest Life* 31 (October 1925): 602.

27 Killan and Warecki, "Battle for Wilderness," 330–31; Searle, *Saving Quetico-Superior*, 53.

28 Ernest C. Oberholtzer, "A University of the Wilderness: A Proposal to Perpetrate by Treaty the Ontario-Minnesota Border Lakes," *American Forests and Forest Life* 35 (November 1929): 693. Following the transfer of natural resource management authority from the federal government to Canada's Prairie provinces, Manitoba established the Whiteshell Forest Reserve in 1931, the forerunner of the provincial park designated in 1961.

29 Oberholtzer, "University of the Wilderness," 692.

30 Ibid. This model continues to gain followers.

31 Ibid., 690.

32 Oberholtzer, quoted in Joe Paddock, *Keeper of the Wild: The Life of Ernest Oberholtzer* (St. Paul, MN: St. Paul Historical Society Press, 2001), 43.

33 Oberholtzer refers to a news article in the autumn of 1927. Oberholtzer, "University of the Wilderness," 691.

34 Ibid., 690.

35 Saleem H. Ali, ed., *Peace Parks: Conservation and Conflict Resolution* (Cambridge, MA: MIT Press, 2007); U.M. Goodale et al., eds., *Transboundary Protected Areas: The Viability of Regional Conservation Strategies* (New York: Food Products Press, 2003).

36 Searle, *Saving Quetico-Superior*, 70.

37 Killan and Warecki, "Battle for Wilderness."

38 Ibid., 335.

39 The US legislation, the Shipstead-Nolan Act, also introduced a requirement for federal approval of dam projects affecting the area. Killan and Warecki, "Battle for Wilderness," 332.

40 Ibid., 331–32.
41 Wightman and Wightman, *Land Between*, 201–2.
42 Ibid., 249.
43 International Joint Commission (IJC), *Final Report on the Rainy Lake Reference* (hereafter *Rainy Lake Reference*) (Ottawa: King's Printer, 1934).
44 Ibid., 7.
45 Hearings transcripts are now available electronically.
46 "Oppose Storage Dams Project," *Kenora Miner and News*, 30 September 1925, 3.
47 Ibid.
48 Searle, *Saving Quetico-Superior*, 49.
49 Backus quoted in Searle, *Saving Quetico-Superior*, 48.
50   Ibid.
51 Quoted in ibid., 49–50.
52 Quoted in ibid.
53 Quoted in ibid.
54 Quoted in ibid.; "Hearings of the International Joint Commission on the Reference by the United States and Canada in Re Levels of Rainy Lake and Other Upper Waters of the Lake of the Woods Watershed and Their Future Regulation and Control, Being Public Hearings at International Falls, Minn., 28–30 September 1925" (hereafter "Hearings of the IJC"), 133.
55 IJC, *Rainy Lake Reference*, 24.
56 "Oppose Storage Dams Project," *Kenora Miner and News*, 30 September 1925, 3.
57 Quoted in Searle, *Saving Quetico-Superior*, 50.
58 Quoted in ibid.
59 Quoted in ibid., 52.
60 Quoted in ibid., 52.
61 The engineers submitted their final report to the IJC in April 1932. IJC, *Rainy Lake Reference*, 10.
62 Searle, *Saving Quetico-Superior*, 95–96.
63 Ibid.; IJC, Report of Engineers, 10–14, 34–41.
64 Searle, *Saving Quetico-Superior*, 96.
65 Ibid., 97.
66 Ibid.
67 "Waterways Commission Will Open Hearings Here Today on Raising of Water Levels," *Winnipeg Free Press*, 5 October 1933, 2.
68 Ibid.
69 Ibid.
70 "Manitoba and Ontario in Whole-Hearted Agreement on Storage in Rainy Lake," *Winnipeg Free Press*, 6 October 1933, 2.
71 Ibid.
72 "Witnesses at Joint Commission Hearing Agree on Lake Levels," *Winnipeg Free Press*, 7 October 1933, 1.
73 Ian M. Drummond, *Progress without Planning: The Economic History of Ontario from Confederation to the Second World War* (Toronto: University of Toronto Press, 1987), 83.
74 "Manitoba and Ontario in Whole-Hearted Agreement," 2.
75 "Strong Opposition Voiced to Raising Boundary Lake Levels by Building Dams," *Winnipeg Free Press*, 10 October 1933, 3.

76 Ibid.
77 Ibid.
78 Wightman and Wightman, *Land Between*, 248–50.
79 "Strong Opposition Voiced."
80 Ibid.
81 For a detailed account of the passage of the Shipstead-Nolan Act, see Searle, *Saving Quetico-Superior*, 72–89.
82 "Strong Opposition Voiced."
83 Ibid.
84 "Witnesses at Joint Commission Hearing," 6.
85 Ibid.
86 "Opponents of Rainy Lake Power Project Complete Arguments Before Inquiry," *Winnipeg Free Press*, 12 October 1933, 5.
87 Ibid.
88 IJC, *Rainy Lake Reference*.
89 Ibid., 49.
90 Ibid.
91 Ibid.
92 Searle, *Saving Quetico-Superior*, 90–93.
93 Wightman and Wightman, *Land Between*, 232.
94 IJC, *Rainy Lake Reference*, 51.
95 Ibid., 52.
96 Ibid.
97 *Convention between Canada and the United States of America Providing for Emergency Regulation of the Level of Rainy Lake and of the Level of Other Boundary Waters in the Rainy Lake Watershed*, 15 September 1938, Canada: Treaty Series 1940 No. 9, United States of America: Treaty Series No. 961, Article 1.
98 IJC, "In The Matter of Emergency Regulations of the Level Of Rainy Lake and Other Boundary Waters in the Rainy Lake Watershed, Order Prescribing Method of Regulating the Levels of Boundary Waters, June 8, 1949."
99 Ibid., 6.
100 Ibid., 1 October 1957. Supplementary and consolidating orders were issued in 1970, 2000, and 2001.
101 David McNab, "Wilderness and Extinction: The Lac La Croix and the Sturgeon Lake First Nations," in *Circles of Time: Aboriginal Land Rights and Resistance in Ontario* (Waterloo, ON: Wilfrid Laurier University Press, 1999), 89–99. Lac La Croix residents have continued to seek employment opportunities within the Quetico wilderness. See Bruce W. Hodgins and Kerry A. Cannon, "The Aboriginal Presence in Ontario Parks and Other Protected Places," in *Changing Parks: The History, Future and Cultural Contexts of Parks and Heritage Landscapes*, ed. John S. Marsh and Bruce W. Hodgins (Toronto: Dundurn Press, 1998), 63–67.
102 LAC, Cabinet Conclusion, International Joint Commission Reference on Lake of the Woods Watershed, 16 May 1951, RG 2, Privy Council Office, series A-5-a, vol. 2648.
103 Killan and Warecki, "Battle for Wilderness," 341.
104 H.H. Chapman, "The Quetico-Superior Program," *National Parks Magazine*, January–March 1945, 4; H.H. Chapman, "A Factual Analysis of the Quetico-Superior Controversy," *Journal of Forestry* 43, 2 (1945): 97–103. Chapman later produced *A Historic Record*

of Development of the Quetico-Superior Wilderness Area and the Chippewa National Forest (Minnesota, 1961) that was "edited and approved" by Chester Wilson.

105 Killan and Warecki, "Battle for Wilderness," 343.

106 Kennedy, *Report of the Royal Commission on Forestry*, 12.

107 Don Delaplante and Melwyn Breen, "Northern Ontario: Canada's Waiting Bonanza," *Saturday Night*, 13 March 1951.

108 Killan and Warecki, "Battle for Wilderness," 345.

CHAPTER 10: WE ARE ALL IN THIS TOGETHER

1 Canada, House of Commons, *Debates*, 7 April 1920, 1030–32.

2 Some knowledge of potential deposits dated back to the 1860s and a brief period of production by the Atikokan Iron Company took place in 1911. See W. Robert Wightman and Nancy M. Wightman, *The Land Between: Northwestern Ontario Resource Development, 1800 to the 1990s* (Toronto: University of Toronto Press, 1997), 245, referring to *The Globe*, 28 September 1865.

3 V.A. Sowa, R.B. Adamson, and A.W. Chow, "Water Management of the Steep Rock Iron Mines at Atikokan, Ontario, during Construction, Operations, and after Mine Abandonment," *Proceedings of the 25th Annual British Columbia Mine Reclamation Symposium*, Campbell River, BC, 2001, 104–15. For discussion of hydroelectricity requirements associated with Steep Rock, including the contribution of the Ogoki diversion, see Matthew Evenden, *Allied Power: Mobilizing Hydro-electricity during Canada's Second World War* (Toronto: University of Toronto Press, 2015), 85–86.

4 LAC RG2, A-1-a, Vol 1787, PC 11693, 31 December 1942.

5 "Big Fish Catch Is Being Made at Steep Rock," *Globe and Mail*, 16 July 1943.

6 "A Great New Ore Supply: Steep Rock Mine in Canada Reaches Big-Scale Production," *Life*, 24 October 1949, 90.

7 Don Delaplante and Melwyn Breen, "Northern Ontario: Canada's Waiting Bonanza," *Saturday Night*, 13 March 1951; Donald F. Putnam, ed., *Canadian Regions: A Geography of Canada* (London: J.M. Dent and Sons, 1952), 336. Wightman and Wightman, *Land Between*, 259–60.

8 Sowa, Adamson, and Chow, "Water Management."

9 "Inland Steel Company of Chicago Leases Rights of Steep Rock 'C' Ore Body," *Kenora Miner and News*, 13 January 1949.

10 "Iron Ore Riches: Dredge Steep Rock Lake to Get at 60 Million Tons," *Globe and Mail*, 22 January 1952.

11 Ontario Hydro, Design and Development Division, "Proposed Atikokan Generating Station: Environmental Analysis," May 1976, 4–2 to 4–4. The legislations authorizing these actions were the Steep Rock Iron Ore Development Act, 1942, S.O. c. 35; Steep Rock Iron Ore Development Act, 1943, S.O. c. 29; Steep Rock Iron Ore Development Act, 1949, S.O. c. 97; and Seine River Diversion Act, 1952, S.O. c. 98.

12 Archives of Ontario (hereafter OA), Ontario Pollution Control Board (hereafter OPCB), R.H. Millest and I.G. Simmonds, "Report, Industrial Waste Survey, Steep Rock Iron Mines, Ltd. Atikoken, Ontario," 1–2 August 1952; "Benidickson Refers Pollution Problem to Joint Commission," *Fort Frances Times*, 31 May 1951.

13 "Benidickson Visits Town; Discusses Lake Pollution," *Fort Frances Times*, 26 July 1951.

14 William R. Edmonds, "United States-Canada Boundary Water Pollution Studies," *Journal (Water Pollution Control Federation)* 35, 10 (1963): 1341.

15 OA, Ontario Water Resources Commission (hereafter OWRC), Sulphur Fumes Arbitration Records, "A Programme for Pollution Control in Ontario," revised 10 January 1952, 4.

16 OA, OPCB, Millest and Simmonds, "Report, Industrial Waste Survey."

17 Ibid.

18 Jamie Benidickson, "Water Supply and Sewage Infrastructure in Ontario, 1880–1990s: Legal and Institutional Aspects of Public Health and Environmental History," Issue Paper for the Walkerton Inquiry, Toronto, 2002.

19 OA, "Public Hearing: OWRC, Kenora, Rainy River, Thunder Bay 1956," RG 84–12, TBE 197.

20 OA, RG 84-12, TBE "Brief Submitted at a Hearing of the Ontario Water Resources Commission held in the City of Port Arthur on Thursday, September 20th, 1956 by the Municipal Council of the Corporation of the Town of Kenora."

21 Wightman and Wightman, *Land Between*, 321.

22 OA, RG 84-12 "Public Hearing: OWRC, Kenora, Rainy River, Thunder Bay 1956."

23 Jamie Benidickson, "KVP v. McKie," in *Property on Trial: Canadian Cases in Context*, ed. Eric Tuffer, James Muir, and Bruce Ziff (Toronto: Irwin Law, 2012), 71–92.

24 SO 1949 c. 48, s. 6, amending The Lakes and Rivers Improvements Act, RSO 1937 c. 45, s. 30.

25 OA, OWRC, Sulphur Fumes Arbitration Records, "A Programme."

26 Benidickson, "Water Supply and Sewage Infrastructure"; Keith Hawkins, *Environment and Enforcement: Regulation and the Social Definition of Pollution* (Oxford: Clarendon Press, 1984).

27 OA, "File: Pulp and Paper Wastes, 1963," Industrial Wastes Branch, OWRC, "Brief re: Pulp and Paper Waste Treatment and Disposal in Ontario," 14 May 1963, 1, RG 84–12, TBE 198.

28 Ibid.

29 Ibid., Appendix, "Pulp and Paper Mills Requiring Primary Treatment."

30 Ibid.

31 Ibid., 4.

32 Wightman and Wightman, *Land Between*, 317.

33 Ibid., 318.

34 Clarence Dusang, "From Our Files: 1965 Survey Completed – Kenora Sewage Discharged without Treatment," *Kenora Daily Miner and News*, 31 January 1985.

35 IJC, *Final Report of the International Joint Commission on the Pollution of Boundary Waters Reference: Washington-Ottawa* (hereafter *Boundary Waters Reference*) (Washington, DC: Government Printing Office, 1918).

36 OA, Cabinet Conclusion, Pollution of Rainy River and Lake of the Woods; reference to International Joint Commission, 19 October 1957, RG 2, Privy Council Office, series A-5-a, vol. 1893.

37 Ibid.

38 IJC, *Report of the International Joint Commission, United States and Canada, on the Pollution of Rainy River and Lake of the Woods* (hereafter *Pollution of Rainy River*), February 1965, 7.

39 IJC, "Report of the Advisory Board on Water Pollution, Rainy River and Lake of the Woods to the International Joint Commission United States and Canada on the Pollution of International Boundary Waters, 1960–1962 Investigations," April 1963.

40 IJC, "Preliminary Report of the Advisory Board on Water Pollution, Rainy River and Lake of the Woods to the International Joint Commission United States and Canada on Pollution of International Boundary Waters, 1960–1962 Investigations: Rainy River and Lake of the Woods, Minnesota and Ontario," October 1962.

41 Edmonds, "United States-Canada Boundary Water Pollution Studies," 1339.

42 Ontario Department of Health, *Annual Report 1937*, 133. See also Edmonds, "United States-Canada Boundary Water Pollution Studies," 1341.

43 Harald Leverin, *Industrial Waters of Canada* (Ottawa: King's Printer, 1942), 46.

44 Edmonds, "United States-Canada Boundary Water Pollution Studies," 1341.

45 Ibid.

46 IJC, "Report of the Advisory Board," 63.

47 Ibid. 32.

48 IJC, *Pollution of Rainy River*, 16.

49 Ibid., 9.

50 Ibid.

51 Ibid., 8–9.

52 Ibid., 9.

53 Ibid.

54 Ibid., 10.

55 Ibid.

56 Ibid.

57 "Sable Island Channel Proposal Turned Down," *Kenora Miner and News*, 10 January 1963; "Turtle Portage Dredging Program Aids Navigation," *Kenora Miner and News*, 23 November 1961; "Ottawa to Chart Rainy Lake," *Kenora Miner and News*, 4 March 1964.

58 IJC, *Pollution of Rainy River*, 10.

59 Ibid., 13

60 Ibid.

61 Ibid.

62 Ibid.

63 Ibid., 14.

64 Ibid., 14–15.

65 Ibid., 15.

66 Ibid.

67 Ibid., 16.

68 Ibid.

69 Ibid.

70 Ibid., 16–17.

71 Ibid., 19.

72 OA, Cabinet Conclusion, "Recommendations of the International Joint Commission For Controlling Pollution of The Rainy River," 23 July 1965, RG 2, Privy Council Office, series A-5-a, vol. 6271.

73 OA, "Liaison with Ontario-Minnesota Industries Pulp and Paper Plant, Kenora," (hereafter, "Ontario-Minnesota Liaison"), Mrs. S.M. Dorothy Bolton to Hon. J.P. Robarts, 27 January 1967, RG 12–29, TB 27.

74 Ibid.

75 A.K. McDougall, *John P. Robarts: His Life and Government* (Toronto: University of Toronto Press, 1986), 48–50. Two years before Dorothy Bolton solicited his assistance, Premier

Robarts had toured northwestern Ontario extensively with a group of legislators. See "Touring Group Viewed the Borderland," *Kenora Miner and News*, 7 July 1965.

76 OA, "Ontario-Minnesota Liaison," F.R. Phoenix, Division of Industrial Wastes to F.G. Williams, 13 August 1966.

77 OA, "Ontario-Minnesota Liaison," E.W. Turner, "Report: Ontario-Minnesota Pulp and Paper Company Limited 15 May 1966," 2.

78 Ibid., 7–8.

79 OA, "Ontario-Minnesota Liaison," Millest to Sharpe, 6 September 1966, 3–5.

80 OA, "Ontario-Minnesota Liaison," R.H. Millest to K.H. Sharpe, "Ontario-Minnesota Pulp and Paper Company Limited (Fort Frances and Kenora)," 14 September 1966.

81 J.P. Erichsen-Brown, "Legal Aspects of Water Pollution Control in Ontario," in *14th Ontario Industrial Waste Conference: Proceedings, June 18–21, 1967*, Niagara Falls, ON, 91.

82 OA, "Ontario-Minnesota Liaison," Landis to Macdonnell, 6 November 1967.

83 OA, "Ontario-Minnesota Liaison," D.P. Caplice to K.H. Sharpe, 18 October 1967.

84 OA, "Ontario-Minnesota Liaison," E.W.C. Turner, "Meeting to Discuss Waste Treatment at the Two O-M Ontario Installations at Fort Frances and Kenora," 25 April 1967, 2.

85 Ibid.

86 Ibid., 3.

87 OA, "Ontario-Minnesota Liaison," H.A. Clarke, Division of Industrial Wastes to E.W.C. Turner, 6 November 1967.

88 OA, "Ontario-Minnesota Liaison," James A. Vance, "Prosecution of the Ontario-Minnesota Pulp and Paper Company Limited," 13 November 1967.

89 For a survey of continuing environmental impacts, see OA, "Ontario-Minnesota Liaison," E.W.C. Turner, "Ontario Minnesota Pulp and Paper Company, Kenora," 21 October 1966; "Statement of Facts: Prosecution of the Ontario-Minnesota Pulp and Paper Company Limited," n.d., 5.

90 OA, "Ontario-Minnesota Liaison," James A. Vance, "Prosecution of the Ontario-Minnesota Pulp and Paper Company," 13 November 1967, 2.

91 OA, "Ontario-Minnesota Liaison," Landis to Caverly, 17 November 1967.

92 Boise Cascade acquired O&M in the mid-1960s but continued to operate under the O&M name at this time.

93 OA, "Ontario-Minnesota Liaison," Landis to Caverly, 17 November 1967.

94 OA, "Ontario-Minnesota Liaison," E.W.C. Turner, minutes of a meeting with the Ontario-Minnesota Pulp and Paper Company Ltd. at OWRC offices, 19 December 1967.

95 OA, "Ontario-Minnesota Liaison," Burton to Landis, 29 December 1967.

96 OA, "Ontario-Minnesota Liaison," Landis to Burton, 22 December 1967.

97 OA, "Ontario-Minnesota Liaison," Landis to Burton, 27 December 1967.

98 OA, "Ontario-Minnesota Liaison," G.M. Gotts, "Ontario-Minnesota Pulp and Paper Company Limited – Kenora," 29 November 1967, 9.

99 Legislative Assembly of Ontario, *Debates*, 11 June 1968, 4302.

100 OA, "Ontario-Minnesota Liaison," Thatcher to D.S. Caverly, GM, OWRC, 6 February 1967.

101 OA, "Ontario-Minnesota Liaison," Sharpe to Thatcher, 7 February 1967.

102 OA, "Ontario-Minnesota Liaison," D.P. Caplice, Director, Division of Industrial Wastes, to J.F. MacKeller, VP and GM, O&M, Fort Frances, 20 April 1967.

103 Wightman and Wightman, *Land Between*, 321.

104 T.J. Bell, speech, "ABITIBI: Company Is Moving and Making News President T.J. Bell Reports," *Globe and Mail*, 16 May 1968. See also Robert Schmon, "Pulp and Paper Is

Concerned about Water Pollution," in *Economic Thinking and Pollution Problems*, ed. D.A.L. Auld (Toronto: University of Toronto Press, 1972), 103.

105 John Saunders, "$250 Million Price-Tag on This Pollution Problem," *Toronto Star*, 24 January 1970. See generally J.H. Dales, *Pollution, Property and Prices* (Toronto: University of Toronto Press, 1968) and Auld, *Economic Thinking and Pollution Problems*.

106 Legislative Committee of the Province of Ontario, Standing Committee on Resources Development, *Final Report on Acidic Precipitation, Abatement from Emissions from the International Nickel Company Operations at Sudbury: Pollution Control in the Pulp and Paper Industry, and Pollution Abatement at the Reed Paper Mill in Dryden*, October 1979, 55; Ontario Ministry of Industry and Tourism, *Report of the Special Task Force on Ontario's Pulp and Paper Industry*, 16 November 1978; Ontario Ministry of Natural Resources, *The Ontario Pulp and Paper Industry – Status and Outlook*, April 1978.

107 As Boise Cascade Canada pursued an extensive modernization initiative in the early 1980s, environmental considerations were the third dimension of the program, following product quality improvement and cost reduction. "Kenora's Mill Modernization Is Moving Full Steam Ahead," *Kenora Daily Miner and News*, 25 September 1984.

108 Ontario, *Final Report on Acidic Precipitation*, 59.

109 Ibid., 74.

110 Ibid.

111 Ibid., 75.

112 Ibid., 74–75.

113 Ontario, Ministry of Natural Resources, "Lake of the Woods Planning Area: Information Package," May 1974, 44.

114 Author's Collection, R.M. Watt, Lake of the Woods Control Board, to Fred Kelly, Grand Council Treaty #3, enclosure in Hon. Judd Buchanan to W.M. Benidickson, 24 October 1975.

CHAPTER 11: "SLOWLY TO THE RESCUE AS A COMMUNITY FAILS"

1 Canada, House of Commons, *Debates*, 16 May 1977, 5667.

2 Ibid., 5670.

3 See Jamie Benidickson, "KVP v. McKie," in *Property on Trial: Canadian Cases in Context*, ed. Eric Tuffer, James Muir, and Bruce Ziff (Toronto: Irwin Law, 2012), 71–92.

4 Russell L. Winget and Russell O. Blosser, "The Pulp and Paper Pollution Abatement Program in the United States," in Ontario Water Resources Commission, *Proceedings of 4th Industrial Waste Conference*, June 1957, Honey Harbor, ON, 110.

5 *New York Times*, 25 July 1970, quoted in H.R. Jones, *Mercury Pollution Control* (Rahway, NJ: Noyes Data Corporation, 1971), 1. Under anaerobic conditions such as those resulting from pollution by fibrous materials, metallic mercury might be methylated. This organic derivative of metallic mercury wastes can then enter the food chain, where it becomes increasingly concentrated. See Roger Suffling and Greg Michalenko, "The Reed Affair: A Canadian Logging and Pollution Controversy," *Biological Conservation* 17 (1980): 8.

6 R. Howard, *Poisons in Public: Case Studies of Environmental Pollution in Canada* (Toronto: James Lorimer, 1980), 19.

7 W. Eugene Smith and Aileen M. Smith, *Minamata* (New York: Holt, Rinehart and Winston, 1975).

8   Norvald Fimreite, "Mercury Contamination in Canada and Its Effects on Wildlife" (PhD diss., University of Western Ontario, 1971).

9   Hugh Winsor, "Cool Clear Water? Yep. If the OWRC Has Its Way," *Globe and Mail*, 23 May 1970. George Hutchison and Dick Wallace describe Fimreite's research contribution in *Grassy Narrows* (New York: Van Nostrand Reinhold, 1977), 21–38.

10 Sylvia Cosway, *The Grassy Narrows and Islington Band Mercury Disability Board: A Historical Report 1986–2001* (Kenora, ON: Grassy Narrows and Islington Band Mercury Disability Board, 2001), 16.

11 Cosway, *Grassy Narrows*, 16.

12 Jones, *Mercury Pollution Control*, 4; David H. Klein, "Sources and Present Status of Mercury Problem," in *Mercury in the Western Environment*, ed. Donald R. Buhler, proceedings of a workshop, Portland, OR, 25–26 February 1971 (Corvallis, OR: Continuing Education, c. 1973), 5.

13 Katherine Montague and Peter Montague, *Mercury* (San Francisco: Sierra Club, 1971), 76–77.

14 Frank M. D'Itri, *The Environmental Mercury Problem* (Cleveland, OH: CRC Press, 1972), 96.

15 David H. Klein, "Sources and Present Status of the Mercury Problem," in Buhler, *Mercury in the Western Environment*, 10.

16 For US experience, see William H. Rodgers, "Industrial Water Pollution and the Refuse Act: A Second Chance for Water Quality," *University of Pennsylvania Law Review* 119 (1971): 761.

17 Fishermen's Assistance and Polluters' Liability Act, S.M. 1970, c. 32.

18 Ibid., s. 4 (1).

19 Ibid., s. 4 (2).

20 *Interprovincial Cooperatives and Dryden Chemicals Limited v The Queen*, [1975] 5 W.W.R. 382 (S.C.C.).

21 Joost Blom, "The Conflict of Laws and the Constitution – *Interprovincial Co-operatives Ltd. v The Queen*," *University of British Columbia Law Review* 11 (1977): 144–57.

22 *Interprovincial Cooperatives*, 398.

23 Ibid., 413.

24 Ibid., 416.

25 Donald N. Dewees, "The Effect of Environmental Regulation: Mercury and Sulphur Dioxide," in *Securing Compliance: Seven Case Studies*, ed. M.L. Friedland (Toronto: University of Toronto Press, 1990), 367–70.

26 Ibid., 354.

27 D'Itri lists measures presumed necessary in the circumstances. D'Itri, *Environmental Mercury Problem*, 69.

28 See Chapter 5 in this volume.

29 On the expansion of the facilities, see Legislative Committee of the Province of Ontario, Standing Committee on Resource Development, *Final Report on Acidic Precipitation, Abatement of Emissions from the International Nickel Company Operations at Sudbury: Pollution Control in the Pulp and Paper Industry and Pollution Abatement at the Reed Paper Mill in Dryden*, October, 1979, 85.

30 On the 1962 discharge, see Anastasia M. Shkilnyk, *A Poison Stronger Than Love: The Destruction of an Ojibwa Community* (New Haven, CT: Yale University Press, 1985), 189; Warner Troyer, *No Safe Place* (Toronto: Clarke, Irwin, 1977), 4.

31 Ontario, *Final Report on Acidic Precipitation*, 86–87.

32 OWRC, Annual Report, 1970, 63.

33 Quoted in Ontario, *Final Report on Acidic Precipitation*, 87.

34 N.S. Haines, "Whitedog Falls and Caribou Falls Generating Stations," *Engineering Journal* (October 1959): 83. See also Dorothea Belanger, "The Whitedog Falls Power Project: 1956–1958," with Willy Gollub, in *Common Ground: Stories of Lake of the Woods II – Celebrating Another Five Years of Storytelling* (Kenora: Lake of the Woods Museum, 2015), 67. Downstream impacts of the Whitedog Generating Station affected members of the Dalles First Nation along the Winnipeg River and were later acknowledged in a formal apology from Ontario Power Generation.

35 On compensation, see Joseph A. Radocchia, "Resource Development and First Nations in Ontario, North of 50: The Right to Participate in Self-Determination" (master's thesis, Faculty of Environmental Studies, York University, North York, ON, 1993), 98n147–49.

36 Ibid., 106n161; Anna J. Willow, *Strong Hearts, Native Lands: The Cultural and Political Landscape of Anishinaabe Anti-clearcutting Activism* (New York: State University of New York Press, 2012), 73.

37 "Indians Get Land 30 Years after Flood," *Globe and Mail*, 7 December 1988; Geoffrey York, "Ojibway Band Gets Compensation 32 Years after Dam Flooded Land," *Globe and Mail*, 19 October 1989; Radocchia, "Resource Development," 102n157.

38 Radocchia, "Resource Development," 98–100n149.

39 Shkilnyk, *Poison Stronger Than Love*, 189–90. See also Troyer, *No Safe Place*, 99–105.

40 Shkilnyk, *Poison Stronger Than Love*, 189–90; "Reed Closes Mercury-Cell Chloralkali Plant Here," *Dryden Observer*, 23 October 1975. Cosway provides a detailed description of the reduction of mercury discharges, treatment of waste, and eventual closure of the chloralkali plant in 1994. Cosway, *Grassy Narrows*, 20. See also Canada, House of Commons, *Debates*, 27 January 1971, 2829.

41 Understanding the extraordinary challenges associated with attempting to restore or rehabilitate the contaminated water system may have been a factor influencing the appeal and abandonment of the idea of creating a national park in the area surrounding Grassy Narrows and Whitedog. See Troyer, *No Safe Place*, 92–93.

42 Cosway, *Grassy Narrows*, 4.

43 Ibid., 14.

44 Ibid., 2.

45 Ibid., 14–15.

46 Ibid., 60. For criticism of limitations in the sampling, testing, and surveying, see Troyer, *No Safe Place*, 133–49.

47 Cosway, *Grassy Narrows*, 60; Mario Faieta et al., "The Grassy Narrows and Islington Bands Mercury Disability Board," chap. 33 in *Environmental Harm: Civil Actions and Compensation* (Markham, ON: Butterworths, 1996).

48 Cosway, *Grassy Narrows*, 66.

49 Ibid., 66–68.

50 Ibid., 81.

51 Ibid., 67–68.

52 Ibid., 89.

53 Ontario, Royal Commission on the Northern Environment (RCNE), *Issues: A Background Paper on Behalf of the Royal Commission on the Northern Environment* (Toronto: Ontario Ministry of the Attorney General, 1978), 158.

54 Ibid., 194

55 Quoted in J.E.J. Fahlgren, *Final Report and Recommendations of the Royal Commission on the Northern Environment* (Toronto: Ontario Ministry of the Attorney General, June 1985), 3–25.

56 Quoted in Robert Williamson, "Credibility: Closing the Gap on Mercury," *Globe and Mail*, 4 October 1975.

57 Quoted in Marci McDonald, "Massacre at Grassy Narrows," *Maclean's*, 20 October 1975, 30.

58 Peter Mosher, "Indians Take Demands to Ministers, Get Few Promises," *Globe and Mail*, 30 September 1975.

59 "Indian Band Vows to Barricade Road Until Fishing Banned," *Globe and Mail*, 15 June 1976.

60 John Aitken, "Don't Drink the Water, Don't Eat the Fish," *Weekend Magazine*, 10 January 1976, 4. For discussion of hesitant action and limited communication relating to health risks from fish consumption, see Troyer, *No Safe Place*, 66–83.

61 Peter Whelan, "Pollution-Hit Indians Offered Jobs, Food," *Globe and Mail*, 1 November 1975.

62 Interview with Louis Cameron, in *Ojibway Warriors' Society in Occupied Anicinabe Park, Kenora, Ontario, August 1974* (Toronto: Better Read Graphics, 1974), 7–9.

63 Gail Singer and Bob Rodgers, "Mercury: The Hidden Poison in the Northern Rivers," *Saturday Night*, October 1975, 19. See also Smith and Smith, *Minamata*, 141–42.

64 Stan Oziewicz, "Sport Fishing Ban Cost Is Set at $3 Million," *Globe and Mail*, 21 January 1977.

65 Michael Moore, "Indians Back Down on Closing Mercury-Polluted River," *Globe and Mail*, 27 April 1978.

66 Kai Erikson, Foreword, in Shkilnyk, *Poison Stronger Than Love*, xvii. See also Kai T. Erikson and Christopher Vecsey, "A Report to the People of Grassy Narrows," in *American Indian Environments*, ed. Christopher Vecsey and R.W. Venables, 152–61 (Syracuse: Syracuse University Press, 1980).

67 Willow, *Strong Hearts, Native Lands*, 79.

68 Robert J. Sharpe, "Islington and Grassy Narrows Bands Pre-Litigation Study: Final Report," (July 1984), 197.

69 Ibid., 139–40.

70 Ibid., 201.

71 E.P. Hartt, *Interim Report of the Royal Commission on the Northern Environment* (Toronto: RCNE, 1978), 25.

72 "Band Chiefs and Government Join in Signing Ceremony in Northwestern Ontario," Indian and Northern Affairs, Communique, 15 December 1978.

73 Ken MacQueen, "Nobody Cares about Us Says Whitedog Chief," *Kenora Miner and News*, 30 April 1982.

74 OA, RG 22-5800, Emmett Hall, Affidavit, 18 June 1986, appendix 18 to *Isaac Mandamin et al and Simon Roy Fobister et al v Reed Limited et al.*, Ontario Supreme Court, 1977; No. 14716. See also Glenn Sigurdson, *Vikings on a Prairie Ocean: The Saga of a Lake, a People, a Family, and a Man* (Winnipeg: Great Plains, 2014) 256–60.

75 Ibid., para. 8.

76 Ibid., para. 12.

77 Ibid.

78 "Reserve in Despair: Part 1," editorial, 2 July 1985; "Reserve in Despair: Part 2," editorial, *Globe and Mail*, 3 July 1985.

79 "Slowly to the Rescue as a Community Fails," editorial, *Globe and Mail*, 7 May 1973.
80 Emmett Hall, Affidavit, para. 20 and Appendix D.
81 Ibid., para. 31.
82 Ibid., para. 21.
83 Grassy Narrows and Islington Bands Mercury Pollution Claims Settlement Act, S.C. 1986, c. 23; English and Wabigoon River Systems Mercury Contamination Settlement Agreement Act, 1986, S.O. 1986, c. 23. Commentaries include Leigh West, "Mediated Settlement of Environmental Disputes: Grassy Narrows and White Dog Revisited," *Environmental Law* 18, 1 (1987): 131.
84 Faieta et al., "Grassy Narrows and Islington Bands," 465–70.
85 Remediation by dredging, or by covering mercury sediments, was contemplated prior to the compensation settlements but not pursued. Jayme Poisson and David Bruser, "Province Ignored Minister's 1984 Recommendation to Clean Up Mercury in River near Grassy Narrows," *Toronto Star*, 4 July 2016. Less disruptive clean-up initiatives are now under consideration. "Promise to Clean Up Waters at Grassy Narrows Is Long Overdue," editorial, *Toronto Star*, 23 November 2016; Gloria Galloway, "Grassy Narrows Chief Urges Trudeau to Clean Up Mercury in River," *Globe and Mail*, 1 January 2017. See also the Grassy Narrows and Islington Bands Mercury Disability Board website at http://www.mercurydisabilityboard.com/about/.
86 Ontario, *Final Report on Acidic Precipitation*, 67; Arthur Johnson, "Pollution Pays for Pulp and Paper Mills, Report Says," *Globe and Mail*, 30 November 1976; Jonathan Manthorpe, "Kerr Should Get Hot under the Collar," *Toronto Star*, 30 November 1976. See also Troyer, *No Safe Place*, 221–23.
87 Ontario, *Final Report on Acidic Precipitation*, 95.
88 Ibid., 87.
89 Mayor T.S. Jones, quoted in Ontario, *Final Report on Acidic Precipitation*, 87.
90 Emmett Hall, Affidavit, para. 27. Great Lakes Forest Products, which had agreed to purchase Dryden Paper and Dryden Chemicals in 1979, provided $250,000 to assist Grassy Narrows in purchasing the fishing resort.
91 *Carey v Ontario*, [1986] 2 S.C.R., 640–41.
92 Ibid., 639.
93 Ibid., 683. The *Globe and Mail*, "Minaki Lodge Case Put Off after Cabinet Files Released," on 20 January 1988, indicated that the documents eventually released supported Carey's claim that he had government assurances of continuing support.
94 Hon. Claude Bennett, minister of Industry and Tourism, cited in "Statement by Mr. J.E.J. Fahlgren, Chairman of the Board of Directors, Minaki Lodge Resort Limited, at Minaki, Ontario, April 23, 1976," *Minaki News*, 30 April 1976, 1; "Minaki Millions," editorial, *Globe and Mail*, 28 April 1980.
95 Duncan McMonagle, "Sell Minaki Lodge at $40 Million Loss, MPPs' Report Urges," *Globe and Mail*, 8 January 1986.
96 Ibid. For debate in the Legislative Assembly of Ontario, see *Hansard*, Official Records, 8 December 1986, http://www.ontla.on.ca/web/house-proceedings/house_detail.do?locale=en&Sess=2&Parl=33&Date=1986-12-08#P39_9653.
97 Bud Wildman, quoted in Estanislao Oziewicz, "Lavish Lodge Was Product of Grand Dreams," *Globe and Mail*, 13 October 2003; originally quoted in Stanley Oziewicz, "Minaki Lodge Sold to Four Seasons for $4 Million," *Globe and Mail*, 9 December 1986.
98 "The Mystery of Minaki," editorial, *Globe and Mail*, 9 January 1986.

99   Orland French, "Intriguing Uses Given for Minaki," *Globe and Mail*, 13 August 1986.
100 Orland French, "Baby Doc Perfect for Minaki," *Globe and Mail*, 21 February 1986.
101 Geoffrey York, "Can a White Elephant Be Taught New Tricks?" *Globe and Mail*, 7 August 1987.
102 In October 2003, Minaki's main building, uninsured at the time, burned to the ground following the outbreak of fire thought to have occurred in the vicinity of an enclosed pool where work was underway to winterize the premises. Aldo Santin, "Minaki Lodge Fire Remains a Mystery," *Winnipeg Free Press*, 17 January 2004. Recent investors have pursued. condominium proposals or cottage lot developments. Murray McNeill, "Minaki's Next Incarnation: Condos," *Winnipeg Free Press*, 25 September 2010, http://www.winnipegfree press.com/business/minakis-next-incarnation-condos-103777124.html. Minaki on the River secured redevelopment approval in April 2016. For continuing challenges to redevelopment see: https://www.winnipegfreepress.com/business/cottage-development-plan-mired-in -red-tape-disputes-457380703.html.
103 Ministry of Natural Resources, "Lake of the Woods Planning Area: Information Package" (May 1974), 7.

Chapter 12: Lumbering towards Sustainability

1   Gro Harlem Brundtland, "Chairman's Foreword," in *Report of the World Commission on Environment and Development: Our Common Future* (Oxford: Oxford University Press, 1987), ix.
2   Brundtland, *Our Common Future*.
3   W.E. Johnson and J.R. Vallentyne, "Rationale, Background, and Development of Experimental Lake Studies in Northwestern Ontario," *Journal of the Fisheries Research Board of Canada* 28, 2 (1971): 123.
4   Ibid., 126.
5   "Dividing the volume by the outflow yields the theoretical water replenishment time in years. Using a first order equation (based on constant 50% removal times) one can calculate the approximate 90% removal times for conservative pollutants (those that, like sodium ions, follow the movements of water) by multiplying the theoretical water replenishment time by a factor of 3." Jack Vallentyne, "The Canadian Experimental Lakes Area," n.d., http://ces.iisc.ernet.in/energy/water/proceed/section1/paper2/section1paper2.htm.
6   Ontario Hydro, Design and Development Division, "Proposed Atikokan Generation Station: Environmental Analysis," May 1976, 1–2.
7   Ontario Hydro, "Proposed Atikokan Generating Station," 4–2. Mining developments at Steep Rock are described in Chapter 10 of this volume.
8   Ontario, Royal Commission on the Northern Environment (RCNE), *Issues: A Background Paper on Behalf of the Royal Commission on the Northern Environment* (Toronto: Ontario Ministry of the Attorney General, 1978), 131. As of 2015, Ontario prohibited coal-based electricity generation.
9   Ibid., 129–30.
10   J.E.J. Fahlgren, *Final Report and Recommendations of the Royal Commission on the Northern Environment* (Toronto: Ontario Ministry of the Attorney General, 1985), 5–9.
11   Fahlgren, *Final Report*, chap. 5, 8–12.
12   Stan Oziewicsz and Peter Mosher, "Ready to Die to Block Reed Timber Deal, Indians Warn," *Globe and Mail*, 30 October 1976.

13 "Text of Remarks by Grand Chief Andrew Rickard," Westbury Hotel, Toronto, 28 June 1976, 3. See also Grand Council Treaty #9, press release, 11 February 1976; Andrew Rickard, "Speech Presented to the Ontario Federation of Labour Annual Convention," 23 November 1976.

14 Sieciechowicz, Krystyna. "The People and the Land Are One: An Introduction to the Way of Life North of 50," Grand Council Treaty Number 9 (Timmins, Ontario, n.d.): 16–20; Stan Oziewicz, "Indians Won't Participate in Environmental Hearing on Reed Project," Globe and Mail, 11 November 1976.

15 Roger Suffling and Gregory Michalenko, "The Reed Affair: A Canadian Logging and Pollution Controversy," Biological Conservation 17, 1 (1980): 12.

16 Peter Mosher, "Davis Cools Some Critics of Reed Deal; Special Chairman to Conduct Hearings," Globe and Mail, 29 October 1976. Fahlgren, Final Report, 5–10.

17 Norman Webster, "Indians Don't Trust Anyone," Globe and Mail, 11 November 1976.

18 Stan Oziewicz, "The Reed Timber Deal: 'Death' for the Indians or New Economic Life?" Globe and Mail, 30 October 1976.

19 K.A. Armson, Forest Management in Ontario (Toronto: Ministry of Natural Resources, 1976). See also Stan Oziewicz, "Report Criticizes Big Forest Licences," Globe and Mail, 4 November 1976, and J.A. Donnan and P.A. Victor, Alternative Policies for Pollution Abatement: The Ontario Pulp and Paper Industry, 3 vols. (Toronto: Ministry of the Environment, 1976).

20 "Lost in the Woods," editorial, Globe and Mail, 26 October 1976.

21 Fahlgren, Final Report, 5–11. For further discussion of the RCNE, see Paul Driben, "Revisiting the RCNE: An Evaluation of the Recommendations Made by the Royal Commission on the Northern Environment Concerning the Native People in Northern Ontario," Native Studies Review 2 (1986): 45–67, and Suffling and Michalenko, "Reed Affair," 5.

22 Fahlgren, Final Report, 5–3.

23 Ibid., 5–1.

24 Ibid.

25 Ontario, RCNE, Issues: A Background Paper, 67.

26 Wilf Wingenroth, quoted in ibid., 67.

27 Fahlgren, Final Report, 5–5.

28 Ibid.

29 Ibid., 5–6.

30 Ibid., 5–7.

31 See, for example, Peter M. Kareiva et al., Natural Capital: Theory and Practice of Mapping Ecosystem Services (Oxford: Oxford University Press, 2011).

32 Fahlgren, Final Report, 5–15.

33 Ibid., 5–16.

34 Ibid., 5–29 to 5–33.

35 Ontario, Environmental Assessment Board, Reasons for Decision and Decision: Class Environmental Assessment by the Ministry of Natural Resources for Timber Management on Crown Lands in Ontario (EA-87–02), 20 April 1994.

36 Crown Forest Sustainability Act, 1994, c. 25, s. 1.

37 Ibid., s. 2(3).

38 At the time of writing, the most current edition is Forest Management Planning Manual (Toronto: Queen's Printer, 2017), https://files.ontario.ca/forest-management-planning-manual.pdf.

39 For a discussion of indicators and the *Forest Management Planning Manual*, see Arbex Forest Resource Consultants (Arbex), *Kenora Forest: Independent Forest Audit, 2003–2008* (Toronto: Queen's Printer, 2009), 29n9. The role of forests in global ecological cycles was subsequently added as a sixth criteria for evaluation to account for impacts on planetary carbon cycles.

40 Regulation 160/04 of the *Crown Forest Sustainability Act*, S.O. 1994, c. 25 (*CFSA*) sets out the specific requirements for conducting the audits.

41 Arbex, *Kenora Forest*, 1.

42 Ibid., 8–9.

43 Ibid., 9–10.

44 Ibid., 19. The following First Nations are found within the Kenora Forest: Iskatewizaagegan Independent First Nation (Shoal Lake #39); Northwest Angle #33 First Nation; Northwest Angle #37 First Nation; Ochiichagwe'Babigo'Ining First Nation (Dalles); Shoal Lake #40 First Nation; Wabaseemoong Independent First Nation; Wauzhusk Onigum First Nation (Rat Portage); Washagamis Bay First Nation; Naotkamegwanning First Nation (Whitefish Bay); Big Grassy First Nation; Onigaming First Nation; Big Island First Nation.

45 KBM Forestry Consultants, *Whiskey Jack Forest: Independent Forest Audit, 2004–2009 – Final Report* (Toronto: Queen's Printer, 2010), 3, http://cpcml.ca/Tmlw2011/F11-1940.PDF.

46 Weyerhaeuser received CSA (Canadian Standards Association) certification in 2005 and was subsequently audited prior to reregistration in 2008. See Arbex, *Kenora Forest*, 14. Sustainability considerations have been applied to Canadian forest management through certification procedures that are largely independent of government procedures. For a valuable discussion of this development, see Chris Tollefson, *Setting the Standard: Certification, Governance and the Forest Stewardship Council* (Vancouver: UBC Press, 2008).

47 Arbex, *Kenora Forest*, 61–65.

48 Based on an assessment of available information and review in the audit context, the Kenora Forest management operations were considered to be sustainable. Ibid., 66–67, 69–70.

49 Ibid., 51.

50 American White Pelican Recovery Team, *American White Pelican (*Pelecanus erythrorhynchos*) in Ontario: Ontario Recovery Strategy Series*, prepared for the Ontario Ministry of Natural Resources, Peterborough, Ontario, February 2011, http://www.ontla.on.ca/library/repository/mon/25008/305606.pdf; *Pelecanus erythrorhynchos* (American White Pelican), *Minnesota Department of Natural Resources*, 2018, http://www.dnr.state.mn.us/rsg/profile.html?action=elementDetail&selectedElement=ABNFC01010.

51 Arbex, *Kenora Forest*, 12.

52 Ontario, *Resource-Based Tourism Policy*, n.d., http://www.mtc.gov.on.ca/en/publications/RBT_Policy.pdf; *The Timber Management Guidelines for the Protection of Tourism Values* (Toronto: Ontario Ministry of Natural Resources and Ministry of Tourism and Recreation, 1987); Larry Watkins, *The Forest Resources of Ontario 2011*, prepared for Ontario Ministry of Natural Resources, Sault Ste. Marie, ON, Forest Evaluation and Standards Section, Forests Branch (Toronto: Queen's Printer, 2011), http://www.web2.mnr.gov.on.ca/mnr/forests/public/publications/FRO_2011/forestresources_2011.pdf.

53 RSA Working Group and RSA Steering Committee, *Tourism and Forestry Industry Memorandum of Understanding*, 7 June 2000, https://dr6j45jk9xcmk.cloudfront.net/documents/2991/policy-tourismmou-eng-aoda.pdf.

54 Ontario, Ministry of Natural Resources, *Tourism and Forestry Industry: Guide to Resource Stewardship Agreements*, Forest Management Authority, 15 June 2001, https://dr6j45jk9xcmk.

cloudfront.net/documents/2993/policy-resourcestewardship-agr-eng-aoda.pdf. For an assessment of Ontario's experience with RSAs, see Sarah Anne Browne, "Engaging the Tourism Industry in Forest Management Planning: An Evaluation of Ontario's Resource Stewardship Agreement Process" (master's project, Simon Fraser University, School of Resource and Environmental Management, Report No. 391, 2006).

55 Arbex, *Kenora Forest*, 32.

56 Ibid., 32.

57 Ibid., 36.

58 Joseph F. Castrilli, "The Ontario Forest, Land Use, and Mining Initiatives of 1999 and the Management of Public Land in Canada in the Twenty-First Century: One Step Forward, Two Steps Back," *Canadian Environmental Law Reports*, n.s., 43 (2002): 11–105.

59 Ontario, Ministry of Natural Resources, *Lake of the Woods Conservation Reserve (C2366): Resource Management Plan*, August 2006, 6, http://www.ontla.on.ca/library/repository/mon/15000/267564.pdf.

60 Arbex, *Kenora Forest*, 73.

61 Ibid., 37.

62 The framework for cooperative management of the Kenora Forest takes the form of the Miitigoog Limited Partnership.

63 Anna J. Willow, *Strong Hearts, Native Lands: The Cultural and Political Landscape of Anishinaabe Anti-clearcutting Activism* (New York: State University of New York, 2012). The use of chemical ground treatments and aerial spraying significantly declined in the Kenora Forest following a decision to delay treatments until crop trees were sufficiently high to remain above competing species after treatment. The decision was also based on public opposition and the shortage of qualified contractors. See Arbex, *Kenora Forest*, 46, 48, 68.

64 At the time of audit, Whiskey Jack encompassed administrative areas previously known as the Pakwash Forest and the Patricia Forest, each of which had had its own management plan. Having acquired Canadian properties from Boise Cascade, Abitibi-Consolidated Company of Canada (ACCC) held the Sustainable Forest Licence during the audit period. A contingency plan for 2009–12 was required to synchronize the planning schedules for the Whiskey Jack Forest and the adjoining Kenora Forest prior to amalgamation. KBM, *Whiskey Jack Forest*, 3.

65 Ibid., 23–24.

66 Ibid., 5–6.

67 Operational conditions later improved for both Trus Joist and Kenora Forest Products.

68 Ibid., 16.

69 Ibid. Further discussion of the FRT Fund arrangement may be found in the "Contractual Obligations" section of KBM, *Whiskey Jack Forest*, 23.

70 Some indication of the scope and complexity of financial constraints facing Abitibi is illustrated in litigation: *Newfoundland and Labrador v AbitibiBowater Inc.* 2012 S.C.C. 67.

71 Grassy Narrows specifically asserted an interest in a Traditional Land Use Area covering over 672,000 hectares in the context of negotiations following mercury contamination. Willow, *Strong Hearts, Native Lands*, 97; Jean Teillet, *The Role of the Natural Resources Regulatory Regime in Aboriginal Rights Disputes in Ontario*, Final Report for the Ipperwash Inquiry, 31 March 2005, 43n134, http://www.attorneygeneral.jus.gov.on.ca/inquiries/ipperwash/policy_part/research/pdf/Teillet.pdf.

72 Willow, *Strong Hearts, Native Lands*, 142. On supporting organizations, see Amnesty International, "The Law of the Land: Amnesty International Canada's Position on the Conflict over Logging at Grassy Narrows," Public Briefing, 20 September 2007, 17; Kate Harries, "Loney's Absence Felt Strongly at Grassy Narrows," *Globe and Mail*, 10 December 2005; Martin Mitelstaedt, "Groups Take Aim at Ontario's Logging Industry," *Globe and Mail*, 2 March 2006.

73 Willow, *Strong Hearts, Native Lands*, 150, 174.

74 KBM, *Whiskey Jack Forest*, 15.

75 Ibid., 15.

76 "Open Letter from the Community of Grassy Narrows to Weyerhaeuser, Abitibi, Their Customers, Investors and Bankers," 7 February 2006. See also "Open Letter from Grassy Narrows Chief and Council et al to Abitibi Consolidated, Weyerhaeuser Corporation et al," 17 January 2007, https://intercontinentalcry.org/grassy-narrows-declares-moratorium -on-industrial-development/.

77 Michael William Aiken, *After the Mill: From Confrontation to Cooperation* (Winnipeg: Aboriginal Issues Press, 2011), 20–31. Following a sale to Resolute Forest Products, Fort Frances operations were curtailed and declined amidst deteriorating market conditions.

78 The 12 May 2008 agreement between MNR and the Asubpeeschoseewagong Netum Anishinabek (ANA) anticipated a government-to-government relationship and collaborative arrangements for the sustainable management, protection, and use of the Whiskey Jack Forest. The parties further agreed to encourage a self-sustaining community for the ANA by supporting cultural, economic, and capacity building.

79 KBM, *Whiskey Jack Forest*, 5–6.

80 Ibid., 7.

81 The Kenora Forest audit details communications by mail, telephone, and email, alongside invitations to contribute information, to attend meetings, or to review and comment on draft documentation. See also KBM, *Kenora Forest*, 20 and 85.

82 Ibid., 19. For further discussion of the agreement, see René Dussault and Georges Erasmus, *Report of Royal Commission on Aboriginal Peoples*, vol. 2: *Restructuring the Relationship*, part 2, chap. 4, Appendix 4B: "Co-management Agreements."

83 KBM, *Whiskey Jack Forest*, 7–8. Wabaseemoong was allocated nine thousand cubic metres for pole-sized material from the Whiskey Jack Forest and the same amount from the Kenora Forest.

84 Arbex, *Kenora Forest*, 21, 25.

85 Ibid., 21.

86 The Kenora Forest audit itself was no more successful in eliciting First Nations' involvement in the assessment of forest planning and operations. Arbex, *Kenora Forest*, 5.

87 Ibid., 22–23.

88 Ibid.

89 Grand Council Treaty #3, Manito Aki Inakonigaawin, available at: http://gct3.ca/land/manito-aki-inakonigaawin/.

90 First Nations in the region have continued to elaborate the Resource Law and the Great Earth Law and to promote acceptance on the part of developers.

91 *Wawatay News*, 7 April 2011.

92 "Grassy Narrows, province working on forest management deal," Wawatay News, available at: http://www.wawataynews.ca/home/grassy-narrows-province-working-forest-management -deal.

93 KBM, *Whiskey Jack Forest*. Chief Fobister continued to protest MNR's proposals for the area. His interview on *As It Happens*, CBC Radio, 30 September 2013, is available at "Grassy Narrows Chief Fobister on CBC Rejecting New Logging Plan," *Free Grassy Narrows*, http:// freegrassy.net/2013/10/30/grassy-narrows-chief-fobister-on-cbc-as-it-happens-rejecting -new-logging-plan/.

94 *Keewatin v Minister of Natural Resources* 2006 CanLII 35625 (O.S.C.).

95 *Keewatin v Minister of Natural Resources* 2011 O.N.S.C. 4801, para. 14.

96 Ibid., paras. 19 and 25.

97 Quoted in ibid. para. 1.

98 Ibid., para. 65.

99 Ibid., para. 68; *R. v Sparrow*, [1990] 1 S.C.R. 1075.

100 *Keewatin v Minister of Natural Resources* 2011 O.N.S.C. 4801, para. 762.

101 Ibid., para. 8.

102 Ibid., para. 182.

103 On the continuing reluctance through 1871, see ibid., paras. 263–65, 294; for newspaper reports to same effect, see paras. 277–82, 285.

104 Ibid., para. 770.

105 Ibid., para. 781. See also paras. 812–13; 819–23. In para. 823, Sanderson sets out her reasoning step by step.

106 Ibid., para. 833.

107 Ibid., para. 794.

108 Ibid., para. 917.

109 Ibid., para. 62.

110 Ibid., paras. 553–68, 660, 669.

111 Ibid., para. 742.

112 Ibid., paras. 838–39, 843.

113 Ibid., para. 846.

114 Ibid., para. 848.

115 Ibid., para. 849. The Ontario Court of Appeal would later express the view that certain of the trial judge's factual findings amounted to "palpable and overriding error." *Keewatin v Ontario (Natural Resources)* 2013 O.N.C.A. 158, paras. 162-72. It is nevertheless my view that Justice Sanderson's extensive and elaborate review of the voluminous body of documentary and oral evidence presented in the trial demonstrates exemplary diligence and respect for the complex historical record presented to the court.

116 *Keewatin v Minister of Natural Resources* 2011 O.N.S.C. 4801, para. 1221.

117 Ibid., para. 1224.

118 *Keewatin v Ontario (Natural Resources)* 2013 O.N.C.A. 158, para. 135.

119 Ibid.

120 Ibid., para. 160.

121 *Grassy Narrow First Nation v Ontario (Natural Resources)* 2014 S.C.C. 48, para. 30. For a thoughtful and comprehensive discussion of the implications of the Keewatin decision for the relationship between Canada's constitutional division of powers and treaty making by the Crown, see Nigel Bankes, "The Implications of the *Tsilhqot'in* (*William*) and *Grassy Narrows* (*Keewatin*) Decisions of the Supreme Court of Canada for the Natural Resources in Industries," *Journal of Energy and Natural Resources Law* 33 (2015): 208–17.

CHAPTER 13: FISHING CONTESTS

1   George H. McIvor, *Report of Commission of Inquiry into Freshwater Fish Marketing* (Ottawa: Queen's Printer, 1966), 9.
2   An Act to Regulate Interprovincial and Export Trade in Freshwater Fish and to Establish the Freshwater Fish Marketing Corporation, SC 1969, c. 21.
3   Legislative Assembly of Ontario, *Debates*, 28 April 1969, 3673.
4   Novel legal proceedings were launched in court on behalf of those seeking compensation for the effects of the new marketing arrangements on their businesses or livelihoods. See Jim Phillips and Jeremy Martin, "*Manitoba Fisheries v The Queen*: The Origins of Canada's De Facto Expropriation Doctrine," in *Property on Trial: Canadian Cases in Context*, ed. Eric Tucker, James Muir, and Bruce Ziff (Toronto: Irwin Law, 2012), 261–68.
5   Lori Nelson, "Recalling the Halcyon Days of Kenora Fish Market," *Kenora Enterprise*, 6 July 1997, 15.
6   G.F. Adam and D.P. Kolenosky, *Out of the Water: Ontario's Freshwater Fish Industry* (Toronto: Fisheries Branch, Ontario Ministry of Natural Resources, 1979), 60–61.
7   Ontario, Ministry of Natural Resources, Kenora District Office, "Shoal Lake Commercial Harvest (Including Labyrinth Bay) 1949–1978."
8   Michael Moore, "For These Indians, It's Break the Law or Go on Welfare," *Globe and Mail*, 26 April 1978.
9   Ibid.
10 *Times News* (Thunder Bay), 16 March 1979.
11 Herb Redsky, quoted in Moore, "For These Indians." For discussion of the headland-to-headland claim, see Richard H. Bartlett, *Aboriginal Water Rights in Canada: A Study of Aboriginal Title to Water and Indian Water Rights* (Calgary: Canadian Institute of Resources Law, 1988), 101–9.
12 E.S. Rogers, *Ojibwa Fisheries in Northwestern Ontario* (Toronto: Ontario Ministry of Natural Resources, Division of Fish and Wildlife, Commercial Fish and Fur Branch, 1972), 44.
13 Author's Collection, "Notes on the Fishing Problem in Shoal Lake, Lake of the Woods, Kenora Area," n.d., reporting on the situation as of October 1963.
14 Moore, "For These Indians." Competition between commercial, sport, and subsistence fishing interests was certainly not confined to this region. See Alan B. McCullough, *The Commercial Fishery of the Canadian Great Lakes* (Ottawa: Supply and Services Canada, 1989), 105–7.
15 Michael Moore, "Province Postpones Shoal Lake Quotas," *Globe and Mail*, 19 May 1978. The decision to postpone implementation of the quotas was communicated to band members by letter, dated 18 May 1978 from the district manager, MNR. *Re Shoal Lake Band of Indians No. 39 and the Queen*, (1979) 101 D.L.R. (3d), 132.
16 Re Shoal Lake Band of Indians No. 39 and the Queen, (1979) 101 D.L.R. (3d), 132 at 136.
17 Ibid.
18 Ibid., 132.
19 Anthony J. Usher, "Ontario Lake of the Woods Fishery: Economic and Social Analysis," *Transactions of the American Fisheries Society* 116, 3 (1987): 353.
20 Ibid.
21 Ibid., 354. See also Fikret Berkes, "Subsistence Fishing in Canada: A Note on Terminology," *Arctic* 41, 4 (1988): 319–20.

22 Ontario Ministry of Natural Resources and Minnesota Department of Natural Resources, *Minnesota-Ontario Boundary Waters Fisheries Atlas for Lake of the Wood, Rainy Lake, Rainy River* (July 1984), 55–56.

23 Ibid., 56.

24 Ibid., 55.

25 Usher, "Ontario Lake of the Woods Fishery," 354.

26 Ibid., 357.

27 Ibid.

28 Ibid.

29 Ibid.

30 Ibid., 359.

31 Northwestern Ontario Commercial Fisheries Task Force, "The Northwestern Ontario Fisheries Situation Report," (December 1978) 11.

32 Ibid., 15.

33 Author's Collection, A.J. Herridge, Assistant Deputy Minister, Resources and Recreation, MNR, to John Kelly, President, Grand Council Treaty #3, 12 January 1978.

34 E.P. Hartt, *Interim Report of the Royal Commission on the Northern Environment* (Toronto: RCNE, 1978), 19.

35 This summary is derived from F. Berkes and D. Pocock, "The Ontario Native Fishing Agreement in Perspective: A Study in User Group Ecology," *Environments* 15, 3 (1983): 19.

36 "Furor over Fishing Rights Marked by Court Battles," *Globe and Mail*, 3 February 1983.

37 See Paul Driben, "Fishing in Uncharted Waters: A Perspective on the Indian Fishing Agreements Dispute in Northern Ontario," *Alternatives: Perspectives on Society, Technology, and Environment* 15, 1 (1987): 19–26.

38 Berkes and Pocock, "Ontario Native Fishing Agreement," 19. See also Ontario, Ministry of Natural Resources, "Listing of Bands Licensed in the Province of Ontario, 1982," n.d., J. Ridgely, Client Services Section, Toronto.

39 Berkes and Pocock, "Ontario Native Fishing Agreement," 23.

40 Ibid., 24.

41 Subsistence fishing operations continued. See John Seyler, "Changes in the Fish Community of Shoal Lake: A Review of Historical and Recently Collected Data" (North Bay, ON: Anishinabek/Ontario Fisheries Resource Centre, 2004).

42 Rudy Platiel, "Indians Drop Support for Fishing Pact," *Globe and Mail*, 9 June 1983.

43 Berkes and Pocock, "Ontario Native Fishing Agreement," 25.

44 Thomas Claridge and Rudy Platiel, "Bid to Resolve Native Disputes Seeds Political Storm," *Globe and Mail*, 3 February 1983.

45 *Globe and Mail*, 1 March 1983, quoted in "Indian Fishing Agreements: Background and Rationale" (Library of Parliament, n.d.), 21.

46 *The Fishing Rights of Treaty #3 Indians* (Kenora: Grand Council Treaty #3, 1986).

47 Ibid.

48 See "Public Consultation on Indian Fishing Agreements Enters Second Phase, MNR," Fact Sheet, Ontario MNR, September 1986.

49 "Indian Fishing Agreements," 26.

50 *R. v Jack*, [1980] 1 S.C.R. 294, 313.

51 Driben, "Fishing in Unchartered Waters," 20–21; Author's Collection, "Indian Fishing Advisory Committee Report," (November 1988), 58–63.

52 Ibid.
53 Quoted in ibid., 3.
54 Ibid., 10.
55 Ibid., 17.
56 Ibid., 12.
57 Ibid., 34.
58 Ibid., 19.
59 Ibid., 20.
60 Ibid., 22–23.
61 Ibid., 26.
62 Ibid., 30.
63 Ibid., 50–54.
64 Christopher J. Pibus, "The Fisheries Act and Native Fishing Rights in Canada: 1970–1980," *University of Toronto Faculty of Law Review* 39, 1 (1981): 44.
65 *R. v Sparrow*, [1990] 1 S.C.R. 1075.
66 *R. v Bombay*, [1993] 1 C.N.L.R. 92.
67 Seyler, "Changes in the Fish Community of Shoal Lake," 2–4. According to the Shoal Lake Watershed Management Plan, existing commercial quotas allowed a total annual catch of 83,515 pounds (37,882 kg) of all species from Shoal Lake waters. First Nations were allocated 100 percent of the whitefish and 50 percent of the northern pike. Shoal Lake Watershed Working Group (SLWWG), *Shoal Lake Watershed Management Plan*, April 2002, 8, https://www.gov.mb.ca/waterstewardship/water_quality/quality/shoal_lk_report_index.html.
68 Seyler, "Changes in the Fish Community in Shoal Lake."
69 Ibid., 8.
70 SLWWG, *Shoal Lake Watershed Management Plan*, 37.
71 The Lake of the Woods was declared "the greatest sturgeon pond in the world" in Barton Warren Evermann and Homer Barker Latimer, "The Fishes of the Lake of the Woods and Connecting Waters," *Proceedings U.S. National Museum* 39, 1778 (1910): 126. For recent assessment of the state of the Shoal Lake fishery and potential, see SLWWG, *Shoal Lake Watershed Management Plan*, 55–58. Illegal pickerel sales continue to undermine the recovery process. "First Nation Pair Fined, Banned from Fishing over Illegal Walleye Sale," *CBC News*, 2 June 2015, http://www.cbc.ca/news/canada/manitoba/first-nation-pair-fined-banned-from-fishing-over-illegal-walleye-sale-1.3097630.
72 June Bland, "Battle over Fish," *Kenora Daily Miner and News*, 27 July 1999; Barrie McKenna, "The Gourmet Fish War," *Globe and Mail*, 24 July 1999.
73 North American Free Trade Agreement (NAFTA), "Article 1202: National Treatment," *Government of Canada*, http://www.international.gc.ca/trade-commerce/trade-agreements-accords-commerciaux/agr-acc/nafta-alena/fta-ale/12.aspx?lang=eng. The agreement entered into force 1 January 1994.
74 Quoted in Rossella Brevetti, "Minnesota Group Files Section 301 Alleging Discriminatory Fishing Practices by Ontario," *International Trade Reports* 16, 12 (1999): 495.
75 James Brooke, "The Walleye War; A Trade Dispute Roils the U.S.-Canadian Border," *New York Times*, 26 November 1999, http://www.nytimes.com/1999/11/26/business/the-walleye-war-a-trade-dispute-roils-the-us-canadian-border.html; James Southwick, "State and Provincial Regulations with Cross-Border Impact," *Canada-United States Law Journal* 27 (2001): 239.

76 Robert Franklin, "Canada's Fishing Rules Spur More Creative Bills," *Star Tribune* (Minneapolis), 30 March 1999.

77 Tim O'Brien, *In the Lake of the Woods* (New York: Penguin, 1995), 286.

78 Helene Cooper, "To Catch a Fish, You Have to Stay the Night in Canada – Minnesota Angles for a Deal to Save Walleye Lovers from Motorboat Mounties," *Wall Street Journal*, 19 August 1999.

79 David Roberts, "Jesse Meets Joe in the Political Ring," *Globe and Mail*, 22 May 1999.

80 Gillian Livingston, "Minnesota Governor Attacks Fishing Laws," *Globe and Mail*, 22 February 1999.

81 *Ontario Federation of Anglers and Hunters v Ontario* (2002), 211 D.L.R. 4th 741 (O.C.A.); leave to appeal refused (2003), 313 NR 198 (note). The basis of public concern leading to the Crown's decision to close the hunt is explained at para. 47:

> Between 1990 and 1997, approximately 4,100 black bears per year were killed during the spring hunting season. Approximately 30% (1230) were females, and approximately 492 of the females were over 5 years of age. Ninety-eight per cent of the bears were hunted at bait sites, where the hunters remain hidden approximately 15 to 20 meters from the bait, and wait for the bears to approach the bait site. Up to 274 bear cubs per year may be orphaned during the spring hunting season, with the likely numbers being in the range of 20 to 90.

82 Heather Scoffield, "Fishing Rules Violate NAFTA, U.S. Charges," *Globe and Mail*, 30 July 1999.

83 John Gray, "Pulling the Plug on His Way of Life," *Globe and Mail*, 24 July 1999.

84 Legislative Assembly of Ontario, *Debates*, 3 December 1987.

85 June Bland, "Battle over Fish," *Kenora Miner and News*, 27 July 1999.

86 Brooke, "Walleye War."

87 John Ibbitson, "Ontario Cooks Up a Solution to Fish War," *Globe and Mail*, 30 September 1999.

88 Rossella Brevetti, "U.S. Ends Case against Canada Targeting Discriminatory Fishing Rules," *International Trade Report* 16, 45 (1999): 1884.

89 Brooke, "Walleye War." Barshefsky's news release was headlined "U.S. Prevails in Dispute with Canada over Sport Fishing and Tourism Services."

90 Quoted in Brooke, "Walleye War."

91 Quoted in McKenna, "Gourmet Fish War."

92 Quoted in Brooke, "Walleye War."

93 United Nations, "Convention on the Law of the Non-navigational Uses of International Watercourses," General Assembly resolution 51/229, annex, Official Records of the General Assembly, Fifty-first Session, Supplement No. 49 (A/51/49). The convention was adopted by the General Assembly of the United Nations on 21 May 1997 but only came into force on 17 August 2014.

CHAPTER 14: "FOR WATER KNOWS NO BORDERS"

1 Shoal Lake Watershed Working Group (SLWWG), *Shoal Lake Watershed Management Plan*, April 2002, 14, http://www.gov.mb.ca/waterstewardship/water_quality/quality/shoal_lk_report_index.html.

2 Frank Miclash, Legislative Assembly of Ontario, *Debates*, 25 June 1992, 1677.
3 Editorial, *Winnipeg Free Press*, 12 June 1989. This was not the first time Manitobans had sought assurances about water quality from the neighbouring province. See "Manitoba/Ontario Memorandum of Understanding Concerning Present and Future Development on High Lake and in the Immediate Vicinity of Shoal Lake," 26 May 1981.
4 Robert V. Parsons, Letter, *Winnipeg Free Press*, 24 June 1989, 23.
5 Canada, House of Commons, *Debates*, 10 May 1989, 1540–41.
6 *Ontario Gazette* 122, 36 (9 September 1989): 5117; Publications under the Regulations Act, 9 September 1989; Environmental Assessment Act, O. Reg. 486/89 – "Designation – Mines at Stevens Island, Cameron Island and Shoal Lake" (made 10 August 1989; filed 24 August 1989); Fiona Christensen, "Consolidated Professor Renews Interest in Its Dupont [sic] Gold Project," *Northern Ontario Business*, May 1994, 24.
7 "Shoal Lake Mine on Filmon's Agenda with Rae," *Winnipeg Free Press*, 8 November 1990.
8 Allison Bray, "City Water Still at Risk, Group Fears," *Winnipeg Free Press*, 19 November 1990.
9 "Filmon Denies Softening Stand on Proposed Shoal Lake Mine," *Winnipeg Free Press*, 14 February 1991.
10 Claude Huot, "Mixed Message," letter, *Winnipeg Free Press*, 24 February 1991.
11 Zena Olijnyk, "EPC Urges More Money for Clean Water Group," *Winnipeg Free Press*, 7 December 1989; 21 December 1989.
12 Radha KrishnanThampi, "Group Fighting Shoal Lake Mine Gets Nod for Grant," *Winnipeg Free Press*, 4 October 1989.
13 Ruth Teichroeb, "'Strict' Rules for Mine Review Issued," *Winnipeg Free Press*, 2 August 1990.
14 Helen McCullough, "Bleak Report," letter, *Winnipeg Free Press*, 29 January 1990.
15 Helen McCullough, "Water Supply," letter, *Winnipeg Free Press*, 22 November 1990; letter from Helen McCullough. The detailed criticism was outlined in a letter dated 5 November to Environment Minister Robert de Cotret and copied to the *Winnipeg Free Press* on 7 November.
16 Terry Weber, "Funding Refusal Threat to Mine Fight," *Winnipeg Free Press*, 31 July 1990.
17 G.R. Cunningham-Dunlop, "Firm Guarantees no Adverse Effect on City's Water Supply," letter, *Winnipeg Free Press*, 23 September 1989.
18 G.R. Cunningham-Dunlop, "Drinking Water," letter, *Winnipeg Free Press*, 22 February 1990.
19 *114957 Canada Ltée (Spraytech) v Hudson (Town)* 2001 S.C.C. 40.
20 SLWWG, *Shoal Lake Watershed Management Plan*, 68.
21 Gerald Flood, "High Lakeside Cyanide Level Cited," *Winnipeg Free Press*, 15 August 1989.
22 Gerald Flood, "Cummings Wants Ban to Lake Development to Protect City's Water," *Winnipeg Free Press*, 16 August 1989.
23 Gerald Flood, "Police Probe Cyanide in Pond," *Winnipeg Free Press*, 19 August 1989.
24 Gerald Flood, "Cyanide Cleanup Poses Problems," *Winnipeg Free Press*, 22 August 1989.
25 Dan Lett, "Pond Spiking Ruled Out," *Winnipeg Free Press*, 21 September 1989.
26 Kent Gerecke, "Water Gathering," letter, *Winnipeg Free Press*, 30 August 1989.
27 Patrick McKinley, "Dam Retreat Raises Fears for Water," *Winnipeg Free Press*, 2 September 1989.
28 Legislative Assembly of Manitoba, *Debates*, 19 November 1990, 1396–98. Later, as premier, Doer faced a revived proposal for gold mining on Stevens and Cameron Islands led by Halo Resources of Vancouver, with support from Shoal Lake Band #39.

29 Donald Campbell, "Shoal Helpless to Spill," *Winnipeg Free Press*, 19 April 1990.
30 Patrick McKinley and Nick Martin, "Liberal Calls on Province to Probe Spill," *Winnipeg Free Press*, 5 May 1990.
31 William Leiss and Douglas Powell, *Mad Cows and Mothers' Milk: The Perils of Risk Communication* (Montreal and Kingston: McGill-Queen's University Press, 2004) 184, 188–91.
32 Radha Krishnan Thampi, "City Admits Liquor Link to Shoal Lake Spill," *Winnipeg Free Press*, 14 June 1990.
33 Val Werier, "City's Claim to Clean Water Must Be Protected," *Winnipeg Free Press*, 29 June 1991.
34 Quoted in Radha Krishnan Thampi, "Global Water Management Plan Needed, Councilor Says," *Winnipeg Free Press*, 19 August 1991.
35 Dennis R. O'Connor, *Report of the Walkerton Inquiry, Part 2: A Strategy for Safe Drinking Water* (Toronto: Ontario Ministry of the Attorney General, 2002).
36 "Ontario Side Not Polluting Shoal Lake," *Winnipeg Free Press*, 20 August 1991.
37 "MDs Seek Shoal Lake Mining Ban," *Winnipeg Free Press*, 16 July 1991. For a flurry of correspondence, see *Winnipeg Free Press*, 20 July 1991.
38 Donald Campbell, "Water Group Flays '20% Solution,'" *Winnipeg Free Press*, 6 June 1991.
39 Dan Lett, "Rules to Limit Mines at Shoal Lake Flayed as '11% Solution.'" *Winnipeg Free Press*, 22 June 1991.
40 Quoted in Larry Kusch, "'Gold Rush' Critics Stall Opportunity," *Winnipeg Free Press*, 17 March 1993. In 2004, Halo Resources of Vancouver concluded an arrangement with Sheridan Platinum Group with the support of Shoal Lake Band #39 to acquire the Duport property. The band anticipated royalties and employment opportunities. Michael William Aiken, *After the Mill: From Confrontation to Cooperation* (Winnipeg: Aboriginal Issues Press, 2011), 42.
41 Jean Chrétien, *Straight from the Heart* (Toronto: Key Porter Books, 1994), 220.
42 Michael Tenszen, "Here's Mud in Your Eye," *Globe and Mail*, 4 October 1984.
43 Quoted in Larry Krotz, "Water Woes in Cottage Country," *Globe and Mail*, 8 September 1984.
44 CBC, *Sunday Morning*, 14 December 1986. John Redsky replaced his brother Herb in this period. Geoffrey York and Ritchie Gage, "Chrétien to Negotiate for Manitoba Indians in Battle over Compensation for Cottages," *Globe and Mail*, 12 January 1987.
45 "Speaking Notes for the Hon. Jean Chrétien, Re: Shoal Lake," 30 April 1987, Canadian Water Resources Association, Manitoba Branch.
46 Ibid.
47 For discussion of payments for ecosystem services, see Thomas Greiber, ed., *Payments for Ecosystem Services: Legal and Institutional Frameworks*, IUCN Environmental Law and Policy Paper No. 78 (Gland, Switzerland: International Union for Conservation of Nature and Natural Resources, 2009).
48 "Speaking Notes."
49 Gary Doer, Legislative Assembly of Manitoba, *Debates*, 1 May 1987, 1546, 1547.
50 "Memorandum of Agreement between the Shoal Lake Band No. 40, the Province of Manitoba, and the City of Winnipeg 30 June 1989," http://winnipeg.ca/waterandwaste/pdfs/water/Shoal_Lake_Memorandum_of_Agreement.pdf.
51 The Shoal Lake #40/Canada Agreement Respecting the Economy and the Environment was concluded in September 1990.
52 "Memorandum of Agreement," para. 16.

53 Ibid., para. 30.
54 Ibid., para. 22. For information on water consumption and treatment facilities for First Nations circa 2000, see SLWWG, *Shoal Lake Watershed Management Plan*, document 19–20.
55 "Draft Guiding Principles for the International Watersheds Initiative," *International Watersheds Initiative, IJC*, http://www.ijc.org/php/publications/html/guiding_principles_e.htm; IJC, *The International Watershed Initiative: Implementing a New Paradigm for Transboundary Basins* (January 2009), 12.
56 IJC, *Transboundary Watersheds: First Report to the Governments of Canada and the United States under the Reference of November 19, 1998 with Respect to International Watershed Boards* (Ottawa and Washington, DC: IJC, December 2000); IJC, *A Discussion Paper on the International Watershed Initiative: Second Report to the Governments of Canada and the United States under the Reference of November 19, 1998 with Respect to International Watershed Boards* (Ottawa and Washington, DC: IJC, June 2005); IJC, *International Watershed Initiative*. See Murray Klamen, "The IJC and Transboundary Water Disputes: Past, Present and Future," in *Water without Borders: Canada, the United States and Shared Waters*, ed. Emma S. Norman, Alice Cohen, and Karen Bakker (Toronto: University of Toronto Press, 2013), 70.
57 IJC, *Discussion Paper*, 21–26.
58 International Lake of the Woods and Rainy River Watershed Task Force (IJC Task Force), *Final Report to the International Joint Commission on Bi-national Management of the Lake of the Woods and Rainy River Watershed* (Ottawa and Washington, DC: IJC, 2011), 1, 38–45, and Appendix K. The report is also reproduced in full in International Joint Commission, *Report to the Governments of the United States and Canada on Bi-national Water Management of the Lake of the Woods and Rainy River Watershed* (Ottawa and Washington, DC: IJC, 2012). Background scientific literature includes Huirong Chen et al., "First Assessment of Cyanobacterial Blooms and Microcystin-LR in the Canadian Portion of Lake of the Woods," *Lake and Reservoir Management* 23, 2 (2007): 169, and Canada, *Environment Canada's Lake of the Woods Science Initiative, 2008 to 2011 – Summary* (Ottawa: Environment Canada, 2014), http://publications.gc.ca/collections/collection_2017/eccc/En164-49-1-2014-eng.pdf.
59 In 2015, the Waakebiness-Bryce Institute for Indigenous Health at the University of Toronto announced a long-term study of cancer rates in regional communities. Cara McKenna, "Cancer Rate to be Studied among Ontario Aboriginals," *Globe and Mail*, 28 July 2015.
60 IJC Task Force, *Final Report*, 1.
61 Resolute Forest Products scaled back paper-making at Fort Frances in 2012 and announced final closure of the facility in May 2014. Greg Keenan, David Parkinson, and Brent Jang, "The Fall of Forestry: An Industry in Retreat," *Globe and Mail*, 6 December 2014.
62 IJC Task Force, *Final Report*, 2.
63 Margot W. Parkes et al., "Towards Integrated Governance for Water, Health and Social-Ecological Systems: The Watershed Governance Prism," *Global Environmental Change* 20 (2010): 693. See Jacqueline A. Oblak, *Water and Health in Lake of the Woods and Rainy River Basins*, prepared for Health Professionals Task Force, IJC, 23 June 2009, http://www.ijc.org/files/publications/Water%20and%20Health%20in%20Rainy-LoW%20Basins.pdf.
64 Karen Bakker, Emma S. Norman, and Gemma Dunn, "Recent Developments in Canadian Water Policy: An Emerging Water Security Paradigm," *Canadian Water Resources Journal* 36 (2011): 53.

65 See *Journal of the Fisheries Research Board of Canada* 28, 2 (1971): 123–301, for articles on the ELA and early research results.
66 J.R. Vallentyne, "Cut Really Amputation," *Winnipeg Free Press*, 18 June 1995; Andrew Nikiforuk, "Canada Is Starving Its World-Famous Freshwater Institute," *Globe and Mail*, 9 March 1996.
67 Quoted in Carol Sanders, "PM Delivers Lake Clean-up Cash" *Winnipeg Free Press*, 3 August 2012.
68 "It's Best to Benefit All Lakes," *Winnipeg Free Press*, editorial, 3 August 2012. Extensive further consultation eventually preserved the ELA and sustained its operations under the leadership of the International Institute for Sustainable Development.
69 IJC Task Force, *Final Report*, 2.
70 "Canada-US Data Hamonization Provides New Tools – StreamStats in Development for Rainy River," *International Joint Commission*, 8 April 2014, http://www.ijc.org/en_/blog/2014/04/08/data_harmonization_new_tools_streamstats_rainy_river/.
71 IJC Task Force, *Final Report*, 6.
72 Ibid., 7.
73 Ibid., 28. The higher the BOD level, the less dissolved oxygen is available for aquatic life.
74 Ibid., 30.
75 International Rainy Lake Board of Control, *Final Report: Review of the IJC Order for Rainy and Namakan Lakes* (26 October 1999); IJC Task Force, *Final Report*, 30. For further detail, see 30–35. Arrangements in support of rule curve review were initiated in 2009.
76 Ontario MNR and Minnesota DNR, *Ontario-Minnesota Boundary Waters Fisheries Atlas*, 4th ed. (Toronto: Queen's Printer, 2004), iii.
77 Ibid., 2.
78 Ibid., 3.
79 This is presumably why, in order to encourage sleep, people are advised to count sheep rather than fish.
80 Ibid., 4.
81 Ibid., 9.
82 Ibid., 4.
83 "The Sturgeon Returns," *Northern Sportsman*, editorial, August 1961, 5.
84 Ontario MNR and Minnesota DNR, *Ontario-Minnesota Boundary Waters Fisheries Atlas*, 10. "Peaking" refers to a practice by hydroelectric power facilities of adjusting their daytime and evening water outflows for the purpose of maximizing efficiency during periods of high electricity demand. This causes adverse affects on shoreline property and aquatic organisms that may be sensitive to fluctuating water levels. "These shifts in water levels alter fish spawning habitat and eggs and larvae in shallow regions can be exposed or desiccated or stranded. Water level fluctuations also leave eggs susceptible to fungal infection and predation at reduced water levels. In addition, drastic temperature changes often occur when water levels change, which may influence the timing and length of spawning periods." D. O'Shea, *Water Management Recommendations for the Rainy River Stream Habitat Program, Final Advisory Report*, Rainy River Peaking Group (St. Paul, MN: Minnesota Department of Natural Resources, Division of Ecological Services, 2005), cited in Anna M. DeSellas et al., *State of the Basin Report for the Lake of the Woods and Rainy River Basin*, March 2009, 107, http://www.rainylakeconservancy.org/Resources/Documents/2009_State_of_the_Basin_Report.pdf. Ownership changes and new operating arrangements for hydroelectric

power facilities at Fort Frances and Kenora in 2009 gave rise to further legal action on the part of Treaty 3 to safeguard the sturgeon fishery and the wild rice crop.

85 Ontario MNR and Minnesota DNR, *Ontario-Minnesota Boundary Waters Fisheries Atlas*, 3. Water level regulation appropriate to sturgeon remains an ongoing regulatory concern. See International Rainy and Namakan Lakes Rule Curves Study Board, *Managing Water Levels and Flows in the Rainy River Basin: A Report to the International Joint Commission*, June 2017, 23.

86 D.B. Stewart and F.N. Hyntka, eds., *Proceedings of the Lake Sturgeon Research and Recovery Workshop, Winnipeg, Manitoba, March 10–12, 2010* (Winnipeg: Department of Fisheries and Oceans, 2011), 21–25.

87 Ontario MNR and Minnesota DNR, *Ontario-Minnesota Boundary Waters Fisheries Atlas*, 34–35.

88 Stewart and F.N. Hyntka, *Proceedings*, 22–23.

89 "A population would be considered to be 'recovered,' if it possessed age, size, abundance, and brood stock characteristics, similar to unexploited or lightly exploited populations." Ontario MNR and Minnesota DNR, *Ontario-Minnesota Boundary Waters Fisheries Atlas*, 10.

90 Ibid.

91 Ibid., 33.

92 Ibid., 34–35. For further discussion, see COSEWIC, *COSEWIC Assessment and Update Status Report on the Lake Sturgeon (Acipenser fulvescens) in Canada* (Ottawa: Committee on the Status of Endangered Wildlife in Canada, 2006).

93 Denton (Denny) Newman Jr., "Recovery of Minnesota's Dinosaur-Like Lake Sturgeon Continues," *Brainerd Dispatch*, 1 May 2014. Minnesota Department of Natural Resources, "Lake Sturgeon Continue Recovery in Rainy River and Lake of the Woods," press release, 15 January 2015. The Minnesota DNR's 2004 changes included the following:

> One sturgeon per licence year; a harvest slot of 114 to 127 cm (45–50 inches) total length; or one fish over 190 cm (75 inches); licence validation when a sturgeon is harvested; a reduced harvest season from April 24 through May 7 and from July 1 through September 30; and catch and release angling seasons from May 8 through May 16 and from October 1 through April 23.

Ontario MNR and Minnesota DNR, *Ontario-Minnesota Boundary Waters Fisheries Atlas*, 39.

94 Endangered Species Act, 2007 S.O. 2007, c. 6. See also Golder Associates Ltd., *Recovery Strategy for Lake Sturgeon (Acipenser fulvescens) – Northwestern Ontario, Great Lakes-Upper St. Lawrence River and Southern Hudson Bay-James Bay Populations in Ontario*, prepared for the Ontario Ministry of Natural Resources, Peterborough, Ontario, 2011, http://files.ontario.ca/environment-and-energy/species-at-risk/stdprod_086034.pdf.

95 Donald Campbell, "Cummings to Plead Case," *Winnipeg Free Press*, 15 December 1992; Donald Campbell, "Gold Mine Put on Hold," *Winnipeg Free Press*, 7 January 1993.

96 Paul Sarnyn and George Nikides, "Shoal Lake Study Rejected," *Winnipeg Free Press*, 26 January 1993.

97 "Shoal Lake Watershed Agreement Between Big Island First Nation and Iskutewisakaygun #39 Independent FN and Northwest Angle #33 FN and Northwest Angle #37 FN and Shoal Lake #40 FN and Her Majesty the Queen in Right of Ontario," September 1994; "Ontario Balks at Mine Pledge," *Winnipeg Free Press*, 16 January 1994; "Water Plan 'Good Step'," 3 September 1994.

98 SLWWG, *Shoal Lake Watershed Management Plan.*
99 Ibid., 46.
100 John Sinclair and Dale Hutchison, "Multi-Stakeholder Decision-Making: The Shoal Lake Watershed Case," *Canadian Water Resources Journal* 23, 2 (1998): 167–79.
101 Compensation claims are under consideration. See Gordon W. Walker (Canadian Chair, IJC) and Lana Pollack (US Chair, IJC), to Christopher Wilkie and Sue Saarnio, 3 November 2014, http://www.sl40.ca/docs/Shoal%20Lake_Letter%20to%20Gov'ts_Nov%203_2014_.pdf. A Freedom Road linking Shoal Lake #40 First Nation with the Trans-Canada Highway has been contemplated for a number of years and figured prominently in the 2015 federal election campaign. Joyanne Pursaga, "Road to Freedom," *Winnipeg Sun*, 11 August 2015, and Mary Agnes Welch, "A Lack of Principle," *Winnipeg Free Press*, 12 August 2015. At the time of writing, engineering issues appear to have been resolved and funding commitments from the City of Winnipeg, the Province of Manitoba, and the Government of Canada are in place.
102 V.A. Sowa, R.B. Adamson, and A.W. Chow, "Water Management of the Steep Rock Iron Mines at Atikokan, Ontario, during Construction, Operations, and after Mine Abandonment," Proceedings of the 25th Annual British Columbia Mine Reclamation Symposium in Campbell River, BC, 2001, 104–15.
103 David Boileau et al., *2004–2014 Seine River Water Management Plan*, 31 March 2004, http://seineriverwmp.com/ApprovedWMP_28May2004.pdf, 49.
104 Jeff Walters, "Northern Ontario's Steep Rock Mine Water to Overflow by 2070," *CBC News*, 20 April 2016, http://www.cbc.ca/news/canada/thunder-bay/atikokan-steep-rock-1.3543495.
105 Princesa VanBuren Hansen et al., *2010 Minnesota Water Plan* (St. Paul, MN: Minnesota Environmental Quality Board, 2010), https://www.eqb.state.mn.us/sites/default/files/documents/2010_Minnesota_Water_Plan.pdf, 4.
106 Deborah L. Swackhamer et al., *Minnesota Water Sustainability Framework* (St. Paul, MN: Water Resources Center, University of Minnesota, 2011), https://www.wrc.umn.edu/sites/wrc.umn.edu/files/minnesota_water_framework.pdf.
107 The proposed schedule for the initial cycle is as follows: Little Fork River Watershed (2008); Big Fork River Watershed (2010); Lake of the Woods Watershed (2012); Rainy River Headwaters Watershed (2014); Vermillion Watershed (2015); Rainy River/Rainy Lake Watershed (2016); Rainy River Manitou Watershed, Rapid River Watershed, and Rainy River/Baudette Watershed (2017).
108 IJC Task Force, *Final Report*, 32.
109 Lake of the Woods Water Sustainability Foundation, *State of the Basin Report, 2009*, 43.
110 Ibid., 39; IJC Task Force, *Final Report*, 32.
111 IJC Task Force, *Final Report*, 29–30.
112 Ibid., 36.
113 Princesa VanBuren Hansen et al., *2010 Minnesota Water Plan*, 27–56.
114 IJC Task Force, *Final Report*, 28.
115 Ibid., 2.
116 Ibid., iii.
117 Ibid., 62.
118 Ibid., 65.
119 Ibid.

120 Ibid., 66–67.
121 Diane Kelly, Grand Chief, Grand Council Treaty #3 to International Joint Commission, 18 August 2011; IJC Task Force, *Final Report*, 67.
122 IJC Task Force, *Final Report*, 68.
123 Ibid., 69.
124 IJC, *Report to the Governments of the United States and Canada*.
125 IJC Task Force, *Final Report*, 40. This is followed by a more detailed discussion of the form and functions of the proposed board.

CONCLUSION

1 International Joint Commission (IJC), *A Water Quality Plan of Study for the Lake of the Woods Basin* (Ottawa and Washington, DC: IJC, 2015).
2 Shafiqul Islam and Lawrence E. Susskind, *Water Diplomacy: A Negotiated Approach to Managing Complex Water Networks* (New York: Routledge, 2013).
3 IJC, *Water Quality Plan of Study*, ii.
4 Julia Martin-Ortega et al., *Water Ecosystem Services: A Global Perspective* (Cambridge: Cambridge University Press, 2015). For the latest elaborate expert examination of water level regulation affecting the Rainy-Lake of the Woods region, see International Rainy and Namakan Lakes Rule Curves Study Board, *Managing Water Levels and Flows in the Rainy River Basin: A Report to the International Joint Commission*, June 2017, http://ijc.org/files/tinymce/uploaded/RNLRCSB/IRNLRCSB_Final_Report_2017l.pdf.
5 For an introduction to climate change considerations in the Great Lakes context, see Victoria Pebbles, "Incorporating Climate Adaptation into Transboundary Ecosystem Management in the Great Lakes Basin," in *Transboundary Water Governance: Adaptation to Climate Change*, ed. Juan Carlos Sanchez and Joshua Roberts, IUCN Environmental Policy and Law Paper No. 75 (Gland, Switzerland: International Union for Conservation of Nature, 2014), 197–217.
6 In 2005, the US Bureau of Reclamation, in a study conducted pursuant to the Dakota Water Resources Act of 2000, identified the Lake of the Woods as one of the water sources that would be available in response to potential shortages in the Red River basin, including the communities of Fargo and Grand Forks, ND, as well as Moorhead and East Grand Forks, MN. The hypothetical shortages – possibilities that might be imagined over a time horizon extending out to the middle of this century or in the context of drought conditions reminiscent of the 1930s – served as foundations for an array of pipeline developments, some up to four hundred miles in length, to facilitate water imports from the Lake of the Woods to the Red River basin. US Department of Interior, *Reclamation: Managing Water in the West – Final Report on Red River Valley Water Needs and Options* (Bismarck, ND: US Department of Interior, Bureau of Reclamation, Dakotas Area Office, 2005).
7 It is one thing to agree with Justice Dennis O'Connor's observation that "watersheds are an ecologically practical unit for managing water" and another to suggest that this might be easy. Dennis R. O'Connor, *Report of the Walkerton Inquiry, Part 2: A Strategy for Safe Drinking Water* (Toronto: Ontario Ministry of the Attorney General, 2002), 94.
8 An international environmental treaty, the Minamata Convention on Mercury, was agreed in 2013. Article 12(4) encourages parties to "co-operate in developing strategies and implementing activities for identifying, assessing, prioritizing, managing, and, as appropriate, remediating contaminated sites." Ontario committed $85 million to remediation

of the Wabigoon-English river system following further review of possible continuing contamination in 2016. See John Rudd, Reed Harris, and Patricia Sellers, *Advice on Mercury Remediation Options for the Wabigoon-English River System: Final Report*, prepared for Asubpeeschoseewagong Netum Anishinabek (Grassy Narrows First Nation) – Ontario – Canada Working Group on Concerns Related to Mercury, 21 March 2016.

9 Note, in particular, D. Russi et al., *The Economics of Ecosystems and Biodiversity for Water and Wetlands* (London and Brussels: Institute for European Environmental Policy; Gland, Switzerland: Ramsar Secretariat, 2013), http://www.teebweb.org/publication/the-economics -of-ecosystems-and-biodiversity-teeb-for-water-and-wetlands/.

10 Margot W. Parkes et al., "Towards Integrated Governance for Water, Health and Social-Ecological Systems: The Watershed Governance Prism," *Global Environmental Change* 20, 4 (2010): 696.

11 IJC, *The International Watersheds Initiative: Implementing a New Paradigm for Transboundary Basins* (Ottawa and Washington, DC: IJC, 2009), 12.

12 For a thoughtful brief exploration of the evolution of the watershed approach, see Alice Cohen and Seanna Davidson, "The Watershed Approach: Challenges, Antecedents, and the Transition from Technical Tool to Governance Unit," *Water Alternatives* 4, 1 (2011): 1–14.

13 Tun Myint, *Governing International Rivers: Polycentric Politics in the Mekong and the Rhine* (Cheltenham, UK: Edward Elgar, 2012), 80.

14 "Directive to International Rainy-Lake of the Woods Watershed Board," 1 April 2013, para. 4(a), http://www.ijc.org/files/tinymce/uploaded/Directive%20to%20ILWRR%20 Watershed%20Board%20(3).pdf.

15 For the IRLWWB mandate, see "International Rainy-Lake of the Woods Watershed Board: Mandate," *IJC*, 2018, http://ijc.org/en_/RLWWB/Mandate. For details, see "Directive to International Rainy-Lake of the Woods Watershed Board." These arrangements avoid a source of confusion noted in some analyses of watershed governance: "As the concept of watershed boundaries was adopted into water governance efforts, this technical tool – which was not designed to address the broader components of water governance – became a governance unit, but without an attendant focus on the governance or procedural elements of the new watershed approach." Cohen and Davidson, "Watershed Approach," 7.

16 Bev J. Clark and Todd J. Sellers, eds. *Rainy-Lake of the Woods State of the Basin Report*, 2nd ed. (Kenora, ON: Lake of the Woods Water Sustainability Foundation, 2014), 156–57. For the text of the Arrangement, see IJC, *Report to the Governments of the United States and Canada on Bi-National Water Management of the Lake of the Woods and Rainy River Watershed* (Ottawa and Washington, DC: IJC, 2012), Appendix J. With regard to the anticipated benefits of improved information support, see Christina Leb, *Cooperation in Transboundary Water Resources* (Cambridge: Cambridge University Press, 2013), 114.

17 IJC, *Report to the Governments of the United States and Canada*, 29–35. St. Cloud State University and Rainy River Community College have been valuable contributors on the educational front. For general discussion of institutional innovation involving stakeholder participation, see K. Bakker and C. Cook, "Water Governance in Canada: Innovation and Fragmentation," *International Journal of Water Resources Development* 27, 2 (2011): 278–79.

18 Jutta Brunnée and Stephen J. Toope, "Environmental Security and Freshwater Resources: A Case for International Ecosystem Law," *Yearbook of International Environmental Law* 5, 1 (1995): 46. See also Rob de Loe, Jeji Varghese, and Cecilia Ferreyra, *Water Allocation*

and Water Security in Canada: Initiating a Policy Dialogue for the Twenty-First Century (Guelph, ON: Guelph Water Management Group, University of Guelph, 2007).

19 Jutta Brunnée and Stephen J. Toope, "Environmental Security and Freshwater Resources: Ecosystem Regime Building," *American Journal of International Law* 91, 1 (1997): 27.

20 Cameron Holley and Andrew Lawson, "Implementing Environmental Law and Collaborative Governance: Water and Natural Resource Management," in *Implementing Environmental Law*, ed. Paul Martin and Amanda Kennedy (Cheltenham, UK: Edward Elgar, 2015), 238–59; Bradley C. Karkkainen, "Post Sovereign Environmental Governance," *Global Environmental Politics* 4, 1 (2004): 72.

Suggested Readings

Detailed chapter notes will guide curious readers to specific sources of information and quotations found in the text. These references include archival records and official documents as well as newspaper stories and academic publications.

This section on suggested readings addresses other considerations. It is intended, from one perspective, to highlight key materials that may be of particular interest to anyone who wishes to follow up one or more of the interwoven themes in this book – water management, environmental history, federal-provincial and trans-boundary relations, institutional development, and so on. In addition, this list of suggested readings gives me the opportunity to acknowledge further some of my own debts as a researcher who has benefited from other explorers of this terrain.

The broad themes of regional history that this volume has elaborated and brought up to date are outlined in Grace Lee Nute, *Rainy River Country: A Brief History of the Region Bordering Minnesota and Ontario* (St. Paul, MN: Minnesota Historical Society, 1950). Later regional studies that have greatly enhanced awareness of resource, environmental, and water-related issues include W. Robert and Nancy M. Wightman, *The Land Between: Northwestern Ontario Resource Development, 1800 to the 1990s* (Toronto: University of Toronto Press, 1997); R. Newell Searle, *Saving Quetico-Superior: A Land Set Apart* (St. Paul, MN: Minnesota Historical Society, 1977); and Gerald Killan and George Warecki, "The Battle for Wilderness in Ontario: Saving Quetico-Superior, 1927–1960," in *Patterns of the Past: Interpreting Ontario's History*, ed. Roger Hall, William Westfall, and Laurel Sefton MacDowell, 328–55 (Toronto: Dundurn Press, 1988).

Without necessarily contributing in detail to this account of the environmental history of the Rainy-Lake of the Woods watershed, a number of works can be acknowledged for their general influence or inspiration. I have benefited over many years from Roderick Nash's *Wilderness and the American Mind*, originally published in 1967 and now in its fifth edition (New Haven, CT: Yale University Press, 2014), and the same should be said of Donald Worster's *Nature's Economy: A History of Ecological Ideas* (Cambridge: Cambridge University Press, 1985). *Fishing the Great Lakes: An Environmental History, 1783–1933* (Madison, WI: University of Wisconsin Press, 2000), by Margaret Beattie Bogue, and *The Great Lakes Forest: An Environmental and Social History* (Minneapolis, MN: University of Minnesota Press, 1983), edited by Susan L. Flader, have provided insight and guidance on methodology or scope in environmental history. I have also drawn encouragement from more recent scholarship in the environmental history field, notably Ted Steinberg's *Gotham Unbound: The Ecological History of Greater New York* (New York: Simon and Schuster, 2014) and Claire Elizabeth Campbell's *Shaped by the West Wind: Nature and History in Georgian Bay* (Vancouver: UBC Press, 2005).

Along with newspaper records, numerous local and community-oriented publications are the source of valuable insights on social, economic, and environmental developments. Two recent examples are *Common Ground: Stories of Lake of the Woods* (Kenora: Lake of the Woods Museum, 2010) and Michael William Aiken, *After the Mill: From Confrontation to Cooperation* (Winnipeg: Aboriginal Issues Press, 2011). Although there is much more to be done, a few biographical studies illuminate the character and careers of prominent regional figures: Elizabeth Arthur, "Dawson, Simon James," *Dictionary of Canadian Biography*, vol. 13 (1901–10); Elizabeth Arthur, *Simon J. Dawson, C.E.* (Thunder Bay, ON: Singing Shield Productions, 1987); and Mark Kuhlberg, "'Eyes Wide Open': E.W. Backus and the Pitfalls of Investing in Ontario's Pulp and Paper Industry, 1902–1932," *Journal of the Canadian Historical Association*, n.s., 16, 1 (2005): 201–33.

In terms of governmental records and reports, the work of all those who contributed as witnesses, consultants, researchers, and authors to the International Joint Commission's *Final Report of the International Joint Commission on the Lake of the Woods Reference* (Ottawa and Washington, DC: Government Print Office, 1917) is highly noteworthy. More recent IJC reports continue this tradition, one example being *A Water Quality Plan of Study for the Lake of the Woods* (2015). Equally valuable is official input from a wide range of natural resource managers as consolidated in state-of-the-basin reports, such as Bev J. Clark and Todd J. Sellers, eds. *Rainy-Lake of the Woods State of the Basin Report*, 2nd ed. (Kenora, ON: Lake of the Woods Water Sustainability Foundation, 2014). The trial level decision of Justice Sanderson in *Keewatin v Minister of Natural Resources*, 2011 ONSC 4801, reflects an exemplary consideration of official and Aboriginal perspectives on resource activity and treaty negotiations from the late nineteenth century.

The search for archival materials cited throughout this volume involved visits to numerous libraries and record centres, each offering distinctive insights. Depending on particular areas of interest and the relevant time frame, valuable insights might be gleaned from the records of the Hudson's Bay Company, the diaries of John Mather, and correspondence and reports in the files of the department of Indian Affairs, some now accessible online. Primary records and archival sources referred to in this volume include the following from the Archives of Ontario: Ontario Provincial Board of Heath; Ontario Water Resources Commission; Ontario Pollution Control Board; Lake of the Woods Milling Company

Papers; the papers of Premiers Whitney, Ferguson, and Drury; Aemilius Irving Papers; and the records of the Ontario Lumberman's Association. Relevant materials from Library and Archives Canada include the John E. Read Papers, Blake and Redden Papers, Sifton Papers, and Meighen Papers. Business records and diaries of John Mather may be found at the Archives of Ontario, the University of British Columbia, and the Lake of the Woods Museum, where the Letterbooks of W.D. Lyons may also be consulted. In addition to the Hudson's Bay Company Archives, other useful records at the Archives of Manitoba include Lake of the Woods papers in the Premiers' Series, the H.N. Ruttan Papers, and corporate records of the Keewatin Lumbering and Manufacturing Company. Other primary materials used include the Matheson Papers at the Metropolitan Toronto Reference Library and Records of the Joint Committee Relative to the Preservation of Fisheries in Waters Contiguous to Canada and the United States at the US National Archives at College Park, MD, as well as selected case reports at the Supreme Court of Canada.

Partly as a consequence of the underlying federal-provincial boundary dispute on the Canadian side and partly as a result of the litigiousness of certain protagonists, Rainy-Lake of the Woods issues frequently found their way to court. Thus, judicial decisions from all levels of courts not only offer distinctive perspectives on regional developments but also give rise to or elaborate legal principles of ongoing national significance. Three such decisions of particular note are *St. Catharines Milling and Lumber Co. v R.* (1887) 13 S.C.R. 57; *Fort Frances Pulp and Power Co. v Manitoba Free Press* [1923] A.C. 695; [1923] 3 D.L.R. 629; and *Interprovincial Cooperatives and Dryden Chemicals Limited v The Queen* [1975] 5 W.W.R. 382 (SCC).

These legal decisions have attracted considerable commentary for their general significance in the fields of Aboriginal and constitutional law. Although this form of analysis falls generally outside the scope of this volume, some broader historical discussion of these cases has also appeared. Notable in this regard are S. Barry Cottam, "Indian Title as a 'Celestial Institution': David Mills and the *St. Catherine's Milling* Case," in *Aboriginal Resource Use in Canada: Historical and Legal Aspects*, ed. Kerry Abel and Jean Friesen, 247–86 (Winnipeg: University of Manitoba Press, 1991) and Sidney L. Harring, *White Man's Law: Native People in Nineteenth-Century Canadian Jurisprudence* (Toronto: University of Toronto Press/Osgoode Society, 1998).

The International Joint Commission is simultaneously an agent in and observer of the history of the Rainy-Lake of the Woods region and a subject of interest from the perspective of interjurisdictional water management and institutional innovation. Useful references from a very extensive body of literature on the IJC include L.M. Bloomfield and G.F. Fitzgerald, *Boundary Waters Problems of Canada and the United States* (Toronto: Carswell, 1958); William R. Willoughby, *The Joint Organizations of Canada and the United States* (Toronto: University of Toronto Press, 1979); and Murray Klamen, "The IJC and Transboundary Water Disputes: Past, Present and Future," in *Water without Borders: Canada, the United States and Shared Waters*, ed. Emma S. Norman, Alice Cohen, and Karen Bakker (Toronto: University of Toronto Press, 2013).

Management challenges associated with the watershed concept, especially in the transboundary context, are by no means unique to the Manitoba-Ontario-Minnesota border country with which this volume deals. Insightful framework studies that have contributed to my understanding include the following: Laurence Boisson de Chazournes, Christina Leb, and Mara Tignino, eds., *International Law and Freshwater: The Multiple Challenges* (Cheltenham, UK: Edward Elgar, 2013); Alistair Rieu-Clarke, Ruby Moynihan, and Bjørn-Oliver Magsig, *UN Watercourses Convention: User's Guide* (Dundee, Scotland: IHP-HELP Centre for Water Law, Policy and Science, University of Dundee, 2012); Alice Cohen and Seanna Davidson, "The Watershed Approach: Challenges, Antecedents, and the Transition from Technicial Tool to Governance Unit," *Water Alternatives* 4, 1 (2011): 1–14; Stephen C. McCaffrey, *The Law of International Watercourses* (Oxford: Oxford University Press, 2007); Juan Carlos Sanchez and Joshua Roberts, eds., *Transboundary Water Governance: Adaptation to Climate Change*, IUCN Environmental Policy and Law Paper No. 75 (Gland, Switzerland: International Union for Conservation of Nature, 2014); Margot W. Parkes et al., "Towards Integrated Governance for Water, Health and Social-Ecological Systems: The Watershed Governance Prism," *Global Environmental Change* 20, 4 (2010): 693–704.

Aboriginal rights, history, and resource uses are ubiquitous themes in the ongoing regional story. Among numerous studies that were particularly useful in the course of my research are these: David T. McNab, "The Administration of Treaty 3: The Location of the Boundaries of Treaty 3 Indian Reserves in Ontario 1873–1915," in *As Long as the Sun Shines and the Water Flows*, ed. Ian A.L. Getty and Antoine S. Lussier (Vancouver: UBC Press, 1983), 145–57; Anastasia M. Shkylnik, *A Poison Stronger Than Love: The Destruction of an Ojibwa Community* (New Haven, CT: Yale University Press, 1985); John Sinclair and Dale Hutchison, "Multi-stakeholder Decision-Making: The Shoal Lake Watershed Case," *Canadian Water Resources Journal* 23, 2 (1998): 167–79; Jean Teillet, *The Role of the Natural Resources Regulatory Regime in Aboriginal Rights Disputes in Ontario*, Final Report for the Ipperwash Inquiry, 31 March 2005; Leo G. Waisberg and Tim E. Holzkamm, "'Their Country Is Tolerably Rich in Furs': The Ojibwa Fur Trade in the Boundary Waters Region 1821–71," *Papers of the Algonquian Conference* 25 (1994): 493–513; Anna J. Willow, *Strong Hearts, Native Lands: The Cultural and Political Landscape of Anishinaabe Anti-clearcutting Activism* (New York: State University of New York Press, 2012).

Resource development and environmental issues have been and remain central to the social, economic, and political evolution of the Rainy-Lake of the Woods region, with water management of increasing significance. Among particularly valuable contributions are the following: C. Armstrong, *The Politics of Federalism: Ontario's Relations with the Federal Government, 1867–1942* (Toronto: University of Toronto Press, 1981); Andrew J. Chapeskie, "Indigenous Law, State Law and the Management of Natural Resources: Wild Rice and the Wabigoon Lake Ojibway Nation," *Law and Anthropology* 5 (1990): 129–66; A. Ernest Epp, "The Lake of the Woods Milling Company: An Early Western Industry," in *The Canadian West: Social Change and Economic Development*, ed. Henry C. Klassen (Calgary: Comprint, 1977), 147–62; H.V. Nelles, *Politics of Development: Forests, Mines and*

Hydro-electric Power in Ontario, 1849–1941 (Toronto: Macmillan, 1974); John J. Van West, "Ojibwa Fisheries, Commercial Fisheries Development and Fisheries Administration, 1873–1915: An Examination of Conflicting Interests in the Collapse of the Sturgeon Fisheries of the Lake of the Woods," *Native Studies Review* 6, 1 (1990): 31–49; Morris Zaslow, *The Opening of the Canadian North, 1870–1914* (Toronto: McClelland and Stewart, 1971).

The environmental backdrop against which land use, resource development, and water management decisions must ultimately be measured has both local and global dimensions as illustrated in publications such as the following: W. Eugene Smith and Aileen M. Smith, *Minamata* (New York: Holt, Rinehart and Winston, 1975); Victoria Pebbles, "Incorporating Climate Adaptation into Transboundary Ecosystem Management in the Great Lakes Basin," in *Transboundary Water Governance: Adaptation to Climate Change*, ed. Juan Carlos Sanchez and Joshua Roberts, IUCN Environmental Policy and Law Paper No. 75 (Gland, Switzerland: International Union for Conservation of Nature, 2014), 197–217; Julia Martin-Ortega et al., *Water Ecosystem Services: A Global Perspective* (Cambridge: Cambridge University Press, 2015); John L. Riley, *The Once and Future Great Lakes Country: An Ecological History* (Montreal and Kingston: McGill Queen's University Press, 2013); Warner Troyer, *No Safe Place* (Toronto: Clarke, Irwin, 1977).

Index

NATURE|HISTORY|SOCIETY
GENERAL EDITOR: GRAEME WYNN

Justin Page, *Tracking the Great Bear: How Environmentalists Recreated British Columbia's Coastal Rainforest*

Daniel Macfarlane, *Negotiating a River: Canada, the US, and the Creation of the St. Lawrence Seaway*

Ryan O'Connor, *The First Green Wave: Pollution Probe and the Origins of Environmental Activism in Ontario*

John Thistle, *Resettling the Range: Animals, Ecologies, and Human Communities in British Columbia*

Carly A. Dokis, *Where the Rivers Meet: Pipelines, Participatory Resource Management, and Aboriginal-State Relations in the Northwest Territories*

Jessica van Horssen, *A Town Called Asbestos: Environmental Contamination, Health, and Resilience in a Resource Community*

Nancy B. Bouchier and Ken Cruikshank, *The People and the Bay: A Social and Environmental History of Hamilton Harbour*

Jonathan Peyton, *Unbuilt Environments: Tracing Postwar Development in Northwest British Columbia*

Mark R. Leeming, *In Defence of Home Places: Environmental Activism in Nova Scotia*

Jim Clifford, *West Ham and the River Lea: A Social and Environmental History of London's Industrialized Marshland, 1839–1914*

Michèle Dagenais, *Montreal, City of Water: An Environmental History*

David Calverley, *Who Controls the Hunt? First Nations, Treaty Rights, and Wildlife Conservation in Ontario, 1783–1939*